Dreyfus: The Prisoner of Devil's Island

William Harding

DREYFUS:

E PRISONER OF DEVIL'S ISLAND

DREYFUS:

'HE PRISONER OF DEVIL'S ISLAND

CAPTAIN ALFRED DREYFUS.

DREYFUS:

THE PRISONER OF DEVIL'S ISLAND

A Full Story of the Most Remarkable Military
Trial and Scandal of the Age .. ..

BY

WILLIAM HARDING

Cable Editor Associated Press

Profusely illustrated with Portraits of the Principal
Actors, and Photographic Reproductions of the Places
and Scenes of Dreyfus's Trial and Exile   .. ..

WESTERN W. WILSON

14 Thomas Street, ...   New York

Copyright 1899,
BY
J. A. JONES

Dedication

To the Men of America
Whether Jew or Gentile
Who abhor Persecution
Who believe in the Reign of Justice
Who rejoice when the sword of Truth is drawn
And will not see it sheathed

This History

Of the Sorrows and Persecutions of

Captain Alfred Dreyfus

Is dedicated by the Author
To whom the Atlantic Cables
By Day and Night for Months and Years
Have told the Marvelous Story.

INTRODUCTION

THE case of Alfred Dreyfus is the most remarkable episode of modern times. It is an incident *of its own kind*, without an antecedent and without a parallel. Superficially it seems to be an imbroglio of what Carlyle would call "despicable personalities"; but under the surface are playing some of the most powerful forces of human history. The fact is, that the real causes of this strange outbreak and upheaval in France are as universal as the present political constitution of the world, and as old as the flight of Abraham from Ur of the Chaldees.

The echo of the Dreyfus case has been heard as far as the confines of civilization. The headlines have been cried in Tokio and Buenos Ayres. The name of this Franco-Hebrew captain has been spoken and his fate discussed by the trappers of the Yenisei, by the Peruvian silver miners, by the alcaldes of Guatemala, by the priests of Thibet, and by the gamblers of Monte Carlo. Every cabinet, every ministry, from that of Calcutta to that of The Hague, has felt the vibrations and weighed the consequences of the case of Dreyfus. Every monarch of Asia has taken time to learn at least the pronunciation of the name of the prisoner of Devil's Island. Every schoolboy from Siberia to Texas has heard something of the trial of Dreyfus, and of Zola and Esterhazy.

As a result of the thousands of columns printed about this *cause célèbre*, the ordinary mortal has floundered about in a sea of doubt and speculation. Unable to afford the time to follow carefully all the exciting developments in the drama, the average man or woman has had to be content with getting a glimpse, now and then, of the actors on the stage, or of the doings behind the scenes. Meanwhile, both men and nations have looked forward to the time when a calming of the swiftly whirling waves might enable the interested mind to sift the true from the false in the turbulent whirlpool of news.

In the following pages it has been our task to attempt this work of condensation, elimination, and construction. In this work, we give all due credit to The Associated Press and its most able General Manager, Melville E. Stone, to whose effective direction the newspapers of this country have been so greatly indebted in presenting to the American public such complete accounts of the famous trial at Rennes.

The author of this work, from the official position which he has held, has had the invaluable opportunity to gather from the ever-flowing volume of cable intelligence all the essentials of the remarkable event which he has attempted to narrate in the following pages. It is but justice to say that no position other than that which he has held could have afforded like opportunities. The general American offices of The Associated Press have been for years the fleece of Jason, heavy with the golden sands of intelligence. If the volume of news sometimes flows by leaving vast deposits of sediment, the golden grains are ever in the current; and these may be caught and molten into the rich bullion of human history.

The Dreyfus case has ended. The writer of this volume has done his part to transmit a knowledge of the proceedings to the American people day by day, as the cause has unfolded itself; and now he has reviewed and recorded in these pages the whole course of the event—the conspiracy, the crime, the suffering, the ignominy, which have been brought to light in the trial hall at Rennes.

This book contains the results of the author's gathering and inquiry; it also contains his interpretations and deductions. He now sends the story of the prisoner of Devil's Island to the public, with the hope that the liberty-loving and truth-seeking people of his country may find in the perusal as much instruction and interest as the author has found in the preparation of this volume.

WILLIAM HARDING.

CONTENTS

CONTENTS

CONTENTS

LIST OF ILLUSTRATIONS

DREYFUS:

THE PRISONER OF DEVIL'S ISLAND

Chapter I.

THE CAUSE OF IT ALL

IF you had asked any Frenchman, after the disastrous war with Germany of 1870–71 (when, instead of the eagles of France swooping down upon Berlin, the eagles of Germany fluttered over Paris), the reason for this state of affairs, he would have replied most promptly:

"*Nous sommes trahis.*" ("We are betrayed.")

Here we have the situation in a nutshell. France is continually being betrayed, or fancying she is being betrayed, which is about the same thing, to all intents and purposes; for the idea, as much as the fact, keeps the people in a continual state of turmoil, almost boiling with its superheated lava.

The very suggestion that a French general could be incompetent is protested against with angry derision by Frenchmen; therefore treachery alone must be allowed to explain the military defeats and other reverses suffered by French arms and French diplomacy.

In addition to this, the feeling against the Jews which first developed in Algeria shortly after the Franco-German war, owing to the enfranchisement of all the Jews in that French colony, to the detriment of all other foreigners, including the Arabs, has been steadily growing ever since, and has reached such a point that the most overheated Frenchmen have actually been thinking of the possibilities of a St. Bartholomew massacre, in which all sympathizers with the Jews, as well as all Jews, would be killed.

The pulse of France may be said to be the army, for nearly all French-

2

men have to draw lots on coming of age to decide whether they are not to serve under the colors. The army permeates into every hole and corner of France. Red-tape and officialdom reign supreme. Nearly every family in France is in some way connected, or likely to be connected, with the army. Consequently when the feeling against the Jews spread to the army, the paths of the Jewish soldiers and officers were far from being strewn with roses.

It is unnecessary to dwell further upon the reasons which led to this antipathy in France against the Jews. It is not a question of religion, though religion has had something to do with the state of affairs existing. The average Frenchman, however, cares little or nothing for any man's religion, though there are many good Catholics in France, and some of them have taken part in the popular crusade against the Jews. But it seems to be that a sort of feeling of envy, or jealousy of the growing wealth of the Jews in general, coupled with complaints against their so-called aggressiveness and prominence in commercial life, grows stronger and stronger. Eventually a number of Anti-Semitic newspapers appeared, principal among them being the *Libre Parole* (Free Speech), edited by M. Drumont, a Catholic, which added considerable fuel to the flames.

The alliance, or understanding arrived at between France and Russia also served to add to the bitterness against the Jews. In Russia the Jews are despised and oppressed, and therefore Frenchmen, after the understanding with Russia, fancied it was but natural, in view of the "alliance," to heap red-hot coals on the heads of the Jews in France.

And so the feeling in France against the Jews grew stronger day by day and began to express itself in violence.

Chapter II.

GLANCING BACKWARD

HERE it is necessary to take a glance at the political situation just previous to the outbreak of the famous Dreyfus case. In November, 1893, soon after the reassembling of Parliament, a crisis in the Ministry arose on account of objections to the Ministerial programme of the premier, M. Dupuy, who was desirous of conciliating the Moderates, and on account of the abuse of three Radical members of the Cabinet, MM. Viette, Peytral, and Carriere. M. Dupuy was unable to conciliate, and it was agreed that the three Ministers should leave the Cabinet. But the discord in the Ministry leaked out, and owing to the failure of the Government supporters to carry a vote of confidence in the Ministry, M. Dupuy and his colleagues resigned November 26th, and M. Casimir-Périer formed a Cabinet, being succeeded as President of the Chamber of Deputies by M. Dupuy.

An extraordinary scene occurred in the Chamber of Deputies on December 10, 1893. An Anarchist named Vaillant flung a bomb, filled with nails, among the members of the Chamber of Deputies, more or less seriously injuring forty-seven persons. Vaillant was promptly captured, tried, condemned, and executed. The affair served still further to inflame the public mind.

The next day, M. Casimir-Périer managed to pass through the Chamber of Deputies four bills, modifying the Press Law, the Criminal-Conspiracy Law, and the Explosive Law, and formed a fund for the preservation of order and the prevention of such outrages as the one which had so startled the world.

Soon afterward, M. Clémenceau, a popular leader, began the publication of a series of "revelations" tending to show the unpreparedness of the Toulon Arsenal in case of war and the general unsatisfactory condition of the Navy of France, which did not tend to calm the public mind. The Government appointed a Commission to inquire into the alleged mismanagement in the Navy Department, and a resolution of confidence in the Ministry was passed by a large majority. This was in January, 1894.

Early in March, 1894, there was an exciting debate in the Chamber of Deputies over a slight incident which occurred at St. Denis, where the mayor, a Socialist, prohibited a display in the streets of any religious symbol or emblem. The Minister of Public Works, M. Spuller, declared this was imprudent and tyrannical, and he announced that a new spirit would animate the Government in its treatment of matters at issue between the laity and the clergy, namely the spirit of tolerance. The Radicals were furious at such a suggestion, and a resolution, violently hostile to the clergy, was proposed by M. Brisson. The Government, however, triumphed, and for some time this "new spirit" was in evidence, and was by some people interpreted as further concessions to the Jews, thus arousing more ill-feeling against them.

After gaining further victories over the Socialists and Radicals, M. Casimir-Périer fell from office on account of an adverse vote in the Chamber of Deputies over an interpellation regarding leave of absence being given to the railroad employees, who are government servants, to attend a congress of the Railroad Workmen's Federation.

M. Dupuy formed a new Cabinet on May 28, 1894, his place as President of the Chamber of Deputies being taken by M. Casimir-Périer.

For a time the political sea was smooth. But France and the world at large, on June 24th, was plunged into excitement and indignation by the cowardly assassination of President Sadi-Carnot, at Lyons, whither he had gone to open an exhibition. He was stabbed to death by Caserio Santo, an Italian anarchist, who claimed he was inspired to commit the deed by a desire to avenge his fellow anarchists who had been previously executed in France.

M. Casimir-Périer was elected June 27th, to succeed M. Carnot. He obtained 451 votes out of the total of 851 votes cast, M. Dupuy receiving 97 votes.

The Dupuy Ministry resigned on the election of the new President, but the Cabinet was asked to remain in office. A bill was introduced into the Chamber by the Government, giving the law more extended powers against anarchists and restricting the press from publishing full reports of the trials of anarchists, much to the disgust of many of the irreconcilables.

Chapter III.

WHAT WAS FOUND IN A WASTE-BASKET

THIS was about the state of affairs in France when, in September, 1894, there was brought to the Intelligence Department of the French War Office a mysterious document, torn into pieces, which was said to have been stolen from a waste-basket at the German Embassy, where, at that time, Colonel von Schwartzkoppen was the military attaché. This document was carefully pasted or pieced together by members of the Intelligence Department, and was shown to the Minister of War, General Mercier; the Chief of the Headquarters Staff, General de Boisdeffre; and the Assistant Chief of the Headquarters Staff, General Gonse.

Colonel Sandherr was then Chief of the Intelligence Department of the War Office, and among his assistants was Lieutenant-Colonel Henry. The former soon died, the latter committed suicide after confessing a forgery. On the Headquarters Staff were three officers, Lieutenant-Colonel Picquart, Lieutenant-Colonel Du Paty de Clam, and Captain Dreyfus, a Jew.

This finding of the pieces of paper in the waste-paper basket led to the great scandal of the century, which began at that time, and which is not yet ended. This document has since been known as the *bordereau*, or *pièce de conviction*, and it was this which sent an unfortunate man to five years of torture, and which may yet have the most serious consequences for France.

When pieced together, the *bordereau* read:

"Without news indicating that you wish to see me, I am sending you, nevertheless, sir, some interesting information:

"1. A note on the hydraulic brake of the 120 gun and on the way in which this piece behaved.

"2. A note on the covering of troops (*troupes de couverture*). Some modifications will be entailed by the new plan.

" 3. A note on a modification in artillery formations.

" 4. A note relative to Madagascar.

" 5. The project for a Firing Manual for field-artillery, March 14, 1894.

" This last document is extremely difficult to procure, and I can only have it at my disposal for a very few days. The Minister of War has sent a limited number of copies to the several corps, and these corps are responsible for it; each officer is to send his copy back after the manœuvres. If, therefore, you will take from it what interests you, and hold it afterward at my disposal, I will take it, unless you should desire that I should have it copied *in extenso* and then send you the copy. I am about to go to the Manœuvres."

For some time after the discovery of the bordereau, the matter was kept secret and certain investigations were made. Gradually rumors of the discovery of treason by the War Office officials became current, and the words " *Nous sommes trahis !* " began to be heard outside of official circles.

Finally, M. Drumont, editor of the *Libre Parole*, is said to have obtained the first authentic details of the affair through a letter, addressed to M. Papillaud, of his staff, that a traitor had been found among the officers of the General Staff at the Ministry of War, and, it was added, the traitor was a Jew. The writer of this anonymous letter intimated that if a search was made among "the Dreyfuses, the Meyers, and the Levys," the traitor could be identified. Later, during the latter part of October, 1894, M. Papillaud received another letter, apparently from the same source, saying the name of the traitor was Captain Alfred Dreyfus, of the Fourteenth Regiment of Artillery, and adding that the traitor had been confined in the Cherche-Midi prison since October 15th. The letter contained the words:

" People say he is travelling, but they lie, because they would like to smother the business. All Israel is astir. *Tout à vous*, Henry."

The staff of the *Libre Parole* were then alive to the importance of the story, and gradually many of the facts in the case leaked out. The prisoner, it appeared, was accused of having sold important documents relating to the national defence to the agents of a foreign power, Germany. He was arrested on October 15th, by Lieutenant-Colonel Du Paty de Clam,

The following is a reduced facsimile of a portion of the famous *bordereau* :

REDUCED FACSIMILE OF A PORTION OF THE "BORDEREAU"

acting under the orders of General Mercier, the Minister of War, had been imprisoned in the Cherche-Midi Prison, and the most extraordinary precautions had been taken to keep the affair secret, even from Dreyfus's own family. Madame Dreyfus, his wife, it developed later, was frightened into silence by Du Paty de Clam.

France, naturally, became greatly excited, and those who had been the most bitter in their denunciations of the Jews found ample material for "I-told-you-so" statements. All kinds of sensational reports were circulated. Some rumors had it that the whole country had been betrayed, from first to last, army and navy, and that France was almost at the mercy of her enemies. People even went so far as to declare that war with Germany was imminent. The recall of the German Ambassador was openly demanded, and all kinds of pressure was brought to bear on the Government to clear up the mystery without delay and let the public know the whole truth. But, the authorities maintained an air of mystery; the darkest hints were dropped, the name of Russia began to be bandied about, and the War Ministry was said to have in its possession secrets which, if divulged, would practically cause the upheaval of Europe.

Chapter IV.

THE INITIAL PASSAGE

WHEN the outburst of public feeling could no longer be withstood, the Government made up its mind to let the world know something about what was going on, and, at a Cabinet Council, November 1, 1894, the Minister of War, General Mercier, formally announced his intention of ordering proceedings against Captain Alfred Dreyfus, of the Fourteenth Regiment of Artillery, attached to the General Staff, for disclosing secret War Office documents to foreigners.

A despatch from Paris to the London *Times*, announcing this fact, added:

"Although the arrest of Captain Dreyfus has made a great sensation, every one feels that the honor of the French army will not be impugned if one solitary officer should be convicted of treachery."

The developments of the case showed this correspondent to be somewhat in error; for it is impossible to imagine a darker showing of dishonorable transactions among French officers than has since been disclosed.

Dreyfus, a name which must now go down to all future ages as that of the central figure of the greatest trial of this age, was born in 1859, at Mülhausen, Alsace, one of the provinces given up to Germany by France as a result of the outcome of the war of 1870–71. His parents were Alsatian Jews of good standing and considerable wealth, and his brothers conducted a large cotton-spinning factory at Mülhausen. This, incidentally, seems to have been one of the causes which led to suspicions against Dreyfus. Although he does not appear to have been of a particularly inquisitive turn of mind, it has been shown that while in the army he made a number of inquiries, since classed as suspicious, but which appear to have really been founded on nothing more than a desire to obtain information which would lead to perfecting the spinning machinery of the family cotton factory. He is shown to have asked, for instance, Robin, the inventor of the Robin shell, a number of questions on this subject, but his enemies tried to turn this to an entirely different intention.

After the cession of Alsace and Lorraine to Germany, the inhabitants of those provinces, by agreement between the two countries, were given the option, or privilege, of declaring for French or German nationality.   In other words, if they chose to become German subjects they were at liberty to do so, while if they elected to become citizens of France there was no objection to that.   Dreyfus chose to remain a French citizen, and, when he reached the proper age, he entered the Polytechnic School, where he was educated.   This school, by the way, is the nursery of French officers, just as West Point is the school for American officers.   In 1880 Dreyfus entered the artillery as a sub-lieutenant.   He cannot have been backward in his study or have shown any objectionable characteristics at that time, for in 1882 he became a lieutenant, and in 1889 was promoted captain. Later, he was appointed to a position in the offices of the General Staff at the French War Office, being the first Jew to be so honored.

During his early years in the French army, Dreyfus, like most other French officers, seems to have led a pretty gay life, and, possibly, he obtained more credit for this than he really deserved, if some reports are to be believed, by boasting of conquests and claiming to have lost large sums in gambling, whereas it appears that while he had relations with a married woman, a Mrs. Bodson, while a lieutenant, he never gambled, and his conduct was most exemplary after his marriage, which occurred in 1889.

The pay of French officers and men is ridiculously small, and any officer having private means, as Dreyfus had, is naturally envied by those who are not similarly blessed.   This, undoubtedly, had something to do with the feeling which was aroused against Dreyfus.   General de Boisdeffre, the Chief of the Headquarters Staff, for instance, received a salary of only $5,000 a year, while Lieutenant-Colonel Henry's pay was but $1,000 a year.   In spite of these meagre stipends, French officers have to make a great deal of show, or, if they do not have to do it, they fancy it is incumbent upon them.   Under these circumstances a man handicapped by the fact that he depended entirely on his pay could hardly fail to feel a little jealousy of those like Dreyfus the Jew, who did not depend on their pay alone.

Captain Dreyfus still further improved his position financially when be married, for his wife is the daughter of M. Hadamard, a wealthy diamond merchant. They had two children and occupied expensive apartments in the Avenue du Trocadéro.

An entirely impartial opinion of Dreyfus is that he was a man of easy temper, of no particular ability, unlikely to shine in the military world, and easily depressed and discouraged. A good husband and father, he adored his family and took life easy. In return he was beloved by his wife and family, and loved by his brothers. These facts would seem to show that the man certainly possessed admirable qualities, for no woman could exhibit the steady, loyal devotion to a husband that Madame Dreyfus has exhibited unless the object of her affection possessed some sterling qualities. Indeed, the brightest feature of the whole tragedy is the grand spirit of loyalty shown by Madame Dreyfus toward her husband, her implicit belief in his innocence, the heroic manner in which she pointed out to him the path of duty, telling him, for the sake of his children, to go to his distant, pestilential island prison, there to await the hour when his innocence would be established. Had it not been for this wifely devotion, there is no doubt Dreyfus would not have lived to stand his second trial.

The brothers of Dreyfus, in fact all his relatives and friends, have shown steadfastness in this loyalty, which would seem still further proof that the man was not made of the material from which spies are moulded. Besides, the paltry sums, forty and sixty dollars, paid by the agents of foreign powers for valuable French military secrets, as subsequently shown, were certainly no attraction to Dreyfus, the well-to-do officer, happy in his home and family, and wanting for nothing. However, the above is but a pen-picture of the famous prisoner as he appeared; subsequent events and his trials must complete this light sketch of the prisoner of Devil's Island.

Chapter V.

THE PLOTTING BEGINS

AFTER the announcement of the intention of the French Government to prosecute Dreyfus on the charge of treason, the whole machinery of the War Office was set in motion to establish a case against the prisoner. The day after the official declaration to this effect (November 2d), the French authorities intercepted a telegram sent by Major Panizzardi, the Italian military attaché at Paris, whose name had been mentioned in connection with Dreyfus, to the Italian Government. The exact wording of this despatch was not made known. It was understood in the first instance to have been a request upon the part of Panizzardi that his Government deny, if it had no relations with Dreyfus, any connection with the prisoner, and asking that the Italian Ambassador at the French capital might be instructed to publish a statement to this effect in order to silence certain statements which were appearing in the press. This despatch seems to have been twisted in translations so as to convey an entirely different meaning to that of the writer, and was later used, surreptitiously, at the court-martial of the prisoner, and without the knowledge of his counsel or of himself, in obtaining his conviction.

After the prisoner's guilt was suspected he was subjected to a series of tests. For instance, he was asked to write under dictation a letter which contained terms similar to those of the *bordereau*. The dictation was given by Colonel Du Paty de Clam, with the Chief of Detectives, M. Cochefert, hiding behind the drapings of the room.

As a result of this dictation test, Dreyfus's arrest was decided upon by Colonel Du Paty de Clam. It was a cold day and, as the prisoner explained later, his hand may have shaken somewhat, which was taken as a *semblance* of guilt by Colonel Du Paty de Clam, who cried:

"*Vous tremblez!*" ("You tremble!")

"No," replied Dreyfus, "my fingers are cold."

The following is a portion of the test letter dictated to Dreyfus by Colonel Du Paty de Clam:

RÉPUBLIQUE FRANÇAISE.

THE TEST LETTER DICTATED TO CAPTAIN DREYFUS BY COLONEL DU PATY DE CLAM

But with a flourish of trumpets, it may be said, Paty de Clam made the signal agreed upon; the Chief of the Detectives entered, and M. Cochefert exclaimed, as he touched Dreyfus on the shoulder:

"I arrest you in the name of the Minister of War."

Captain Dreyfus submitted quietly to his arrest. He seemed, as he afterward exclaimed, to be completely dazed, and had no clear recollection of what occurred. When he asked to be informed regarding the charge against him he was put off with mysterious phrases, and it was not until some time later that he became aware he was charged with treason.

The prisoner was taken to the Cherche Midi, or military prison, of which institution Major Forzinetti was then the governor. He was escorted to the prison by Lieutenant-Colonel Henry and the detectives, and he was handed into the custody of Major Forzinetti with an order from the Minister of War by which the prisoner, described as being accused of high treason, was not to have his name entered on the prison books, but was to be kept in secret confinement, and was not to be allowed to hold any communication with anybody in the prison, much less outside of it, with the exception of Major Forzinetti and the chief keeper of the prison. These officials were strictly prohibited from telling anybody of the arrest of the prisoner.

A book could be written upon what transpired in the Cherche Midi while Dreyfus was confined there.

Major Forzinetti, at a later date, gave some idea of what occurred during that period. He said, in brief:

"On October 14, 1894, I received a confidential despatch from the War Office. It informed me that on the following morning a field-officer would call at the prison in order to acquaint me with a secret communication. On the 15th, Lieutenant-Colonel d'Abeville, in full uniform, handed me a despatch, informing me that Captain Dreyfus, of the Fourteenth Regiment of Artillery, serving on the General Staff of the army, would be imprisoned on the charge of high treason, and that I was personally responsible for his safe custody. Colonel d'Abeville asked me to give my word of honor that I would strictly carry out the minister's injunctions. The prisoner was to have no sort of communication with the outer world, and was to have neither knife, paper, pen, ink, nor pencil. He was to be treated in the matter of food as an ordinary criminal, but this order was cancelled upon my remark that it was illegal. The colonel, without going into particulars, ordered me to take whatever precautions I might deem necessary to prevent the fact of the prisoner's arrest being known in the prison or outside. He asked to see the cells set apart for officers, and selected one for Captain Dreyfus. He told me to be on my guard against the intrigues of the *haute Juiverie* (high Jewdom) as soon as the news of arrest should reach their ears. I saw nobody and nobody attempted to get at me. I never visited the prisoner except in company of the head keeper, who alone had the key of the cell. Nobody saw the prisoner during his detention except in my presence. When, after his arrival, I went to see the prisoner, he was in a state of excitement impossible to describe—like a madman. His eyes were bloodshot, and he had upset everything in his room. I was able at length to quiet him. I felt that he was innocent."

A further insight into the methods of the military inquisitors may be gathered from the following additional statement of Major Forzinetti:

"Du Paty de Clam, who had arrested Dreyfus at the War Office, called at the prison from October 18th to October 24th, with the special authority of the Minister of War [Mercier] to examine the prisoner. He asked me whether he could not enter Dreyfus's cell noiselessly with a bull's-eye sufficiently powerful to throw a flood of light on the face of the prisoner, whom he wanted to take by surprise in order to upset him. I said it was not possible. He examined the prisoner twice, and each time dictated to him sentences taken from the famous document (the bordereau) in order to compare the two writings.

"During the whole of this period Captain Dreyfus was in a state of terrible excitement. In the hall one could hear him moaning, crying, talking aloud, protesting his innocence. He knocked against the furniture, against the walls, and did not seem aware of the injuries he was inflicting upon himself. He had not a moment's rest, and when overcome with fatigue and agony he lay, dressed, on his bed. His sleep was haunted by horrible nightmares. He had such convulsions during his sleep that he sometimes fell on the floor. During this agony of nine days he took nothing but beef tea and a little wine with sugar.

"On the 24th, in the morning, his mental state, bordering on insanity, seemed so serious, that, anxious to screen my responsibility, I reported it, to the Minister of War [Mercier] and to the Governor of Paris. In the afternoon I was summoned by General de Boisdeffre, and accompanied him to the War Office. The general asked me my opinion. I replied without hesitation that Dreyfus was not guilty. General de Boisdeffre entered the minister's room alone, and, coming out again, looking annoyed, he said to me: ' The general is leaving Paris to attend his niece's wedding, and gives me full powers during his absence. Try and keep Dreyfus alive until his return, and the minister will do what he pleases.' General de Boisdeffre told me to send the prison doctor to Dreyfus. He prescribed some soothing drugs.

"Du Paty de Clam called nearly every day after the 27th, to examine Dreyfus and to get new specimens of his handwriting. His real object was to wring an admission of guilt, against which Dreyfus never ceased to protest.

"After the verdict Dreyfus was taken back to his cell, where I saw him about midnight. On seeing me he burst into sobs, and said: ' My only crime is to be born a Jew.' His despair was such that I was afraid for his mind, and had him watched day and night.

"I have been for many years at the head of military prisons, and have some knowledge of prisoners, and I can assert emphatically that a dreadful mistake has been committed. My superiors have known my opinion from the first. Several generals and statesmen are just as certain as I am of Dreyfus's innocence, but cowardice prevents them from speaking."

Chapter VI.

THE FIRST COURT-MARTIAL

CAPTAIN ALFRED DREYFUS was tried by secret court-martial, at the Cherche-Midi Prison, the trial beginning on December 19, 1894. At the time nothing was allowed to transpire regarding the proceedings, but all the main facts in the case have since become known.

The first code of military justice, which was in force at that time in France, was promulgated in 1857, and leaves much to be desired so far as obtaining justice for an accused person is concerned.

The principle which governs the composition of councils of war is as follows:

No military man can be judged by his subordinates. He has the right to the jurisdiction of his superiors or his peers. That is to say, following the rank of the accused, the composition of a court-martial varies. Captain Dreyfus, for instance, was tried by a court-martial presided over by a colonel, Maurel-Pries, and had among its members a lieutenant-colonel, three chiefs of battalion (majors), or chiefs of squadrons (majors), and two captains. The commissary of the Government, or prosecutor, has to be of a rank at least equal to that of the accused. The defence is provided for in the presence of a lawyer or through an officer, according to the choice of the accused. The members of the court-martial sit in full uniform, while the accused appears in undress uniform and without arms.

As to the procedure before a French court-martial, it is about the same as before French civil tribunals. The president of the court, before interrogating the accused, warns him that the law gives him every latitude to explain matters and present his defence. But the president remains sole master of the interrogatory, the other members of the court-martial being only authorized to put, through the president, any questions which may seem to them to be of a nature likely to throw light on the case and which the president's questioning may have omitted.

3

The witnesses depose according to the ordinary customs of France. That is to say, they mount to the witness stand and practically make a speech for the prisoner or against him, and make almost any allegations they choose.   In fact, the prisoner is practically looked upon as guilty, and it is considered his duty to prove himself not guilty.

After each deposition, the president of the court is called upon to put the following question to the witness:

" You affirm that you have been speaking of the accused, here present. Do you formally declare you recognize him? "

After taking the testimony, the commissary of the Government makes his plea for the punishment of the accused, and counsel for the defence replies, after which the members of the court-martial retire and deliberate in private.   The votes of the court are received according to the ranks of the members, beginning at the lowest grade, the president being the last to make his opinion known.

After the judgment of the court has been drawn up, the members of the Council of War re-enter the court, stand upright, and when the president begins the initial formula of the announcement of the judgment, " In the name of the French people," the members of the court salute and the military guard on duty present arms.

The judgment of the court is then read, the presence of the accused not being permitted, though the sentence is made known to him later by a special ceremony, the clerk of the court reading the sentence to him before the guard, under arms.

The members of the first Dreyfus court-martial were: Colonel Maurel-Pries, President; Lieutenant-Colonel Echemann, Majors Florentine, Patron, and Gallet, and Captains Roche and Freystaetter.

Major Brisset acted as Government commissary, and prosecuted the prisoner in behalf of the Government.

The greatest interest was taken in the trial, and great efforts were made on the part of the public to get a glimpse of the prisoner.   The approaches to the prison were crowded, and the greatest military and police precautions were taken to prevent a disturbance.   As previously noted, the word " treason " has an almost magical effect upon the French public, and, therefore, when it became known that " *Nous sommes trahis* " for once had apparently some foundation in fact, the excitement was very great.

Dreyfus was taken to the prison before the crowd had time to assemble, and all sorts of erroneous rumors were set afloat in order to complicate matters and divert the attention of the populace from the trial.

Dreyfus entered the court escorted by Republican Guards. He was apparently cool and calm, bowed to the court, and quietly advanced to the seat set apart for him. It has been claimed, however, that his eyes were filled with tears, and that it was with difficulty he preserved his self-control.

In this connection a curious theory was advanced and found a number of believers. It was to the effect that Dreyfus was more of a German hero and martyr than a French traitor. It was asserted that he "opted," or pronounced himself in favor of French citizenship, at the time his native province, Alsace, was turned over to Germany; entered the French Military School, Army, and Ministry of War, all with one fixed purpose, namely. to serve the Germany he loved against the France which he hated. It was added that he was not more than eighteen years of age when he formed this project, and that he had carefully weighed all his chances— except the fearful imprisonment on Devil's Island. Since that time, however, no evidence has been forthcoming to substantiate this theory, while there has been abundant testimony to prove that Dreyfus was actuated by feelings of hearty loyalty to France. Indeed, it has been the writer's experience with Alsatians and Lorrainers to find them ultra-loyal to France. With but few exceptions (perhaps only a single exception—an Alsatian soldier who was eventually sentenced to penal servitude for life as a result of his bitter hatred for France), the Alsatians and Lorrainers of France appear to detest the Germans more bitterly than the French of the interior, which is a matter not easily accounted for.

Chapter VII.

FOUND GUILTY AND CONDEMNED

COLONEL MAUREL-PRIES, president of the court, began the proceedings with interrogating the prisoner in the usual stereotyped manner, the latter saying his name was Alfred Dreyfus, that he was thirty-five years of age, a captain of artillery, and born at Mülhausen, Alsace.

At the opening of the proceedings the court was filled with officers of all grades and arms, and some fifty reporters were present. But when this stage had been reached, the president called upon Major Brisset, the Prosecutor, or Government Commissary, to make a formal charge against the prisoner; whereupon the major arose, and, to the astonishment of probably all but the members of the court, requested that the proceedings be conducted *in camera*, or in secret, otherwise behind closed doors. He advanced in support of his plea the statement that the publicity which would be given to the testimony, if allowed to be printed in the press, would be "against the public interests," meaning that matters would be revealed which it was advisable that the enemies of France should not know. A plea of this description has great weight with any French court, and there was no doubt of the outcome from the moment the prosecutor addressed the president.

Dreyfus, at these proceedings, was represented by Maître Demange, a lawyer of considerable ability, who had been retained by the relatives of Dreyfus. Although not a brilliant lawyer, in the sense the term is generally accepted, Maître Demange proved himself to be a steady, hardworking seeker after the truth and a conservative adviser of great value. It was not his first experience in such cases, which was probably the reason which led to his being selected to defend Dreyfus. He had defended other men charged with treason, and had the confidence of the authorities.

At the conclusion of the plea of Major Brisset, Maître Demange strongly opposed having the trial of the prisoner conducted in secret. He entered into a lengthy argument on the subject, and presented a number of good reasons why the trial should be in public. Subsequent events showed that his contention was well based, and France would have been spared a great deal of trouble and loss of prestige, from a judicial, political and military standpoint, if the arguments of the lawyer had been allowed to prevail. But there seems to be no doubt now that no amount of argument would have changed the predetermined opinion of that court-martial on the subject of the secret sitting. Beyond doubt, orders were issued from high quarters to have the trial conducted in secret.

The president of the court insisted that the lawyer must not make any reference in his plea to the actual charge against the prisoner, which almost disarmed the latter's counsel at the outset.

A long controversy followed between the lawyer, the president, and the prosecutor.

"There are other interests at stake," cried the prosecutor, "than those of the defence and of the prosecution."

That some inkling of the Government's case had reached the counsel for the defence was evidenced by the fact that Maître Demange, at one stage of his argument, referred to the "solitary document" brought forward against the prisoner, whereupon he was instantly silenced by the president, and as the lawyer insisted, in spite of this rebuff, upon referring to the "solitary document," though loyally refraining from entering into details, the court rose, and when the members of the court-martial returned to the trial hall the president, after severely reprimanding Maître Demange for having "persistently insisted" upon "raising the discussion of the essentials of the case," announced that the trial of Dreyfus would take place behind closed doors.

In spite of the veil of secrecy thrown over the proceedings, enough has since transpired to show that the following was the procedure:

The indictment of the prisoner, which had been prepared by Major d'Ormescheville, was read, and then the court took the testimony of three experts in handwriting, MM. Pelletier, Charavay, and Teysonniere, who had been called upon to examine the handwriting of the bordereau and Dreyfus's handwriting, particularly the test dictation prepared by Du Paty de Clam.

The first of the experts, Pelletier, testified that the handwriting of Dreyfus was identical with that of the bordereau.

The second expert, M. Charavay, testified that the two documents were written by the same person, adding, however, that he would never have any one condemned to imprisonment for life on such testimony as he was then able to give.

The third expert, M. Teysonniere, also thought the bordereau might have been written by Dreyfus.

Du Paty de Clam testified elaborately to the many experiments, some of them of the most ridiculous nature, which he had made in connection with Dreyfus, particularly referring to the prisoner's "nervous movements of the foot when interrogated," and to the "trembling of his hand," when asked to write from dictation.

Colonel Henry, chief of the Intelligence Department, told the court he was persuaded the prisoner was guilty. He added that he had other reasons than those which appeared in the indictment to show Dreyfus was the traitor. But when he was urged to speak out and explain what he meant, Henry drew back and exclaimed:

"I am a soldier, and my képi must ignore what is in my head."

The verdict was rendered the same evening. The prisoner was pronounced "Guilty," and was sentenced to perpetual imprisonment in a fortified place, and to military degradation.

Night had fallen when this act in the drama was ended. The news soon spread with the public outside of the Cherche-Midi prison, and there were hideous cries of "Down with the Jews!" "Down with the traitors!" "Vive la France!" "Vive l'Armée!" which must have reached the unhappy prisoner.

The sentence was read to Dreyfus by gaslight, in the dully illuminated hall of the prison, with the military guard presenting arms and every accompaniment of military horror which it was possible to imagine. The prisoner listened, speechless, to the words which sent him to a living tomb. He appeared utterly unnerved, helpless, friendless—plunged into the deepest despair. His face was almost as white as it was possible to be, and drops of cold perspiration gathered on his brow. His lips were parched and of a dull, blue color. His eyes were bloodshot and glared with the expression seen in those of hunted animals. Apparently the prisoner was stupefied, for he did not seem to realize that the scene transpiring in that dark prison was not a horrible nightmare. A few words of comfort from his lawyer, a whispered message from his wife, and the crushed, wincing man was led back to the room which he was not to leave again until taken to the scene of his degradation.

"I am innocent!" he cried hoarsely, the words choking him. "I am innocent!" "My God! You have condemned an innocent man!"

But, the military inquisitors had already turned their backs on the hapless captain, and with fierce mutterings against the traitor they hurried away to their different haunts, while France was supposed to have breathed sighs of relief, as evidenced by the hoarse cries in the streets: "Down with the Jews!" "Down with the traitor!" "Vive la France!" "Vive l'Armée!" "Vive la République!"

Such were the cries which broke the stillness of the night.

Throughout the evening Paris was in a state of the greatest agitation. The evening papers, briefly announcing the verdict, sold like the proverbial "hot cakes" on the boulevards. The cafés were crowded with people eagerly discussing the case. The military and other clubs were packed with excited people, and it may be said hardly a voice, hardly a murmur was raised in behalf of Dreyfus, the convicted traitor.

But in a darkened room in a pretty apartment on the Avenue du Trocadéro knelt a weeping woman. By her side were two men of stern bearing and a stout, honest-looking personage, a lawyer. The woman wept and prayed, but the men soothed her as much as possible, and assured her of their unalterable sympathy.

Two children, in their nursery, had been put to bed, lulled into slumber by the legend that their father, a captain of artillery, had been sent away on foreign service, and would not return for a long time, perhaps for years. By this pleasant tale the mother's grief and agitation was accounted for, and the next day the children were taken away to a distant spot, far from the cruel echoes of the noisy world, where they have since grown up, praying nightly for the return of the absent father, so long away "on foreign service."

Dreyfus, in his prison room, passed the night with his head upon his table, now and then writing short, feverish-worded notes; but his thoughts were fixed upon those rooms in the Avenue du Trocadéro where his wife and children waited and prayed.

Chapter VIII.

THE DEGRADATION

THE degradation of Captain Dreyfus took place on the Square of the Military School, at Paris, at nine o'clock on the morning of January 5, 1895, in the presence of 5,000 troops, a number of newspaper representatives and others.   It was described by cable as follows, at the time:

Some time before daylight detachments from all the regiments in the district of Paris were on the march to the parade ground.   These detachments comprised raw recruits, veterans, and men of all grades of the service, and as they arrived at the École Militaire they took the positions assigned to them.

The weather was clear and bright, but cold.

Workingmen, who were hurrying down the Rue Cherche-Midi about seven o'clock on the morning of the degradation of Dreyfus, stopped for a moment to stare at the prison van, surrounded by mounted soldiers, which was standing outside the Military Prison waiting to convey Captain Dreyfus to the École Militaire.   Many of the men shook their fists in the direction of the condemned man's quarters and uttered deep curses upon the head of the traitor.

About 7:40 A.M., a veteran soldier, employed as janitor in the prison, threw back the iron gates, and Captain Dreyfus, flanked by two soldiers carrying guns with fixed bayonets, walked out and hurriedly mounted the steps of the van between lines of Republican Guards. The van, which was driven by a trooper, took its course across the Rue Dupin and down the Rues de Babylone and d'Estrées, crossing the Avenue de Breteuil, to the École Militaire, where it arrived at five minutes of eight.

Dreyfus mounted the van with perfect unconcern.   He stood erect, and his cheeks were not whitened by the customary pallor of prisoners. His appearance was more like that of a man going on parade than that of a prisoner condemned to life imprisonment and official degradation.   At

8:30 A.M., General Darras, commanding the troops, arrived. He was assisted by Colonel Fayette and a major of the Paris garrison. The troops formed a square, facing the main entrance to the parade ground, where a band composed of drums and bugles was stationed.

The Thirty-ninth Regiment, having Captain Dreyfus in charge, was one of the first bodies of troops to arrive at the parade ground.

At precisely nine o'clock the prisoner was led out from the left wing of the square. He was accompanied by a squad of artillery soldiers. He was pale, but with a firm step marched, with his sword in his right hand, to the centre of the square, where he was awaited by General Darras. Dreyfus halted before the general and stood at "attention."

The adjutant of the Republican Guard then read the verdict of the court-martial which had condemned Captain Dreyfus. While the verdict was being read Dreyfus flushed somewhat, but otherwise he showed no sign of losing his composure.

After the reading of the verdict General Darras addressed the prisoner, saying:

"Dreyfus, you are unworthy to carry arms. In the name of the people of France we degrade you."

The adjutant then walked up to Dreyfus, and took from him his sword, which, with a quick, sharp movement, he broke across his knee, casting the pieces upon the ground. He then cut the buttons and insignia of rank from the uniform of the condemned captain, and threw them also upon the ground.

At this point in the proceedings, Dreyfus was for a moment moved by a sense of his humiliation, but he quickly suppressed his emotion and shouted in a loud voice: "*Vive la France!*"

Continuing, he said: "You have degraded an innocent man! I swear that I am innocent!"

He seemed about to speak further, but his voice was drowned by the rolling of the drums, which was not loud enough, however, to drown a ringing shout from the crowd, in the rear of the soldiers, of "*À mort le traître!*" ("Death to the traitor!")

The ceremony up to this time had lasted just four minutes. The drums then beat, and the degraded man began his march along the four sides of the square, in what is known as "*la parade de l'execution.*"

The scene was very impressive, and many of the younger soldiers turned their heads away.

Dreyfus marched in a firm and soldierly way, with a quick, short step, and when he reached the delegation of officers from the Reserves, he raised his hand and said:

"Tell the whole of France that I am innocent!"

Turning to the left from the position of the Reserve officers, he came before the members of the press, to whom he said in a firm voice:

"I declare that I am innocent!"

The end of the march was reached at twenty minutes past nine, after which the condemned man was taken to the barrack gate and turned over to the civil authorities.

A large crowd of people had gathered at the entrance of the parade ground, and from among them came not one word of sympathy, but the cry of "*À mort le traitre!*" ("Death to the traitor!") was taken up by them and repeated until the miserable man was out of the hearing of his tormentors.

Dreyfus was received from his escort at the barrack gate by four gendarmes, who placed him in an ordinary prison van, and at half-past nine the troops marched out of the parade ground, back to their respective quarters.

As a measure of preparation for stripping the prisoner of his insignia of rank, etc., the prison tailor on the day before removed all the buttons and stripes from Dreyfus's tunic, the red stripes from his trousers, and the regimental number and braid from his collar and cap. These were all replaced with a single stitch, so that they could be torn away readily.

The condemned man's sword was also filed almost in twain, in order that it might be easily broken. The adjutant's quick movement and apparent effort in breaking the sword was consequently mere pretence, as only a mere touch was necessary.

As the prison van sped through the streets the people stood on the sidewalks and with uplifted hands menaced and cursed the unfortunate officer.

It is stated that when Dreyfus spoke to the officers of the Reserve, protesting his innocence, the latter retorted: "Down with the Judas!" "Silence, traitor!" etc.

Dreyfus became greatly excited at this, and turned again appealingly to the officers, but the soldiers escorting him quickly seized him and forced him to continue his humiliating march.

Another report said that when the officers of the Reserve cried out, "Down with the Judas!" "Silence, traitor!" etc., Dreyfus was stunned for a moment, but, quickly recovering himself, he looked upon them through his eye-glasses, which he wore throughout the ceremony, and with a smile of contempt said in a clear, firm voice:

"You are cowards!"

Before the ceremony of degradation began the vast space in the Place de Fontenoy, facing the courtyard of the École Militaire, was crowded with men and women. Many persons climbed the base of the hexagonal granite monument erected to the memory of the Parisians who were killed in 1870, and others hired places upon step-ladders at the rate of five francs each and maintained their positions throughout in the biting wind.

Toward the end of the ceremony the sky became overcast with snow clouds, which the sun occasionally pierced, but the air was extremely cold.

Although the ceremony of degrading the condemned officer presented a theatrical aspect to civilians, it had so profound an impression upon the military spectators that during the short time it lasted a newspaper representative who was present counted within a few feet of him six officers, whose trembling limbs were scarcely able to hold them up, while hundreds of others, officers and privates, stood with blanched cheeks and straining eyes, utterly unable to control their feelings.

The crowds outside, who kept up a continual shout of "Death to the traitor!" became almost delirious, and had the ceremony taken place in an open space like the Esplanade des Invalides it is absolutely certain that twenty at least of the most violent of these fanatics would have broken through the square and tried to lynch Dreyfus.

Generally ninety-nine out of every hundred men who are thus degraded weep like children during the ceremony, but Dreyfus was firm throughout. During the entire ceremony he appeared to be less affected than almost any person present. Except that he was stung for an instant by the taunts of his fellow-officers, he was perfectly cool.

Dreyfus, upon reaching the prison depot, said to the governor of the institution:

"My innocence will be recognized some day. I have confidence that Providence in its own time will reveal the real culprit."

After Dreyfus's height and other dimensions were taken, he was transferred to the Prison de la Santé, where he remained until deported for confinement in a fortress, in accordance with his sentence.

Chapter IX.

ANOTHER ACCOUNT OF THE DEGRADATION

THE following account of the degradation of Dreyfus, written by "Jacques St. Cere," the famous correspondent of the New York *Herald*, is interesting as it gives the impressions formed at the time by the writer:

"The degradation of Captain Alfred Dreyfus from his military rank and honors took place this morning (January 5, 1895), on the parade ground of the École Militaire.

"By order of General Saussier, Military Governor of Paris, no card of admission was issued to the correspondent of any foreign paper. Nevertheless the representative of the *Herald* was present throughout the whole ceremony.

"The scene was one that can never be forgotten. When the adjutant tore away the insignia of his rank from his cap, Dreyfus shouted: '*Vive la France!*' and this cry he repeated when his sword was broken. This caused a profound emotion. Then he was led, bareheaded, his uniform stripped of all its gold lace and buttons, along the front of the troops.

"When he arrived in front of the group of two hundred journalists and civil officials who were permitted to witness the ceremony, Dreyfus cried out:

"'Tell the whole of France that I am an innocent man!'

"The way in which this cry was given, and the appearance of the prisoner, who held himself very erect in his mutilated uniform, his red face, his bloodshot but dry eyes, produced a profound impression even on those who were the most thoroughly convinced of his guilt. Dreyfus had in every respect the appearance of a man protesting against a great injustice.

"There certainly is a great deal of mystery about this case. On the one hand the officials of the ministry of war affirm that Captain Dreyfus is guilty, while on the other hand Maitre Demange, whose position as a leading member of the French bar is above question, solemnly asserts that his client is innocent, something which, now that the case is at an end, there is no reason for his doing unless he is convinced that such is the fact.

"At the end of the ceremony of degradation the prisoner, with handcuffs on his wrists, was placed in a prison van, and removed to the police dépôt. His name was struck from the army rolls, and he was henceforth treated like any ordinary criminal.

"The degradation of Dreyfus caused a profound excitement among the Parisian public. Not less than twenty thousand persons, who were kept at a distance from the scene, surrounded the square and hooted at the prisoner throughout the ceremony, shouting:

"'Death to the traitor!' 'Death to the Jews!'

"Such days are bad for the people and bad for the Government, which is now being driven into making a cleaning away of persons prominent in journalistic and political circles, who are suspected simply because of the race to which they are supposed to belong.

"'Casimir wants to clean up,' is a favorite expression just now among those who belong to the '*entourage*' of the President of the French Republic.

"Public opinion is passionately worked up over the Dreyfus case. Here is some information in regard to it which comes to me from a very good source. There is no doubt as to the prisoner's guilt. His arrest was decided on the unanimous vote of the eleven ministers, who at the same time pledged themselves not to reveal anything contained in the report demanding the prosecution of Dreyfus, which was signed by General Mercier, Minister of War; General de Boisdeffre, Chief of the General Staff, and General Gonse, the Assistant Chief of the General Staff.

"The secrets betrayed by Dreyfus are of such importance that the Government will ask the chamber to pass a law providing for the imprisonment of Dreyfus, not at Noumea, from which an escape is possible, but on an island of French Guiana, where he will be strictly watched.

"It is believed that Dreyfus was the centre of the German espionage system in France, and it is asserted that no less than twenty-seven attempts were made by German diplomacy, both at the Ministry of Foreign Affairs and at the Ministry of the Interior, to get the affair hushed up.

"These facts, which I have upon the best authority, force me, in spite of the way in which Dreyfus faced the ordeal, to believe in his guilt."

Chapter X.

THE "SYNDICATE OF SILENCE"

IN order that the situation in France at the time of the first Dreyfus court-martial may be more clearly understood, it is necessary to refer to the corruption existing in the French press, and particularly to the famous "Syndicate of Silence."

No sooner was the news of the arrest of Dreyfus made public than Madame Dreyfus, a wealthy woman in her own right, was besieged by representatives of certain of the Paris newspapers with offers to "give publicity to anything she might wish to publish regarding the arrest of her husband," etc., etc., not on the honest basis of the American press, which would print free anything a woman so unfortunate might be willing to say, but—for a consideration. Distracted with grief, Madame Dreyfus is said to have disbursed a large amount of money, in sums varying from one hundred to one thousand francs, to the first dozen or so of these journalistic vultures. But her eyes were opened to the true state of affairs by her friends.

At about this time, M. Henri Rochefort, editor of the *Intransigéant*, referred to France, his native land, as the "*Pays de Chantage*," otherwise the "Land of Blackmail." M. Rochefort claimed that blackmail was not only a prominent characteristic of the modern press of France, but that it was the strongest weapon of the Government of that day (1894–95) He added:

"Since the time when the lists of Arton and Reinach (the Panama lobbyists) were made public, the reactionary government of the country has obtained all its concessions from the Chamber of Deputies merely by the terror of divulgation."

That there may have been truth in this assertion would seem likely from the exposure in December, 1894, of the "Syndicate of Silence." It appears that Allez Brothers, a well-known hardware firm of Paris, contracted early in December of that year to supply the minister of war with

a number of water-cans for the use of the army.   Later, the firm sublet
the contract to another house, and when the cans were delivered the inspector of the War Department refused to accept them, as being too light and
made of inferior metal.   The cans were offered again by Allez Brothers,
whereupon the inspector discovered that false bottoms had been put in the
cans in order to bring them up to the required weight, and he again
refused them.   Allez Brothers were informed by the Minister of War,
General Mercier, that they would be prosecuted, and the story got into
the public press.   But, in some manner not clearly explained, seven Paris
newspaper men formed a "Syndicate of Silence."   The object of the organization was to prevent the newspapers of Paris from publishing references
to the alleged fraud due to the action of Allez Brothers.   The head of
that firm is said to have been visited by the head of the "Syndicate of
Silence," who is reported to have said to him:

"If you will hand over to me 100,000 francs ($20,000) I will
guarantee the silence of the Paris press upon this little matter of the
water-can contract.   I will undertake to organize a press campaign in
favor of the house of Allez Brothers.   Further, a certain number of
deputies shall be influenced in such a way as to force the Minister of War
to accept the false-bottomed cans already tendered, and if General Mercier
should show himself at all obstinate he will be politely requested to resign
his portfolio."

Still, according to the story, Allez Brothers jumped at the offer and
paid this large sum demanded without much protest, and the head of the
syndicate, it is asserted, handed $2,500 to each of his associates and kept
$5,000 for himself.

But, the next day, Allez Brothers discovered that many of the Paris
newspapers continued to demand the prosecution of the firm.   In fact, it
became apparent that only seven out of the forty or fifty newspapers had
been "silenced," whereupon the firm complained to the Minister of War
and insisted upon the prosecution of the blackmailers.

General Mercier, it seems, decided to proceed against the seven members of the "Syndicate of Silence," and even began to take steps in that
direction, when, it was pointed out at the time, a Higher Power in the
State intervened, explaining to the general that it would be "unwise, at
this moment, to raise another Panama scandal."

"Call upon the seven to refund the one hundred thousand francs," the Higher Power is alleged to have said, "and let the matter drop, so far as the Government is concerned."

This, it is added, was done, and six of the members of the "Syndicate of Silence" took their $2,500 share to their chief, but they were dumfounded when the latter told them he had spent his $5,000 in paying his debts, and that in order to settle the matter they would have to contribute that amount from their own pockets in order to make up the 100,000 francs; and this was done also!

Some of the papers insisted that an inquiry should be made into the matter, and it seems at least one of the seven conspirators was himself asked to sit in judgment upon the affair, while the man appointed president of the committee of inquiry was described as occupying a prominent position upon a Paris newspaper which was inscribed upon the Panama Canal lobbying list as having received 1,500,000 francs. As the committee had no power to investigate or authority to search for evidence against the guilty parties, those in possession of the facts refused to appear before the tribunal.

Finally, it is charged that the committee was purposely constructed so as to frustrate the object it was intended to accomplish; and the inquiry of course collapsed.

4

Chapter XI.

EXILED TO DEVIL'S ISLAND

SHORTLY after his degradation, Dreyfus was taken to the fortress of Île de Ré, off the coast of France, preparatory to being shipped to the French penal settlement of Cayenne, French Guiana, off which place lay the Îles du Salut (Salvation Islands), of which Île du Diable (Devil's Island), which was to be his permanent prison, formed a part.

Thus, for four years, disappeared from view the degraded officer, the man denounced as a traitor from one end of France to the other, but beloved and believed in by those who knew him best.

Before he was put on board the ship which took him to Devil's Island, Dreyfus was allowed to have a probably last interview with his faithful wife. In this interview he broke down and talked of suicide. But the noble woman arose to the occasion and pointed him out the path of duty. She told him that, for the sake of his children and for her sake, as well as for the sake of his loyal friends, he must put up with everything and trust to them to prove his innocence in due course of time.

Just before leaving France Dreyfus wrote a letter to his wife which contained the following words:

"In promising you to live, to keep firm until my name is rehabilitated, I have made you the greatest sacrifice that a man of feeling—a man of honor—from whom they have torn his honor, can make. Provided only that God help me, that my physical strength does not leave me. The will is there, and my conscience, which reproaches me with nothing, bears me up. So, then, my darling, do all in the world you can to find the true culprit; never relax your efforts for a moment. It is my only hope."

Madame Dreyfus was faithful to her husband's solemn charge. From that time on she devoted herself to the rehabilitation of her husband. The brothers of Dreyfus and her relatives spared no trouble and no money in seeking for enlightenment. The brothers freely offered their whole fortune in the efforts made, and a systematic campaign was opened in behalf of the prisoner. Madame Dreyfus made superhuman efforts to touch the hearts of the great army chiefs, but they were obdurate, saying they were firmly convinced of the guilt of the prisoner. In fact, the War Office authorities seemed to think they had done a very clever piece of work, and Du Paty de Clam was promoted for his share in the affair.

Dreyfus, on his way to his island prison, was treated with the greatest harshness and contempt. Nobody has any sympathy or respect for a traitor; and Frenchmen less than any other people. He arrived at his destination, however, in fairly good health, though much depressed in spirits and still vainly protesting his innocence.

In this manner two years passed, and this gives us an opportunity to glance at the Salvation Islands.

The Salvation Islands comprise three small islands off the coast of French Guiana, a few degrees north of the equator, and, except by a narrow sea frontage, is covered with tropical forests. The climate is simply murderous, (certain death being the result of standing bareheaded in the sun even for a short time.) From November to June is the wet season, during which the average rainfall is 180 inches; yet the temperature is never less than 85°, and rises to 115° during the four dry months. Convict ships bound for these "Islands of the Cursed" generally sail either from the Île de Ré, in the Bay of Biscay, or the Île d'Aix, in the Mediterranean. A month is occupied by the voyage, the horrors of which are a fit prelude to those yet to come.

Dressed in their convict garb, the prisoners are confined in batches of fifty in great iron cages on the spar deck. Benches are placed around the sides of the cage, and hammocks are slung at night. But day and night they are watched by guards standing beside loaded *mitrailleuses*, (rapid-firing guns), ready to fire at the first sign of mutiny. Sometimes, indeed, such outbreaks do occur; but they are invariably quelled with remorseless severity. The horrors of the passage are too repulsive for description, the scenes resembling rather those observable a century or two ago than what one would expect in the present times.

On the arrival of the prisoners at the Îles du Salut they are taken to the "camp," a clearing occupied by strongly built iron-barred huts, furnished with double rows of hammocks. But at night the fetid atmosphere within, combined with the noisome vapors of the outer air and the ever-present swarms of stinging insects, render any but the sleep of exhaustion impossible.   From the moment of his arrival the convict has no name. He is known only by the number of his hammock.   The new arrivals are put to the most severe tasks—draining marshes and clearing ground—"to break their spirits."   They are conducted to their work by armed guards, who are ordered to fire at the least attempt at flight.   Hardly any try to escape, for they know that, if they evade the bullets of the guards and their pursuit, it will be necessary to traverse the virgin forest and the sea. At every step will lie in wait of them death by hunger, by fatigue, by disease, or by the poisoned arrows of the natives, who receive a reward for every convict they bring back, dead or alive.   Meanwhile, with their bodies broken by their awful toil in a climate where a walk of a hundred yards is a formidable task, they labor in the blazing sun with spades and picks.   About their heads hang clouds of stinging insects.   Great red ants cover their bare legs, and sometimes poisonous serpents twist about their ankles and inflict mortal wounds.   They stand in trenches up to their knees in water and mire, and the exhalations rising from the earth consume them with fever, or set their teeth chattering as with cold, while the sweat rolls from their foreheads.

Occasionally, in their despair, some of the convicts revolt, in the hope, which is seldom disappointed, of finding in the bullets of their custodians a relief from this living torture.   Others again go mad, or end their lives by deliberately exposing themselves to the sun, while very few ever succeed in escaping.   Indeed, only once have any fugitives reached civilized countries again, and even then their period of freedom was comparatively brief.

Chapter XII.

LIFE ON DEVIL'S ISLAND

ONLY a week previous to Dreyfus's arrival his particular island (Devil's Island) was used as *a hospital for lepers*, all of whom, however, had been removed, and their huts burnt down.

The island on which the man convicted of betraying his country was seemingly destined to pass the rest of his days is a very small one, shaded by a few cocoanut trees, and, small though it be, he was not allowed to set foot on more than a part of it, the only point from which he could by any possibility escape being prohibited to him. His modern hut, measuring four yards square, comprised but one room, in which a couple of guards were ever with the prisoner, who at night was shut in his den, which was constantly lighted up, a hole in the door enabling the watchman to keep an eye on his every movement.

With regard to food Dreyfus was treated at first, it appears, in the same way as French soldiers in the colonies, and on that score he had nothing to complain of.

Naturally the view was a distant one; for on the Île du Diable (Devil's Island) no one debarks. But from either of the other islands—from the Île St. Joseph, where the bulk of the convicts are confined, and where the executioner has his habitat, or from the Île Royale, where the marines who constitute the garrison are quartered—the prisoner on the intermediate rock could be made out distinctly enough through an opera-glass, and the more readily that he alone was privileged to wear white clothes. The one white-clad figure, bearded now, and bent and listless, among the blue uniforms—that is surely he.

Dreyfus's movements in 1896 were under less restraint than was at first the case. The length and breadth of the rock was his exercise during certain hours. He was master of his dreary time. He could employ it as he pleased, and he seemed to have mapped it out with the idea of getting through as much of it as possible.   He read steadily and smoked as steadily, walked much, ate little, drank no stimulants, and slept seven hours out of the twenty-four.   His health under this régime held out, perhaps, as well as could be expected against a climatic dispensation of tropical rain and torrid sun, by no means conducive to longevity.

His literature was as ample as his friends could make it.   He had books of all sorts, and periodicals by the bale, but never a newspaper. Yet somehow he heard of the Cauvin case, and laid considerable stress on that rehabilitation of an unjustly condemned man in one of the many memorials he addressed to the powers at home.

The burden of all the prisoners was the same.   Dreyfus admitted appearances were against him, but he maintained that he was the victim of a ghastly judicial error.   For fear of diplomatic complications, the court that tried him sat with closed doors; it was those closed doors, he averred, that shut out the truth.   But the time, he never ceased to declare, was bound to come when his innocence would appear clear as the sun at noonday.   And there was always the same calm assurance of this, and no heat, or anger, or acrimony.

The prisoner's attitude was as disquieting as were his more passionate protests that January morning in the square of the École Militaire.

Certainly it disquieted M. Chautemps, Minister for the Colonies in the Ribot Cabinet.   He was moved to wire to the governor of French Guiana to know if it were not possible for the prisoner to have his wife with him.   But the governor had his own responsibility to consider, and opposed so formal a negative that M. Chautemps's efforts ended there.

In a house opposite the prisoner's lived his bodyguard.   It consisted of six picked ex-noncommissioned officers under a sergeant.   The men were on duty two at a time for four-hour stretches, from dawn to dark. At dark one man entered a sort of cage in the prisoner's house, whence he commanded a view of the prisoner's bedroom.   That man remained on duty all night and never sat down.

One man took this watch every night for a whole year.   He so nearly went mad over it that the system had to be altered, and afterward only one night watch for each guard per week was exacted.

But, by night or by day, no matter what happened, no word could be addressed to the captive.

The total cost of keeping Dreyfus where he was may be put down at something like $10,000 a year. This included the cost of the periodical cablegram from Cayenne (which is in telephonic communication with the island) at $2.50 per word, to the Colonial Office, Paris, to inform the minister that "no change has taken place in the prisoner's situation."

Chapter XIII.

THE DOCTOR'S STORY

DR. VEUGMON, the physician who had Dreyfus in charge while the prisoner was on Devil's Island, in an interview at Cayenne, in March of the year 1899, said:

"Dreyfus is a neuropathic subject, and the régime to which he has been submitted has made him more so; isolation, idleness, boredom, and discouragement irritate his nervous system. His malady displayed itself about a year after his imprisonment had commenced, and took the form of cerebral depression. He was beset by unconquerable sadness; he clenched his teeth; he complained of dyspepsia, exhaustion, and prolonged insomnia, caused by moral preoccupations, more particularly by the 'fixed idea' of disculpating himself from the charge of treason. Next came headaches and pains in the neck, and finally, last year, I was called in to treat him for fainting fits of considerable duration, which I put a stop to by subcutaneous injections of morphia. In my presence Dreyfus was always self-possessed.

"Under his strength of will one could detect, however, stormy symptoms, and his jailers said that often, when first awaking of a morning, he would break out into furious passion, bursting into tears, gesticulating like a madman, and shouting unintelligible words. These violent rages usually resulted in utter exhaustion and general torpor, and sometimes in syncope, when, of course, I was sent for. Unfortunately, I could only put him through an illusory sort of treatment, prescribing good nourishment, tonics, work in his little garden, and plenty of walking exercise, to fatigue his body and distract his mind. But the only palliative remedies for acute neurasthenia—which I consider incurable—are bracing air, amusement, active life—a treatment, in short, not to be dreamed of in his case.

"The irritability of Dreyfus's character has increased since he has been told of the application to revise his trial. This proceeding haunts him;

he is a prey to feverish restlessness; a thousand conjectures torment his fancy, ignorant as he is of the evidence advanced by his defenders to obtain a new trial."

"Do you believe," the doctor was asked, "that if the application for revision be rejected, Dreyfus is strong enough to get over his disappointment?"

Dr. Veugnon smiled, hesitated, and then replied:

"I think we had better not consider such an eventuality. Dreyfus has repeatedly expressed his intention to put an end to his life. His words have been reported to the authorities, and even M. Deniel, fearing an attempt at suicide, has ordered Dreyfus's jailers not to lose sight of him for a second. After carefully searching his habitation they carried off even perfectly harmless objects, such as kitchen utensils."

"Was Dreyfus in earnest?"

"I can mention a characteristic circumstance which took place early in 1898, and justified the belief that he meant what he had said. He sent for me one day, complaining of violent headache, and besought me to give him a quantity of antipyrin, the only drug, he said, that gave him relief. Struck by a sudden suspicion, I acquiesced in his request, but, observing that a portable medicine case did not contain what he wanted, I left him, and soon returned with a dozen perfectly harmless cachets. These I recommended him to use very cautiously, not more than two per diem. Next day I visited him again. His headache had disappeared, and when I asked him to give back the balance of the cachets I had handed to him, he pretended to look for them, and presently told me that he could not remember where he had put them. I dropped the subject, and never thereafter even alluded to the incident, which I consider conclusive. My instructions were to converse with him exclusively about his health, and he never mentioned the offence he was expiating except to protest his innocence.

"At the present time I do not think that Dreyfus will try to kill himself, for the possibility of 'revision' has shed a ray of hope upon his tortured soul. But should he be disappointed, and hurled back into a slough of despond, I should not be surprised were he to carry out his sinister projects and commit an act of desperation."

The head keeper of the Cayenne penal settlement, at about the same time, was questioned confidentially as to whether Dreyfus knew of the efforts being made in France.   He said:

"I can positively assert that Dreyfus is ignorant of what has taken place in France since his incarceration, except what has been written to him by members of his family, for every imaginable measure has been taken to preclude indiscretion.   Before his arrival here it had been arranged to isolate him completely and cut him off from all external communication.   It may be said with truth that a tomb closed upon him as soon as he came hither.   In the bureaux a special service was organized under the control of a chief inspector to supervise his food and all his appurtenances, of which he himself drew up a list that was handed to a Cayenne storekeeper.   They were all minutely examined before being forwarded to the island.   All the clothes sent to Dreyfus are unsewn and turned inside out to make sure that no written matter is hidden under the seams or in the lining.   His provisions are rigorously searched; meat cans and other tins are opened and resoldered; his cigars—he smokes a good deal—are unrolled and made up again, as they might contain slips of paper.   Even the labels on the wine bottles are removed to make certain that nothing is written on them.   His letters are read; whatever allusion they contain to his case is pitilessly suppressed, and before delivery to him they are subjected to great heat, in order to detect any sympathetic or other special ink.

"If you take into consideration that Dreyfus is in the custody of incorruptible warders, always in fear of dismissal and punishment at the least infraction of standing rules, you will recognize, as I do, the impossibility that outside rumors should ever reach the former captain.   It is not so in the penitentiary, where the convicts enjoy relative freedom; but the situation of Dreyfus and of these common malefactors has absolutely nothing in common."

Chapter XIV.

LETTERS OF DREYFUS TO HIS WIFE

DREYFUS, while in the prison of Cherche Midi, the prison of La Santé, on the Île de Ré, and on Devil's Island, wrote a number of touching letters to his wife which were afterward published by Harper & Brothers. Therefore we shall only touch upon them briefly, referring more particularly to the letters written from Devil's Island, as they furnish links in the chain which we now attempt to construct. The following is one of the letters referred to:

TUESDAY, March 12, 1895.

MY DEAR LUCIE:

Thursday, February 21st, some hours after your departure, I was taken to Rochefort and put on shipboard.

I shall not speak to you of my voyage; I was transported in the manner in which the vile scoundrel whom I represent deserved to be transported. It was only just. They could not accord any pity to a traitor, the lowest of blackguards; and as long as I represent this wretch I can only approve their conduct.

My life here must drag itself out under the same conditions.

But your heart can tell you all that I have suffered—all that I suffer. I live only through the hope in my soul of soon seeing the triumphant light of my rehabilitation. That is the only thing that gives me strength to live. Without honor a man is not worthy of life.

On the day of my departure you assured me that the truth would surely come soon to light. I have lived during that awful voyage, I am living now, only on that word of yours—remember it well. I have been disembarked but a few minutes, and I have obtained permission to send you a cablegram.

I write in haste these few words, which will leave on the 15th by the English mail. It solaces me to have a talk with you, whom I love so profoundly. There are two mails a month for France—the 15th the English, and the 3d the French mail.

And in the same way there are two mails a month for the Iles—the English mail and the French mail.   Find out the days of their departure and write to me by both of them.

All that I can tell you more is that if you want me to live, have my honor given back to me.   Convictions, whatever they may be, do nothing for me; do not change my lot.   What is necessary is a decision which will reinstate me.

I made for your sake the greatest sacrifice a man can make, in resigning myself to live after my tragic fate was decided.   I did this because you had inculcated in me the conviction that the truth must always come to light.   In your turn, my darling, do all that is humanly possible to discover the truth.   A wife and a mother yourself, try to move the hearts of wives and mothers, so that they may give to you the key of this dreadful mystery.   I must have my honor if you want me to live.   I must have it for our dear children.   Do not reason with your heart; that does no good.   I have been convicted.   Nothing can be changed in our tragic situation until the decision shall have been reversed.   Reflect, then, and pursue the solution of this enigma.   That will be worth more than coming here to share my horrible life.   It will be the best, the only means of saving my life.   Say to yourself that it is a question of life or death for me, for our children.

I am incapable of writing to you all.   My brain will bear no more; my despair is too great.   My nervous system is in a deplorable condition, and it is full time that this horrible tragedy should end.

Now my spirit alone is above water.

Oh, for God's sake, hurry, work with all your might!

Tell them all to write to me.

Embrace them all for me; our poor darlings, too.

And for you a thousand tender kisses from your devoted husband,

ALFRED.

MARCH 28, 1895.

I was hoping to receive news of you at about this time; as yet I have heard nothing.   I have already written you two letters.

I know nothing as yet beyond the four walls of my chamber.   As for my health, it could not be very brilliant.   Aside from my physical miseries, of which I speak only to cite them, the cause of this condition of my health lies chiefly in the disorder of my nervous system, produced by an uninterrupted succession of moral shocks.

You know that no matter how severe they might be at times, physical sufferings never wrung a groan from me, and that I could look death coolly in the face if only my mental sufferings did not darken my thoughts.

My mind cannot extricate itself for an instant from the horrible drama of which I am the victim, a tragedy which has struck a blow not only at my life—that is the least of evils, and truly it would have been better had the wretch who committed the crime killed me instead of wounding me as he has—but [he struck] at my honor, the honor of my children, the honor of you all.

This piercing thought of my honor torn from me leaves me no rest either by day or by night. My nights, alas! you can imagine what they are! Formerly it was only sleeplessness; now the greater part of the night is passed in such a state of hallucination and of fever that I ask myself each morning bow my brain still resists. This is one of the most cruel of all my sufferings. Add to this the long hours of the day passed in solitary communion with my thoughts, in the most absolute isolation.

Is it possible to rise above such preoccupation of the mind? Is it possible to force the mind to turn aside to other subjects of thought? I do not believe it; at least I cannot. When one is in this, the most agitating, the most tragic plight that can possibly be conceived for a man whose honor has never failed him, nothing can turn the mind from the idea which dominates it.

Then when I think of you, of our dear children, my grief is unutterable; for the weight of the crime which some wretch has committed weighs heavily upon you also. You must, therefore, for our children's sake, pursue without truce, without rest, the work you have undertaken, and you must make my innocence burst forth in such a way that no doubt can be left in the mind of any human being. Whoever may be the persons who are convinced of my innocence, tell yourself that they will change nothing in our position; we often pay ourselves in words and nourish ourselves on illusions; nothing but my rehabilitation can save us.

You see, then, what I cannot cease reiterating to you, that it is a matter of life or of death, not only for me, but for our children. For myself I never will accept life without my honor. To say that an innocent man ought to live, that he always can live, is a commonplace whose triteness drives me to despair.

I used to say it and I used to believe it. Now that I have suffered all this myself, I declare that if a man has any spirit he cannot live under such circumstances. Life is admissible only when he can lift his head and look the world in the face; otherwise, there is nothing left for him but to die. To live for the sake of living is simply low and cowardly.

I am sure that in this you think as I do; any other opinion would be unworthy of us.

The situation, already so tragic, becomes each day more tense. You have not to weep, not to groan, but to face it with all your energy and with all your soul. To make clear this situation, we must not wait for a happy chance, but we much display all-absorbing activity. Knock at all doors. We must employ all means to make the light burst forth. All forms of investigation must be tried; the object we have in view is my life, the life of every one of us.

Here is a very clear bulletin of my state, moral and physical. I will sum it up:

A pitiable nervous and cerebral excitability, but extreme moral energy, outstretched toward the one object which, no matter what the price, no matter by what means, we must attain—vindication. I will leave you to judge from this what struggles I am each day forced to make to keep myself from choosing death rather than this slow agony in every fibre of my being, rather than this torture of every instinct, in which physical suffering is added to agony of soul. You see that I am holding to my promise that I made you to struggle to live until the day of my rehabilitation. It remains for you to do the rest, if you would have me reach that day.

Then away with weakness. Tell yourself that I am suffering martyrdom, that each day my brain is growing weaker; tell yourself that it is a question of my honor—that is to say, of my life, of the honor of your children. Let these thoughts inspire you, and then act accordingly.

Embrace every one, the children, for me.

A thousand kisses from your husband, who loves you,

ALFRED.

How are the children? Give me news of them. I cannot think of you and of them without throbs of pain through my whole being. I would breathe into your soul all the fire that is in my own, to march forward to the assault that is to liberate the truth. I would convince you of the absolute necessity of unmasking the one who is guilty by every means, whatever it may be, and above all without delay.

Send me a few books.

Chapter XV.

FURTHER EXPRESSIONS OF THE PRISONER

HAVING given our readers some idea of the manner in which Dreyfus wrote to his wife, we shall now submit a few extracts from other letters of the prisoner to Madame Dreyfus, so as to convey as far as possible, a pen picture of the workings of his mind while on Devil's Island.

In a letter date May 8, 1895, Dreyfus wrote:

A profound silence reigns around me, interrupted only by the roaring of the sea; and my thoughts, crossing the distance which separates us, carry me to your midst, among all those who are dear to me, whose thoughts must of a truth be often turned toward me. Often I ask at such an hour, "What is my dear Lucie doing?" and I send you by my thoughts the echo of my immense affection. Then I close my eyes, and it seems to me that I see your face and the faces of my dear children.

For three months now I have been without news of you, of the children, of our families.

I believe that I have already told you that I advised you to ask permission to leave your letters at the Ministry eight or ten days before the departure of the mails; perhaps in that way I shall receive them sooner. But, my good darling, forget all my sufferings, overcome your own, and think of our children. Say to yourself that you have a sacred mission to fulfil, that of having my honor given back to me, the honor of the name borne by our dear little ones. Moreover, I recall to my mind what you told me before my departure. I know, as you repeated to me in your letter of February 17th, what the words of your mouth are worth. I have an absolute confidence in you.

Then do not weep any more, my good darling; I will struggle until the last minute for you, for our dear children.

The body may give way under such a burden of grief, but the soul should remain firm and valiant, to protest against a lot that we have not deserved. When my honor is given back to me, then only, my good darling, we shall have the right to withdraw from the field. We will live for each other, far from the noise of the world; we will take refuge in our mutual affection, in our love, grown still stronger in these tragical events. We will sustain each other, that we may bind up the wounds of our hearts; we will live in our children, to whom we will consecrate the remainder of our days. We will try to make them good, simple beings, strong in body and mind. We will elevate their souls so that they may always find in them a refuge from the realities of life.

May this day come soon, for we have all paid our tribute of sufferings upon this earth! Courage, then, my darling; be strong and valiant; carry on your work without weakness, with dignity, but with the conviction of your rights. I am going to lie down, to close my eyes and think of you. Good night and a thousand kisses.

On May 18, 1895, Dreyfus wrote as follows to his son:

DEAR LITTLE PIERRE:

Papa sends good big kisses to you, also to little Jeanne. Papa thinks often of both of you. You must show little Jeanne how to make beautiful towers with the wooden blocks, very high, such as I made for you, and which toppled down so well. Be very good. Give good caresses to your mamma when she is sorrowful. Be very gentle and kind also to grandmother and grandfather. Set good little traps for your aunts. When papa comes back from his journey you will come to the railway station to meet him, with little Jeanne, with mamma, with every one.

More good big kisses for you and for Jeanne. Your

PAPA.

Here is another touching extract from a letter of Dreyfus to his wife:

I do not know anything of what is passing around me. I live as in a tomb. I am incapable of deciphering in my brain this appalling enigma. All that I can do, then, and I shall not fail in this duty, is to sustain you to my last breath—is to continue to fan in your heart the flame which glows in mine, so that you may march straight forward to the conquest of the truth, so that you may get me back my honor, the honor of my children. You remember those lines of Shakespeare, in "Othello." I found them again not long since among my English books. I send them to you translated (you will know why!)

> "Celui qui me vole ma bourse,
> Me vole une bagatelle.
> C'est quelque chose, mais ce n'est rien.

THE GREAT ACTORS:

1. Zola.   2. Clemenceau.
3. Mercier.   4. Carrière.

COLONEL PICQUART IN THE CHERCHE-MIDI PRISON.

FIRST SCENE OF THE TRAGEDY:

1. M. Cochefert, Chief of the Secret Service.
2. Major Du Paty de Clam dictating Trial Passages of the Bordereau to Captain Dreyfus before his arrest.

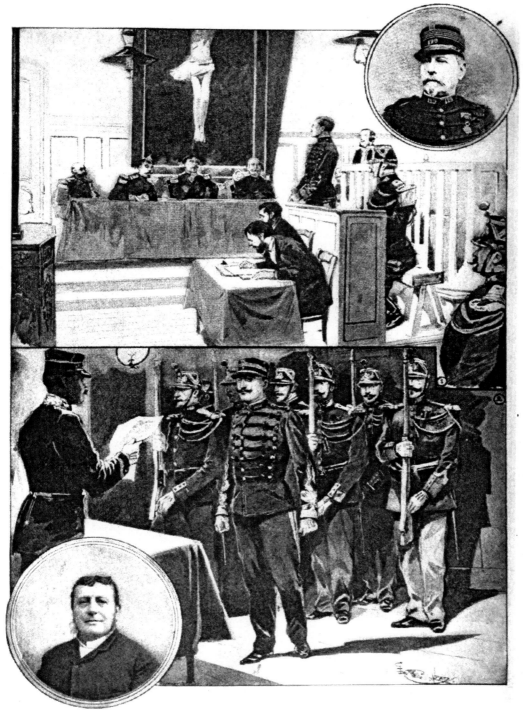

THE SECRET COURT-MARTIAL.

1. Dreyfus before the Court.
2. Reading the Verdict.

3. Maurel-Pries.
4. Maître Demange.

OPENING OF THE TRIAL: DREYFUS DECLARES HIS INNOCENCE.

MADAME DREYFUS AND HER CHILDREN.

MAITRE LABORI.

MADAME DREYFUS AND HER CHILDREN.

MAITRE LABORI.

CONFESSION OF COLONEL HENRY TO WAR MINISTER CAVAIGNAC.

Elle était à moi, elle est à lui et
    A était l'esclave de mille autres.
Mais celui que me vole ma bonne renommée,
Me vole une chose que ni l'enrichit pas,
    Et que me rend vraiment pauvre."

Ah, yes! he has rendered me "vraiment pauvre," the wretch who has stolen my honor! He has made us more miserable than the meanest of human creatures.

The quoted verses are a rendering of—

"Who steals my purse steals trash; . . .
But he who filches from me my good name
Robs me of that which not enriches him,
And makes me poor indeed."

Under date of June 16, 1895, the unhappy prisoner wrote:

To-day a more peculiarly intimate sadness invades my soul, because on this day, Sunday, we used to be together all day, and we used to end it with your dear parents. But my heart, my conscience, and my reason, too, tell me that these happy days will return to us. I cannot admit that an innocent man can be left to expiate indefinitely, for a guilty wretch, a crime as abominable as it is odious; and then, to sum it up in one word, what must give you, as it gives me, unconquerable energy, is the thought of our children, as I have already told you before; for ideas which emanate from such a subject must, from their nature, repeat themselves. We must have our honor, and we have not the right to be weak; without it, it would be better to see our children die.

As for our sufferings, we all suffer alike. Do you think that I do not feel what you suffer—you, who are struck doubly, in your honor and in your love? Do you believe that I do not feel how your parents suffer, your brothers and your sisters, for whom honor is not an empty word? But I hope that our anguish is to have an end, and that that end is near. Until that day we must guard all our courage, all our energy.

Thank Mathieu for those few words he wrote to me. How the poor boy must suffer; he who is honor incarnate! But tell him that I am with him in thought—that our two hearts suffer together. There are moments when I think that I am the plaything of a horrible nightmare; that all this is unreal; that it is only a bad dream; but it is, alas! the truth. But for the moment we ought to put aside every weakening thought. We ought to fix our eyes upon one single object; our honor. When that is returned to me, and when I know the meaning of what is now for me an

5

unsolvable problem, perhaps I shall understand this enigma which baffles my reason, which leaves my brain panting.

I will wait, then, for that moment, sure that it will come. I wish for us all that it may come soon; I even hope it, so immovable is my faith in justice. Mystery has no place in our century. Everything is brought to light, and must be brought to light.

My Sunday has seemed less long to me, my dear Lucie, because in this way I have been able to talk with you. As for our children, I have no advice to give you. I know you; our ideas on this subject are alike, both in regard to their bringing up and in regard to their education. Courage always, dear Lucie, and a thousand kisses.

Do not forget that I am answering letters dated three months ago, and that my replies may therefore seem out of date to you.

ALFRED.

On July 15, 1895, Dreyfus wrote:

My energy is occupied in stilling the beatings of my heart, in containing my impatience, to learn at last that my innocence is recognized everywhere and by every one. But if my energy is altogether passive, yours ought, on the contrary, to be all active and animated by the ardent spirit which gives strength to my own.

If it were merely a question of suffering it would be nothing. But it is a question of the honor of a name, of the life of our children, and I do not wish, you understand, that our children should ever have to lower their heads. Light, full, complete, must be let in upon this tragic story. Nothing, therefore, should rebuff or tire you. All doors open, all hearts beat for a mother who begs only for the truth, so that her children may live.

It is almost from the tomb—my situation here is comparable to that, with the added grief that my heart still beats—that I write these words to you. Thank your dear parents, our brothers and sisters, as well as Lucie and Henri, for their good and affectionate letters. Tell them all the pleasure which I take in reading them, and tell them that if I do not answer directly it is because I could do nothing but keep on repeating what I have already said. Kiss your dear parents for me; tell them all my affection. Long, tender kisses for the children. As for you, my dear and good Lucie, your letters are my daily reading. Continue to write me long letters; with them I come nearer to living with you, with our dear children, than I could by my own thought alone, which, indeed, never leaves you for an instant.

The prisoner, on September 7, 1895, wrote:

Should it last much longer either one or the other will give way under it. Well, my dear Lucie, that must not be! We must before all else get back our honor, the honor of our children. We must not allow ourselves to be overcome by a fate so infamous when it is so unmerited. However natural, however legitimate, may be the cries of pain of souls who suffer far beyond all imaginable suffering, to groan, my dear Lucie, will do no good. If, when you receive this letter, the mystery has not been made clear, then, I think, it will be time, when the courage, the energy which duty gives, with the invincible force which innocence gives, for you to take personal steps, so that at last light may be thrown upon this tragic story. You have neither mercy nor favor to ask for, but only a determined search for the truth, a search for the wretch who wrote that infamous letter, and, in one word, justice for us all! And you will find in your own heart words more eloquent than any that could be contained in a mere letter. We must, in a word, find at last the key to this mystery. Whatever may be the means, your position as a wife and a mother gives you every right, and should give you every courage.

From what I myself feel, from the state of my own heart, I know but too well how it must be with you all, and in my long nights I see you suffering, agonizing with me.

It must end. Men cannot, in a century like ours, leave two families in agony without clearing up a mystery like this. The truth can be made known, if only they are willing to have it so.

In the course of a long letter dated May 22d, Dreyfus said:

It is from the thought of you, the thought of our dear children, from my determined resolve to sustain you, to live to see the day when our honor shall be given back to us, that I draw all my strength. When I sink under the united burden of all my woes, when my brain reels, when my heart can bear no more, when I lose all hope, then to myself I murmur three names—yours, those of our dear children—and I nerve myself again against my agony, and not a sound passes my silent lips. To tell the truth, I am physically very weak, it could not be otherwise. But everything is effaced from my mind, hallucinations of memories, sufferings, the atrocities of my daily life, before so exalted, so absolute a preoccupation, the thought of our honor, the patrimony of our children. So I come again, as always, to cry to you with all my strength, with all my soul, "Courage, and still courage, to march steadfastly onward to your goal—

the unclouded honor of our name"—and to wish for both our sakes that this goal may soon be reached. The dear little letters written by the children always move me deeply, cause me extreme emotion; I often wet them with my tears, but I draw from them also my strength. In all my letters I read that you are raising these dear little children admirably. If I have never spoken of this to you it has been because I knew it, because I knew you.

To speak of my love for you, the love that unites us all, would be useless, would it not? Still, let me tell you again that my thought never leaves you for an instant day or night, that my heart is always near to you, to our children, to you all, ready to sustain you, to animate you with my unconquerable will. I embrace you with all my strength, with all my heart, and also the dear children.

Finally Dreyfus began to give way to despair. After addressing a heartrending appeal to the governor of French Guiana, in September, 1898, no encouragement was forthcoming, and he broke down. But there was already sunshine in the distance, as the following letter shows:

If my voice had ceased to make itself heard, this would have been because it had forever died away. If I have lived, it has been for my honor, which is my property and the patrimony of our children; it has been for my duty, which I have done everywhere and always; and as it must ever be accomplished when a man has right and justice on his side, without fear of anything or of anybody. When one has behind one a past devoted to duty, a life devoted to honor, when one has never known but one language, that of truth, one is strong, I assure you, and atrocious though fate may have been, one must have a soul lofty enough to dominate it until it bows before one. Let us, therefore, await with confidence the decision of the Supreme Court, as we await with confidence the decision of the new judges before whom this decision will send me. At the same time as your letter I have received a copy of the petition for revision, and of the decree of the Court of Cassation, declaring it acceptable. I read with wonderful emotion the terms of your petition, in which you expressed admirably, as I have already done in mine, the feelings by which I am animated in asking that an end shall be put to the punishment of an innocent man—I may add to that of a noble woman, of her children, of two families, of an innocent man who had always been a loyal soldier, who has not ceased, even in the midst of the horrible sufferings of unmerited chastisement, to declare his love for his native land.

Chapter XVI.

THE PRISONER HEARS GOOD NEWS

THE Procureur-Général of Cayenne, M. Darius, on November 15, 1898, entered the hut occupied by Dreyfus on Devil's Island and said to him:

"Dreyfus, the Court of Cassation has decided to revise your case. What have you to say?"

The prisoner was almost overwhelmed by the good news, it is admitted. But, according to the Procureur-Général, the prisoner contented himself with replying:

"I shall say nothing until I am confronted by my accusers in Paris."

But, from a letter written by Dreyfus to his wife, later, in November, 1898, he said:

MY DEAR LUCIE:

In the middle of the month I was told that the petition for the revision of my judgment had been declared acceptable by the Court of Cassation, and was invited to produce my means of defence. I took the necessary measures immediately. My requests were at once transmitted to Paris, and you must have been informed of this some days ago. Events must therefore be moving rapidly. In thought I am night and day, as always, with you, with our children, with all, sharing our joy at seeing the end of this fearful drama approaching rapidly. Words become powerless to describe such deep emotions . . . According to information which I sent you in the last mail, all will be over in the course of December. Therefore, when these lines reach you I shall be almost on the point of starting for France.

We will conclude this series of extracts from the letters of Dreyfus with the letter received by his counsel, Maître Demange, December 31, 1894, made public when sent to the Minister of Justice, M. Sarrien, July 11, 1898, as showing the lines the prisoner indicated for those who were engaged in the work of attempting to establish his innocence:

Du Paty de Clam came to-day, Monday, December 31, 1894, at 5:30 P.M., after the rejection of my appeal, to ask me, on behalf of the minister, whether I had not, perhaps, been the victim of my imprudence, whether I had not meant merely to lay a bait . . . and had then found myself caught fatally in the trap. I replied that I never had relations with any agent or attaché, . . . that I had undertaken no such process as baiting, and that I was innocent. He then said to me on his own responsibility that he was himself convinced of my guilt, first from an examination of the handwriting of the document brought up against me, and from the nature of the documents enumerated therein; secondly, from information according to which the disappearance of documents corresponded with my presence on the General Staff; that, finally, a secret agent had declared that a Dreyfus was a spy, . . . without, however, affirming that that Dreyfus was an officer. I asked Paty de Clam to be confronted with this agent. He replied that it was impossible. Paty de Clam acknowledged that I had never been suspected before the reception of the incriminating document.

I then asked him why there had been no surveillance exercised over the officers from the month of February, since Commandant Henry had affirmed at the court-martial that he had been warned at that date that there was a traitor among the officers. Paty de Clam replied that he knew nothing about that business; that it was not his affair, but Commandant Henry's; that it was difficult to watch all the officers of the General Staff. . . . . Then, perceiving that he had said too much, he added:

"We are talking between four walls. If I am questioned on all that I shall deny everything."

I preserved entire calmness, for I wished to know his whole idea.

To sum up, he said that I had been condemned because there was a clue indicating that the culprit was an officer, and the seized letter came to give precision to that clue. He added, also, that since my arrest the leakage at the ministry had ceased; that perhaps . . .* had left the letter about expressly to sacrifice me, in order not to satisfy my demands.

He then spoke to me of the remarkable expert testimony of M. Bertillon, according to which I had traced my own handwriting and that of my

---

* The leaders indicate an omitted name.

brother in order to be able, in case I should be arrested with the letter on me, to protest that it was a conspiracy against me. He further intimated that my wife and family were my accomplices—in short, the whole theory of M. Bertillon.

At this point, knowing what I wanted to discover and not wishing to allow him to insult my family as well, I stopped him saying:

"Enough; I have only one word to say, namely, that I am innocent, and that your duty is to continue your inquiries."

"If you are really innocent," he exclaimed, "you are undergoing the most monstrous martyrdom of all time."

"I am that martyr," I replied, "and I hope the future will prove it to you."

To sum up, it results from this conversation:

1. That there have been leakages at the ministry.

2. That . . . must have heard, and must have repeated to Commandant Henry, that there was an officer who was a traitor. I do not think he would have invented it of his own accord.

3. That the incriminating letter was taken at . . . From all this I draw the following conclusions, the first certain, the two others possible:

First, a spy really exists . . . at the French ministry, for documents have disappeared.

Secondly, perhaps that spy slipped in in an officer's uniform, imitating his handwriting in order to divert suspicion.

Thirdly [here four lines and a half are blank].

This hypothesis does not exclude the fact No. 1, which seems certain. But the tenor of the letter does not render this third hypothesis very probable. It would be connected rather with the first fact and the second hypothesis—that is to say, the presence of a spy at the ministry and imitation of my handwriting by that spy, or simply resemblance of handwriting.

However this may be, it seems to me that if your agent is clever he should be able to unravel this web by laying his nets as well on the . . . side as on the . . . side. This will not prevent the employment of all the methods I have indicated, for the truth must be discovered.

After the departure of Paty de Clam I wrote the following letter to the minister:

"I received, by order, the visit of . Paty de Clam, to whom I once more declared that I was innocent, and that I had never even committed an imprudence. I am condemned. I have no favor to ask. But in the name of my honor, which I hope will one day be restored to me, it is my duty to beg you to continue your investigations. When I am gone let the search be kept up; it is the only favor that I solicit."

Chapter XVII.

WORKING FOR THE TRUTH

WE must now leave Dreyfus on Devil's Island and turn back to the events which followed his degradation, January 5, 1895.

For about two years little or nothing was heard of the case of the unhappy prisoner. But loyally, steadily, and fearlessly, his devoted wife, his brother Mathieu and others persisted in their efforts to get at the truth.

As for the War Office officials, they were quite pleased with the result of their efforts, so much so that some of those concerned, particularly Du Paty de Clam, were promoted.

M. Méline was then Premier, M. Hanotaux was Minister of Foreign Affairs, M. Lebon was Minister of the Colonies, and the Minister of War was General Billot. Colonel Picquart was head of the Intelligence Department.

During the month of March, 1896, there came into the possession of Colonel Picquart, a fearless, intelligent, and apparently honest officer, a French post-card, or *petit bleu*, torn into fragments (as was the case with the bordereau which brought about the conviction of Dreyfus), which, strange to say, had also been found by a spy who had investigated the contents of the waste-paper basket of the German Embassy at Paris.

When pieced together, the *petit bleu* read:

"I await before everything a more detailed explanation than that which you gave me the other day upon the question at issue. I beg you, therefore, to give it to me in writing, so that I can judge if I may continue my relations with the firm of R—— or not."

This post-card, (or *petit bleu*) was addressed to Major Esterhazy, 27 Rue de la Bienfaisance, Paris, an infantry officer whose reputation was somewhat shady, to put it as mildly as possible.

The full title of Esterhazy was "Major Count Ferdinand von Walsin

Esterhazy." He claimed to be a direct descendant of the noble Esterhazy family of Austria, but the head of that house protested against this claim and even threatened to prosecute Major Esterhazy for bearing the name of the family.

However, to continue our story, the interest of Colonel Picquart was aroused by the wording of the *petit bleu*, and he started an investigation of the matter. He obtained specimens of Esterhazy's handwriting, and, to the astonishment of the head of the Intelligence Department, he found on comparing the major's writing with that of the bordereau that Esterhazy was seemingly the author of the document which had sent Dreyfus to Devil's Island. A sample of Esterhazy's handwriting was submitted to M. Bertillon, the head of the Anthropometric Department of the Paris Prefecture of Police, who had previously, in 1894, identified the handwriting of Dreyfus as being that of the author of the bordereau, and at this time he pronounced Esterhazy's writing to be that of the author of the bordereau.

Further investigation convinced Colonel Picquart that Esterhazy and not Dreyfus was the writer of the bordereau, and Picquart appealed to General Gonse, Deputy-Chief of the Headquarters Staff, and to General de Boisdeffre, Chief of the Headquarters Staff, urging immediate action. The generals consulted, and, instead of promptly taking steps to establish, if possible, the innocence of Dreyfus, they seem to have arrived at the conclusion that the best thing to do was to hush the matter up, in order to "protect the honor of the army," and save certain high personages from apparently well-merited condemnation. Therefore General Billot, the Minister of War, took no steps toward possibly clearing Dreyfus. But, on the contrary, he seems to have hampered the work of those who were moved to pity the prisoner and who urged the detection of the real traitor.

In the case of two men in the War Office, Du Paty de Clam and Lieutenant-Colonel Henry, there was a feeling of consternation at the discovery of the resemblance of the handwriting of Esterhazy to that of the bordereau.

For a while this important discovery was kept secret, but the news eventually leaked out, and further inquiry into the Dreyfus affair was imminent. Picquart became the champion of the prisoner of Devil's Island, and Du Paty de Clam and Henry, as persecutors of Dreyfus, were placed on the defensive, with the result that the whole Headquarters Staff, and those of the Intelligence Department involved in the condemnation of Dreyfus, banded together to defend themselves by any means against the disgrace which threatened them. In this effort, it has since been shown, forgery and even murder were resorted to in order to heap up evidence against Dreyfus.

Lieutenant-Colonel Henry was the leader of this gang of conspirators. At all hazards Picquart must be discredited, for the Minister of War was slowly being interested in the new developments.

A press campaign, ostensibly against Picquart but really directed against Dreyfus, was opened in some of the newspapers of Paris.

The *Éclair*, in September, 1896, printed an article setting forth that Dreyfus had really been convicted on documents which had been secretly communicated to the court-martial of 1894, and one of these documents was referred to as having actually mentioned Dreyfus by name—which has since been proved incorrect. This was the document known as " *Cette canaille de D——* " document, no name being given, but Dreyfus being inferred, though it has since been shown to have probably referred to a spy named Dubois. The first version printed was that the document contained the words :

" *Décidément cet animal de Dreyfus devient trop exigéant.*" ("Decidedly that animal Dreyfus is becoming too exacting.")

The second version was that the document read :

" *Cette canaille de D——* " etc., etc. ("That rascal D——" etc., etc.)

Then facts about the secret *dossier*, or secret batch of papers used at the court-martial of 1894, began to appear in the papers and, in due course of time, M. Bernard Lazare was bold enough to publish a pamphlet in favor of Dreyfus.

This was followed, November 10, 1896, by the publication in the *Matin* of a facsimile of the bordereau, or incriminating document, which the paper mentioned obtained from M. Teyssonieres, one of the three experts in handwriting who testified at the Dreyfus court-martial. This inflamed public curiosity, and sides were formed for and against Dreyfus. Up to about that time, only the faithful few were believers in the innocence of the prisoner. From that time on people began to compare the handwriting for themselves, and the number of Dreyfus's friends increased.

As the interest of the public in the case increased, Generals de Boisdeffre and Gonse continued to block the efforts made by Colonel Picquart in behalf of Dreyfus, representing to General Billot, the Minister of War, that Picquart had been in the habit of consulting a lawyer, named Leblois, about the secret papers in the case. This was a serious accusation, as it rendered Picquart open to the charge of communicating to a civilian secret documents belonging to the War Office.

At the same time hints crept into the papers of a corruption fund of 35,000,000 francs having been raised abroad for the war chest of those working in behalf of the prisoner, and it was intimated that a suspicious-looking American vessel had been sighted off Devil's Island. This caused the authorities to redouble their precautions; the life of Dreyfus on his prison island was made more burdensome than ever; his exercise was restricted. A guard, pistol in hand, with orders to shoot the prisoner on the slightest evidence of an attempt to escape, was stationed in his room, and decoy letters were sent to the unhappy man in the hope of getting him to answer them, and thus, possibly, giving the authorities an excuse to shoot him.

Finally, M. Castelin, a member of the Chamber of Deputies, representing the district of Aisne, gave notice that he would interpellate the Government, on November 18, 1896, regarding the various Dreyfus rumors afloat and the action the Government was taking or contemplated taking in the case.

Chapter XVIII.

COLONEL HENRY TO THE RESCUE

THE announcement of an interpellation in the Chamber made the military authorities more and more anxious. Something had to be done. Lieutenant-Colonel Henry came to the rescue of his chiefs. As he afterward admitted before committing suicide, Henry forged a note, in bad French, purporting to be from Major Panizzardi, the Italian military attaché, to Colonel Schwartzkoppen, the military attaché of Germany. It read:

MY DEAR FRIEND:

I read that a deputy is going to interpellate upon Dreyfus. If . . . I shall say that I never had relations with that Jew. That is agreed. If you are asked, say likewise, for no one must ever know what has passed with him.

This forgery was shown to Generals de Boisdeffre and Gonse, who, in turn, showed it to General Billot, but it was not shown to Colonel Picquart. The Minister of War, however, referred to the so-called Panizzardi note in a conversation with Picquart, who immediately expressed doubts as to its authenticity. This did not have any weight with General Billot. He appeared in the Chamber of Deputies and, replying to the interpellation, said the Dreyfus court-martial was regularly composed, that the appeal was rejected unanimously, that the affair was a thing already passed upon by the court, otherwise a *chose jugée*, and that the state reasons which, in 1894, made it necessary to hear the case in secret still prevailed. This mysterious statement had weight with the deputies, who received the announcement with approval; and once more the military authorities breathed freely.

The governments of Germany and Italy were not so easily satisfied. They entered protests against the authenticity of the documents, but their protests were not allowed to become public at that period, and General Billot congratulated himself upon having saved "the honor of the army."

It now remained to get rid of Colonel Picquart, who was entirely too honest-minded for the position he held. Therefore it was arranged to send him away from Paris on various pretexts, termed "missions." First he was sent to Nancy, then to Besancon, next to Algiers, and finally to the frontier of Tunis, where he was given command of the Fourth Regiment of Algerian sharpshooters. Besides this, it was proposed to send him on a "mission" into a district from which it is more than likely he would never have returned. But Colonel Picquart slipped out of the trap set for him, appealed to his immediate superior, placed the case plainly before him, met with some sympathy, did not go on the "mission," and thereby, in all probability, saved his life; for Picquart had no doubt it was intended to get rid of him by foul means or fair.

Lieutenant-Colonel Henry, having thus disposed of his rival Picquart, was promoted to his place as Chief of the Intelligence Department. The friends of Picquart could obtain no news of him; his most private letters were opened at the War Office, and every effort was made to suppress him effectually.

Picquart, in May, 1897, protested to Lieutenant-Colonel Henry against the mystery which was made to surround his whereabouts, and Henry replied in a threatening manner, saying the mystery was the result of Picquart's own action in opening letters and in attempting to prevail upon officers to give testimony as to a certain document being in the handwriting of a person other than Dreyfus. There were other statements in the letter which so alarmed Colonel Picquart that he succeeded in obtaining leave of absence from his friendly general in Tunis, and went to Paris, where he placed the case before M. Leblois, his friend and lawyer. Picquart also placed in the lawyer's hands the threatening letter sent him by Henry, and letters which he had received from General Gonse, after which he returned to his post in Tunis.

With Picquart out of the way, the enemies of Dreyfus thought the proposed further inquiry into the case would be dropped.

But they reckoned without faithful Madame Dreyfus, who was working incessantly for the prisoner of Devil's Island. The facts in the case, especially the new developments, were placed before M. Scheurer-Kestner, an

Alsatian countryman of Dreyfus and one of the vice-presidents of the Senate. He became so impressed with the statements made to him that he soon developed into a champion of Dreyfus, and with Mathieu Dreyfus, a brother of the prisoner, he denounced Esterhazy as being the author of the bordereau.

Affairs were now beginning to look much brighter for the prisoner, and the hope of his friends mounted still higher when M. Émile Zola, the famous novelist and author of "Nana," joined the ranks of the Dreyfusards, or friends of the prisoner.

M. Mathieu Dreyfus, in November, 1897, wrote to the Minister of War and squarely denounced Esterhazy as the author of the bordereau. He also firmly insisted that justice be done to his brother. In this matter, M. Mathieu Dreyfus acted on the advice of M. Scheurer-Kestner.

There are various stories told as to how this vice-president of the Senate was converted from a believer in the guilt of Dreyfus into a staunch champion of the prisoner. One version is that, while at dinner one day, he expressed wonder at the fact that an officer holding such a high position as Dreyfus and being so well provided with the world's goods could have become a traitor, whereupon an officer who was present said the reason could be found in the fact that Dreyfus had purchased a house in Paris, for which he had agreed to pay 228,000 francs, and that he was in need of money. This officer also said he had this "fact" from one of the officers who composed the Dreyfus court-martial. M. Scheurer-Kestner, it is further asserted, investigated this matter and found it to be absolutely false. He afterward met M. Leblois, Picquart's lawyer, who placed before the vice-president of the Senate all the letters which he had in his possession in connection with the affair. Some time afterward M. Scheurer-Kestner called upon the Minister of War and urged him to make inquiries in the matter, telling him of his own investigations, and saying he was convinced Dreyfus was innocent. This was in July, 1897.

The next step was taken by the *Figaro*, probably the most influential paper in France, which came out boldly for a revision of the Dreyfus trial. M. Scheurer-Kestner then headed the campaign which was destined to end in a victory for the Dreyfusards, so far as obtaining a revision of the trial was concerned.

In the mean while, Major Forzinetti, governor of the Cherche-Midi prison, where Dreyfus was confined after his arrest, was removed from active service and sent into the army reserve for declaring to M. Henri Rochefort, editor of the *Intransigéant*, his belief that Dreyfus was innocent.

The private apartments of Picquart were searched, and he was recalled from Tunis, in order to be examined by General Pellieux, who had been detailed by the Government to inquire into the charges so openly brought in the press and elsewhere against Esterhazy. The latter, driven to desperation, was finally compelled to demand a trial by court-martial, which was accorded him. It took place in January, 1898, but, subsequent developments show, he had previously been assured of protection from high quarters, as was the case when he fought a duel with Picquart, which, as is the case of most French duels, was not a very desperate affair.

Before the court-martial Esterhazy was charged with having written the bordereau, and with having been in treasonable correspondence with Colonel von Schwartzkoppen. Esterhazy admitted that the handwriting of the bordereau was his own, but he claimed it was in the result of a tracing made by Dreyfus upon his (Esterhazy's) writing, which the prisoner of Devil's Island afterward put together. The *petit bleu*, it was asserted before the court, was a forgery perpetrated by Picquart.

The statements made by Esterhazy were accepted by the court as accurate in every respect, and he was promptly acquitted, and left the court with his mistress, Mademoiselle Pays, on his arm. They received an ovation in the street, the crowds shouting: "Vive l'armée!" "Vive la France!" "Down with the Jews!" "Down with traitors!" etc., etc., which must have made Esterhazy feel uncomfortable.

The acquittal of Esterhazy was followed by the arrest and imprisonment of Colonel Picquart, who was brought before a Military Court of Inquiry, where he was accused of showing and divulging documents connected with the national defence and other matters, to his lawyer, M. Leblois, and with showing the latter his correspondence with General Gonse. Only the latter charge was proved, and Picquart was dismissed from the army.

This was a sad blow, apparently, to the friends of Dreyfus, and his enemies were correspondingly elated.

Chapter XIX.

ZOLA TO THE FRONT

It was at this stage of the campaign that Emile Zola came to the front. In January, 1898, the novelist caused to be published in the *Aurore*, a newspaper owned by a friend of his, a series of formal accusations, addressed to the President of the Republic, each beginning with " J'accuse," (" I accuse,") against the courts-martial which had tried Esterhazy and Dreyfus. The object of Zola in making these accusations was to bring about his prosecution and thus cause light to be thrown upon the Dreyfus affair.

The Minister of War was compelled to prosecute M. Zola for these denunciations; but, in order to prevent the reopening of the Dreyfus case, which was the object the novelist had in view, the minister confined his attention to the following paragraph:

" I accuse the first court-martial of having violated the law in condemning an accused person on a document kept secret. And I accuse the second court-martial of having by order screened this illegality, committing in its turn that which in a judge is a crime—knowingly acquitting a guilty person."

M. Zola was accordingly tried in February, 1898, before the Assize Court, whose president, M. Delegorgue, did everything possible to prevent the witnesses of the defence from giving testimony bearing on the Dreyfus case. He had plenty of weapons at his command, including the ever-present gag of " state secrets " and the equally effective *chose jugée* and " professional secrecy."

Maître Labori, an able and fearless lawyer, was counsel for M. Zola. Although heavily handicapped by the rulings of the president of the court, he succeeded in bringing out valuable points in favor of Dreyfus, notably the illegal manner in which the prisoner was condemned, the apparent error in attributing the bordereau to Dreyfus, and the seeming identity of its real author, Esterhazy.

6

President Delegorgue again and again announced that he could not admit rebutting testimony on certain vital points raised by the prosecution, or on the charges made by M. Zola in his famous "I accuse" letter. This so exasperated the novelist that, during the second day of the trial, he heatedly announced that he wished to be treated at least as fairly as thieves or murderers were treated. He claimed that while such criminals had the right to defend themselves, he, M. Zola, was deprived of such rights. But the court ruled against the defence, and there was nothing to do but submit.

One of the witnesses at the trial of M. Zola was M. Casimir-Perier, who had resigned the presidency of the Republic, and had been succeeded by M. Felix Faure, who died suddenly on the 16th of February, 1899, and was in turn succeeded in the presidency by M. Émile Loubet.

On being sworn, M. Casimir-Perier said:

"Excuse me, but I cannot tell the truth. That is just what I may not tell. It is my duty not to tell the truth."

The resignation of M. Casimir-Perier, it became known later, was in some manner connected with the Dreyfus case, his friends holding that he resigned in order not to become further mixed up in the matter.

General de Boisdeffre, the Chief of Staff, caused a sensation at the Zola trial, by saying that, according to his view of the case, the guilt of Dreyfus was certain, adding that there were facts both anterior and subsequent to the trial which made this certainty unshakable.

General Mercier, the former Minister of War, advanced the opinion that Dreyfus had been legally and justly condemned.

Major Esterhazy practically confined himself to refusing to reply to the questions put to him, on the ground of professional secrecy, and General Pellieux made an excited speech, during which he dropped dark hints of danger threatening the fatherland, etc., etc., in the usual refrain of the French.

The examination of Colonel Picquart was obstructed throughout by the judges, but Maître Labori succeeded in making a fierce and effective attack on the enemies of Dreyfus, which caused the Headquarters Staff to make a rally and wave the old fiction of mystery above their heads. Generals de Boisdeffre and Pellieux proved themselves equal to the occasion. General Pellieux, turning to the jury, said:

"If the chiefs of the army are to be discredited in the eyes of the soldiers, your sons, gentlemen, will be led to the slaughter."

General de Boisdeffre went a step further. He actually threatened that the chiefs of the army would resign unless, practically, they were allowed to have their own way.

As a last shot, the new "secret document,"—the forged Panizzardi despatch—was presented to the court, and Generals de Boisdeffre and Gonse confirmed the fact that it had been "intercepted by the vigilance of the Government."

Maître Labori, however, was not permitted to see this document. But Colonel Picquart declared it to be a forgery. It was produced in court at the very moment the prosecution was endeavoring to show that Esterhazy was not the author of the bordereau.

Maître Labori, in his summing up for the defence, said:

"Zola's letter was a cry for justice and truth. It has rallied all save some disturbers around what France counts the greatest and purest. Do not be alarmed or allow yourselves to be intimidated. The honor of the army is not involved. They tell you of dangers near. Do not believe in these dangers. These brave officers, who have made a mistake, will yet fight with the highest courage and lead us to victory. Do not strike Emile Zola. Gentlemen, you know well that he stands for the honor of France. It is by the heart, by moral energy, that great battles are won, and I also cry ' Vive l'armée!' when I ask you to acquit Zola. I cry at the same time ' Long live the Republic!' ' Long live the right!' 'Long live eternal justice and truth!' "

M. Clemenceau, for the defence, reviewed the testimony which confirmed his conviction that Dreyfus had been illegally condemned, and protested against the idea that this constituted an insult to the army. The only person who had insulted the army, he declared, was Esterhazy, and it was high time to distinguish between the cry of "Vive l'armée!" and that of "Vive Esterhazy!"

"Many Frenchmen are saying," he continued, "that it is possible that Dreyfus was condemned irregularly, but that he was justly condemned, and that suffices. That is the sophistry of reasons of state. We dance every 14th of July upon the ruins of the Bastile. These reasons of state, if they prevail, will constitute another and lower Bastile. It was a reason of state which, by the guillotine, stopped the magnificent movement of 1789. There is no justice outside of the law. It is sad, no doubt, to come into conflict with the military, brave men, who believed that they were doing right. This happens to civilians without uniforms, it happens to civilians in uniforms, for soldiers are nothing else.

"Gentlemen, render the country the service of stopping a religious war at its commencement. You have seen what happened in Algiers. Say in the name of the French people that justice must be done even to the Jews. Say to the religious war which has just begun: ' Thus far shalt thou go and no further.' We appear before you, gentlemen; you are appearing before history."

By a vote of eight to four, the jury rendered a verdict against M. Zola, and he was sentenced to pay a fine of 3,000 francs and to undergo a year's imprisonment.

The case was carried to the Court of Appeal, which quashed the judgment of the Assize Court on the ground that the case should have been brought by the court-martial which M. Zola had libelled, and not by the Minister of War. Consequently a second trial took place, but M. Zola declined to be present; he was again sentenced to the fine and imprisonment, and left France for England, where he remained until the revision proceedings before the Court of Cassation enabled him to return to France.

Chapter XX.

M. CAVAIGNAC AND THE DREYFUS CASE

THE Méline Cabinet, in June, 1898, was succeeded by the Brisson Cabinet. M. Sarrien became Minister of Justice, M. Cavaignac became Minister of War, with the firm intention of settling into oblivion for all time the Dreyfus case, whose echoes were then heard all over the world.

Replying to an interpellation in the Chamber of Deputies, M. Cavaignac made a memorable speech in which he attempted to put the quietus upon the Dreyfus case. He outlined the result of his investigations, and said considerations superior to reasons of law made it necessary to the Government to bring before the Chamber and the country the facts which confirmed the conviction of Dreyfus. The minister said there was absolutely no doubt as to the guilt of the prisoner, which was based on his own confessions and on documents on file in the Intelligence Department of the War Office.

This so-called confession was a remark attributed to Dreyfus by Captain Lebrun-Renault, of the Republican Guard, who had charge of the prisoner at the Military School just previous to his degradation. He is alleged to have said, after vigorously protesting his innocence, that if he had handed over documents to the agents of a foreign power *he did so in order to obtain more important papers in return*, and, in any case, the documents he had surrendered were unimportant papers.

In short, M. Cavaignac reviewed the whole of the Government case, already outlined, and wound up by saying that absolute proof, if it had previously been needed, was furnished by the Panizzardi despatch.

The Chamber of Deputies was enthusiastic over the speech of the Minister of War, and passed a resolution to the effect that it should be printed and placarded in every Commune throughout France, of which there are about thirty-six hundred.

But this was not all M. Cavaignac did. In his efforts to crush utterly the friends of Dreyfus, he ordered Esterhazy to be brought before a Court of Military Inquiry to justify his military career, owing to a serious indiscretion upon the part of the major.   Among other charges brought against him, it was said that, in 1882, he wrote to Madame de Boulancy, his cousin, a letter which was afterward seized by General Pellieux as a result of the proceedings previous to the court-martial of Esterhazy.   This letter showed that Esterhazy had very bitter feelings against the French army and the French nation.   He said that the French were an "accursed people," and expressed the opinion that they were "not worth even the cartridges for killing them!"

Continuing, this French officer said it would please him greatly to be slain as a captain of Uhlans (Prussian Lancers) while he was sabreing the French, and he said his favorite dream was to see Paris "beneath the red sun of battle, given over to pillage by a hundred thousand drunken soldiers."

It was also asserted that Esterhazy had written certain letters to the President of the Republic, and he was charged with certain irregular proceedings before and after his court-martial.

The Military Court of Inquiry was asked to pronounce upon the following questions:

Ought Esterhazy to be cashiered for habitual misconduct?

There was three votes in the affirmative and two in the negative.

Ought Esterhazy to be cashiered for grave offence against discipline?

The court unanimously decided in the negative.

Ought Esterhazy to be cashiered for offence against honor?

One member of the court voted yes, and four members of the court voted in the negative.

The Military Governor of Paris, General Zurlinden, in forwarding the finding of this court to the Minister of War, M. Cavaignac, pointed out that, as the decision was not unanimous, in accordance with army customs it would be sufficient to inflict only a disciplinary punishment upon the accused, by withdrawing him from the active list of the army.

The minister, however, decided that Esterhazy should be cashiered; and some time afterward the name of Du Paty de Clam was also removed from the active list of the army.

Having apparently settled the cases of Esterhazy and Du Paty de Clam, M. Cavaignac turned his attention to Colonel Picquart, who had informed the Premier that he could prove that one of the three documents referred to by M. Cavaignac in the Chamber of Deputies, as proof of the guilt of Dreyfus, was a forgery. The Minister of War ordered Picquart to be proceeded against, and he was arrested and lodged in prison.

For a while, things ran smoothly for the Headquarters Staff. But, in August, 1898, the generals had a rude awakening. They were informed that Lieutenant-Colonel Henry, the head of the Intelligence Department, the backbone of the prosecution of Dreyfus, who had in court dramatically pointed to Dreyfus as the traitor, had broken down and confessed to having forged at least one of the documents quoted by M. Cavaignac before the Chamber of Deputies as furnishing absolute proofs of the guilt of the prisoner of Devil's Island.

This was followed by the news of the arrest of Henry and his imprisonment in Mont Valérien, where, it is claimed, he cut his throat with a razor.

We purposely use the words "it is claimed," in referring to the death of Henry, because the suicide theory has never been accepted in the best-informed circles at Paris. Men who are versed in military customs are well aware that a prisoner of such importance, arrested after making such a startling confession, would never have been allowed to have a razor or other weapon within his reach, and, as in the case of a detective of the Government, Lemercier-Picard, who was found strangled to death by hanging in his apartments, the opinion has prevailed that Henry was murdered by the anti-Dreyfus clique's agents in order to save the honor of the army.

At this point it may be interesting to refer to a legend current in Paris in 1894, which had it that General de Boisdeffre one day entered the bureau in which Dreyfus was at work, and, placing a document before him, asked the captain if he would copy it, to which Dreyfus is said to have replied, "Certainly." Continuing, the story says Dreyfus had no sooner cast eyes on the paper than he turned deadly pale and exhibited signs of the greatest emotion, whereupon General de Boisdeffre is said to have placed a revolver on Dreyfus's desk, with the words:

"I will return in five minutes' time."

The general, it is further said, did return at the expiration of the time mentioned, and, finding Dreyfus still alive, remarked:

"What, not yet?"

The arrest of Dreyfus is said to have been ordered immediately afterward.

Of course this is only one of the many fairy tales in circulation at that time, for General de Boisdeffre has never referred to the matter, and he certainly would have done so had the story been true. It is true, however, that a pistol was placed near Dreyfus when he was arrested. He saw it, but declined to make use of it.

The death of Henry sealed the fate of M. Cavaignac as Minister of War, and he was sensible enough to recognize it; for he resigned. It also sent General de Boisdeffre into the background, for, as chief of the staff and main adviser of the minister, he was compelled to resign with M. Cavaignac, and General Zurlinden, then Military Governor of Paris, was appointed Minister of War.

Zurlinden followed the example of M. Cavaignac in some respects. He started to study the documents in the Dreyfus case. But it would seem he did not derive much satisfaction from them, for, after about a week in office, he resigned and resumed the military governorship of the city of Paris. General Chanoine succeeded General Zurlinden as Minister of War, and Esterhazy, possibly on account of his health, left France, and from that time on he may said to have been a wanderer on the face of the earth, making confessions, for considerations, to any one willing to pay for them, that he wrote the bordereau, and offering to prove this and other matters of an equally important nature.

At this point there is one question that is not quite clear, and that is, how was it that Henry was compelled to admit that he had committed forgery. The generally accepted answer to this question is that the governments of Germany and Italy, which had previously denounced the Panizzardi-Schwartzkoppen correspondence as forgery, took steps to impress this upon the French Government in unmistakable terms. Previous to this the French Government and the French War Office had paid no attention to the repudiations of the German and Italian governments, though they strongly denied having had any connection with Dreyfus.

Another version of the affair is that Captain Cuignet, of the Intelligence Department, ascertained, with the use of an extra strong lamp, that the Panizzardi document had been "doctored," and was not identical with the paper upon which the rest of the correspondence appears.

The details are not of great importance. The main facts, that Henry had confessed to forgery, and that his death had resulted from his action, were fully established, and higher and higher rose the hopes of the friends of the prisoner of Devil's Island.

The new minister of justice, M. Sarrien, in conjunction with Colonel Picquart, now began in earnest the work of inquiring as to whether it was not advisable to revise the Dreyfus court-martial of 1894. The Brisson Cabinet became committed to a revision, though the Minister of War was opposed to it.

Picquart, from his prison, wrote a letter to the Minister of Justice asking permission to tell him all he knew of the Dreyfus affair. The minister replied that he was willing to hear anything the prisoner had to say, and thereupon Picquart entered into a long description of the secret dossier as he knew the document in 1896, and charging that the fact that papers had been secretly communicated to the members of the Dreyfus court-martial was well known to General Mercier, General de Boisdeffre, the late Colonel Sandherr, General Gonse, Lieutenant-Colonel Henry, and Colonel Du Paty de Clam.

When the Minister of War, Zurlinden, heard of this, he sent the Minister of Justice a note tending to show that Picquart was not to be trusted, and that he ought to be tried by court-martial for forging the *petit bleu*. In addition, General Zurlinden applied to the Cabinet for permission to try Picquart by court-martial, but the minister refused to allow him to do so.

At a ministerial council held in the middle of September, 1898, under the presidency of the President of the Republic, M. Sarrien referred to Paragraph IV., Article 443, of the Code of Criminal Procedure, which provides for reopening a case, if, after a condemnatory verdict, fresher evidence is discovered tending to show that the innocence of the person condemned may be established. The minister then pointed to the confession of Henry as being of a nature to throw a legitimate suspicion upon the evidence which he furnished before the court-martial which sentenced Dreyfus.

The ministers were divided upon the question of reopening the case. The Minister of War was decidedly against such a step, and so was the Minister of Public Works, M. Tillaye, while the President was somewhat undecided.   In the end the question was referred to the Permanent Commission of Revision of the Ministry of Justice, to decide whether the case should or should not be re-tried by carrying it to the Court of Appeals. The commission could not agree, and then the Brisson Cabinet applied, through the Procureur-Général, to the Court of Appeals direct.   Eventually M. Bard, one of the members of the court, was instructed to report upon the case, and thus was taken the first great step toward revision.

Chapter XXI.

BEFORE THE COURT OF CASSATION

ABOUT a month after the revision question had been taken before the Court of Appeal, probably better known as the Court of Cassation, there was a debate in the Chamber of Deputies on October 25, 1898, on the action of the Government, during which the Minister of War, General Chanoine, ascended the tribune and announced that, representing as he did the army, he could not be a party to a revision of the Dreyfus case. The resignation of the Brisson Cabinet followed. It was succeeded on October 31st by a Cabinet presided over by M. Dupuy, who held office at the time of the court-martial of Dreyfus, and M. de Freycinet was the Minister of War. This ministry was not favorable to Dreyfus, and on September 21st Colonel Picquart was brought before the tribunal on the charge of communicating War Office documents to a civilian, M. Leblois, his lawyer. The Military party, however, demanded that Picquart should be surrendered to the military authorities so that he might be prosecuted for forging the *petit bleu*. The civil judge yielded, and Picquart was turned over to the military authorities, whereupon he loudly exclaimed in court:

" I absolutely oppose my being surrendered. I submit my case to your wisdom, but I have something further to say. It is only here, and a few minutes ago, that I learned the reality of the abominable plot in which this morning I still could not believe. It is the charge of forgery in regard to the *petit bleu*. You would have understood the matter more plainly if this trial had taken place, for it would have enlightened you with regard to the good faith of my accusers. I shall perhaps this evening go to the Cherche Midi, and now is probably the last time prior to secret trial that I can say a word in public. I would have people know, if there be found in my cell the rope of Lemercier-Picard, or the razor of Henry, that I have been assassinated. For a man like myself cannot for an instant think of suicide. I shall face this accusation erect and fearless, and with the same serenity with which I have ever met my accusers. That is what I had to say, Monsieur le President."

These utterances were received with cheers for Picquart upon the part of the Dreyfusards and with cries of "Down with the forgers!" from the anti-Dreyfusards.

There was little doubt that the bold statement made by Picquart in court saved his life.

The Criminal Chamber of the Court of Cassation met October 27, 1898, to consider the report of M. Bard.

After referring to the party passions aroused by the case and the prejudice, even before the verdict, expressed against the prisoner, M. Bard said:

"The echoes from outside cannot disturb that fear, for we have but a single passion, that of justice and truth."

Continuing, the reporter of the court said the bordereau was the essential document in the case against Dreyfus, and that the word of Lieutenant-Colonel Henry, a self-confessed forger, was the only guarantee of its origin. The forgery of Henry, under the circumstances, left nothing of the original trial of 1894 intact, especially as the handwriting experts of 1897 completely contradicted the testimony of the handwriting experts of 1894.

M. Bard then said:

"It is not too much to affirm that the accusation is now entirely nullified. It might indeed be asked, whether, as an acquittal was incumbent, the court ought not to certify as it did last January, in quashing a judgment of an Algiers court-martial, that there was no crime, and simply annul the judgment without ordering a fresh trial.

"Whatever might be the opinion of the court on the judgment of 1894, it would not forget that the military authorities were opposed to revision. It was the function of the Court of Appeals to bring the truth to light. It was a delicate task, but it would be derogatory to the court to suspect it of shirking its duty. Already there have been too many derelictions of duty in this long series of incidents. Free from all considerations or suggestions which had inspired others, and solely anxious for justice, the court has a great duty before it, and it will follow the dictates of its conscience."

When M. Bard had concluded his report the court was addressed by the Procureur-Général, M. Manau, and by counsel for Madame Dreyfus, M. Mornard.

The court, on October 29, 1898, delivered judgment as follows:

"In view of the letter of the Minister of Justice of September 20, 1898;

"In view of the arguments submitted by the Public Prosecutor attached to the Court of Cassation, denouncing to the court the condemnation pronounced by the first court-martial of the Military Court of Paris, on December 22, 1894, on Alfred Dreyfus, then captain of artillery, attached to the General Staff of the army;

"In view of all the documents of the case, and also of Article 443 to 446 of the Code of Criminal Procedure, amended by the law of June 10, 1895, on the admissibility, in proper form, of an application for revision—

"Whereas, the court has had the matter brought before it by its Public Prosecutor, in virtue of an express order of the Minister of Justice, acting after having taken the opinion of the Commission established by Article 444 of the Code of Criminal Procedure;

"Whereas, the application comes within the category of cases provided for by the last paragraph of Article 443, and has been introduced within the period fixed by Article 444;

"Whereas, finally, the judgment, the revision of which is asked for, has the force of a *chose jugée*.

"As regards the state of the case:

"Whereas, the documents produced do not place the court in a position to decide on all the merits of the case, and there is ground for making a supplementary inquiry;

"For these reasons, the court declares the application in proper form and legally admissible; states that it will institute a supplementary inquiry; and declares that there is no ground for deciding at the present moment on the Public Prosecutor's application for the suspension of the penalty."

Chapter XXII.

HOPES GROW STRONGER

THE Criminal Chamber of the Court of Cassation, October 29, 1898, began taking testimony in the revision proceedings. All was not smooth sailing, however. M. Quesnay de Beaurepaire, President of the Civil Section of the court, joined in the attacks made upon his colleagues, and matters became so complicated and feverish that, after a great deal of squabbling, the adjudication of the Dreyfus case was transferred to the United Chambers of the Court of Cassation. This was practically declaring that the highest criminal court in the country was incapable of dealing with the case.

Matters had reached this stage, when M. Félix Faure, President of the Republic, died suddenly, and the country was thrown into a state of turmoil. All parties looked upon the President's death as an opportunity to create disturbances, and they did so in their own ways. The Royalists and Bonapartists actively plotted against the Government, and M. Déroulède, founder of the League of Patriots, attempted to incite a detachment of troops to march upon the Elysée Palace. These troops were commanded by General Roget, and had taken part in the funeral procession. The soldiers paid no attention to M. Déroulède, and he and others were arrested and acquitted of inciting soldiers and troops to rebellion, although he pleaded guilty to the charge.

While the question of revision was before the Court of Cassation the usual number of rumors was circulated. The anti-Dreyfusards and a majority of the court were against the revision, and this had a depressing effect upon the Dreyfusards. Here the *Figaro* stepped into the breach and managed to publish all the evidence taken in secret before the Court of Cassation. Thus did the press throw its searchlight upon the mysteries of the Headquarters Staff, and up went the hopes of the friends of Dreyfus.

When the judges of the United Chambers of the Court of Cassation met in the Palace of Justice to hear the report of M. Ballot-Beaupré, President of the Civil Section of the court and successor of M. Quesnay de Beaurepaire, who had resigned, there was a period of expectancy throughout the world. The report, which was an exhaustive one, dealt with the bordereau as the one question at issue. Was the bordereau in the handwriting of Dreyfus? In reply M. Ballot-Beaupré said:

"Gentlemen, after a profound study of the question, I, for my part, have come to the conviction that the bordereau was not written by Dreyfus, but was written by Esterhazy."

It then became known that there existed two letters, written in 1892 and 1894, written by Esterhazy upon the same kind of water-mark and filigree tracing paper as that upon which the bordereau was written, which fact does not appear to have been known to the members of the court-martial of 1894.

In conclusion, M. Ballot-Beaupré said:

"I do not ask you to proclaim the innocence of Dreyfus, but I say that a fact unknown to the judges of 1894 tends to prove it. This suffices to ordain the sending of the prisoner before a new court-martial to bring in a definite verdict with a full knowledge of the case."

The Procureur-Général, M. Manau, took the same ground. He said the paper upon which the bordereau was written had spoken and established the innocence of Dreyfus, so far as the authorship of the bordereau was concerned. He added:

"What remains is that, whoever may be guilty, a crime of treason has been committed, but Esterhazy, having been acquitted of having written the bordereau, cannot be prosecuted again, were he a hundred times guilty. As to the innocence of Dreyfus, I do not ask you to proclaim it—that is for the new court-martial, to which, if the court so decides, the case will be referred. Your mission, gentlemen, is another—to say whether there ___fficient elements to prove that the judgment of the court-martial of ___is tainted with suspicion. It being now established that Dreyfus had nothing to do with the bordereau, we will dispense ourselves from entering upon a technical discussion of the facts. That will be for the new court-martial. It will be for them to reconcile the opinions of the former Ministers of War on that point, and to discuss with their special science the things which are unknown to us."

The Procureur-Général, during the course of his argument, pointed to the lack of incentive to commit such a crime in the case of Dreyfus, showing that he was well-to-do, and had married a wealthy woman, while Colonel Du Paty de Clam had admitted in his report that Dreyfus led a regular life, and did not live beyond his means. It was also shown that the prisoner had a splendid future before him. His position was compared with that of Esterhazy, the needy adventurer, who was seeking money in all directions.

M. Manau wound up with the statement that there was nothing in the secret dossier to incriminate Dreyfus, adding:

"We do not yet understand why there was so much delay in submitting these documents to investigation. They were secret only for Dreyfus, and they cannot be brought up against him. He knows, as the basis of his indictment and conviction, solely the bordereau and his alleged confession. The examination of the secret papers results in showing that of the three documents by which M. Cavaignac (when Minister of War) sought to justify the condemnation of the prisoner, two are forgeries, and the third does not apply to Dreyfus.

Finally, the Procureur-Général touched upon the alleged confessions of Dreyfus to Captain Lebrun-Renault, who had charge on the prisoner on the day of his degradation. He said that it was only in November, 1897, that the story of the alleged confession was brought up at the request of General Billot, and he held that this was clear proof that the so-called confession was not made by Dreyfus.

M. Manau severely criticised M. Cavaignac, who, he said, had depended for the proof of Dreyfus's guilt on a sheet from a note-book destroyed by Captain Lebrun-Renault. The Procureur-Général then remarked:

"I have the right to say that these confessions never existed, and I should like to know whether the incomprehensible evidence of M. ▉▉il-lon was not the first cause of Dreyfus's condemnation."

M. Manau alluded to the accounts of officials who had been in contact with Dreyfus, and who all affirmed their belief in his innocence, and quoted letters written from the Devil's Island wherein the prisoner repelled the imputations brought against him. He had been told in 1894 that "superior interests" were opposed to any search for the real culprits. In his letters he asked that, notwithstanding these interests, honor might be restored to the name he bore, and that he should be restored to his family. What was there more human? The chief officer of Devil's Island declared that Dreyfus was an abominable being, loving neither his wife nor his children. If so, how could he write such letters?

In conclusion, M. Manau said:

" I decline to believe that the court can refuse Dreyfus the supreme relief which is being solicited for him. The country, the world, and history are awaiting the decision; they will pass a judgment without appeal. Before them and before the court we assume the responsibility of our conclusions as magistrates and as citizens with the consciousness of having done our duty. These conclusions are:

" We affirm the existence of several new facts which are of a nature to establish the innocence of Dreyfus. Consequently, let it please the court to pronounce the abrogation of. the judgment of December 22, 1894, and to send Dreyfus, in the quality of an accused person, to such court-martial as it may be pleased to designate."

No sooner were the facts of the alleged confession first published, early in 1895, than M. de Civry, managing editor of the *Echo de l'Armée*, wrote an article on the subject, directed against Dreyfus, and, incidentally, sent the proof to the late Colonel Sandherr, then head of the Intelligence Department of the War Office, for revision before publication. The reply of Colonel Sandherr to M. de Civry is quite an important piece of evidence in favor of Dreyfus. It is as follows:

SATURDAY, January 5, 1895.

MY DEAR DE CIVRY:

-No, do not publish the article which Georgin has just submitted to me. It would open the door to needless discussions; for, I tell you frankly, it is not correct. Dreyfus did not make confessions to the captain of the Republican Guard, as he has told you. Hence, no capital can be made out of the confessions, and you must not set them against the public protestations of the condemned man. The latter simply recalled the words of the minister which Major Du Paty de Clam had been deputed to convey to him. The captain, who, without proper reason, has noised abroad the conversation held by him with the condemned man before the degradation, has involuntarily omitted to put in his mouth the words ' he said ' in speaking of these remarks of the minister: ' If I have furnished documents,

7

he said, it was to obtain others.' I do not know the full text of these remarks, but rest assured they are the words of the minister; not of Dreyfus. This mistake might elicit protestations from the defence or the family. Pass this incident over, therefore, in silence. The less you speak of this sad affair in the *Echo de l'Armée* the better will it be for us. You have better things to do. Georgin agrees with me."

Thus ended the great fight for the revision of the Dreyfus case.

Chapter XXIII.

DREYFUS BROUGHT BACK TO FRANCE

No sooner had the Court of Cassation pronounced in favor of the revision than the then Minister of War, M. de Freycinet, resigned, as a protest against the court's action, and M. Krantz, a man of more moral courage, succeeded him, and orders were sent to the Governor of French Guiana to ship Dreyfus back to France.

Then all thoughts were turned toward Devil's Island, and more and more sympathy for the prisoner was aroused, due in great measure to the publication of the testimony before the Court of Cassation of M. Lebon, the Minister of the Colonies, who admitted having ordered the sick man to be placed in double irons and subjected to other punishments, because it was feared he might be rescued. The French cruiser *Sfax* was ordered to take the prisoner on board, and there were many heartfelt good wishes for Dreyfus when it became known that he was homeward bound.

He was embarked at Cayenne on June 8, 1899, and was landed at Aliquen, on the Quiberon Peninsula, during the night of July 1st, and in very stormy weather. But it is to be presumed that the elements did not affect the prisoner's joy at once more setting foot on French soil. He saw ahead of him his honor vindicated, and a reunion with the faithful wife who had labored so gallantly in his behalf for five long and wearisome years in spite of every cruel obstacle thrown in her path.

The captain of the *Sfax*, referring to Dreyfus after the prisoner had been landed, said:

"There is extraordinary energy in this man. During the twenty days we were at sea he gave no sign of weakness."

And this was in spite of the fact that he was confined in a cabin, with the window closed and an armed sentry at the door.

A member of the crew of the *Sfax*, in his diary, described the embarkation of Dreyfus as follows:

"In a steam launch we perceived a civilian attired in a suit of dark blue cloth, and wearing a cork helmet. He hid his head in his hands. Sometimes he rose and took a couple of steps, and then he sank down on a bench. He seemed exhausted. We wondered who this personage could be. All sorts of rumors were current among the crew, and, after an hour's interval, the officers left the captain's cabin and orders were given for a boat to go alongside this launch and fetch the man on board the *Sfax*. This was done, and ten minutes later we saw former Captain Dreyfus ascending the ladder with difficulty, and with uncertain steps, followed by the gendarmes, who had revolvers in their belts. He staggered as he reached the deck, but he recovered his composure. With a still trembling hand he saluted in the military style, drawing himself up with a quick movement, as he was very bent. He had gray hair and a dark-red beard. His general appearance was fairly good, in spite of the seasickness from which he was suffering."

After his arrival on board the *Sfax*, Dreyfus was taken to his cabin by the second officer of that cruiser, and was furnished with a wardrobe, table, washstand, and bed. The port-hole of the cabin was strongly barred.

The *Sfax* weighed anchor June 10th, without having had time to take on board her full supply of coal or water, and sailed for the island of St. Vincent.

Dreyfus was watched night and day. During the day-time he was allowed to take three turns on deck, in the morning from nine until ten, from eleven until noon, and in the afternoon from four until five o'clock. All the officers and sailors were expressly forbidden to hold any communication with the prisoner. His meals were sent to him in his cabin from the officers' table.

The prisoner spent his time in reading and writing, though sometimes he looked long out of the port-hole, apparently plunged in deep thought. His baggage consisted of two portmanteaus, containing linen, books; several packages of chocolate, small biscuits, and several bottles of toilet vinegar. He generally went to bed at seven, arose about midnight to smoke a cigarette, and got up regularly at five o'clock in the morning.

June 13th, at 2:30 P.M., the *Sfax* arrived off the island of St. Vincent, from which place no letters or telegrams were allowed to be sent, as the

DREYFUS BROUGHT BACK TO FRANCE

journey of Dreyfus was to be kept a secret. The cruiser arrived at Aliquen July 1st.

The fishermen of that place were the first to make out the cruiser, and
they spread the news of her coming, resulting in the whole population,
about one hundred and fifty persons, rushing off to the pier, where a closed
carriage drawn by two white horses was drawn up. In the vehicle was
M. Viguier, Director of the Criminal Department. The One Hundred and
Sixteenth Regiment of the Line stood waiting in the rain for the landing
of Dreyfus. Shortly before two o'clock a launch approached the pier.
Dreyfus got out of the boat, and, between two gendarmes, with slow and
weary steps, he ascended the side of the pier, and reached the carriage of
M. Viguier. As the prisoner entered the carriage it was surrounded by
troops, and he was driven at a rapid pace, still in the pouring rain, to the
Quiberon railroad station, about a kilometer from Aliquen.

A special train was waiting at Quiberon. It consisted of four carriages,
and started in the direction of Rennes as soon as the prisoner was on
board. The train, however, was stopped at La Rablais, a level crossing a
mile or so outside the city. Carriages were in waiting there. The prisoner and his immediate escort entered the vehicles, and Dreyfus was
driven rapidly to the prison at Rennes. His carriage was surrounded by
gendarmes, and as it approached the prison the gates were opened and two
hundred gendarmes, who had been on duty inside, suddenly rushed out
and barred the street on either side of the entrance. Those who were able
to obtain a glimpse of Dreyfus as he was hurried into the prison noticed
that he looked startled and tired. He wore a blue suit with a gray overcoat and a soft felt hat. His hair was gray, and his beard was trimmed
to a point. The eyes of the prisoner seemed to lack expression. He first
looked at the ground, then at his escort, and afterward at the prison, but
he seemed to see nothing, or to be in a dream. A moment later Dreyfus
was again in a prison, not to reappear again until brought before the second court-martial which was finally to decide his fate.

Some days previous to this Madame Dreyfus had arrived at Rennes,
and a well-known resident of the place, Madame Godard, placed her house
at her disposal.

Madame Dreyfus was immediately informed of the arrival of her husband at Rennes, and was accorded permission to visit him. As may be

supposed, the meeting between the long-separated and long-suffering husband and the wife was touching in the extreme.

The prisoner was also allowed to see the lawyers who had been provided for him, and the next few days were spent in talking over the events of the past five years, of which the prisoner was profoundly ignorant. But he was deeply distressed when told of the machinations of which he had been a victim, and for a time seemed very much discouraged. The cheering words of his wife and the advice of his friends and lawyers eventually gave him more nerve, and he began to prepare for the trying ordeal to which he was to be subjected.

Chapter XXIV.

HOW M. LEBON TREATED DREYFUS

ONE of the features of the case which aroused the foreign press a great deal against the persecutors of Dreyfus, was the treatment to which he was subjected to by M. Lebon, the Minister of the Colonies, while the prisoner was on Devil's Island, and the minister was so severely criticised that, on July 12, 1899, although no longer a member of the ministry, he felt compelled to issue a full statement of his position, which certainly did not change the opinion people had formed about him. In this document, M. Lebon said:

"M. Louis Havet having substituted definite charges for the system of vague insults of which I have been the object for two years, and M. Guillian having dispelled some of the legends which there is an attempt to substantiate with reference to the Ile du Diable, I feel bound to break the silence which I have hitherto imposed upon myself from respect for the work of justice now going on, and to explain myself as clearly as I can as to the measures which I adopted and my reasons for them. I shall say nothing, moreover, which cannot be verified by the records of the Colonial Office, and I declare once for all that I accept entire responsibility for my acts, and that I entirely indorse the action of my old subordinates in the execution of my orders or in the acts which they reported to me, and which I did not blame at the time.

"I first recall certain facts outside my own administration. The public degradation of Dreyfus having taken place early in January, 1895, M. Guérin, then Minister of Justice, and M. Delcasse, then Minister for the Colonies, asked Parliament on the 11th of that month to indicate the Iles du Salut as a place of transportation in a fortified enclosure, together with the Ducos Peninsula, in order, as the preamble of the bill said, ' to increase the guarantee of supervision, and thus render the repression as effective as possible.' The bill was promulgated on February 9th, and

was countersigned by MM. Traireux and Chantemps.   It was in the spring
of the same year, 1895, that general instructions were given for the new
transportation service, and I did not become Minister for the Colonies
until a year later, at the end of April, 1896.   During the first months of
my ministry I had no occasion to pay any attention to the system established at the Île du Diable.   The measures to be taken for the pacification
of Madagascar, with the choice of a suitable man to be sent there, occupied my whole time, and I had no inclination to display ' fury or hatred
or the instinct of an executioner,' which M. Louis Havet deigns to admit
are totally lacking in me.   I will add, in order to reassure him immediately as to the reasons for my action, that I should never have dreamed
that I should one day be accused of having yielded to the ' fear of journalists.'   In the mistakes I may have made during my public life it is
rather in the contrary direction that I seem to myself to have erred.

"What, then, were my motives?   And first, how did matters stand in
the summer and autumn of 1896, as regards the Dreyfus affair?   In the
excitement of the past few months this question would appear to have
been totally forgotten.   No one then publicly defended the innocence,
true or supposed, of the prisoner.   No one disputed the authority of the
chose jugée.   Everybody, except a few who had special knowledge, was
anxious that Dreyfus should not escape, and was eager to discover the accomplices who were almost universally thought to have helped him.   It
was by no means my duty to listen to outside rumors nor to substitute
any personal opinion for the decisions of those who had been qualified to
express one.   I had in his case, as in that of all transported convicts,
merely to insure the execution of the decrees of justice and of the laws.
How did I come to think that there might be some doubt of the effectiveness of the system at Devil's Island, and how was I led, a full year
before the commencement of the revisionist agitation, and without making
the slightest mention of it to the journalists, as can easily be shown, to
adopt the measures for which I am now blamed?

"Within the space of a few weeks I learned that, one after another, two
service telegrams relative to the prisoner had been communicated to the
press; that another sent, like the first, by one of my predecessors had
never reached its destination; that, finally, a person connected with the
penitentiary administration could not be counted upon for the faithful exe-

cution of his duties, but that he frequently spoke of the possibility of procuring Dreyfus's escape. It was at this moment, early in September, that the English papers disseminated broadcast a report that an American ship had carried off Dreyfus, and then for the first time I obtained explanations of the organization of Devil's Island, and easily discovered that such a rescue was physically possible.

"Now, I did not wish that Dreyfus should escape, nor was I anxious to have his sentinels obliged to apply the general orders which permit recourse to the most extreme measures in order to prevent a prisoner from escaping. Hence my telegram of September 4th, to the Governor of Guiana. Here is its complete text as regards the point in question:

"'You will keep Dreyfus until further orders in hut, double staple at night. You will surround perimeter court round hut with solid palisading, with sentinel inside.'

"In order thoroughly to indicate the essentially temporary character of this measure of rigor, I telegraphed that the prisoner should be carefully informed that it was a measure of security, not of punishment; and, believing that my orders were already on the point of being fulfilled, I telegraphed again on the 19th, to say that as soon as the palisading was finished the double staple should be removed. Unfortunately, the work was done with less celerity than I had hoped, but neither then nor afterward was I apprised of the slightest disorder in the prisoner's health.

"Was I right or wrong in being so anxious as to the possibility of escape? All I can say is that during my two years' tenure of office hardly a month passed in which similar projects were not brought to my attention, either by the Prefecture of Police, by the Detective Department, or by diplomatic or consular agents. The external defence of the island being henceforth assured, none of these projects affected the prisoner's treatment. On the contrary, the work hastily done in September, 1896, having modified the hygienic conditions of his hut, a new building more spacious and healthier was prepared for him early in 1897, at the instance of one of the very agents now being most unjustly attacked.

"What is now called the Weyler forgery had nothing whatever to do with all this, though it was contemporaneous with it. It was, however, the cause of other measures which I felt bound to take as regards the prisoner's correspondence. The tenor of that document, and the way in which it reached the Colonial Office, have been sufficiently indicated in the inquiry of the Supreme Court.   I will only say that no one then, not even a certain eminent personage in the Intelligence Bureau, affirmed or approved it to be a forgery, and that it gave ground for believing that, apart from the prisoner's regular correspondence, then submitted, like that of all prisoners, to the control of the Penitentiary Department, there existed between Dreyfus and his friends or family other relations which escaped all supervision.   This suspicion was confirmed by other facts, either concomitant or subsequent, and gave rise toward the end of 1897 to a very suggestive report by the head of the local service as to the removal at the beginning of 1898 of a suspected sentinel.   If I had shown in the affair that blind passion now attributed to me I should, perhaps, have adopted measures other than those which I had definitely adopted.   I decided that copies of the letters exchanged between Dreyfus and his family should be transmitted instead of the originals, so that the apparent and known text should alone reach its destination.   But as to having attempted by means of subordinates, as is insinuated, to undermine the condemned man's confidence in his family by suppressing, mutilating, or deliberately delaying any of their letters, I affirm that such an idea prevailed neither in Paris nor Guiana.

"Such is the strict truth free from all dissimulation or amplification.   I am surprised that in facts which have been so long known to the parties concerned, and on which no one ever ventured to present an interpellation, such tardy accusations should be revived.   I might, moreover, show by relating either a conversation held or a correspondence exchanged with certain leaders of the sad controversy now witnessed by us, the signal bad faith which has been employed; but having no personal concern in this, and being only anxious to show that a servant of the Republic is not the ' sinister torturer ' represented, I limit myself to this too long explanation."

Chapter XXV.

DREYFUS'S FINAL APPEAL FOR JUSTICE

A MONTH after Dreyfus had been landed in France and a week before the opening of the court-martial at Rennes, the Paris *Figaro* published some most interesting correspondence, showing how steadily the prisoner maintained his innocence and how clearly he met all the points of his accusers. The letters, however, were not sent to their addresses, by order of Premier Méline.

The first letter of the series referred to follows:

ILE DU SALUT, February 28, 1898.

On the very morrow of my condemnation, now more than three years ago, when Major Du Paty de Clam came to see me on behalf of the Minister of War, to ask me, after I had been condemned for an abominable crime which I had not committed, whether I was innocent or guilty, I declared that not only was I innocent, but that I wished for the light, the complete light, and I asked immediately for the aid of all the customary means of investigation, either through the military attachés or in any other mode at the disposal of the Government. I was told that interests superior to mine, owing to the origin of this lamentable and tragic history and owing to the origin of the incriminating letter, prevented the customary means of investigation, but that the inquiry would be continued. I have waited for three years in the most terrible situation conceivable, suffering continuously and without cause, but these researches never end. If, then, interests superior to mine are to prevent, and must always prevent, the use of the only means of investigation which can finally put an end to this horrible martyrdom of so many human beings and throw complete light on this tragic business, these interests can surely not require that a woman, children, and an innocent man should be sacrificed to them. Otherwise we must go back to the darkest ages of our history, when the truth and the light are stifled. A few months ago I submitted the whole tragic and undeserved horror of this situation to the high equity of the Government. I now do the same to the high equity of *Messieurs les*

Députés to ask them for justice for me and mine, the life of my children, and an end to this frghtful martyrdom of so many human beings."

The prisoner wrote a similar letter to the Senators.

Dreyfus, on March 21st, wrote as follows to the Minister of War:

A few months ago, probably in consequence of a report on the accusation, I was told that this was based—(1) on a charge against my family. This document was unknown to me. It was never communicated to me, so I could not reply. It is, moreover, as atrocious as it is calumnious. (2) The presumption drawn from the handwriting. I declared that I was not the author of the incriminating letter; I showed from its contents that I could not be. (3) The trembling of the hand. At the court-martial Major Du Paty de Clam, in reply to a question, affirmed that it was warm at the time. M. Cochefort, a few moments later, declared with me that it was piercingly cold. (4) The rest of the accusation. Another document. At the court-martial the straightforward protest of Captain Besse against the interpretation given to his deposition, and the explanation given by Major Mercier, forced the Government commissary to abandon this portion of the accusation. Moreover, at the court-martial the oral evidence and the explanations brought out by the defence reduced this entire portion to nothing. (5) Moral causes—gaming, and women. I can only refer to my own declaration, in opposition to which no serious proof was given, no signed deposition. The court upheld none of the atrocious anonymous documents which had been appended to the dossier. In a letter to the Minister of Justice a few months ago I asked, in the name of the imprescriptible rights of truth and justice and in the interests of my wife and children, that a serious inquiry should be made to elucidate definitively all the anonymous gossip and reports. To sum up, I appeal, Monsieur le Ministre, to General de Boisdeffre's loyalty and to that of those who obtained my condemnation, that it may be made known that at the court-martial, where the minister was represented, the accusation, save for the first document—of which I had no knowledge, and which was communicated therefore solely to the judges—the accusation was reduced by discussion to a presumption as to handwriting.

No. 1 in this letter refers to M. Bertillon's theory that the bordereau was both in Captain Dreyfus's hand and in that of his brother.

The following letter was written by Dreyfus to President Faure. It is dated February 14, 1897, but was never finished nor sent:

I venture once more to appeal to your high justice. For more than two years, innocent of an abominable crime the very-thought of which revolts my whole being, I have been undergoing the most frightful torture imaginable. I cannot possibly tell you, Monsieur le President, how I have suffered; my heart alone knows. Another pen than mine is needed to describe tortures such as these. And if I have lived, holding down my heart, keeping myself in check, swallowing insults and affronts, it is because I would have wished to be allowed to die tranquil, knowing that I should be leaving to my children a pure and honored name. But, alas! I have been too great a sufferer. I can endure it no longer. Ah! Monsieur le President, I know not how to find words to tell you how I suffer, to describe the horrors of every minute in every hour of the day, horrors against which I succeeded in bearing up only in the supreme hope of beholding once more for my dear children the day when honor will be restored to them. And in this profound distress of my whole being, in this agony of my whole strength, it is to you, Monsieur le President, to the Government of my country, that I throw again this supreme cry of appeal, sure that it will be heard. And this supreme cry of appeal from a Frenchman, a father, who now for more than two years has lain on a bed of torture, is ever the same—namely, for the truth of this terrible drama, for the unmasking of the man or men who committed the infamous crime. . . .

On January 6, 1898, Dreyfus wrote to the Governor of Guiana:

I venture to send you the enclosed letter, asking you if it would not be possible to have it transmitted at my expense by telegraph to the President of the Republic.

The enclosed letter was as follows:

Not having received any letters from my family now for two months, my brain maddened, I once more affirm to you that I never was, that I am not, and that I cannot possibly be the culprit.

The following is the letter written by Dreyfus to the head of the local penitentiary service in October, 1896, on learning that he was to be put in irons:

I have just been warned that I shall be put in irons at night. I should be very grateful to you if you would tell me what fault I have committed.   Since I have been here I believe that I have strictly obeyed all the rules, all the orders.   All that has been told me I have executed in its integrity.   I take the liberty, therefore, of asking you what I must do to avoid so terrible a punishment.   I have been living only out of duty to my wife and children.   If I am to die, the sooner the better.

Chapter XXVI.

OPENING OF THE SECOND DREYFUS COURT-MARTIAL

THE second trial by court-martial of the prisoner of Devil's Island opened at 7:10 A.M., on Saturday, August 7th, in the Lycée, at Rennes, France.

The Prefect of Police and the Chief of the Secret Police, M. Viguier, arrived at the Lycée shortly before 6 A.M., and began superintending the police measures. At that hour only half a dozen gendarmes were visible about the building. They were stationed about the entrance of the Lycée and inside the garden in front of it. The garden is separated from the sidewalk of the Avenue de la Gare, on which the Lycée is situated, by a high iron railing, within which no one was allowed to pass until Dreyfus was transferred from his quarters in the military prison to a room within the Lycée building, where he awaited the summons to appear before the court.

Strong detachments of gendarmes, mounted and on foot, began to arrive at about six o'clock, and took up positions in the side avenues about the Lycée and in all the by-streets leading to the Avenue de la Gare.

At 6:15 A.M., the Prefect gave orders to close the Avenue de la Gare for three hundred yards in front of the Lycée, and also to close all the streets leading into the avenue. Consequently, gendarmes were immediately drawn up across the avenue, and the space mentioned was cleared of all spectators.

A detachment of infantry was then stationed across the avenue in two double lines, leaving between them a passage for Dreyfus to cross the avenue from the prison to the entrance to the Lycée. The crowd, which by that time had increased to a few hundreds, was kept by gendarmes at a distance of one hundred and fifty yards on either side of this passage.

Dreyfus soon afterward emerged from the military prison escorted by a lieutenant and four gendarmes. The party crossed the roadway quickly and disappeared within the Lycée, the hedges of soldiers hiding the prisoner from view.

From 6:30 to 7 A.M., the principal personages participating in the court-martial arrived. The various generals interested passed into the building, with hardly a cheer from the spectators, General Mercier (who was Minister of War when Dreyfus was originally convicted) alone being greeted with a few cries of "Vive l'Armée!" "Vive Mercier!" as he drove up in a closed carriage.

Colonel Picquart (the former Chief of the Secret Intelligence Bureau of the French army, whose favorable attitude toward the prisoner did so much to bring about a revision of the latter's sentence) arrived at the Lycée on foot, at 6:40, wearing a high silk hat and a black frock coat, with the red ribbon of the Legion of Honor in his buttonhole. There was no demonstration when he appeared, but Picquart seemed to be in a most cheerful mood, smiling and chatting with his friends.

The scene inside the court-room was most animated. Every inch of space was filled a quarter of an hour before the proceedings opened.

The large, airy, well-lighted room in which the trial took place was in the form of a concert hall, with a stage and proscenium. The platform of the stage had been brought forward beyond the footlights. The room was painted a light brown. The names of famous Bretons, such as Le Sage, Renan, and Châteaubriand were inscribed in golden letters on an ornamental band about midway between the floor and ceiling. A long table covered with dark-blue cloth was ranged in front of the stage, behind which were the seats of the members of the court-martial, a higher-backed armchair having been provided for the president. The seats were of polished mahogany, and were upholstered in dark-red cloth.

Behind the members of the court sat the Supplementary Judges, who must attend all sittings and be able to replace any member who may be ill or otherwise be unable to be present. Behind the Supplementary Judges were a few privileged members of the public.

On a portion of the stage extending in front of the proscenium was placed the bar at which the witnesses were heard. The bar had a wooden frame of light polished oak. It stood out prominently against the dark cloth-covered table of the judges.

On the right end of this extended platform stood a table for the use of

ÎLE DU DIABLE: DREYFUS IN HIS CELL

COURT OF CASSATION: ASSEMBLING TO HEAR BEAUPRE'S REPORT IN FAVOR OF REVISION.

DREYFUS'S OUTBURST OF PASSION: "I AM INNOCENT!"

COURT OF CASSATION: ASSEMBLING TO HEAR BEAUPRE'S REPORT IN FAVOR OF REVISION.

DREYFUS'S OUTBURST OF PASSION: "I AM INNOCENT!"

DEVIL'S ISLAND: SHOWING DREYFUS'S HUT AND THE WATCH-TOWER.

RETURN OF DREYFUS: ARRIVAL ON BOARD THE "SFAX."

RETURN OF DREYFUS: LEAVING THE TRAIN AT RABLAIS NEAR RENNES.

SOME OF THE PRINCIPAL PERSONAGES IN THE DREYFUS CASE.

1. M. Scheurer-Kestner, vice-president of the Senate.—2. M. Ranc, senator for the Seine.—3. General Billot, War Minister.—4. M. Darlan, Minister for Justice.—5. M. de Castro, who was the first to assert that the bordereau was written by Major Esterhazy.—6. Maître Leblois, counsel for Lieutenant-Colonel Picquart.—7. Lieutenant-Colonel Picquart.—8. Colonel Panizzardi, Italian military attaché in Paris.—9. M. Mathieu Dreyfus, brother of Alfred Dreyfus.—10. Lieutenant-Colonel Henry.—11. Colonel Schwartzkoppen, German military attaché in Paris.—12. M. Henri Rochefort, director of the *Intransigeant.*—13. M. Castelin, deputy for the Aisne.—14, 15, 16, and 17, MM. Gobert, Pelletier, Charavay, and Crépieux-Jamin, handwriting experts.

THE DEGRADATION OF DREYFUS: BREAKING THE SWORD.

Maîtres Labori and Demange, counsel for the prisoner, and their two secretaries.   At the left side was placed a table for Major Carriere, the Government Commissary, or official representative of the Government, and his assistants.

MM. Labori and Demange, on entering, were greeted with warm handshakes from numerous friends in the court-room.

Former President Casimir-Perier entered shortly before seven. An officer met him at the door, and conducted him to the velvet-covered chairs reserved for witnesses.   The ex-President found himself between Generals Billot and Chanoine, both in parade uniform.   Other ex-Ministers of War—Generals Mercier and Zurlinden, and M. Cavaignac—were seated in a row behind them.

The widow of Lieutenant-Colonel Henry, dressed in deep mourning, was present in court, and replied to her name in the roll-call of witnesses.

M. Mathieu Dreyfus and Dreyfus's father-in-law, M. Hadamard, were among the audience.

On either side of the hall was a solid mass of newspaper men, for whom rough pine tables and benches had been provided.

In the centre of the hall were placed chairs for the witnesses.   Behind these was another batch of the privileged public, and then a row of soldiers, in parade uniform, drawn across the hall, with fixed bayonets.

A narrow space between the troops and the back of the hall was filled with the "general public," which consisted of a few journalists and detectives, with gendarmes sprinkled among them.   Back of the stage hung a crucifix, before which the witnesses took the oath.   Facing this, at the back of the hall, was an emblem of the Republic, with the letters " R. F." (République Française).

At seven o'clock MM. Labori and Demarge and Major Carriere, with their assistants, took their seats, and the witnesses followed.   Then sharp words of command rang out from the officer in charge of the row of soldiers at the back of the court:

"Carry arms!"

"Present arms!"

There was a rattle of arms, and a moment later Colonel Jouaust, followed by the other members of the court, walked on to the stage from a

8

room behind and took seats at the table.   Deep silence fell upon the audience, who up to then had been engaged in a buzz of conversation.

Colonel Jouaust and his colleagues were in full parade uniform, with plumes in the front of their peaked shakos.   Colonel Jouaust's aigrette was white; the others were tri-color.   On the right hand of Colonel Jouaust sat Lieutenant-Colonel Brongniart, Major de Breon, and Captain Parfait, all of the artillery.   On his left hand were Majors Profillet and Merle and Captain Beauvais, also of the artillery.

An interesting figure, seated behind the judges, was the famous and mysterious lady known as La Dame Blanche (the White Lady), who never absented herself from any of the proceedings connected with the Dreyfus affair, including all sessions of the Esterhazy, Zola, and Picquart trials, and the proceedings of the Court of Cassation.   All the actors in the drama are known to her.   She is a pronounced Dreyfusarde, very rich, and wears splendid pearls.   She was dressed that day in a "picture" hat with black and white trimmings and a pink bodice.   Her name is Mlle. Blanche de Comminges, whose salon Colonel Picquart frequented, and whom Henry and Du Paty de Clam attempted to implicate in an alleged plot of the Dreyfusards to substitute Esterhazy for Dreyfus as the author of the bordereau.

The splendid, gold-laced uniforms of the generals summoned as witnesses, and the uniforms of the judges, soldiers, and various officers present, combined to light up the dark tints with which the walls of the hall were painted, and gave a bright appearance to the court-room.

Immediately after Colonel Jouaust was seated he gave the order to bring in the prisoner.   All eyes were then turned to the right of the stage, beside which was a door leading to the room in which Dreyfus was awaiting the summons.   Almost everybody but the most prominent officers stood on his feet.   Some mounted on benches to obtain a better view.

There were subdued cries of "Sit down," amid which the door opened and Captain Alfred Dreyfus, preceded and followed by a gendarme, emerged into the court-room.   His features were deathly pale and his teeth were set, with a determined but not defiant bearing.   He walked quickly, with almost an elastic step, and ascended the three steps leading to the platform in front of the judges.   There he drew himself up erect and brought his right hand sharply to the peak of his képi, or military cap, giving the military salute in a fashion that showed that years of incarceration of Devil's Island and terrible anguish of body and mind had not impaired his soldierly instinct and bearing.

The prisoner then removed his képi and took the seat placed for him, facing his judges, just in front of his counsel's table, and with his back to the audience.   Behind him sat a gendarme holding a sheathed sabre in his hand.   Dreyfus, in a new uniform of captain of artillery, dark blue with red facings, fixedly regarded the judges, with immovable features and without stirring hand or foot, scarcely even moving his head during the whole course of the proceedings, except when he entered and left the court-room.

Dreyfus answered the formal question of the President of the Court, Colonel Jouaust, as to his name, age, and other matters, in a clear, determined voice.   He sat facing the members of the court, with his hands resting on his knees, an apparently impassive figure.

After the formal proceedings, which occupied a couple of hours, Colonel Jouaust began the examination of Dreyfus respecting the famous bordereau, and what Dreyfus did with or could have known of its contents.

When Dreyfus, wearing eyeglasses, rose from his seat for examination, he stood erect, holding his képi in his hand before him.   He looked Colonel Jouaust straight in the face during the whole interrogatory

After the court had decided not to adjourn on account of the absence of certain witnesses, the clerk of the court was ordered to read M. d'Ormescheville's bill of indictment of 1894, which he did in a loud voice, Dreyfus, in the mean while, listening unmoved as the old charges against him were read.

This is the famous *Acte d'Accusation* first made public in *Le Siècle* of Paris, January 8, 1898.   It accused Dreyfus of writing the bordereau, and of transmitting it, together with the documents therein mentioned, to the agent of a foreign power.   It also made serious reflections upon his personal character.

Colonel Jouaust then said:

"It results from the documents just read, that you are accused of having brought about machinations or that you held relations with a foreign power, or with one or more of its agents, in order to procure it means, by delivering to it documents indicated in the incriminating bordereau, to commit hostilities or undertake war against France. I notify you that you will be allowed to state during the course of these proceedings anythin that appears to you useful for your defence."

Colonel Jouaust then added, as he handed the prisoner a long slip of cardboard upon which the bordereau was pasted:

"Do you recognize this document?"

Dreyfus replied, with a passionate outburst:

"No, Colonel! I am innocent! I declare it here as I declared it in 1894. I am a victim——"

His voice here was choked with sobs, which must have stirred every spectator in court. The voice of the prisoner did not seem human. It resembled the cry of a wounded animal, as he ended his reply with the words, "Five years in the galleys! My wife! My children! My God! I am innocent!"

Colonel Jouaust said:

"Then you deny it?"

Dreyfus replied:

"Yes, Colonel."

On the court proceeding to the roll-call of witnesses, the most notable absentees being Esterhazy, Du Paty de Clam, and Mlle. Pays, Dreyfus half turned his head toward the seats of the witnesses, especially when the clerk of the court called Esterhazy. But when no response was received, Dreyfus returned to his previous attitude, looking straight in front of him at Colonel Jouaust.

Esterhazy at the time was in London. Du Paty de Clam was recently released from Cherche-Midi prison, where he was confined pending an investigation to ascertain whether in shielding Esterhazy in 1897–98 he had acted on his own initiative or by orders of his superior officers.

Mlle. Pays is a friend of Esterhazy, who plotted with him to ruin Picquart.

The court afterward retired to deliberate upon the case of the absentee witnesses, the soldiers in the court-room, in response to the word of command of the lieutenant in charge, carrying and presenting arms, the judges leaving and re-entering to the rattle of rifles, as the line of soldiers brought their weapons, like a piece of machinery, smartly to the "Present!" and then dropped the butts heavily to the floor.

This performance was repeated every time the court retired.

Dreyfus was withdrawn into an inner room during the court's retirements.

On the final return of the court, Major Carriere said he thought the absence of Esterhazy ought not to prevent the trial proceeding.

"Let him come or not," he said, "it matters nothing to me."

Colonel Jouaust then proceeded to question Dreyfus as to his knowledge of the "120 brake," a hydro-pneumatic attached to an improved French field-piece. The prisoner, in brief, said he had only a general idea of the brake.

The court then questioned the prisoner about his knowledge of the covering of troops, and Dreyfus replied that he had no knowledge of this question in 1894, though he had certain documents concerning the provisioning and conveying of troops.

Colonel Jouaust then turned to the note referring to Madagascar, and said: "You could have obtained this document from the corporal's desk?"

Dreyfus—That is not usual.

Colonel Jouaust—No, but it could be done. The copying was finished on the 28th, and the bordereau dates from several days later. Now for the fifth document—the proposed Firing Manual for Field Artillery. Did you know the contents of the manual?

Dreyfus (emphatically)—No; never!

Colonel Jouaust—A witness said you communicated it to him.

Dreyfus (vehemently)—No; never!

Colonel Jouaust—A major lent you this Firing Manual?

Dreyfus—No, Colonel. I deny it absolutely.

Dreyfus then entered into an explanation of dates, but his memory failed him.

Colonel Jouaust then took up the famous phrase, "I am starting for the manœuvres." He said:

"You had never been to the manœuvres, because it was the custom only for probationers to go. But at the date of the bordereau you did not know you would not go?"

Dreyfus—There had been fresh orders given.

Originally it was alleged that the bordereau was written in April,

1894. It was subsequently discovered that Dreyfus knew as early as March that he was not to attend the spring manœuvres. The real date was then given, August, 1894. But Dreyfus did not attend the fall manœuvres of that year.

Colonel Jouaust—At the Military School you were reproached for saying the Alsatians were happier as Germans than as Frenchmen?

Dreyfus —No; I never uttered such words.

General de Dionne, who was at the head of the War School in 1892, where Dreyfus was a pupil, made this charge against the prisoner before the Court of Cassation. Thereupon the general was confronted with a report written by him in 1892, in which he spoke of Dreyfus in the highest terms.

Colonel Jouaust—How do you account for the bad note against you written by a certain general?

Dreyfus—He said he wanted no Jews on the General Staff.

Colonel Jouaust—In 1892 you went to Mulhouse, Alsace. What did you do there?

Dreyfus—I went there three times, by way of Basle, without a passport. Once I arrived at my house, I never went out.

Colonel Jouaust—You went there in 1886?

Dreyfus—Yes, possibly.

Colonel Jouaust—Did you follow the German manœuvres?

Dreyfus—No.

Colonel Jouaust—Did you converse with German officers?

Dreyfus—I deny it absolutely.

Colonel Jouaust—What was your object in going to Alsace?

Dreyfus—For instruction.

Colonel Jouaust—You wrote certain information respecting the manufacture of the Robin shell. You said this information was requested by a professor of the Military School. This was false. I am told you asked officers indiscreet questions.

Dreyfus—It is not true.

Colonel Jouaust—Had you relations with a lady living in the Rue Bizet?

Dreyfus—I had no intimate relations with her.

Colonel Jouaust—I do not mean from a moral point of view, but from a military point of view.   This woman was suspected of spying. Why did you visit her?

Dreyfus—I only learned that at my trial, in 1894.   Major Gendrion introduced me to her, and as Gendrion belonged to the Inquiry Bureau he ought to have known if she was suspected.

Colonel Jouaust—Passing through the Champs Elysées in 1891 you remarked: "Here lives a certain lady.   Suppose we call on her.   I have lost heavy sums at her house."

Dreyfus—It is false.   I have never gambled.   Never!   Never!

Colonel Jouaust—Did you know Colonel Du Paty de Clam?

Dreyfus—No.

Colonel Jouaust—Did you know Lieutenant-Colonel Henry?

Dreyfus—No.

Colonel Jouaust—You have no motive for animosity against them?

Dreyfus—No.

Colonel Jouaust—And Colonel Picquart?

Dreyfus—I don't know him.

Colonel Jouaust—And Lieutenant-Colonel Esterhazy?

Dreyfus—I don't know him.

Colonel Jouaust—Colonel Du Paty de Clam said that your writing at his dictation was less firm when he made you undergo a trial on the day of your arrest.

Dreyfus—My writing has not much changed.

Here a non-commissioned officer who was standing in front of Major Carriere crossed the platform and handed Dreyfus his writing on the day of his arrest.

Dreyfus replied by insisting there was nothing to show any perceptible change in his handwriting.

Here occurred one of the most dramatic scenes in the examination. Dreyfus, tremendously excited, swayed to and fro for a moment, and then all his pent-up emotion and indignation burst forth, and he cried in a piercing voice, heard throughout the court and even by those standing outside:

"It is iniquitous to condemn an innocent man.   I never confessed anything!   Never!"

Dreyfus, as he uttered the words, raised his right, white-gloved hand and held it aloft as if appealing to Heaven to vindicate him.

Colonel Jouaust—Did you say: "If I handed over documents it was to have more important ones in return?"

Dreyfus—No.

Colonel Jouaust—Did you say: "In three years they will recognize my innocence"? Why did you say "three years"?

Dreyfus—I asked for all means of investigation. They were refused me. I was justified in hoping that at the end of two or three years my innocence would come to light.

Colonel Jouaust—Why three years?

Dreyfus—Because a certain time is necessary to obtain light.

Colonel Jouaust then said:

"Coming to the day of your degradation, what passed between you and Captain Lebrun-Renault? What did you tell him?"

Dreyfus—Nothing. It was really a sort of broken monologue on my part. I felt that everybody knew of the crime with which I was charged, and I wished to say I was not the guilty party. I wished to make clear that the criminal was not he whom they had before their eyes, and I said: "Lebrun, I will cry aloud my innocence in the face of the people."

Colonel Jouaust—Did you not say, "The minister knows I handed over documents"?

Dreyfus—No. If I spoke of a minister who knew I was innocent, I referred to a conversation I previously had with Du Paty de Clam.

This ended the first day of the second court-martial.

Colonel Jouaust treated Dreyfus brusquely, almost brutally, and it was a matter of satisfaction to the friends of the prisoner when the latter set the judge himself right on certain dates connected with Dreyfus's stay on the General Staff. It was an unimportant point, but it was eloquent testimony to the keenness of Dreyfus's intellect.

The prisoner sat most of the time with his legs stretched out, his spurs resting on the ground, his hands joined and resting on his lap. He repelled the insinuations that he had relations with German officers during his stay in Alsace, in fiercely indignant terms.

Chapter XXVII.

THE PRISONER ASSISTS THE JUDGES

THE court-martial sat in secret session on Monday, August 9th, from 6:30 A.M. until 11:45 A.M., in order to examine the secret documents in the case, and this was continued until August 11th. Several of the documents were written in German, and in the course of the proceedings a German dictionary was sent for. When certain words and expressions could not be exactly understood, even with the aid of the dictionary, Dreyfus, who is a perfect German scholar, volunteered a translation, and was allowed to give explanations, which were of valuable assistance to the members of the court.

The police measures were much more stringent than on the day of the opening of the trial. Strong detachments of infantry instead of gendarmes cordoned the streets leading to the Lycée. Gendarmes alone performed this duty August 7th, and the sightseers, who were much less numerous, barely numbering three hundred persons, were pressed still further back. Even persons standing inside the entrance hall of a house in view of the door of the Lycée were compelled to retire into the interior of the house, and the front door was closed. Absolutely nobody but police and soldiers were thus within one hundred yards of Dreyfus when he crossed the Avenue de la Gare. The police authorities explain the rigor of these measures on the ground that yesterday a few cries against the prisoner were raised while he was crossing the avenue.

Maître Demange, of counsel for Captain Dreyfus, in an interview after the session of August 10th, expressed himself as very well contented with the way in which matters were proceeding, and, judging from his manner, it was apparent that the defenders of the accused had not met with anything very surprising or alarming in the secret dossier.

Naturally Maître Demange declined to give any particulars respecting the contents of the dossier, but he declared that he and his colleague,

Maître Labori, were satisfied of the desire of the members of the court to thresh the whole matter out, and to have full light turned upon the accusations against Dreyfus.

The court-martial concluded its secret sessions at nine o'clock on August 11th, when M. Paleologue of the Foreign Office completed his explanations of the secret dossier.

Chapter XXVIII.

GENERAL MERCIER CONFRONTED BY DREYFUS

THE second public session of the second court-martial of Captain Dreyfus began at 6:30 o'clock August 12th. The red-and-white façade of the Lycée was bathed in sunshine when Dreyfus crossed the Avenue de la Gare from his prison and entered the Lycée. The stringent police precautions observed every day during the week were again taken, but barely twenty persons gathered to witness the prisoner's appearance.

M. Casimir-Perier, ex-President of France, arrived on foot shortly afterward, and was saluted by a crowd in waiting. Then came Colonel Picquart, formerly of the Secret Intelligence Bureau of the General Staff. He was greeted with shouts of "Vive Picquart!" which he smilingly acknowledged.

The curtain rose on the same theatre-like scene as on August 7th. The judges, in uniform, were seated on the stage, behind the dark, cloth-covered table on which, in a row, were képis with gay-colored plumes and heavy gold-lace bands. Every inch of the court was occupied, in expectation of a sensational scene.

The session opened with precisely the same formalities as on August 7th. Dreyfus entered the hall with the same quick, jerky step, and his features were pale and rigid as he took a seat upon the platform. Dreyfus, on entering the court, saluted the president with the same soldierly mien, and Colonel Jouaust returned the salute, and said:

"Sit down, Dreyfus."

The proceedings opened tamely. Matters began to get tedious as M. Casimir-Perier and General Mercier reiterated what had been already shown. But this was only the calm before the storm. When the storm broke, it carried every one in court with it into a whirlpool of the wildest excitement.

Colonel Jouaust, immediately after the court had settled down to work, opened the proceedings by saying to Dreyfus:

"In January, 1895, the director of the penitentiary of the Île de Ré, in the course of duty, searched the clothes you brought from the prison. He found this document in an inside pocket of your waistcoat."

The president here handed Dreyfus a paper, and asked:

"Do you recognize it as having belonged to you?"

Dreyfus—Yes, Colonel.

Colonel Jouaust—Whose was it?

Dreyfus—Mine.

Colonel Jouaust—Will you tell me how and under what circumstances this document came into your possession?

Dreyfus—It is a document I used during my trial. In order to discuss the value of the bordereau I wished to keep it.

Colonel Jouaust—The Military Code gives you the right to have a copy of the documents in your case. This document, therefore, was legitimately in your possession. Why did you wish to keep it?

Dreyfus—As a souvenir of the text of the bordereau?

Colonel Jouaust—That was not proper, and, therefore, it was taken from you. I merely wish to elucidate this point. That will do.

M. de la Roche-Vernet, a secretary attached to the French Embassy at Berlin, was the next witness called. He said he acted as the transmitting agent of the Ministry of War and the Ministry of Foreign Affairs in the translation of the Panizzardi despatch, which was a very minute and complicated matter. Several drafts, he explained, were first made, and finally an official translation was drawn up, which was the same as since published. The original of this despatch was in cipher. It was sent, November 2, 1894, by Colonel Panizzardi, Italian attaché in Paris, to the Italian Headquarters Staff in Rome. Its true construction, which obviously establishes the innocence of Dreyfus, is:

"If the captain has had no relations with you, it would be well to instruct our Ambassador to avoid the comments of the press."

The original has disappeared from the secret dossier. But there exists a version given by Du Paty de Clam "from memory," which reads:

"Captain Dreyfus arrested. The Minister of War has proof of his relations with Germany. All my precautions are taken."

Questioned respectively regarding the draft and the translations, he said they were purely hypothetical, the first only having two words, "Captain Dreyfus," of which the translators were really sure, the sense being to the effect that Dreyfus had been arrested, and that he had no relations with Germany.

M. Paleologue of the French Foreign Office was then called.

The net result of the two witnesses' replies to MM. Labori and Demange was that never, in any translation, was there any question of relations with Germany.

The next witness was M. Casimir-Perier, formerly President of France. He said:

"Monsieur le President, you ask me to speak the truth and all the truth. I have sworn to do it. I will speak it, without reference, without reserve, in its entirety. Whatever I may have said in the past, whatever people may believe and say, which, unfortunately, is not always the same thing, that I alone am aware of incidents and facts which might throw light, and that I have not hitherto said all, justice ought to know that it is false. I will not leave this place without saying all. I intend to do this, not because I can add anything useful to what I have already said, but out of respect to my conscience and the judges and to the opinion of men of good faith. I will not leave this place until I have left an unalterable conviction that I know nothing which might throw light on the case, and that I have said all I know."

When M. Casimir-Perier took the witness-stand at the first Zola trial, he replied:

"I cannot take oath to tell the whole truth, because I cannot tell it."

The witness read the text of the despatch received by Count von Munster-Ledenburg, the German Ambassador at Paris, from Prince Hohenlohe, the German Imperial Chancellor, which the former communicated to M. Casimir-Perier during a visit to the Elysée Palace. It ran:

"His Majesty the Emperor, having every confidence in the loyalty of the President of the Republic and the Government of the Republic, begs your Excellency to tell M. Casimir-Perier that it is proved the German Embassy was never implicated in the Dreyfus affair. His Majesty hopes the Government of the Republic will not hesitate to declare so. Without a formal declaration, the story which here continues to spread regarding the German Embassy would compromise the position of the representative of Germany."

M. Casimir-Perier then recounted how he had expressed to the then Premier and Minister of War his astonishment and indignation at the interview concerning Dreyfus's alleged confession, which Captain Lebrun-Renault gave *Le Figaro* on the subject of Dreyfus.

The witness then related the facts in connection with the futile efforts of M. Waldeck-Rousseau to prevent the first court-martial from sitting behind closed doors, and said he (the witness) had never received any member of the Dreyfus family. M. Casimir-Perier concluded this part of his statement by raising his voice and speaking very excitedly, saying:

"For the honor of the Chief Magistracy, which I occupied, for the honor of the Republic, I will not allow it to be said that I had exchanged a word with a captain in the French army accused of treason."

This statement caused applause in court, which Colonel Jouaust speedily suppressed.

The ex-President ended his statement by saying:

"I affirm, before this tribunal of a soldiers, that my resignation was not connected with the diplomatic incident concerning Germany. It pains me not to be able to second the court in the work of justice confided to it, for from this place must emerge at last, for the sake of the country, reconciliation and peace. I can do no more than tell the truth, the whole truth, and nothing but the truth. As Chief of State, or when a citizen, I have always, in my respect for France, regarded her as free to make a decision as she is herself revered." [Applause, which was quickly suppressed.]

M. Demange then introduced the question of the letter which the anti-Dreyfusards asserted Dreyfus wrote to M. Casimir-Perier respecting him. The witness emphatically replied that he had never entered into any such engagement, as alleged, and he asked that the letter, which was published by the *Éclair* of Paris, should be produced in court, and that the whole matter should be cleared up. M. Casimir-Perier ended this statement with a slap of his hand on the rail of the desk.

Colonel Jouaust then asked Dreyfus if he had anything to say.

Thereupon the prisoner arose and, accompanying his utterances with gestures of his right hand, said:

"My words have certainly been distorted, for I have no recollection of such a letter. The words the former President of the Republic has just uttered are exact. I have never, even in my own mind, supposed there was any engagement undertaken by him, and that he had not held thereto. I can well understand the indignation of M. Casimir-Perier; but such an idea never crossed my mind.

"Will you allow me to explain? M. Demange had asked me at the time of the trial, in conveying through M. Waldeck-Rousseau my request for a public trial, that this publicity should only be on condition that the question of the origin of the documents remained secret. I gave my word of honor not to raise this question, and in that I bowed before the superior interests of my country. In my mind it was with the defence, and not with the President of the Republic, that the word of honor was given. I never had an idea that an engagement was made between the President and myself. Never! Never! Never!"

Colonel Jouaust—Then you declare false these letters in which it is said that the President of the Republic entered into certain engagements with you?

Dreyfus replied:

"In any case, the sense has been completely distorted."

M. Casimir-Perier gave his evidence with a blanched face, but in the determined tone of a man who maintains every word uttered, which inspired confidence in his words. The members of the court-martial listened to him respectfully.

General Mercier, who was attired in the undress uniform of a general —black tunic and red trousers—and wore on his breast the decoration of a Grand Officer of the Legion of Honor, was then called to the stand. As he sat down he placed a brilliant crimson and gold képi on a shelf attached to the witness rail, where it remained, a striking patch of color, during the time he gave his testimony, which lasted from 8:10 A.M. until noon. Beside his képi he placed a black leather wallet full of papers, and he accompanied his remarks with a continual nodding of the head.

His forehead was wrinkled, his eyebrows were contracted, and his eyes peered through slits between his puffy eyelids. His cheeks were sallow, and he spoke almost inaudibly and in a weak, monotonous pitch of voice, which produced a soporific effect upon those who were not able to distinguish his words, but who were within hearing of his voice. This monologue, with hardly a break, except when the clerk read the various documents Mercier presented to the court, lasted nearly four hours, with ten minutes' suspension at eleven o'clock, when there was a general feeling that the witness was going to prove, as the Dreyfusards predicted, an utter fiasco.

At the outset of General Mercier's testimony he prepared the court for a war scare by declaring that the Emperor of Germany personally took an active part in organizing espionage; and then, later, when he defended his action in communicating the secret dossier to the court-martial of 1894, he said:

"I no longer have reason to keep silent, and I am going to accomplish what I consider my duty. In 1894 the diplomatic situation was perilous. M. Hanotaux (then Minister of Foreign Affairs) had indicated this. M. Casimir-Perier had spoken before the Criminal Chamber about the unusual step taken by Count von Munster. He also exposed the somewhat unusual way by which he could double himself into an official personage and a private personage, later giving Count von Munster information that was at first refused him.

"But M. Casimir-Perier amended his deposition, saying he had not said that the same day M. Dupuy and myself remained from 8 in the evening until 12:30 o'clock in his private office at the Elysée awaiting the result of telegraphic communications between the Emperor of Germany and Count von Munster. We remained four hours and a half waiting to see whether peace or war would result from the exchange of programs."

Here M. Casimir-Perier shook his head and hand in emphatic denial of General Mercier's statement.

General Mercier continued:

"I had been warned during the afternoon that the situation was very grave. Count von Munster had an order from his sovereign to ask for his passports if his demands were not conceded. I was prepared to give the order for mobilization. You see, we were within an ace of war. It was only at 12:30 that M. Casimir-Perier notified me that Count von Munster had accepted the insertion of a somewhat vague note declaring the Ambassador was not involved."

M. Casimir-Perier here again made a repudiating gesture, and General Mercier continued to explain that this was the reason for his action regarding the secret dossier.

While he was under examination, General Mercier asked Colonel Jouaust to allow him to present a document showing how an espionage system was organized in France by Colonel von Schwartzkoppen, the former German military attaché at Paris. The document referred to the fortifications of the Meuse. General Mercier then entered into an explanation tending to prove that von Schwartzkoppen was at the head of the German espionage in France. The witness afterward had the clerk read the letter containing the words "Cette canaille de D——" (That scoundrel of a D——).

In the mean while Dreyfus watched Mercier through his eyeglasses apparently unmoved. Dreyfus had listened to General Mercier's pitiless arraignment that morning, until he approached the end of his deposition, with sphinx-like rigidity of features, but watching Mercier like a cat watching a mouse. No one would have suspected the volcano slumbering within Dreyfus, which burst forth when human flesh and blood could stand it no longer. The only sign of the smothered fire within was his heaving bosom and the parching of his lips and palate, which he occasionally moistened with his tongue.

A casual observer might have missed these indications and have imagined that he was an image cut in stone, with the eyes fixed on Mercier. But, when, at last, his feelings obtained the mastery, and he sprang to his feet and faced his accuser, man to man, and flatly denied the charges, already known, which the general reiterated, one appreciated the depth of his previously suppressed emotions; and Mercier, who, startled, had jumped to his feet, at the ringing sound of Dreyfus's voice, from the chair in which he was seated while giving his evidence, recoiled before the terrible look Dreyfus threw at him, and stood aghast wondering whether the prisoner was going to spring upon him.

At the end of his evidence General Mercier said he believed that the only motive of Dreyfus's treason was that Dreyfus had no feeling of patriotism.

This utterance brought forth hisses from the audience, whose blood had been sent up to fever heat by the witness's savage attacks on Dreyfus.

General Mercier, not heeding the hisses, closed by remarking:

"If the least doubt crossed my mind, Messieurs, I would be the first

9

to declare it to you and say before you, to Captain Dreyfus: 'I am mistaken, but in good faith.'"

Then Dreyfus electrified the spectators. He jumped to his feet, as though the words had galvanized him into new life, and shouted with a voice which resounded through the hall like a trumpet note:

"That is what you ought to say!"

The audience burst into a wild cheer, whereupon the ushers called for silence.

General Mercier then stammered:

"I would come and say: 'Captain Dreyfus, I was mistaken, in good faith, and I come with the same good faith to admit it, and I will do all in human power to repair the frightful error.'"

The prisoner then shouted:

"Why don't you then? That is your duty!"

Colonel Jouaust and the other members of the court-martial in the mean time had risen and seized the two men, while the court rang with the cheers of the spectators.

General Mercier, after a pause, when the excitement had partially calmed, said:

"Well, no. My conviction since 1894 has not suffered the slightest weakening. It is fortified by the deepest study of the dossier, and also by the inanity of the means resorted to for the purpose of proving the innocence of the condemned man of 1894, in spite of the evidence accumulated and in spite of the millions of money expended."

The witness referred to the famous "syndicate," which Scheurer-Kestner and Zola were accused of fathering.

"There is a syndicate," wrote Zola at the time; "it is composed of all honest and intelligent persons throughout the civilized world, who have given careful study to this case, who believe in elementary justice, in law, and in the rules of evidence."

Colonel Jouaust then said: "Have you finished?"

General Mercier replied: "Yes."

General Mercier, when he had finished his testimony, according to general opinion had said really nothing, and had proved nothing. The overwhelming proofs he was to have thrown down before the members of the court-martial like a bombshell failed to appear, and he left the court discredited.

Mercier had played the well-worn war scare, but the effect must have been very discouraging to him, for his hearers listened, without stirring a muscle, to his story of how France was on the threshold of a war with Germany.

Colonel Jouaust then announced that the sessions of the court-martial would be resumed August 14th.

M. Casimir-Perier thereupon arose and said:

"After the deposition of General Mercier I shall ask the court to hear me, and I would prefer it to be in confrontation with him."

This announcement caused a sensation. Then followed a thrilling demonstration against General Mercier. As he turned to leave the court the audience rose *en masse* and hissed and cursed him, those at the back of the court standing on chairs and benches in order better to hound him down. The gendarmes placed themselves between the general and the audience, which showed a strong disposition to maltreat the former Minister of War. Though the general was cheered by the crowd outside the court-room on his departure from the Lycée, none of them had witnessed the scene in court or listened to Mercier's weak brief. Moreover, the inhabitants of Rennes have always been anti-Dreyfusard. Counter-shouts of "Vive la République!" and "Vive la Justice!" were raised by those on both sides. The gendarmes, however, cleared the streets, and the crowd quietly dispersed.

Chapter XIX.

ATTEMPT TO MURDER M. LABORI.

A COWARDLY attempt to assassinate Maître Labori, leading counsel for the defence of Dreyfus, was made on Monday, August 14th.

The sitting of the court-martial that was pending seemed big with emotion. M. Casimir-Perier was to be confronted with General Mercier, and all looked forward with impatience to the moment when the great advocate M. Labori, who had revealed himself at the Zola trial as perhaps the most expert and formidable cross-examiner of the French bar, was to exercise his incomparable intellect against the mysterious general whose action in 1894 precipitated upon his country such a host of woes.

Five minutes, ten minutes went by. M. Demange was in his place, but the chair of his colleague was still vacant. This absence was strange, and was generally commented upon.

Hitherto M. Labori had been very punctual. But he must be merely delayed at his house, it was thought. He might have slept late, or he was collecting his notes. However, conjectures were cut short by the entrance of the judges, and Colonel Jouaust, after introducing Dreyfus, asked attention for a few words on the unseemly demonstrations of which the court-room on August 12th was the scene. He would not tolerate, he declared, manifestations of any sort; if need be, he would expel the disturbers of the peace, or even clear the hall.

"If," he continued, "we have given a large space to the journalists, it is in order that as large a number as possible of readers may follow the discussions here, which, however, arouse perhaps too much interest in the public. I hope I shall not be obliged to take action against the press."

It was noted then that for the first time the hall contained a number of gendarmes distributed along the benches. The measure seemed natural enough. The intervention of the president had been anticipated, and was generally approved.

Yet still M. Labori did not come.

Suddenly there was a hubbub at the entrance door. The tall form of M. Taunay, of the judicial police, was seen clambering upon a bench, and then this announcement rang through the court:

"Quick; a doctor! M. Labori is wounded."

It was like a pistol-shot in the court itself.

The faces of half the audience became white with consternation.

Several persons rushed out, among them doctors and surgeons who were present. One of them was M. Paul Reclus.

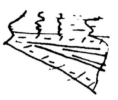

Every one looked at his neighbor in dismay. Cries of "Ah! les misérables!" and other expressions of the general emotion arose all about the court.

And then, in the midst of the general distress, M. Demange rose in his place and said:

"Monsieur le President, painful news has just been spread abroad. It is said that my colleague M. Labori has been wounded." Colonel Jouaust replied, "It is deeply regrettable," while M. Demange went on to ask that the sitting should be suspended pending further information.

It was just on the stroke of seven o'clock. The excitement at this moment was extreme. It was a difficult thing to scrutinize the heart, but, if any of the ordinary outward signs of human feeling are true indications of the inner workings of the soul, there were not two-score persons in that hall who were not profoundly shocked by the news which had just rung through the house.

M. Labori, who had the day before received two letters threatening to kill him, but who had paid as little heed to them as to the scores of others which he had received during the last two years, left his house during the morning of August 14th, at six o'clock, alone, his wife, who attends all the sittings of the court, intending to follow him a few moments later. On the way he met Colonel Picquart and M. Gast, the Colonel's cousin. The three had passed the bridge of La Barbotiere, and, leaving the tow-path, had arrived on the Quai Richemont near the bridge across the Vilaine, when a pistol shot was heard behind them, and M. Labori, uttering the familiar French ejaculation, "Oh, la la!" tottered and fell.

He had received a bullet in the back.

The details which follow were obtained from Colonel Picquart and M.

Gast.   Their first thought was for their companion.   A few moments were therefore lost in assisting Maître Labori.   Moreover, neither Colonel Picquart nor his friend was armed.   With a scrupulous correctness intelligible enough at a moment when the slightest violation of the laws of the land might entail the most serious inconveniences, but with a loyalty which the present event has proved to be Quixotic, and which they profoundly regret at this hour, they were without revolvers, in spite of the threatening letters which the colonel has never ceased to receive for many months. Had they been armed they might have easily killed the assailant.

The would-be murderer, darting off at full speed, had, however, already put one hundred yards between himself and his victim.   Yet as soon as Maître Labori had been laid out on the pavement both his companions started in pursuit.   There were workingmen, early risers, near by, who heard the shot and could help to identify him, but not one of them made the slightest effort to capture him.   M. Gast is a solid, somewhat heavily built man, who soon found pursuit futile, and even Colonel Picquart, although he is more active, and although, in M. Gast's words, he "ran like a deer," had to abandon the chase.

The assailant had dashed along the river unarrested by the slightest obstacle, human or other, until he met on the banks of the Vilaine a company of workingmen unloading a barge.   Seeing a man running toward them, and hearing the cries of "Assassin!" which had followed him from afar, they sought to capture him.   But aiming his revolver he cried:

"Leave me alone!   I have just killed Dreyfus."

It was an "open sesame," and the man rushed on and gained the open fields, making in the direction of Chateaugiron.   The forest of Rennes lay there across country rich in lurking-places, a far finer refuge for a hunted criminal than the clear spaces of the little wood where, in Zola's novel, "Paris," the Anarchist Salvat is surrounded and tracked by the police.

The would-be assassin, who, according to the impression of Colonel Picquart, was not yet thirty, was described as red-haired; he wore a short black coat and a sort of round, white skull-cap, capable, however, Colonel Picquart said, of being rolled down like a turban upon the brow and ears. He sped on into the country, finally followed by no one, left fairly to himself to choose his lair.

Colonel Picquart, who had given up the pursuit and returned to his friend, found Maître Labori still lying on the pavement; but his wife had arrived, and she was holding his head and shoulders on her knees, while with a little Japanese fan, hastily snatched up as she had left the house, she fanned the handsome, pallid face of her husband.

A half-hour passed before a shutter was brought, and it was almost as long before a doctor arrived. Four soldiers had been ordered to the spot with the shutter to transport Maître Labori to his house. He had not lost consciousness, and he spoke to his wife of the trial, urging her immediately to inform the court and to have the proceedings interrupted.

When, at the suspension of the sitting, Maître Demange drove to the house, he found his friend still partially stunned, but not in pain.

"*Mon vieux,*" said Maître Labori to his colleague ,"*je vais peut-etre en crever, mais Dreyfus est sauvé.*" ("Old man, I shall perhaps die from it, but Dreyfus is saved!")

The wound was at first thought to be fatal. It was feared that the bullet had perforated a lung and in its passage perhaps affected the spinal cord. Later, more accurate details were known. The bullet entered the back a little to the right of the backbone, on a level with the fifth or sixth rib. The state of the wound for the moment prevented surgical search for the bullet.

Maître Labori had only just recovered from typhoid fever, during which he was for a time in a critical state. His ardent, nervous, high-strung organism, wrought up as it was to a pitch of terrible tension by his anxieties over work in the Dreyfus affair, was in an extremely unsatisfactory condition for combating this fresh shock.

The worst news would have surprised nobody at Rennes. M. Waldeck-Rousseau, and the Minister of Justice, and the whole world had to wait forty-eight hours at least for any certainty as to his real condition, and then, to the intense relief of all right-minded men, the doctors announced that the wound was not mortal.

There was a terribly suggestive timeliness in that crime, and the course taken by the day's proceedings threw this fact into the light with overwhelming force.

Were the fates combining against Dreyfus they could not have armed among mortals a more efficient agent of their designs than the still unknown man who shot Maître Labori in the early hours of the morning, as he was making for the court-room himself to endeavor to riddle with shot and shatter with his invective and irony and scorn the last arguments of the public accuser Mercier.

It was a master-stroke. The one man indispensable was suddenly thrown *hors de combat* just at the moment when most was expected of him.

With Maître Labori absent the bottom seemed to have dropped out of the defence.

The examination of General Mercier which took place the same day was one of the weakest exhibitions of forensic ingenuity and presence of mind which it was possible to conceive. The witnesses, General Mercier, M. Cavaignac, General Billot, and the rest, had held the floor as did the officers their predecessors in the trial of 1894. M. Cavaignac delivered himself of an impassioned diatribe quite as if he were at the tribune of the chamber. The prisoner was left almost without defence.

Maître Demange was, no doubt, a great lawyer, and it may well be believed that he was under the impression of the terrible event of that morning. But his whole conception of his rôle seemed to be to reply to Dreyfus's adversaries *en bloc* in a final address to the court. But he did not possess the qualities of Maître Labori—his astonishing readiness in repartee, his quick-wittedness in general, his admirable enthusiasm, his courage, his range of eloquence, his unrivalled knowledge of the case, and, above all, his simply incomparable powers of cross-examination.

The formal, old-style methods of Maître Demange stood him in sad stead. It was the great day, the critical moment. It was the day dreaded by all the adversaries of Dreyfus; the day to which General Mercier and M. Cavaignac had looked forward with consternation. They had found in this terrible tragedy, by the initiation and intervention of no one knows what influence, that *deus ex machina* which in the old drama solves problems with a timeliness that has become proverbial. And then, to cap all, the general called on Maître Labori to proffer his sympathy.

The Nationalist Deputy for Rennes M. le Hérissé, signed the same day the following proclamation as Mayor of Rennes:

"Dear fellow-citizens: An abominable outrage, the author of which cannot claim to represent any party, has just dishonored our dear city of Rennes. You will not allow yourselves to be affected by an act of madness which can only serve the interests of the enemies of the work of justice and truth which, with their patriotism and their robust good sense, the members of the court-martial are called upon to accomplish. Resist provocations from whatever quarter, preserve that dignified calm which you have all along maintained. You will thus have deserved well of France and of the Republic, and served the good name of our old Breton town."

General Zurlinden, Colonel Jouaust, and M. Casimir-Perier called on Maître Labori to know how he was getting on.

Several journalists said to have associations with the persons arrested in Paris, among them a member of the staff of M. Cassagnac's paper, *L'Autorité*, were arrested at Rennes.

Maître Labori is young, fair, handsome, and full of lusty life and high spirits. His talents as a speaker are not of the highest order; but no other member of the Paris bar knows better how to use law to defeat its object. He can drive a motor car through the Code. Until he pleaded for Zola his luck was uninterrupted. He then had an attack of typhoid fever, which greatly weakened him and forced him to neglect business. The Zola affair was a great advertisement, but it brought him no direct profit and created for him endless enemies. He refused the handsome fee the novelist offered; nor does he accept pecuniary reward from Dreyfus.

Labori is proud of his wife's beauty. She is equally proud of his good looks and forensic talents, and loses no opportunity to hear him plead. She is an Australian, and received her education as a pianiste in London. She became a player at concerts and made the acquaintance of the deformed but highly gifted Russian pianist, Pachmann, married him, had two children, and then fell in love with Labori. The passion was mutual. She and Pachmann were divorced, and then she married Labori. The children live with her and find a devoted stepfather in him.

Madame Labori had attended all the public sittings of the Rennes court-martial. Her beauty is beyond dispute. She is a striking blonde, and, though her path has not been always strewn with roses, she expresses the joy of life in splendid health and a satisfied heart.

Chapter XXX.

EX-PRESIDENT AND FORMER WAR MINISTER CLASH

THE shooting of Maître Labori took all the life out of the session of the court-martial, August 14th.

On the opening of the court, Maître Demange in a few words officially informed Colonel Jouaust of the attack on Maître Labori, and requested a suspension of the sitting, to which Colonel Jouaust unhesitatingly agreed, adjoining the court until 7:15 o'clock.

Dreyfus must undoubtedly have been profoundly moved by the attack on his champion, who for all he knew might be dead or dying, yet the prisoner maintained the same immovability as hitherto, and did not give the slightest indication of his emotions.

In the course of the short suspension of the proceedings M. Jaures, the Socialist leader, who was in court, remarked that the arrests made in Paris for rioting the previous day had for their sole object to forestall a St. Bartholomew's massacre of the Dreyfusards, and that the attempted murder of M. Labori was one of the acts of the projected massacre.

Others in the audience engaged in violent altercations over the attempted murder. M. Mercier, editor of the *Gaulois*, expressed the opinion that all the newspapers ought to regard themselves as responsible for the outrage, whereupon Mme. Severine loudly protested, saying:

"No; it is you who ought to be held responsible for what has happened?"

The clamor finally became so violent that gendarmes were forced to separate the combatants and take away the tickets of all those present.

On the resumption of the sitting, Colonel Jouaust referred to the outrage, and declared he was personally deeply moved.

Maître Demange announced that, though his colleague's wound was not so serious as at first supposed, it would be impossible for Maître Labori to participate in the proceedings.

General Mercier was then confronted with M. Casimir-Perier, the former President of France. The latter declared that Mercier's story, told on the witness-stand on August 12th, of the imminence of war between Germany and France in 1894, was grossly exaggerated, and complained of Mercier's action in moving 60,000 troops to the frontier without consulting him.

When General Mercier was recalled in reply to the president of the court, he reiterated his belief that Major Count Esterhazy, in spite of the latter's own declaration, was not the author of the bordereau, which the witness claimed was written on tracing paper, and was found in an embassy.

M. Casimir-Perier was then called to the witness stand, but the thoughts of every one in court were directed to the outrage on Maître Labori, and the evidence was followed listlessly. Moreover, Maître Labori was not there to kindle the hidden fires in both men, and they, in addition, were weighed down by the tragedy which had just occurred.

As it had been M. Labori's intention to take General Mercier in hand, M. Demange, associate counsel, was quite unprepared for the task; the few questions the latter put were practically of little effect, and General Mercier escaped cheaply. M. Demange also was deeply affected by the attempt to assassinate his colleague, and was quite unable to do himself justice.

The president of the court asked M. Casimir-Perier to explain the circumstances of the confession Dreyfus is alleged to have made to Captain Lebrun-Renault. M. Casimir-Perier persisted in his statement of August 12th, that he had never received any confidences of this character from Captain Lebrun-Renault. He added that M. Dupuy, the then Premier, was present when Captain Lebrun-Renault called at the Elysée, Paris. "Moreover," said M. Casimir-Perier, "here is a letter from M. Dupuy, which I ask may be read."

The letter asserted that Captain Lebrun-Renault, when questioned by M. Dupuy, replied that General Mercier had sent him to the President to receive a dressing-down for his indiscreet disclosures to the *Figaro*.

General Mercier here interposed, saying:

"Captain Lebrun-Renault spoke to me in regard to the confessions in the presence of General Gonse, who will testify thereto.   It was then that I ordered him to go to the President of the Republic."

Regarding General Mercier's declaration on August 12th, on the witness stand, M. Casimir-Perier said:

"General Mercier had no right whatever to intervene in a diplomatic conversation.   I would have prevented such interference.   It was I alone who conferred with the minister, and I declare that the impression I derived from that conversation was one of complete calm, otherwise the incident would not have been closed by the framing of a note.   We had no telegram from Berlin that evening.   If there had been any news in regard to the matter on the evening of the 6th, we should not have waited until the 8th to publish the note.   There was not a despatch addressed to a friendly power relative to the incident.   The incident has been magnified.   Besides, in the event of diplomatic complications, the president would have communicated with the Minister of Foreign Affairs."

General Mercier replied that he went to the Elysée Palace as Minister of War.   He said General de Boisdeffre could testify in regard to the orders received.

M. Demange seized upon this declaration and insisted that General Mercier repeat the statement that he had given orders to General de Boisdeffre on the 6th, relative to mobilization.

General de Boisdeffre was actually out of Paris on January 6, 1895, for on that day General Gonse wrote him to inform him of Lebrun-Renault's tale about Dreyfus's alleged confession.

M. Casimir-Perier, resuming his testimony, said he did not desire to reply to certain of General Mercier's insinuations.

"I do not wish to answer them," said the witness; "the circumstances are too sad and too tragic for me to desire to envenom the discussion.   I am master of myself and of my conscience.   I would only state that General Mercier has made every effort to mix me as deeply as possible in this affair.   But I have remained aloof."

The former President then complained of the incorrect behavior of his subordinate toward the chief of the state.   "As an instance," he said, "General Mercier undertook to shorten the term of service of 60,000 men without consulting me, thus lacking in the respect he owed to the chief of the state."

M. Casimir-Perier next protested against the assertions made by General Mercier in regard to the rôle adopted by the chief of the state in this affair, whereupon the general interjected the statement that he had spoken of the attitude assumed by M. Casimir-Perier, because he had sworn to tell the whole truth.

M. Demange asked General Mercier if he had explained to the Cabinet how he reconciled the relations of cause and effect, and the patriotic emotion aroused by the treason with the communication of the secret documents to the court-martial.

The general, in reply, repeated his statement of August 12th, as his hypothesis of the situation.

Counsel asked General Mercier why the explanations of the secret dossier were not included in the dossier relating to the revision.

The general replied that he considered these explanations were given for his personal use, and that was why he destroyed the document.

At this M. Demange expressed a sense of astonishment, and asked General Mercier if he did not have reasons for suppressing the document.

The witness repudiated the suggestion.

Dreyfus at this point rose from his seat and asked leave to explain in regard to the assertion that he had traced on a card the itinerary of a certain journey of the General Staff. Both the itinerary and journey, he asserted, were purely fictitious.

General Billot, former Minister of War, was the next witness. He was in uniform, sat with crossed legs, and gave his evidence in a conversational manner. Like everybody else, he added, he had some knowledge of the Dreyfus affair before taking the war portfolio. While feeling deeply on the subject, he remained aloof from the matter until he returned to the Cabinet. In the early days of his ministry, the witness continued, M. Scheurer-Kestner (a former vice-president of the Senate) asked him whether he ought not to investigate the Dreyfus affair. M. Scheurer-Kestner, the general pointed out, had made similar representations to M. de Freycinet, and received the same reply from both, that neither of them was very conversant with the affair.

General Billot dwelt at length upon the action taken by M. Scheurer-Kestner, to whom he said he recommended prudence. M. Scheurer-Kestner finally communicated to General Billot his conviction of the innocence of Dreyfus, but the general found the evidence insufficient, and asked him to investigate the matter further.

General Billot then dealt with the rôle of Colonel Picquart, whom, he said, he holds in the highest esteem. "He is intelligent," said the witness, "and gave me valuable information about the organization of a neighboring army and its artillery. This information showed the necessity of continuing the reforms in our artillery commenced by that great initiator, General Mercier."

"I, who am neither an engineer nor an expert in handwriting," added General Billot, "saw the grand work he accomplished in that direction."

After this General Billot referred to Colonel Picquart's proposition to entrap Esterhazy, whom he suspected, but General Billot forbade this. He added that Colonel Picquart always acted without authorization.

The former Minister of War next referred to the eminent service which Colonel Picquart rendered to the army, leading to his being entrusted with a "confidential mission to the East and afterward to Tunis." He energetically protested against the allegation that he had desired to send Colonel Picquart to a place from which he would never return.

M. Demange then invited General Billot to explain the statements of MM. Barthou and Poincare, former Cabinet ministers, that the general was once so doubtful of the guilt of Dreyfus that he did not sleep for several nights.

General Billot acknowledged that the statements were true.

There was great sensation when M. Demange mentioned the opinion expressed by M. Barthou that General Billot had been forewarned in regard to the forgery of Lieutenant-Colonel Henry. The general acknowledged that the Henry forgery was among the factors arousing his doubts.

M. Cavaignac, former Minister of War, then testified. He said he was the first Cabinet minister to assume responsibility for the Dreyfus affair. He had closely followed the inquiry of the Court of Cassation, and, he continued, still desired to associate himself with the responsibility of those who, in 1894, protected the country and the army against treason. [Sensation.]

Continuing, the witness said that among the principal points upon which he based his conviction was the confession to Captain Lebrun-

Renault, in support of which contention he quoted a passage from an alleged letter of Dreyfus, which was in reality part of General Gonse's report to the Minister of War on Colonel Du Paty de Clam's report of the alleged confession.

The witness also said he found additional proofs of the prisoner's guilt in the technical character of the bordereau, and thought the bordereau alone established the fact that treason had emanated from the bureau of the General Staff, and from an officer who was able to secure all the information desired.

During M. Cavaignac's arraignment Dreyfus was nervous and agitated.

M. Cavaignac next discussed the denials of Dreyfus, and said his excuse of lapse of memory was inadmissible. Dreyfus, he claimed, was aware of the changes in the Bridge Corps belonging to the artillery, and also of the details of the concentration. Why, then, the witness asked, had he denied this knowledge?

It was impossible, according to M. Cavaignac, to believe that Esterhazy was a traitor, even admitting that the bordereau was written by him. Esterhazy, he insisted, could only have acted as an intermediary or an accomplice.

Colonel Jouaust asked M. Cavaignac to explain the discovery of the Henry forgery, and the witness repeated the statements he had already made on the subject.

"The Henry forgery," replied M. Cavaignac, "as alleged, was in order to secure a revision of the case by the Court of Cassation, but was not even alluded to. This forgery, therefore, should remain outside the scope of the questions submitted to this court-martial. This is my opinion."

Counsel for the prisoner then questioned M. Cavaignac in regard to his statement that General de Boisdeffre was absent from Paris on November 6th, when General Mercier declares he was there. The witness replied that General de Boisdeffre was certainly absent on the date.

Colonel Jouaust then told Dreyfus to rise, and asked him if he had any remarks to make upon the evidence. The prisoner replied:

"I am astounded that the man who produced in the tribunal of the Chamber the Henry forgery can come here and base his convictions of my culpability on matters which the Court of Cassation has already disposed of." [Great sensation.]

Dreyfus did not create a very favorable impression when he made this statement, which was delivered in a declamatory fashion, with his hand on his heart.

The speech of M. Cavaignac, however, certainly appeared to make an impression on his hearers.

General Zurlinden, also a former Minister of War, was the next witness. He began by pointing out the obligation resting upon those directing espionage to do everything possible to save those serving them. He then declared he still regarded the bordereau as being decisive proof of the guilt of Dreyfus, and said it would be impossible for those who were prosecuting Dreyfus to be acting from *esprit de corps*, as it would be unjust to say they approved the "odious act just committed in the vicinity."

General Zurlinden then traversed the old ground, and declared that nothing, not even Esterhazy's confessions, had occurred to change his convictions.

The reiteration by General Zurlinden of his belief that Dreyfus wrote the bordereau created a lively excitement.

M. Demange suggested that if Colonel Fabre had not thought of examining the handwriting of the probationers the bordereau would have been eternally buried in the archives of the Ministry of War, "and," he remarked, "if this is the case, it must be evidenced there was nothing in the bordereau which indicated Dreyfus."

General Zurlinden, in a troubled voice, acknowledged this fact, and tried to explain. M. Demange, however, got General Zurlinden to admit that it was not until after the condemnation that the study of the bordereau seemed to indicate that it was the work of a probationer.

In reply to further question, General Zurlinden said that in order to know the whole truth in regard to the bordereau, they must have the four notes therein mentioned. They must be secured.

At this point Dreyfus interjected:

"I associate myself with those words, Colonel. I also desire the truth. I only ask for the truth."

These statements caused excitement in court.

General Chanoine, a former Minister of War, next testified. He briefly affirmed his belief in the culpability of the prisoner.

The appearance of M. Hanotaux, the former Minister of Foreign Affairs, who followed, reawakened the interest of the audience.

M. Hanotaux declared he had nothing to add to his evidence given before the Court of Cassation.   He said he never had cognizance, either as a minister or as a private individual, of any secret dossier.

The former minister denied the allegation that he had told M. Monod he believed Dreyfus was guilty.   He was astounded at M. Monod's statement, but the latter was evidently hazy in his mind regarding the matter, as he had given three versions of the conversation.

M. Demange inquired whether M. Hanotaux was aware of the uncertainties connected with the translation of the telegram, dated November 2, 1894.

The former Foreign Minister replied that uncertainty was the rule in such cases.   He was only aware of the one drawn up in the Foreign Office, which alone was communicated to the War Minister.

The depositions of General Zurlinden, General Chanoine, and M. Hanotaux were listened to closely.   The mass of evidence was directed against Dreyfus.   The lack of trenchant criticism, owing to the absence of the defence's right arm, naturally left an impression unfavorable to the prisoner.

10

Chapter XXXI.

THE PRISONER'S SUFFERINGS ON DEVIL'S ISLAND

THERE was no session of the court-martial on August 15th, that being Assumption Day. But the trial was resumed on August 16th, Major Carriere, the representative of the Government, having refused to agree to the adjournment of the case until August 21st, as asked for by M. De-mange and Captain Dreyfus, owing to the murderous attack upon Maître Labori.

The feature of the day's proceedings was the story of the sufferings of Dreyfus on Devil's Island.

M. Guérin, the former Minister of Justice, was the first witness. He only repeated the evidence he had given before the Court of Cassation.

Ex-Minister Guérin, in reciting his evidence, said that at the end of October, after a Cabinet council, the Premier invited him to his room, where General Mercier joined them, and explained that for some time past documents had been missing from the Headquarters Staff, and that, in consequence of inquiries made, suspicion had attached to Dreyfus. General Mercier added that he was convinced Dreyfus was the culprit. The general said he founded his conviction on three facts:

First, the bordereau, the author of which was undiscoverable until Colonel Fabre, on returning from the manœuvres, immediately after he saw the document, exclaimed:

"Why, it is Dreyfus's handwriting."

Secondly, the nature of the documents enumerated in the bordereau, in conjunction with Dreyfus's employment in the different departments, proved exclusively, according to General Mercier, that Dreyfus alone had cognizance of all these papers, and he alone could have disclosed them.

Thirdly, the dictation test and Dreyfus's perturbation at the time. This referred to the dictation given by Du Paty de Clam to Dreyfus a few moments before his arrest.

General Mercier, M. Guérin then said, in consequence of these convictions declared his intention to ask the Cabinet to authorize the prosecution of Dreyfus. A special Cabinet meeting was held on November 1, 1894, to consider the matter. The witness forgot whether M. Casimir-Perier or M. Dupuy presided. General Mercier handed the Cabinet nothing but the bordereau. After the Minister of War had related his reasons for his suspicions, the Cabinet unanimously authorized the prosecution of Dreyfus.

M. Hanotaux alone made some reserves or diplomatic objections, based on the place where the document was found. But it was agreed that, in the event of court-martialling Dreyfus, measures should be taken to prevent mention of the name of any power.

From that day the witness had learned nothing whatever of the case, personally, as it was in the hands of the military authorities. M. Guérin, at that time, had never heard of the secret documents, and none was ever communicated to the Cabinet. He only first knew during the Zola trial of the existence of the alleged secret documents, and only learned of the alleged confession of Dreyfus to Captain Lebrun-Renault from the newspapers. General Mercier never mentioned the confession to the Cabinet.

Colonel Jouaust then questioned the witness, saying:

"M. Gobert, an expert, has declared you summoned him to your office to give you information about the Dreyfus affair. Do you remember the occurrences? Did he not say, on entering, pointing to the clock:

" 'Monsieur le Ministre de Justice, I fear lest at this hour a grave mistake is being committed'?

"Is it not a fact that you did not reply, but, when M. Gobert was leaving, recommended him to observe extreme caution, as the Government was desirous of keeping the treason secret, dreading particularly indiscretions upon the part of the press, and, above all, upon the part of the *Libre Parole*, as the suspected officer was a Jew?"

M. Guérin replied:

"I cannot affirm whether or not I received M. Gobert, but what I can affirm is that if he came I did not employ the language mentioned, and I made none of the statements he attributes to me."

M. Lebon, the former Minister of the Colonies, then testified in justification of his instructions to treat Dreyfus rigorously, declaring that the extreme stringency only dated from the time he thought an attempt would be made to rescue the prisoner.

M. Lebon, in testifying regarding his treatment of the prisoner, said that when the Cabinet was asked to intervene in favor of a revision he thought the executive should not interfere with the judiciary.

"On my soul and conscience," declared M. Lebon dramatically, "I say I regard the measures I took relative to the prisoner on the Île du Diable as warranted, and if I had to repeat them I would not hesitate."

He admitted that on October 6, 1896, Dreyfus was put in irons and kept in them for two months. At night a lamp was lighted over his head that the jailer might watch the expression of his face. Myriads of tropical insects were thus attracted, which nearly drove the prisoner insane. When Dreyfus learned that he was placed in irons he wrote to the commandant of the Îles du Salut penitentiary, in which he said, among other things:

"I would be grateful to you to let me know of what fault I have been guilty since I have been here. I thought I had conformed rigorously to all the rules. I carried out every order to the letter."

M. Lebon then explained the reasons for the rigorous measures against Dreyfus as already set forth in an earlier chapter. He said a certain telegram sent to French Guiana disappeared. It was traced out of France, but immediately it reached the English lines it disappeared, showing, the witness said, that efforts were being made to enable the prisoner to evade the regulations. Rigorous, even painful, measures were therefore taken to prevent his escape. M. Lebon therefore issued orders that, if necessary, the prisoner was to be fired upon.

In October, 1896, a sham attempt was made by the officials of the Guiana police to rescue Dreyfus. When their boat reached the Île du Diable a loud noise was made. Dreyfus awoke. His jailor immediately levelled his revolver at the prisoner's head. Dreyfus turned his face to the wall and lay very still.

Continuing, M. Lebon said he also issued orders that only copies of the letters addressed to the prisoners should be delivered to him, the originals being retained. The witness was informed, August 19th, that an American vessel passed the Îles du Salut, and orders were then issued that Dreyfus was to be shot on the slightest alarm.

Referring to the Weyler forgery, M. Lebon said he frankly admitted that he believed in its authenticity, as did Colonel Picquart, until long after its production. M. Lebon next referred to the numerous rough drafts the prisoner made of his letters before finally dispatching them.

At this point, M. Demange interrupted the witness and said:

"I pass from a surprise to surprise. August 14th, it was a witness playing the part of prosecutor. To-day, one witness defends himself by saying his conscience is tranquil. He is welcome to a tranquil conscience. But ask him if he finds it surprising that this man, alone out there, on a lost island, should have poured out his soul on paper? I ask again, why you allowed the forged Weyler letter, in which a handwriting was indicated, to reach Dreyfus?"

To this M. Lebon replied:

"We could not give up the original. But, the idea never occurred to any agents of the Administration to subject Dreyfus to the savage and atrocious treatment which has been spoken of."

Colonel Jouaust, addressing Dreyfus, asked:

"Did you receive the letter just referred to?"

Dreyfus replied:

"Yes, Colonel."

"What impression did it make on you?"

"I understood nothing of what it contained," answered the prisoner.

At this juncture some time was occupied in reading a long report from the Minister of the Colonies to the Minister of War, giving the various reports of the governor of French Guiana. Passages describing the dread the prisoner expressed to the doctors when he feared he was losing his reason caused an immense impression. Tears were even seen to glisten in the eyes of General Billot, the former Minister of War.

At the conclusion of the report, M. Lebon asked leave to explain. He said:

"I do not dispute the accuracy of the report, but it is partial. Reference has been most carefully made to the precarious health of the prisoner. But the doctor never made a communication to me on the subject. I do not hesitate to say that if he had done so I should have given orders to have the prisoner treated as all invalids should be treated. It is with deliberate intent that I have been represented as an executioner."

Colonel Jouaust, turning to Dreyfus, then remarked:

" Have you anything to say in regard to this deposition? "

Then the prisoner made vehement reply that he was not there to complain, saying:

" No, Colonel. I am here to defend my honor. I do not wish to speak here of the atrocious sufferings, physical and moral, which, for five years, I, a Frenchman and an innocent man, was subjected to on the Île du Diable. "

These remarks of Dreyfus caused intense excitement in court. The prisoner uttered the words in a loud voice and with tremendous energy.

M. Demange asked that the official report of the treatment of Dreyfus on the Île du Diable should be read. The clerk of the court did so, and in a sympathetic tone, recounted the harrowing tale of Dreyfus's mental and physical sufferings and inhuman treatment, as already pictured in a previous chapter.

Deep-drawn breaths of indignation came from the hearers as the reading proceeded. Dreyfus at first watched the faces of the judges with his usual composure; but gradually, as the story proceeded and incidents of his awful existence were brought up before him, his eyes grew dim and tears glistened in them, and then slowly trickled down his cheeks. Dreyfus could stand it no longer, and, for the first time during his trial, gave way to such emotions and silently wept. The faces of those in the audience expressed sympathy with the prisoner's emotion, and even the captain of gendarmes sitting beside Dreyfus turned and gave him a look of unconcealed compassion.

General Mercier, who, with M. Lebon, was seated in the front row of the witnesses' seats, listened to the reading of the report unmoved, while Colonel Jouaust followed it with an air of bored tolerance.

M. Lebon afterward returned to the stand and added a few more words in justification of his conduct, and then Colonel Jouaust ordered the next witness to be brought in. All eyes were turned toward the door on the right of the stage, and a moment later the form of a woman, dressed in deep mourning, appeared in the doorway, and, accompanied by a non-commissioned officer, advanced to the platform. It was the widow of Lieutenant-Colonel Henry, the French officer who committed suicide in prison after confessing to forging certain documents in the case.

With pale face, and hand upraised before the crucifix, she took the oath to tell the truth.

Madame Henry was of medium height, with a plain cast of features. She at once put herself at ease, leaning forward with both hands resting on the rail of the witness stand. In an attitude of complete self-possession she gave her evidence, accompanying the words with frequent gestures.

In the course of her deposition, Madame Henry admitted the frequent visits of Esterhazy to her husband, and declared her husband told her he had forged one document "in order to save the honor of the country."

Colonel Jouaust, in addressing Madame Henry, said:

"We thought, Madame, that your life in common with your husband has placed you in a position to give interesting information. I beg you to tell the court what you know."

Madame Henry deposed that toward the end of September, 1894, after dinner one evening, her husband told her a very important paper had been handed him. The witness added:

"As he did not return, I retired about eleven o'clock, and I asked him, when he returned, why he was later than usual. He undid a narrow, transparent roll of paper, and said:

"'There is a serious matter here, which I have been requested to investigate this evening.'

"Shortly afterward he re-entered the room, holding papers and a letter, which he had just pieced together. He placed them all in his hat, in order not to forget them in the morning. He left on horseback, as customary, the following morning, saying he had to see Colonel Sandherr as soon as possible."

"What was his impression on seeing the bordereau?" asked Colonel Jouaust.

The witness replied that he, Colonel Henry, did not know the author of it, but said perhaps Colonel Fabre or Colonel d'Abbeville knew.

Continuing, Madame Henry said:

"When my husband returned from the Cherche-Midi Prison, after taking Dreyfus there, I asked why he was on duty, and he answered:

"'I have just carried out the most painful task an officer can have. I have taken to the Cherche-Midi an officer accused of the frightful crime of treason.' Without naming Dreyfus, he added:

" 'I beg you not to speak of it for some time. He is an unfortunate fellow.' "

Before concluding her testimony, Madame Henry returned to the subject of the forgery. She evidently thought she could exonerate her husband by saying that he believed he was justified, in the interests of his country, in inserting in the existing dossier new and convincing material, the proof of which had reached him verbally a few days before.

In answer to a question of Colonel Jouaust, Madame Henry declared she did not know the name of the person who had given the information to her husband.

General Roget, in undress uniform, followed. His evidence was a vitriolic diatribe against Dreyfus from beginning to end. He traversed the old ground, giving his reasons for his conviction of the guilt of Dreyfus. He declared there was no charge against Esterhazy, with the exception of the resemblance of his handwriting to that of the bordereau. Moreover, the witness added, there had been a new fact since the judgment of the Court of Cassation, namely, Esterhazy's confession that he wrote the bordereau. But, he added, Esterhazy advanced and withdrew his confession intermittently. If Esterhazy had rendered services to the Intelligence Department there would have been traces of them in the books. But no money had been paid Esterhazy, though, even supposing he worked out of pure benevolence, he would have been paid. Yet there was no trace of such payments. Esterhazy had first confessed that he wrote the bordereau by the orders of Colonel Sandherr, to a representative of the London *Observer*. The confession was published in that paper on September 25, 1898. Later he made a signed confession, which was published in the *Daily Chronicle*, of London, and later still he confessed to *Le Matin*, in Paris. It was not the fact of the confession that the Court of Cassation deemed a "new fact," but because Esterhazy possessed paper identical with that on which the bordereau was written, and because his handwriting was identical with that of the bordereau.

"But," declared General Roget, "I, who knew Colonel Sandherr, will declare that is false. Colonel Sandherr was absolutely incapable of such an order. I add that it is inadmissible, because Colonel Sandherr was the last person to know of the existence of the bordereau, which was received in the ordinary way. This bordereau was handed to Colonel Henry, and was brought by him to the Intelligence Department. It was shown to others by Colonel Henry after he had pieced it together. Colonel Sandherr only saw it later.

"Esterhazy has also said the document was stolen from an embassy and brought by a porter. It is false to say the Intelligence Department ever had any relations with a porter of that embassy. It is possible Esterhazy is preparing some surprises for us between now and the end of the trial. They won't disturb me any more than other surprises."

Referring to the question of the complicity of Henry and Esterhazy, the witness said:

"If Henry had been the accomplice of Esterhazy, how can it be admitted that he himself brought the bordereau, which might have caused him to be suspected, to the Intelligence Department?"

General Roget while testifying constantly turned toward the prisoner to see the impression made by his deposition, which was virtually a speech for the prosecution. The general discoursed lengthily on the famous scene with Colonel Henry in the office of M. Bertulus, the examining magistrate, and said M. Bertulus asked Henry to inform the witness that he, M. Bertulus, was a friend of the army, and begged the witness to call and see him, when he would communicate the result of his investigations into the "Blanche" and "Speranza" forgeries. "In reply," said General Roget, "I said: 'When you see M. Bertulus, you will thank him in my behalf. Tell him the investigation does not interest me in any way.' I added that I was rather distrustful of this proposal, which I pointed out was perhaps a trap."

The general next dealt with the seizure of papers at the house of Mme. Pays, on which M. Bertulus largely founded his conviction of the guilt of Henry, owing to the mention in them of the name of a spy, Richard Cuers at Basle, where it was well known spies were in the habit of meeting.

Then the general tried to refute M. Bertulus's statements, declaring Henry brought three of these documents to the War Office, and that they did not contain the mention of Basle or Cuers as stated by M. Bertulus. The latter, however, had already shown before the whole Court of Cassation that, while he was mistaken in saying the words appeared in those documents, they did appear in other papers seized at Mme. Pays's residence.

At this point the general thought it desirable to make a declaration that he did not desire it to be said that he questioned the good faith of some of the witnesses who had been heard. He added:

"I make this statement so that there shall be no misunderstanding and in order that my words be not misinterpreted. Nevertheless, their testimony is open to criticism, even as our utterances are criticised."

Continuing, the witness said:

"M. Casimir-Perier deposed before the Court of Cassation that an ambassador called to demand an official denial of the statement that important documents were found at his embassy. The ambassador, however, knew it was a fact. But, admitting that he did not know it, there is nothing surprising in the occurrence, in view of the facility with which Attaché 'A' (I do not mention his name, as the minister has forbidden it) allowed compromising letters to lie around. I read one such letter which was very compromising to a person whose name I cannot mention. Why, therefore, should not the bordereau go astray?"

The general insisted upon the truth of the statements that Military Attachés "A" and "B," under which letters he referred to Colonel Schwartzkoppen, of the German Embassy, and Major Panizzardi, of the Italian Embassy, at the French capital, at the time worked together almost daily, and he quoted a passage from a letter exchanged between them as follows:

"M. Hanotaux, the sly fellow, is glad at the Embassy's denying. The Embassy must deny."

In the same document, declared General Roget, was a name written twice, and the name, he asserted, was that of Dreyfus. The name of Esterhazy, he added, was not found in any of the documents, none of which could be ascribed to him, with the exception of the *petit bleu*, "which Colonel Picquart discovered in such an extraordinary manner."

A certain military attaché, the general said, later informed Colonel Sandherr that there was some one who imitated his handwriting perfectly. The name of Dubois, the witness further said, was found in the correspondence of the military attachés. Dubois, the general explained, was a "unfortunate" who tried to sell the secret of the smokeless powder used in the French army. "If," said General Roget, "no other person can be found to whom the initial 'D' can apply, to whom does it then apply?"

As he made this remark the witness faced about and looked fixedly at the prisoner, who, however, merely shrugged his shoulders.

"No," continued the general, "the explanations furnished on this point by M. Trarieux [former Minister of Justice] troubled me somewhat, but I do not insist."

Here General Roget paused, the excitement under which he was laboring being almost uncontrollable. In a thick, choking voice, he continued:

"And yet in the presence of disinterested testimony like mine, you will not allow preference to be shown to the evidence of persons who have benefited by treason."

At this point the general broke down and tears streamed down his cheeks.

Major Hartmann, a French artillery expert, had exposed before the Court of Cassation that Dreyfus could not have written the bordereau, because there were blunders in the terms used, which Dreyfus, also an expert artillerist, could not possibly have made.

General Roget then repeated the old evidence tending to prove that Dreyfus alone was aware of the secrets of the new artillery guns, of the plans for the concentration of troops, and of the contents of the Firing Manual. He then endeavored to show that Colonel Picquart had recourse to fraudulent methods, with the intent of incriminating some one other than Dreyfus, and declared Picquart spent 100,000 francs with the object of organizing a campaign of surveillance "of an unfortunate officer who was guiltless." This 100,000 francs, he added, was a reserve accumulated by Colonel Sandherr, by strict economy, from the funds at the disposal of the War Office. This reserve had entirely disappeared.

In response to gestures of contradiction from M. Demange, General Roget admitted the figures quoted were perhaps exaggerated.

The witness next accused Colonel Picquart of suppressing documents tending to compromise Dreyfus.

As the general was evidently greatly fatigued, Colonel Jouaust suggested that he continue his testimony the following day, August 17th. The colonel then addressed the prisoner, asking him if he had anything to say in reply to General Roget.

The prisoner, who, during the time of General Roget's fulmination against him, had several times made a movement as if to rise and retort, but was waved down by Colonel Jouaust, then rose, and, in that voice which is not agreeable in ordinary times, but, when strangled with emotion as it was that day, had a thrilling effect on his hearers, he cried:

"No, Colonel. It is frightful that, day after day, for hours, I should thus have my heart, my soul, and my very entrails torn without being permitted to reply. It is a terrible torture to impose upon an innocent and loyal soldier. It is a frightful thing! Frightful! Frightful!"

The audience, profoundly stirred, began to applaud, but the applause was quickly suppressed.

The court then adjourned

As the prisoner passed out in front of the seats assigned to the representatives of the press his face was pale but animated. He seemed to be in a state of great nervous excitement and in a furious temper.

The general impression left by the day's proceedings was unfavorable to Dreyfus, owing to the absence of such cross-examinations as M. Labori would have submitted M. Lebon and M. Guérin to, and owing to the fact that General Roget's arguments received no reply.

Chapter XXXII.

COL. PICQUART AND M. BERTULUS SUPPORT DREYFUS

THE court-martial session of August 17th opened with brighter prospects for the prisoner, as M. Demange, of counsel for the defence, evidently came primed with questions, and subjected General Roget, who resumed his deposition on the opening of the court, dealing with the theft of Esterhazy's letters from Mlle. Pays, to a warm cross-examining fire.

General Roget was unable to conceal his annoyance and anger when M. Demange scored. The ends of the witness's fingers twitched nervously, and he frequently turned for consolation toward Generals Billot and Zurlinden, former Ministers of War, who were seated on the witnesses' seats behind him. The general also threw glances of savage resentment at the audience, when, as happened several times, suppressed titters went round the court-room when M. Demange cornered him.

Finally Roget became quite red in the face, and answered M. Demange in a hollow voice, contrasting strangely with his confident tone of yesterday.

General Roget, on resuming his testimony, criticised the surveillance established by Colonel Picquart over Lieutenant-Colonel Henry. This surveillance, he said, lasted several months and included the interception of letters addressed to Esterhazy. There had also been searches of Henry's house during his absence.

All these measures, the witness asserted, were carried out without the authorization of the Minister of War, who was not even informed of them. Moreover, he asserted, the investigations were carried on at the expense of the Secret Service Fund. The witness also objected to Colonel Picquart's methods of watching Mlle. Pays.

In regard to Esterhazy, General Roget admitted the former was a gambler and an immoral character. But, he asserted, "while I have acknowledged his little failings, I nevertheless maintain that he has been the victim of abominable persecution."

General Roget next spoke of the arrest at Belfort of Quenelli, a spy, declaring that Picquart "doctored" the allegations of spying against Quenelli, in order to attract to himself the approval of his superiors.

M. Demange asked Colonel Jouaust to request General Roget to repeat the explanations which he had given before the Court of Cassation in regard to the part played in the affair by Major Du Paty de Clam, whereupon the witness repeated the tale of Du Paty de Clam's steps to warn Esterhazy of the campaign said to be organizing against him.

The general said he believed the forged "Speranza" letters were either written by Du Paty de Clam or instigated by him. Witness said he had not acted against Du Paty de Clam, because he saw nothing culpable in what he had done to save Esterhazy.

With reference to the "document liberateur," which was a document forged in order to secure the release of Esterhazy when he was court-martialled, General Roget said he only knew how it reached the Ministry of War, adding that its disappearance from that ministry was a mystery. But, he said, doubtless Du Paty de Clam could explain the matter. This document was the "Cette canaille de D——" letter. When, in the autumn of 1897, the General Staff was using every effort to shield Esterhazy, this document was secured from the archives and given to Esterhazy by Du Paty de Clam. Esterhazy made it the subject of a note to the Minister of War. He said it had been given to him by a veiled lady who had explained to him that she had stolen it from Picquart, whose friend she had been. She knew of the plot to ruin Esterhazy, and was overcome with pity for him. By the scheme of the "document liberateur," Du Paty de Clam not only desired to implicate Picquart, but also to draw attention to the "innocent" Esterhazy, who was being "persecuted by the syndicate of treason." General Billot was completely deceived.

Counsel for the defence here wanted to know how, under such circumstances, Du Paty de Clam's intervention in behalf of Esterhazy could be explained. But the witness could only attribute it to Du Paty de Clam's "moral conviction of Esterhazy's innocence."

"What I would like to know," said M. Demange," is how an innocent man like Esterhazy was thought to need this kind of help?" [Laughter.]

"It is certain I should not have done it," said the witness, which caused renewed laughter.

During the course of his remarks, M. Demange referred to the document known as the *petit bleu* and the erasures in it. The general admitted the erasures might have been made with the view of giving the document a suspicious appearance. But, he intimated, Picquart made the erasures and reinserted the name of Esterhazy after taking the photograph exhibited before the Court of Cassation.

Counsel insisted that the falsification occurred after the *petit bleu* left Picquart's hands, and demanded further explanations from the witness.

The general, however, said he was unable to testify as to who falsified the document, or as to why it was done. But he did not think it was done with the view of compromising Picquart.

"How was it you knew," counsel asked General Roget, "that 600,000 francs was offered to Esterhazy if he would confess to being the author of the bordereau?"

"I heard it," the witness replied, "from the Court of Inquiry which tried Esterhazy, and from Esterhazy himself."

"Ah!" exclaimed counsel, "it was Esterhazy who said it. Just so." [Laughter.]

"Why was his residence searched?" M. Demange then asked, and the general answered:

"Esterhazy, at one time, had the document containing the words ' Cette canaille de D——,' and might, therefore, have had others."

"You admit, then," asked M. Demange, "that he might have had other interesting documents?"

"When one is conducting an inquiry," said the witness, "one must expect anything and search accordingly."

"Admitting," counsel then said, "that Esterhazy was the agent of the Dreyfus family, and that he had agreed to assume, as suggested, the prisoner's guilt, how do you explain the fact that Esterhazy upon several occasions wrote statements calculated to compromise the case of Dreyfus?"

"With Esterhazy," replied General Roget, "one can never be sure of anything. [Laughter.] He is such an extraordinary fellow. I do not know what he may be doing to-day, nor what he will do to-morrow."

These statements of the general convulsed the court with laughter and seemed to irritate the witness, who was growing nervous under the searching examination of counsel.

Turning to Dreyfus, General Roget cried, in a loud voice:

"I know very well that if I was accused of an act of treason which I had not committed, I should find arguments with which to defend myself."

This assertion evoked murmurs, but the general shouted:

"Why does he deny even the most obvious things?"

M. Demange shrugged his shoulders, and ejaculated, "Ah!"

Dreyfus, however, arose and emphatically denied point blank some of the general's evidence. He said he never traced on a map any plan of concentration or mobilization, and never had any knowledge of the details of these movements, nor of the plan for the distribution of the various units throughout the departments.

Then came a witness who proved to be a splendid reinforcement for Dreyfus. It was M. Bertulus, the examining magistrate who received the late Lieutenant-Colonel Henry's confession of forgery.

In almost inaudible tones, owing to hoarseness, M. Bertulus gave his testimony, which was a veritable speech for the defence. Coming from a man of the high legal reputation of M. Bertulus, this evidence raised the hopes of the Dreyfusards immensely, as it apparently made a deep impression on the members of the court.

The magistrate had inquired into the charges made against Esterhazy by his cousin, Christian, and it was expected M. Bertulus would be confronted with General Roget, who so tartly criticised the magistrate at the last session.

M. Bertulus described how Major Ravary asked his assistance in examining the secret dossier at the Cherche-Midi Prison, and how, after he had learned the contents of the documents, he declared to Major Ravary that there was a flaw in the dossier which would occasion the collapse of the whole case. Here the witness explained that he meant the *petit bleu*. It must be proved, he told the major, that the *petit bleu* was a forgery, and was the work of Colonel Picquart, and that as long as that was not proved the case could not hold.

Continuing, M. Bertulus recapitulated the evidence he had given before the Court of Cassation, his investigation into Du Paty de Clam's connec-

DREYFUS'S MORNING WALK ON THE "SFAX."

THE RETURN OF DREYFUS: LANDING FROM THE "SFAX" AT QUIBERON.

ON BOARD THE "SFAX": THE CABIN OCCUPIED BY DREYFUS.

ON BOARD THE "SFAX": THE GUARD AT THE DOOR OF DREYFUS'S CABIN.

LEADING ACTORS IN THE DRAMA.

Ex-Minister of War M. Cavaignac.   Ex-President M. Casimir-Périer.

The late President.

General de Freycinet.   M. Félix Faure.   General Gallifet.

LEADING ACTORS IN THE DRAMA.

Colonel Henry.   M. Déroulède.

Major Esterhazy.

General Boisdeffre.   General Roget.

LEADING ACTORS IN THE DRAMA.

Ex-Minister of War M. Cavaignac.   Ex-President M. Casimir-Périer.

The late President.

General de Freycinet.   M. Félix Faure.   General Gallifet.

LEADING ACTORS IN THE DRAMA.

Colonel Henry.   M. Déroulède.

Major Esterhazy.

General Boisdeffre.   General Roget.

Ex-Minister of War M

General de Freyc

PRESIDENT ÉMILE LOUBET.

LEADING ACTORS IN THE DRAMA.

Herr Schwarzkoppen,	Signor Panizzardi,
Attaché of the German Embassy.	Attaché of the Italian Embassy.
M. Scheurer-Kestner,	General Billot.
Ex-Vice President of the Senate.	
Colonel Sandherr.	Major Du Paty de Clam.

PRESIDENT ÉMILE LOUBET.

MAÎTRE LABORI WITH MADAME LABORI AND HIS SECRETARY.

tion with the "Speranza" and "Blanche" telegrams, and the favorable impression he had acquired of Colonel Picquart's honesty during the course of the inquiry.

M. Bertulus then related the notable interviews between himself and Lieutenant-Colonel Henry, on July 18, 1898, shortly before he committed suicide.   This naturally was a painful recital for Madame Henry, the widow, who was much distressed and wept silently as the dramatic scene when Bertulus and Henry proceeded to seal up the seized papers was depicted.   The magistrate repeated the whole story with emphasis, and it had a great effect upon the audience.

After recapitulating his other evidence before the Court of Cassation, M. Bertulus energetically affirmed his belief in the innocence of Dreyfus. He declared the bordereau was in three pieces, and not in little bits.   He also said that it did not reach the War Office by the ordinary channels.

M. Bertulus said his belief in the innocence of Dreyfus was also based on documents in the secret dossier which he had seen.   But what, above all, perturbed the witness was the entire absence of a motive which could have tempted Dreyfus to commit such a crime.   "Without motive," emphatically declared the experienced magistrate, "there was no crime."

This testimony created a profound impression upon his hearers.

"You have been told," said the magistrate, "that Dreyfus is guilty. For myself, I believe, and believe profoundly, in his innocence.   If I come here to tell you so, you will understand that it is because my conscience tells me that in so doing I am performing a duty, an absolute duty.   The Court of Cassation has declared the bordereau to be the work of Esterhazy.   Now, the Court of Cassation is the supreme authority in all matters of justice in France!"

Madame Henry then ascended the platform, and, standing besides M. Bertulus, she said:

"On July 18th, the day my husband called on M. Bertulus, the colonel, in the course of a conversation that evening, told me he had a friendly and charming reception.   He described how the magistrate advanced to meet him and held out his arms.   I said to my husband: 'Are you sure of this man?   Are you sure he is sincere?   I am very much afraid that his kiss was the kiss of a Judas.'"

There was a great sensation in court at this statement.

11

"I was not wrong," she continued, amid the breathless interest of the court; "this man is indeed the Judas I imagined."

Referring to the papers which arrived at the same time as the bordereau, Madame Henry said:

"These papers were not all torn in a thousand pieces. I was able to note that personally. Letters often came entire. M. Bertulus has maintained that everything arrived in pieces. That is false."

M. Bertulus said he did not desire to reply to Madame Henry, adding:

"She is only a woman."

"I am not a woman," exclaimed Madame Henry, furiously; "I speak in the name of my husband."

"How shall I reply to madame?" asked M. Bertulus. "She is defending the name of a dead man and that of her child."

The magistrate then handed the court a letter which he had received the day before, warning him that it was the intention of Madame Henry to create this scene and call M. Bertulus a Judas.

After gazing steadfastly at M. Bertulus, who was greatly moved, Madame Henry descended from the platform and took a seat beside General Zurlinden, and M. Bertulus forthwith left the court.

Colonel Picquart was then called to the witness stand. He protested most formally against all suspicion of having caused the disappearance of any document relating to Dreyfus. Documents, he added, had disappeared, but he was not connected with their disappearance. He also repelled with scorn the assertion that he had endeavored to put another officer in the place of the real author of the bordereau.

"It is true," the witness continued, "that the name of Captain Dorval being mentioned to me as a dangerous man, I had him watched; and do you know, gentlemen, by whom Dorval was denounced? By his own cousin," continued Picquart, "Major Du Paty de Clam."

Colonel Picquart then next proceeded to reply to the various attacks made upon him. "These tactics," he said, "are evidently pursued with the object of lessening the value of my testimony."

The colonel next outlined his connection with Dreyfus at the Military College, and afterward at the Ministry of War, where, owing to the Anti-Semite prejudices of the General Staff, he first appointed Dreyfus to a department where probationers had no direct cognizance of secret documents.

He then described the consternation in the War Office when the treason was discovered, and the relief experienced when it was thought the guilty person had been discovered.   It was then the witness discovered the similarity between the handwriting of Dreyfus and that of the bordereau, and he had recourse to Du Paty de Clam, "who was supposed to have geographical knowledge."   [Laughter.]

Then the witness described what he characterized as the "irregular steps" taken by General Mercier to accomplish the arrest of Dreyfus.

Referring to the dictation test, the witness earnestly and emphatically affirmed that he saw no signs of perturbation in the handwriting of Dreyfus on that occasion, and, moreover, shortly afterward Du Paty de Clam admitted he had not found a fresh charge against Dreyfus.

"Beyond the bordereau," added the witness, "there was nothing against Dreyfus—absolutely nothing."

The colonel next declared that in 1894 he did not know the contents of the secret dossier.   But he believed, like all other officers, that it contained frightful proofs against the prisoner.   But when he became acquainted with its contents he found that his earlier impressions were entirely wrong.

The witness also declared he was quite ignorant of the confessions Dreyfus is alleged to have made to Captain Lebrun-Renault.

Next the colonel examined the bordereau and declared Dreyfus could not have disclosed part of it.

Regarding the Madagascar note, the witness disputed its value, and said he did not believe it was a confidential note.   He added that if Dreyfus, in his capacity of a probationer, had asked the witness for the note, he would have handed it to him immediately.   Therefore, he [Picquart] was unable to understand the sentence in the bordereau reading: "This document was very difficult to obtain."

Colonel Picquart declared he had never seen Dreyfus copy the smallest document in the War Office.   In the opinion of the witness the department where the bordereau was discovered ought to have been searched when the discovery was made.   This, he explained, was the department in which Du Paty de Clam worked, and that was the department which was working on the plan of the concentration of the troops and the Madagascar expedition.   He added:

"It was in Major Du Paty de Clam's department that the search should have been made, or rather in his private room, where he worked quite alone."   [Sensation.]

Du Paty de Clam, continued the witness, had been guilty of grave imprudence in having, contrary to the regulations, had confidential documents copied by simple secretaries, non-commissioned officers, and even private soldiers, whereas the custom was that such work was done solely by officers.

Later on the witness said he wondered if it was not to avoid the risk of punishment that Du Paty de Clam advanced the date of the reception of the bordereau at the Intelligence Department, so as to make it prior to the date of his, Du Paty de Clam's, arrival in the Third Department. [Sensation.]

Chapter XXXIII.

THE PLOTS AGAINST DREYFUS

WHEN the trial of Captain Dreyfus was resumed on August 18th, Colonel Picquart continued his deposition, which was interrupted the preceding day by the adjournment of the court. The colonel gave his testimony in the same loud, fearless tone of voice. He commenced by declaring that he thought it necessary immediately to reply to General Roget's veritable arraignment of him while the latter was on the stand.

Picquart then proceeded to discuss the secret dossier as being the mainspring of the condemnation of Dreyfus.

The colonel practically occupied the whole of the sitting with a masterful presentation of his side of the case. He spoke for five hours, and his voice at the end of that time began to show signs of fatigue.

His testimony was followed with the closest attention by the members of the court-martial and by the audience, and during the brief suspension of the court Generals Mercier, Roget, Billot, and De Boisdeffre, and other witnesses sauntered together up and down the courtyard of the Lycée or gathered in little groups, animatedly discussing Picquart's evidence, which, although it contained but few facts, was so cleverly placed before the tribunal and was spoken so effectively that it could not fail to repeat the impression he had made the day before.

Dreyfus naturally drank in all the witness's words, which came as a balm to the wounds inflicted upon him by Generals Mercier and Roget; and the prisoner frequently and closely scanned the faces of the judges, as though seeking to read their thoughts.

Before resuming his deposition, Colonel Picquart said:

"For the moment I shall confine myself to the following explanation: The Quenelli case occurred between May 30 and July 17, 1896, at which period, on account of a family bereavement, I was able to pay very little attention to my official duties. In my absence, Colonel Henry acted

for me.   Moreover, I devoted most of the month of July to a journey of
the Headquarters' Staff, which also prevented me from attending to my
ordinary duties.   I was, therefore, able to give only very intermittent attention to the Quenelli case.   Besides this, Quenelli was a returned convict, who had contravened a decree of expulsion and had been caught red-
handed in another criminal act.   He was, at first sight, a not particularly
interesting personage.

"I protest absolutely against the allegation that I consented to the
communication of secret documents to the members of the Dreyfus court-
martial without the prisoner's knowledge.   I never ordered such communication, and if it was done it was not with my cognizance.   Having thus
explained certain matters I will continue my deposition."

Then the colonel proceeded to discuss the phrase occurring in the
bordereau, "I am going to the manœuvres."   He said there was no question of probationers going to the manœuvres in September.   This, he
pointed out, would have curtailed their period of probation in an entirely
unusual manner.   It was for this reason that D'Ormescheville, who drew
up the *acte d'accusation*, or indictment, against Dreyfus in 1894, changed
the date of the bordereau from September to April.   When, however, it
was discovered that Dreyfus knew as early as March that he would not
attend the manœuvres, the correct date was resumed.   Later this was
found untenable, and so, in their testimony before the Court of Cassation,
Generals Mercier, Gonse, and de Boisdeffre reassumed the date of the bordereau to have been April.

After dealing with the testimony of the experts at the court-martial
of 1894, Picquart proceeded to examine the secret dossier, a close analysis
of which, he asserted, was particularly necessary, "owing to the weight
the document had with the members of the court-martial in 1894."

"This dossier," continued the witness, "may be divided into two parts.
The first contains three documents: One, a document known as the
d'Avignon document, the terms of which are about as follows: 'Doubt;
proof; service letters; situation dangerous for me with French officer;
cannot personally conduct negotiations; no information from an officer of
the line; important only as coming from the Ministry; already somewhere
else.'"

This is a literal translation of a cipher despatch in German, which was intercepted early in 1894. It was sent by Schwartzkoppen in reply to a message which had been intercepted December 29, 1893, and which contained the words: "The documents; no sign of the General Staff."

"Service letters" in the reply is translated from the German original "patent," *i.e.*, an officer's brevet. Both dispatches have been paraphrased by Picquart as follows: "The documents received. There is no evidence that they come from the War Office."

To which the reply was: "You doubt? My proof is that my informant [Esterhazy] is an officer. I have seen his brevet. True, only a regimental officer; but I assure you he brings his information, every bit of it, from the Intelligence Bureau. I cannot communicate directly with Henry."

"Two, the document containing the words, 'Cette canaille de D——.'"

"Three, a document which is nothing but the report of a journey to Switzerland, and made in behalf of a foreign power.

"The second part of the dossier," continued Picquart, "consisted partly of a supplementary review of the first. It contained the gist of seven or eight documents, one of which, 'Cette canaille de D——,' will serve for the purposes of comparison. It also contained the correspondence of Attachés 'A' and 'B.'" [These initials represent Colonel von Schwartzkoppen, formerly German military attaché, and Major Panizzardi, the former military attaché of Italy, at the French capital.]

The witness next explained why Major Du Paty de Clam's translation of the d'Avignon document, which has been classed as idiotic, was open to doubt and why the document, if it had any meaning whatever, was as applicable to Esterhazy as to Dreyfus. Du Paty de Clam's translation or paraphrasing reads as follows:

"You say the documents do not bear the mark of the General Staff. There are doubts; proof is therefore necessary. I will ask for '*la lettre de service*,' but, as it is dangerous for me personally to conduct the negotiations, I will take an intermediary and tell the officer to bring me what he has. I must have absolute discretion, because the Intelligence Bureau is on the watch against us; there is no good of having relations with a regimental officer. Documents are only of importance when they come from the Ministry; this is why I continue my relations."

Regarding the correspondence of the military attaché, the witness demonstrated the insignificance of the information asked for.

Colonel Picquart then took up the "Cette canaille de D——" document. He called the attention of the court to the fact that it was addressed by Schwartzkoppen to Panizzardi, and not *vice versa*, as long believed.

After giving his reasons for believing Dreyfus was not the person referred to in that document, Picquart showed how Du Paty de Clam endeavored to ascribe the authorship of the document of Panizzardi with the view of establishing a connection which in reality did not exist between the various documents in the indictment against Dreyfus.

The former Chief of the Intelligence Department concluded his examination of the first portion of the secret dossier by saying:

"May I be allowed to express deep regret at the absence of Major Du Paty de Clam? It seems to me indispensable that this officer, who wrote the commentaries on the secret dossier, should be summoned to give evidence here. He would give us his reminiscences, and I would help him." [Laughter.] "But," added Picquart, "since I am dealing with this question of the commentaries of Major du Paty de Clam, permit me to point to you, gentlemen, that this document was not the property of any particular minister. It was classified as belonging to the Intelligence Department, and, as you see, it formed part of a well-defined dossier—a dossier which was shut up in one of the drawers of my desk and which was abstracted from it. This commentary, therefore, is upon a secret dossier document which was improperly removed from my department."

Continuing, the witness remarked: "Mention was made yesterday of the disappearance of documents. That is the case in point."

Turning to the second portion of the dossier, Picquart described a number of documents in it as forgeries, and said the police reports therein contained nothing serious against Dreyfus. He explained that they embodied the theme mostly utilized by police spies in order to dupe the Intelligence Department, and asserted that their information was mostly worthless or false, and prepared in order to make interesting reading.

"In the inquiry made by M. Quesnay de Beaurepaire" (former president of the Civil Section of the Court of Cessation), continued Picquart, "you have an excellent example of the sort of people who can present in the most specious guise what amounts absolutely to nothing. You cannot imagine, gentlemen, what people, in order to get money, if only a modest twenty-franc piece, have brought to the Intelligence Department in the shape of so-called ' information,' which examination has proved to be worthless."

Concluding his examination of the secret dossier, Colonel Picquart explained how he had acquired the conviction that the bordereau was written by Esterhazy, and how he ascertained that the anti-Dreyfus proofs were worthless. He began by detailing how he first learned of the existence of Esterhazy and his efforts to discover something about him. The witness earnestly asserted that the first occasion on which he saw Esterhazy's name was when he read the address of the *petit bleu*. He said he was not acquainted with Esterhazy, and never had Esterhazy watched. Previous to this the utmost efforts had been made to prove the contrary, and to show that Picquart knew Esterhazy before the discovery of the *petit bleu*.

What Picquart gathered about Esterhazy's character, he continued, created the worst impression upon him, but he learned nothing to connect Esterhazy with any act of espionage. Therefore he did not mention his suspicions. An agent, however, was ordered to watch Esterhazy, who had completely compromised himself through his relations with an English company, of which he had agreed to become a director.

"That could not be permitted in the case of a French officer," said Picquart. "Moreover, Esterhazy gambled, led a life 'of debauchery, and lived with Mlle. Pays."

Turning to the leakage at Headquarters, the witness described the negotiations of Major Lauth with the spy Richard Cuers, at Basle, showing how the spy promised to inform him about the leakage, and how he, Picquart, was induced to allow Lieutenant-Colonel Henry to accompany Major Lauth to Basle.

Picquart also described the vague replies of Henry when questioned on the subject of Esterhazy before his departure, and the futility of the visit to Basle, because of Cuers's refusal, when he saw Henry, to impart the promised information. This incident caused the witness to wonder whether, instead of trying to make Cuers speak, Henry and Lauth had not done everything possible to impose silence upon him.

"I affirm," continued Picquart, "that General de Boisdeffre knew that this question was to remain a secret between us, and that I was not to mention it except to the Minister of War. I knew Esterhazy was anxious to enter the War Office, and I did not regard his desire favorably. I communicated my impressions to my chiefs, who approved all my steps, and the application of Esterhazy was rejected.

"His insistence, however, only increased my uneasiness regarding him, and I resolved to obtain a specimen of his handwriting. I was immediately struck with the similarity of his handwriting and that of the bordereau, and forthwith I had the letters of Esterhazy which were in my possession photographed, and showed the photographs to Major Du Paty de Clam and M. Bertillon between August 25th and September 5th."

The colonel emphasized this point, because M. Bertillon affirmed that he saw the photographs in May, 1896, and made a note of them, whereas the letters were not written on that date. The conflicting testimony of Picquart and Bertillon on this point had been used to discredit the former's evidence.

Colonel Picquart also said Du Paty de Clam, on seeing the writing, forthwith declared it was that of Mathieu Dreyfus, the brother of Captain Dreyfus.

The witness, continuing, said:

"'You know,' Du Paty de Clam maintained, 'that the bordereau is the joint work of Alfred and Mathieu Dreyfus.'

"M. Bertillon said: 'That is the writing of the bordereau.'

"M. Bertillon tried to discover where I had obtained the handwriting, but the only information I imparted was that it was current and recent handwriting.

"M. Bertillon then suggested that it was a tracing, and ended by saying that if it was current handwriting it could only have emanated from some one whom the Jews had been exercising for a year in imitating the writing of the bordereau.

"At M. Bertillon's request I left the photographs with him. When he returned them he said he adhered to his opinion and earnestly asked to see the original. When I saw beyond a doubt that the handwriting of the bordereau was Esterhazy's, and seeing that the documents mentioned therein might have been supplied by Esterhazy, that the words, 'I am going to the manœuvres' could perfectly well apply to Esterhazy, and that Esterhazy had secretaries at his disposal to copy a document so voluminous as the Firing Manual, I resolved to consult the secret dossier to see what part of the treachery might be ascribed to Dreyfus, and to assure myself whether the dossier contained anything implicating Esterhazy. I frankly admit I was stupefied on reading the secret dossier. I expected to find matters of gravity therein, and found, in short, nothing but a document which might apply just as much to Esterhazy as to Dreyfus, an unimportant document mentioning d'Avignon, and a document which it seemed absurd to apply to Dreyfus, namely, the 'Cette canaille de D——' document.

"Lastly, I recognized a report appended in the handwriting of Guennée, an agent, which appeared to be at least as worthless as the second document.

"It was then evening. I had stayed late at the office in order to examine the documents thoroughly. I thought it over during the night, and the next day I explained the whole situation to General de Boisdeffre. I took to his office the secret dossier, the facsimile of the bordereau, the *petit bleu*, and the principal papers connected with my investigation of Esterhazy.

"I wonder now if I had one or two interviews? But I still see General de Boisdeffre, as he examined the secret dossier with me, stop before he reached the end, and tell me to go into the country, give an account of the affair to General Gonse, and ask his advice.

"When I informed General Gonse of all which had occurred, he remarked: 'So a mistake has been made?'

"After my interview with General Gonse I did not work any longer on my own initiative. I said nothing more until the return of General Gonse, September 15th. At this time Esterhazy was at the great manœuvres."

Next the witness dwelt on the rumors in September, 1896, of the project of replacing Dreyfus by a man-of-straw, and the discovery of the forged Weyler letter, supposed to be connected with the same project.

At about the same time the campaign for and against Dreyfus was started by the newspapers.

The witness then turned to the newspaper attacks on Dreyfus, saying that the information regarding the bordereau contained in them convinced him that they had been inspired by some one closely connected with the Dreyfus affair. They could not, he added, be attributed to the Dreyfus family, while they contained expressions familiar to Du Paty de Clam, whom it would be interesting to hear on the subject.

The witness next said he asked permission to inquire into the sources of the articles, but was forbidden to interfere in any way whatever.

Describing his interview with General Gonse, on September 15th, Picquart said:

"When I asked General Gonse for permission to continue the investigation, insisting on the danger of allowing the Dreyfus family to proceed with their investigation alone, the general replied that it was impossible, in his opinion and in the opinions of General de Boisdeffre and the Minister of War, to reopen the affair. When I pressed the point, in order to make General Gonse understand that nothing could prevent its reopening if it could be believed Dreyfus was innocent, General Gonse replied:

"'If you say nothing, nobody will know.'

"'General,' I replied, firmly, 'what you tell me is abominable. I do not know what I shall do. But I won't carry this secret with me.'

"I at once left the room," added the witness. "That is what occurred. I know my account is disputed, but I positively swear it," said Picquart, as he emphatically smote the bar in front of the witness box, and looked in the direction of the generals.

The colonel next described his intentions with regard to Esterhazy, which Generals Gonse and de Boisdeffre had forbidden him to carry out. He attached particular importance to this point, as it contained a clue to subsequent occurrences. Later, the witness said, that while Du Paty de Clam evidently acted wrongly in disguising himself during the investigations with a false beard and blue spectacles, perhaps he was authorized to do so.

Colonel Picquart also showed how, through an article in the *Éclair* of September 14, 1896, he was satisfied Esterhazy had been warned of the suspicions against him.

In order to make the proofs complete, the witness continued his investigations with the utmost discretion. In his opinion, the only event of importance in the Dreyfus affair since the discovery of the bordereau was the Henry forgery, perpetrated on October 31st, 1896.   He added that it must have been handed immediately to General Gonse.

Shortly before Henry perpetrated the forgery, the agent Guenée, Henry's right-hand man, prepared a report declaring that M. Castelin (Republican Revisionist, Deputy for Laon, division of Aisne) was about to play the hand of the Dreyfus family by unmasking, in the Chamber of Deputies, the prisoner's accomplices, thus having the affair reopened.

Then, turning to the distant mission upon which he was dispatched, Picquart described the irritation he felt when he saw he was being removed because he was no longer wanted as head of the Intelligence Department. He explained that if this disgrace had been frankly avowed it would have been much less painful to him.   The colonel also said that during his absence his correspondence was tampered with.

Dealing with his mission to Tunis, which Picquart said ought to have been intrusted to a commissary of police, the witness declared it was then that Henry, abandoning his underhand intrigues, began a campaign of open persecution.   Henry wrote to the witness, accusing him of communicating information to the press, with disclosing the contents of secret documents, and with attempting to suborn officers in connection with the *petit bleu*.

It was then Picquart learned of the existence of the forged secret documents directed against himself, and foresaw his own ruin if the Dreyfus affair was reopened; and, to safeguard himself, he intrusted to a lawyer friend, M. Leblois, a certain letter from General Gonse, at the same time acquainting the lawyer with what he knew of Esterhazy, and instructing the lawyer how he should intervene, "if the occasion demanded it."   This lawyer communicated with M. Scheurer-Kestner, then one of the Vice-Presidents of the Senate, and the representations of the latter to Premier Méline's Government followed.

When Picquart's furlough was due, General Leclerc, commanding in Tunis, was ordered to send Picquart to the frontier of Tripoli.   Leclerc commented to the witness on the abnormal order, and Picquart confided to the general the probable reasons for it, and his belief in the innocence of Dreyfus.   General Leclerc thereupon ordered Picquart not to go beyond Gabes.

Picquart created a sensation by incidentally remarking that the judges in 1894 were shamefully deceived in having the document containing the words, "Cette canaille de D——" communicated to them.

Witness then bitterly recited the details of the various machinations with the view of <u>incriminating</u> him, instigated by Henry, Esterhazy, and Du Paty de Clam.

"I have almost finished my task," added Picquart, "but I ask permission to refer to the way the bordereau came to the War Office. I have doubts in regard to the person who brought the bordereau. Two quite different persons could certainly have delivered the bordereau in 1894. But, if an intelligent person had delivered it, he would certainly have insisted on the value of its contents."

In reply to questions of General Roget, Picquart admitted sending documents to Belfort for the use of the Quenelli case. "But," Picquart added, "they were handed to the Public Prosecutor."

General Roget's questions were evidently with the view of eliciting the confession from Colonel Picquart that, in the Quenelli case, he communicated to the judges documents unknown to the defence, as he now accuses the General Staff of doing in the Dreyfus case.

General Mercier promptly replaced General Roget.

"Picquart," Mercier said, "has stated that I ordered him to convey documents to Colonel Maurel-Pries. That is false. I never handed any packet to Colonel Picquart for Colonel Maurel-Pries. I never mentioned secret documents to him."

In reply Colonel Picquart said:

"I remember perfectly that General Mercier handed me a packet for Colonel Maurel-Pries."

General Mercier next denied Colonel Picquart's statement relative to the meeting with General Gonse during the afternoon of January 6, 1895, when the latter was greatly excited at the prospect of war.

Colonel Picquart replied that he adhered to everything he had said. General Gonse, the witness explained, was excited because he knew of the action of an ambassador toward M. Casimir-Perier, then President of the Republic.

General Mercier next referred to Picquart's statement that the D'Avignon document was communicated to the court-martial of 1894. He said:

"I deny it positively. The only documents communicated were the

Panizzardi telegram, Du Paty de Clam's commentary, the note of the Italian attaché in regard to French railroads, and the report of Guenée."

Picquart here pointed out that he had only expressed his belief on this subject.

Maître Demange's cross-examination compelled General Mercier somewhat reluctantly to enumerate the secret documents submitted to the first court-martial.   Among them was the "Cette canaille de D——" letter.

When asked why the commentary of Guenée was not attached to the document, Mercier replied:

"It was supplied for my personal use."

"Then," said Maître Demange triumphantly, "you could not have meant Dreyfus, but did mean Dubois."

M. Demange asked General Mercier why it did not occur to him to append to the comments information of the existence of a man named Dubois, who was suspected of having communicated information to foreign powers.

General Mercier replied.

"Because we had discovered that he could not have been the author of the documents mentioned in the comments."

"Ah," said Maître Demange, "because you considered that Dubois could not be the author, after study of the dossier, of the divulgations, consequently you did not reveal the fact that there was a person called D—— who might be meant?"

General Mercier—Quite so.

The court then adjourned.

Chapter XXXIV.

"THAT IS A MANIFEST LIE," SAID DREYFUS

THE stage of the Lycée at Rennes was occupied, successively, on August 19th, by three enemies of Dreyfus—Major Cuignet, General de Boisdeffre, and General Gonse.   From 6:30 until 11 A.M. they devoted themselves mainly to reiterating what they had said in evidence against the prisoner, who followed them with characteristic composure.

But when the moment came for him to reply, the prisoner delivered one of those brief utterances of indignation which have had such a powerful effect upon his hearers.

General de Boisdeffre, one of the witnesses, is tall, and, like every general who has appeared in court except General Mercier, he boasted of a very conspicuous bald patch, the heads of the other generals being adorned by little more than a rim of gray hair.

De Boisdeffre spoke in a blunt manner and in somewhat gruff tones, but with a certain air of sincerity which had its effect on the judges.

The general was treated with obvious deference by the members of the court-martial, but he did not appear to relish the novelty of being questioned by a junior officer, one of the judges, who wished for a few harmless explanations.

Major Cuignet, charged by Cavaignac, when Minister of War, about a year ago, to examine the secret dossier, was the first witness called.

"Before beginning an account of the special investigations into the case which I was ordered to make by Ministers of War, from M. Cavaignac to M. de Freycinet," said the witness, "I wish to mention a personal fact which, in conjunction with the evidence already heard, will constitute fresh proof of the prisoner's indiscreet behavior when employed on the Headquarters Staff.

"I was on the staff when Dreyfus was a probationer, during the latter half of 1893.   Among other duties, I was connected with the railroad service and the mining of railroads, with the view of interrupting traffic in case of need.   It is hardly necessary to point out the secret character of such matters.   Dreyfus was a probationer on the eastern railroads, and had been ordered specially to study the mining of them.   He possessed information relating solely to them.   One day Dreyfus asked me to give him the general scheme of mining which I possessed, giving as a reason for his request that he was anxious to increase his knowledge, and that it was necessary for him to know the general scheme in order properly to carry out the work entrusted to him.   I replied that I did not see the necessity of giving him the scheme, and that, in any case, he had better apply to his own chief, Major Bertin.   Dreyfus pretended Bertin would not impart any information.   Day after day he pestered me, so that finally, having no reason to distrust him, I began giving him explanations. Dreyfus displayed the keenest interest and took copious notes.   When later his house was searched these notes were not discoverable.   I do not know what became of them.   But it is difficult to believe they were destroyed, considering the importance he seemed to attach to the information and the persistence shown in procuring it."

After making the above declaration, which he apparently considered to be weighty evidence of the treachery of Dreyfus, Major Cuignet proceeded to recount in detail the task assigned to him in May, 1898, of classifying the documents in the Dreyfus, Esterhazy, and Picquart cases.   He then said:

"My conviction of the guilt of Dreyfus is based on three grounds: First, his confession to Captain Lebrun-Renault; second, the technical nature of the contents of the bordereau; third, the results of the examination of the secret dossier.

"I will add to these three points the evidence of the expert Bertillon, [laughter] and, as indirect proof, the means employed by the Dreyfus family to secure the prisoner's rehabilitation.   I protest that a campaign has been undertaken against justice, truth, and our country."

The major's outburst of heroics evoked cynical smiles and indications of dissent, coupled with marks of assent from the assembled generals.

Regarding the confessions said to have been made to Captain Lebrun-Renault, witness said he still believed they were authentic, adding:

"If people do not believe the confessions to Captain Lebrun-Renault, they will believe no human testimony."

12

This question greatly confused the witness, who attempted to explain by saying that it was not for him to judge Du Paty de Clam, etc.

M. Demange pointed out that, in spite of the many arguments Major Cuignet had advanced against Du Paty de Clam, the military judge, Tavernier, threw out the case.

"Now," added M. Demange, "Major Cuignet has advanced as much against Dreyfus. The court will be able to appreciate the value of his arguments."

When Dreyfus was asked if he wished to reply to this witness, he declared he had never asked Major Cuignet for documents except by the desire of his chief, Major Bertin.

"All the details which Major Cuignet has given on this subject," said the prisoner, "sprang out of his own imagination, and are due to the same state of mind which ever prompts unreasoning bitterness against an innocent man."

Amid a buzz of excitement, the name of Major Du Paty de Clam was called out, whereupon Major Carriere said Du Paty de Clam had been officially informed that his presence was necessary to the court-martial, and it was hoped he would be able to come as soon as possible; but the Government Commissary had heard nothing from him since this notification was sent.

General de Boisdeffre, former Chief of the General Staff of the French Army, then advanced to the witness-box and took the customary oath to tell the truth. The general remarked that, in view of the exhaustive evidence already given, he would try to be brief. He hurriedly reviewed the leakage in the Ministry of War, the discovery of the bordereau, the arrest and trial of Dreyfus, and the latter's alleged confessions, before the ceremony of degradation, to Captain Lebrun-Renault. The witness said he believed the confessions were genuine. He next referred to Colonel Picquart's appearance in the Intelligence Department, although the witness hesitated to appoint him because he thought Picquart too self-confident and not sufficiently deferential toward his chiefs.

"It has been said," continued General de Boisdeffre, "that a secret package of papers was shown the judges of the court-martial of 1894. I positively assert that, so far as I am concerned, I never ordered Colonel Picquart to convey any envelope to Colonel Maurel-Pries. I may add that

Colonel Picquart never doubted the guilt of Dreyfus, and never even expressed doubts of his guilt when he took over the duties of Chief of the Intelligence Department.   The first instructions I gave him were to follow up the Dreyfus affair, and it is well known what was the result of these instructions."

The witness discredited Colonel Picquart's statement that the latter asked him not to mention the investigation to General Gonse.

"General Gonse," said de Boisdeffre, "is a friend of thirty years' standing.   I have always had the greatest confidence in him, and should certainly not have entertained a request to leave him in ignorance of what was occurring."

Then the witness briefly referred to the trial and acquittal of Esterhazy and the latter's threats to proclaim himself a tool of the General Staff, after which the general alluded to the Henry forgery and M. Cavaignac's interrogations of Henry.

"You know the result," said he, apparently much moved.   "I will not tell you what I suffered at that moment.   As soon as everything was ended I tendered my resignation, but was asked to withdraw it.   I was told every one could make a mistake.   But I replied that while every one was liable to err, every one had not the misfortune, as I had, to assert to a jury that a document was genuine, when in reality it was forged; that every one ought to stand by one's word, and that when a man happened to experience such a misfortune there was nothing left for him but to go away, and from that moment I have held aloof."

Replying to the court, General de Boisdeffre admitted that the leakage at Military Headquarters continued.   After the condemnation of Dreyfus, he added, it ceased for a year, but in 1895 a paper was discovered proving the communication to foreigners of a document relating to the distribution of the artillery, and showing that a foreign government was perfectly acquainted with the changes made.

General Gonse, who was Under Chief of the General Staff, was next called to the witness-stand.   He explained the motives which influenced his actions during the past few years, and said he believed he was "animated by the loftiest aims, namely, the protection of the army against the criminal attacks made on it from all sides."

In this connection General Gonse dwelt upon the danger to France of the "system of espionage so cleverly organized against her by foreigners," and said that, in spite of Esterhazy's statement, it was impossible for him to have written the bordereau, and still more impossible for him to have secured the information therein contained. He added that no traces of indiscretion were discovered during all the proceedings against Esterhazy.

Continuing, the witness deplored the fact that the court-martial of 1894 was held behind closed doors, adding:

"I regard it as a misfortune, as a great misfortune. The witnesses certainly said much more at the secret trial than they would have done at a public trial, and the judges had a better opportunity of forming an opinion, even though the public might retain doubts. I deplore it keenly."

General Gonse then denied that Esterhazy had received money from the Intelligence Department, and describing the "strange behavior of Dreyfus," and his "frequent acts of indiscretion," the witness begged the court to summon the secretary of the Minister of War, M. Ferret, who surprised the prisoner prying into the offices at a time when there was no business going on there.

The general defended Guenée, the spy, and referred to another spy as an "honorable man," whose name he could not give, as having furnished Military Headquarters with valuable information.

The general then proceeded to defend Du Paty de Clam from the insinuations of Colonel Picquart, and corroborated General Mercier's evidence in regard to the alleged confessions made to Captain Lebrun-Renault.

Replying to M. Demange, the witness admitted he had ordered Colonel Picquart not to concern himself with the handwriting of the bordereau when he commenced his investigations of Esterhazy.

"Then," asked M. Demange, sharply, "when you saw his handwritings were identical with the writing of the bordereau, did that make no impression on you?"

"Evidently," replied the witness, "the two handwritings had a great resemblance."

When Dreyfus was asked the regular question he said:

"I will reply directly to the secretary of the Minister of War, who said he saw me in the offices after service hours. As regards General Gonse, I am surprised that the general officer repeats dinner-table gossip. There is known to be insurmountable difficulty in introducing any one into the Ministry of War, and it is absolutely impossible for an officer to bring any one into the Ministry."

To this the general replied:

"No doubt it is difficult, but it is not impossible. The Ministry can be entered easily enough at certain hours. Dreyfus was in a position to know that." [Sensation.]

The Prisoner—I will reply to Secretary Ferret, who has told a lie. What I have to say to General Gonse is that every time a friend came to see me at the Ministry, even when a French officer, I was obliged to descend to the floor below, and even members of the Chamber of Deputies who called on me could not enter the Ministry. It was consequently absolutely impossible under ordinary circumstances for a subaltern to bring any one into the Ministry.

General Gonse declared that permits could easily be obtained.

At this point Colonel Picquart re-entered the witness box in order to reply to allegations as to the way he performed his duties. He denied a number of General Gonse's assertions regarding the arrests which the witness ordered. Picquart also described the extraordinary methods of investigation employed in the Intelligence Department by his predecessors.

Chapter XXXV.

DREYFUS ANSWERS HIS ACCUSERS

THE third week of the second trial by court-martial of Captain Dreyfus began on August 21st and developed sensational features.

Three points stood out prominently in the day's proceedings. They were Colonel Jouaust's display of partiality, the new attitude taken by Dreyfus, and the contemptible conduct of the last witness, Junck.

General Fabre, former Chief of the Fourth Bureau of the General Staff, was the first witness.

He said that in his official capacity he compared the handwriting of the bordereau with the writing of various officers in his bureau, including the handwriting of a probationer who had been in the bureau during the previous year and who had not favorably impressed his comrades. This probationer, Dreyfus, who was regarded as untrustworthy and insincere in his pretensions, was, according to the witness, equally disliked by his comrades and superiors. He was, Fabre added, constantly endeavoring by all sorts of means to learn the secrets of the plan of concentration of the Eastern Railway system, and in his anxiety to secure information neglected his duties. His official duties, the witness also said, placed it in Dreyfus's power to disclose the documents referred to in the bordereau. The witness could emphatically deny all Dreyfus had said on this subject. When Major Bertin showed the witness the bordereau the latter was struck with the resemblance of the caligraphy. Dreyfus was the only officer who made a bad impression in his bureau, and the opinions of the Chief of Staff and heads of other departments confirmed the witness's belief.

General Fabre, in conclusion, declared he was still as firmly convinced as in 1894 that the prisoner was the author of the bordereau.

After M. Demange had pointed out the discrepancies in Fabre's present statements and those he voiced in 1894, Colonel Jouaust invited Dreyfus to reply.

The prisoner said General Fabre quite correctly described the work on which he was engaged when a probationer, especially emphasizing that he had to keep the dossier relating to the concentration centres on the Eastern Railway system posted up. This was not a fictitious task. The prisoner's reply was made in calm, measured tones, and his frankness seemed to impress the judges favorably.

Colonel d'Abeville, former Deputy Chief of the Fourth Bureau, related how Fabre had showed him a photograph of an anonymous note in which the writer intimated to his correspondent, "evidently foreign to the army," that he had confidential documents to communicate. The witness told Fabre that the documents mentioned showed the writer could only be an artillery officer, belonging to the General Staff, who participated in the expedition of the Headquarters Staff in June and July, 1894. The position of Dreyfus corresponded with these conditions, and, "to their great surprise," a striking resemblance was apparent in the writings of Dreyfus and the anonymous letter.

The witness further declared that only a probationer could possess the information mentioned in the bordereau. It was not only because of the resemblance of the handwriting that suspicions were directed at Dreyfus, but because he was in a position to be acquainted with the documents enumerated.

M. Demange wished to know why Colonel d'Abeville said in 1894 that he thought it necessary to investigate the officers who participated in the expedition of the General Staff that year in order to discover the author of the bordereau.

To this question witness replied that he was induced to do so by the expression in the bordereau, "I am going to the manœuvres," for he considered the expedition of the General Staff equivalent to the manœuvres, although troops were not actually present.

Greater interest in the proceeding was manifested when the name of the next witness was announced, former Chief of the Detective Department Cochefert, who was present when Dreyfus underwent the dictation test in Du Paty de Clam's office.

M. Cochefert declared he knew absolutely nothing of the Dreyfus case when the Minister of War, General Mercier, summoned him to a conference on the subject of the bordereau and the suspicions in regard to Dreyfus. General Mercier, Cochefert continued, asked the witness's advice as to the procedure which ought to be followed, and introduced him to Du Paty de Clam. Subsequently, after M. Bertillon's report, the arrest of Dreyfus was decided upon.

Then the witness proceeded to describe the arrest and the famous scene of the dictation test, saying that from the first remark dropped by Du Paty de Clam the prisoner displayed evident uneasiness. Then, continued the ex-Chief of Detectives, Du Paty de Clam, placing his hand on the prisoner's shoulder, said:

"Captain Dreyfus, in the name of the Minister of War, I arrest you!"

At the time of the examination of Dreyfus the witness gained the impression that he might be guilty, and so reported when the Minister of War asked his opinion.

During this formal examination, Cochefert added, Dreyfus declared his innocence very violently, and declared that he did not know what they wanted or of what he was accused.

M. Gribelin, the principal archivist of the Headquarters Staff, was the next witness. He testified with great volubility, and expressed the opinion that when Dreyfus was arrested in 1894, he was enacting a rôle by systematically denying all the charges against him, even the most obvious and least important things, and in declaring himself ignorant of matters which should have been known to every officer of the General Staff.

The witness said he had cognizance of Dreyfus's relations with women. In support of this assertion he mentioned an alleged voluntary statement made by Mathieu Dreyfus, brother of the prisoner, in the witness's presence, that he had been obliged to pull his brother from the clutches of a woman living near the Champs Elysées.

In regard to the dictation test, the witness recalled Dreyfus's reply to Du Paty de Clam when the latter pointed out that his hands were shaking, namely: "My fingers are cold."

Replying to M. Demange, M. Gribelin admitted having mixed up Du Paty de Clam's and Henry's intrigues in favor of Esterhazy. This admission created a sensation.

It was by order of Colonel Henry, the witness added, that he, Gribelin, put on spectacles and went to the Rue de Douai to hand Esterhazy a letter, to which the latter was to reply "yes" or "no." It was also Henry who ordered witness to accompany Du Paty de Clam to Mont Souris Park at the time Du Paty de Clam masqueraded under a false beard.

The witness thought it would have been much simpler to have summoned Esterhazy to the Ministry of War, especially as it was known Mathieu Dreyfus was about to denounce him publicly.

M. Demange remarked that the denunciation of Mathieu Dreyfus could not well have been foreseen when these "romantic interviews" with Esterhazy were occurring, considering Mathieu himself had not then contemplated a denunciation.

M. Gribelin replied that at any rate it was known measures were in progress against Esterhazy.

M. Demange—Why, then, since it was a question of saving him, were false beards and blue spectacles resorted to?

M. Gribelin—You had better ask Du Paty de Clam when he comes here. [Laughter.]   Do not imagine it amused me.   [Renewed laughter.]

Colonel Picquart, after protesting against the manner in which his correspondence was tampered with, denied that he had given M. Leblois the slightest information regarding the secret dossier, and said the only document of the dossier revealed, and that was not by himself, was the "Cette canaille de D——" document, which had been utilized by the enemies of Dreyfus.   There was also the "liberateur" document, which was delivered to Esterhazy, "who used it to levy the most shameful blackmail on the Government."

Major Lauth followed.   He said that when the bordereau reached the Intelligence Department Henry was absolutely the only officer who knew the agent who furnished it, and was the only officer known to the agent. Henry, he explained, had appointments with the foreign spy in question only in the evenings at eight or nine o'clock, at various places, so it was imposible for Henry to hand the papers received to Colonel Sandherr the same evening.   Therefore, he took them home and brought them to the office in the morning.   Very often these appointments were kept on Saturday, and Major Lauth believed the packet containing the bordereau was handed to Henry on Saturday, September 22d, and was taken to the office on September 24th.

"One morning," said Lauth, "it may have been September 24th or another date, though it cannot matter much, I arrived at the office and was about to enter the room in which I usually work, when Colonel Henry, who was walking in the corridor, called to me and took me into his room. Captain Mathen arrived simultaneously. We had scarcely entered when Colonel Henry showed the packet received, and, exhibiting some pieces he had pasted together, said :

"' It is frightful. Just see what I have found in this packet.'

"We walked to a window, and all three began to read the contents of a paper, which was none other than the bordereau. We discussed who could be the author.

"I must add that M. Gribelin entered the room and was informed regarding the document. At the same time the bordereau was only shown to Colonel Sandherr half or three-quarters of an hour later, when he arrived."

Next, discussing the *petit bleu*, Major Lauth said it reached Colonel Picquart inclosed in a packet, early in March. Incidentally the witness mentioned the mission to Nancy on which Henry went, and said that while he was absent his wife came to the Intelligence Department to ask for his whereabouts, as she knew nothing of his departure.

"It was the same with all the officers of the department," said Lauth. "Our families never knew where we were going when we were sent on a mission, and it was through the department that they corresponded with us. That proves that things were not conducted in the Fourth Bureau as alleged by Colonel Picquart, and the officers were not so negligent and careless as he has asserted.

"I declare," said Lauth, "that if, by inspiring or writing it I had a share in any way whatever in the perpetration of the Henry forgery, I should have avowed it the day Henry committed suicide. I am not even now afraid of the razor, nor the rope of Lemercier-Picard, nor even of a broken-glass omelette."

At the instance of M. Demange, Colonel Picquart again described the alterations of the *petit bleu*, and declared that the last time he saw it, the day before he started on his mission, the *petit bleu* was still in the same condition as when Major Lauth handed it to him in November, 1897. When Picquart saw it in the possession of General Pellieux, former Minister of War, it seemed to him (Picquart) that the handwriting had been somewhat modified, and at the Tavernier inquiry he noticed that alterations of quite a serious character had been made. Ruled lines had been erased. Moreover, experiments showed the address had been written in ink made of gall-nuts, while a superimposed word was written in ink made of logwood.

Replying to the president of the court, Major Lauth said that when he photographed the *petit bleu* he did not notice any sign of erasure.

Colonel Picquart said the plate taken by Major Lauth bore no traces of erasure. The photograph alone had been tampered with.

Colonel Jouaust—Was there an expert examination?

Colonel Picquart—Yes. It was a searching inquiry. Besides, the dossier in the Tavernier inquiry can be referred to.

Captain Junck followed. He said he was a probationer simultaneously with Dreyfus, but in another department of the War Office. He saw the prisoner a great deal, and detailed conversations in which, he alleged, Dreyfus spoke of great sums he had lost in gambling and how much he had spent on women.

"One day," the witness proceeded, "when we were visiting the Concours Hippique, we met three women who bowed to us. Dreyfus returned the greeting, and I said to him: 'Well, for a married man, you have nice acquaintances.' He replied that they were old friends of his bachelorhood, and, pointing to one of them, said her name was Valtesse, and that she had a house on the Champs Elysées, where she gave nice parties, where pretty women were to be met, and where there was much gambling. Dreyfus also boasted of his large means, and spoke with great relish of his comfortable house and travels."

The witness, continuing, said Dreyfus was well acquainted with the scheme for the concentration of troops, and could trace it on any map, as most of the other probationers could.

The witness then detailed the work of the different bureaus, and proceeded to demonstrate that the probationers were cognizant of the plans for the transportation and concentration of the troops, and how Dreyfus was ordered to draw up a report on the German artillery, comparing it with the French artillery, and having access to all the necessary documents.

In regard to the Madagascar note, Dreyfus, Junck claimed, told the witness that his cousin had procured him interesting information.

Captain Junck then spoke of the efforts of Dreyfus to secure the Firing Manual, and discussed the theory that Henry might have divulged the documents in the bordereau. Such a supposition, the captain declared, was utterly impossible.

Later, the witness corroborated the statement that Colonel Picquart proposed post-marking the *petit bleu* with the view of proving its genuineness.

Dreyfus, after being asked the usual question, replied:

" I will not speak to the witness of private confidences he has made to me. If Captain Junck's ideas of honor allow him to divulge private conversation, mine do not. I have clean hands, and I will keep them clean. But there are a number of facts to which I will refer. I will speak first in regard to all the losses it is said I sustained at the club at Mans. I declare I was never a member of the Civil Club at Mans, never visited it, and, consequently, never gambled there. I am convinced that the members of the club are very respectable, and ask you simply to have an inquiry made, in order to know if I am speaking the truth.

" In regard to the lectures in the offices of the Headquarters Staff, at which it is asserted I was present, they occurred in December, 1893. I was absent at that time, and consequently did not attend the lectures."

The prisoner then proceeded to show that in July, 1894, the probationers were informed by an official circular that they were to pass a period of probation in the army, the first-yearers in August and September, the second-yearers in October, November, and December, therefore, at a period when there were no manœuvres.

Regarding the officers directing the dispatch of troops at various points, Dreyfus dwelt upon the fact that he, at that time, was on a mission and was not at the manœuvres at all.

" We must be precise," Dreyfus added, " and not play upon words. In August, 1894, the second-year probationers knew definitely that they were to go to various regiments in October, November, and December, and that consequently they would not attend the manœuvres."

Chapter XXXVI.

LABORI RESUMES THE DEFENCE OF DREYFUS

MAÎTRE LABORI, leading counsel for the defence, who was murderously assaulted on August 14th, was able to resume the defence of Captain Dreyfus when the trial was resumed on August 22d.

The arrival of M. Labori at the Lycée was the signal for scenes of extraordinary enthusiasm. At 6:15 A.M. three carriages, preceded by a number of bicyles, drove up. The first carriage contained M. Labori and his wife and physicians. The others contained friends of the lawyer and some police inspectors. The crowd about the Lycée Building rushed up to M. Labori's carriage, and a number of persons eagerly thrust their hands through the windows to greet the distinguished lawyer.

When M. Labori descended, he was surrounded by friends, and a hundred hands pressed his, while he was assailed with all sorts of questions, to which he smilingly replied:

"I am getting on well, my friends, thank you, thank you."

As M. Labori, still accompanied by Madame Labori and a physician, entered the court-room the audience greeted him by standing up, and there was a general roar of applause, accompanied by the clapping of hands, which was distinctly heard in the streets.

Tears filled the eyes of the wounded man, who was evidently deeply affected by the warm welcome accorded him. Among those who greeted M. Labori were Generals Billot and Mercier, who courteously inquired as to his condition. The lawyer looked very well, considering his recent experience. He walked quite briskly, but held his left arm close to his side, in order not to disturb the wound. He was conducted to a light, well-cushioned armchair, instead of one of the ordinary cane-bottom chairs, behind the table set apart for the lawyers.

Madame Labori, who entered the court-room ahead of her husband, also received a hearty greeting. As she took a seat in court she was surrounded by friends, who overwhelmed her with congratulations on her husband's recovery, to which she smilingly responded.

Dreyfus entered the court-room soon afterward, and, after saluting the judges in the usual manner, he turned to M. Labori with outstretched hand, and a smile of keen pleasure lighted up his pale and usually impassive features. The lawyer took the prisoner's hand and shook it warmly, whereupon Dreyfus gave him another look of gratitude and took his seat in front of the counsel's table with his back toward them.

Colonel Jouaust next read from a paper an address to M. Labori, the tone of the president being quite sympathetic. The lawyer made an impassioned reply. He was deeply affected and his voice was clear, though not so strong as before the outrage. He was very nervous and excited, and swayed to and fro as he delivered his reply, which profoundly impressed his hearers.

The first witness was M. Grenier, the former prefect of Belfort. His testimony was favorable to Dreyfus, inasmuch as his deposition was distinctly hostile to Esterhazy.

Major Rollin of the Intelligence Department was asked during the course of his testimony by M. Labori how a certain document, of a later date than Mercier's ministry, came into General Mercier's possession. Rollin said it was not his business to explain, but counsel insisted, asking whose business it was.

Finally M. Labori asked Colonel Jouaust to request General Mercier to explain.

The general arose and said he declined to answer.

M. Labori insisted emphatically, but Mercier still refused to answer, and Major Carriere, the Government Commissary, supported him, on the ground that the examination was entering upon a matter which ought not, in the interests of the country, to be discussed publicly.

M. Labori then declared in a loud voice that he would reserve to himself the right to take the necessary measure to obtain the desired information.

The next point was made by Dreyfus in his reply to Major Rollin. The latter had remarked that all the prisoner's papers were seized when his rooms were searched in 1894, and Colonel Jouaust said that certain pages from his text-book, "The School of War," were found missing. To this the prisoner retorted:

"Not in 1894, Colonel!"

This caused some sensation, as the obvious interpretation was that the pages were torn out at the War Office, and that then the fact was used against him as an insinuation that he had communicated the missing pages to foreign agents.

M. Ferret, who was alleged to have caught Dreyfus prying into the work of some of his fellow-officers during their absence, then testified that toward the end of 1893, on returning from his luncheon, at an hour the officers were usually out, he found Dreyfus in the Fourth Bureau, standing with a stranger, a civilian, at the table, consulting a document which seemed to the witness to be connected with the transportation of troops.

M. Demange—Why did you not give this evidence in 1894?

Witness said he regretted he had overlooked it.

The prisoner protested against such statements, which, he said, were nothing but "vile insinuations," concocted by a former Minister of War (General Mercier).   [Great sensation.]

"I never went into my office," continued Dreyfus, "at any other time than the hours of duty.   I declare it was impossible, or at least most difficult, for a civilian to enter the offices of the Ministry of War."

Dreyfus added that while his wife was at Houlgate, Normandy, in August or September, 1894, he happened to go to his office at noon, though the usual hour was two o'clock.

Colonel Jouaust questioned Dreyfus relative to his hours of duties and the difficulty of introducing a stranger into the offices, after which General Gonse asked for permission to speak in order to complete his evidence.   He said he received a letter on August 21st from M. Le Chateller, Chief Engineer of the Department of Roads and Bridges, and the general read a letter in which Le Chateller said:

"During six or seven years I had a permit for the Ministry of War, and went there at least a hundred times.   I did not have to show my permit more than ten times.   On another occasion I was accompanied by a friend, who entered without any other formality than opening the gate and saluting the sentry."   [Laughter.]

General Gonse read another letter of similar purport, and Dreyfus said:

"That rule was strict. The letters only prove that certain persons did not observe it."

M. Demange—It also proves that since the Ministry of War was so easily entered, others besides officers could easily procure information. [Murmurs of dissent.]

Lieutenant-Colonel Bertin, who was the head of Dreyfus's office in 1894, was the next witness, and showed himself to be a most virulent enemy of the prisoner. He had evidently learned his testimony by heart, and declared it in a strident, aggressive tone, which grated upon the ears of the audience. Some of his remarks, particularly his declaration that he was convinced of Dreyfus's guilt by M. Bertillon's chart and his introduction of Esterhazy's statements against Dreyfus, elicited general smiles in court.

The witness testified to the prisoner's great zeal at first, and said that later this was replaced by great carelessness in matters of detail.

"In the face of this," said Bertin, "I gradually ceased to consider him an assistant. He left an enormous amount of uncompleted work. Thus, after devoting much time to initiating him into the secrets of the concentration of troops on the Eastern Railway system in time of war, I did not receive any service in exchange."

Witness added that the reports he gave Dreyfus when he left were such that he could never enter the Railroad Department. Proceeding, the witness reiterated that Dreyfus was in a position to acquaint himself with the questions of the Eastern Railroad's mobilization, and described a conversation which he had with Dreyfus in 1893, which, in the opinion of the witness, threw a curious light on Dreyfus's idea of the Fatherland.

Lieutenant-Colonel Bertin also spoke of the comparisons of the handwritings, and then, turning to the prisoner's attitude at the court-martial of 1894, he said it painfully impressed him, and he was convinced of the guilt of Dreyfus by the evidence of M. Bertillon.

Referring to his interviews with M. Scheurer-Kestner, formerly a vice-president of the senate, "whom I always regarded as an honorable man, obeying the dictates of his conscience," Lieutenant-Colonel Bertin controverted part of Colonel Picquart's evidence on the subject, and at the conclusion of his deposition the witness declared he never ordered Dreyfus to procure information concerning the entire network of railroads, "which the prisoner sought to acquire from Captain Cuignet."

13

Replying to questions on the subject of the alleged untimely visit of Dreyfus to his office, witness said that the plans were kept in his office, and that Dreyfus knew the word necessary to open the press containing them.

At this juncture the clerk of the court read a letter from M. Scheurer-Kestner excusing himself from being unable to attend the session of the court. The letter referred to the steps taken by Mathieu Dreyfus to secure the rehabilitation of his brother, and described the writer's investigations and how it was only when Esterhazy's handwriting was shown him that his hesitation ended. The letter also described the moments of anguish the writer experienced during the course of the campaign, and dwelt on the opinion expressed in the judgment of the Court of Cassation and the confessions of Esterhazy that he was the writer of the bordereau.

In conclusion the letter said:

"You will permit an old Alsatian, Monsieur le President, to express the sentiment that the hour of justice will soon strike in the interest of the army, of justice, and of the country." [Great sensation.]

M. Demange reminded Lieutenant-Colonel Bertin of a remark he made to M. Ferdinand Scheurer-Kestner, namely:

"There are only five of us who know this terrible secret. One out of the five must betray it before you can know anything."

Counsel asked if the secret was not that Dreyfus was innocent?

Lieutenant-Colonel Bertin—Oh, no, no!

M. Demange—According to the terms of the conversation?

Lieutenant-Colonel Bertin (energetically)—No, no; and I'll tell you why. I have never concealed two things from any members of the Scheurer-Kestner family: Firstly, that M. Scheurer-Kestner would be doing a great service if his efforts resulted in establishing the innocence of a French officer. Secondly, that I was convinced of the guilt of Dreyfus. [Sensation.]

M. Demange—Did you not once make the following remark: "'This Jew was a thrust at Headquarters, and we had to get rid of him'?"

Lieutenant-Colonel Bertin—No, never. I absolutely deny it. When I was in the War Office the Jewish question was never raised. Dreyfus was regarded as a comrade. I confided all my secrets to him and gave him the password of my locker.

Bertin's testimony was concluded with a sharp passage-at-arms between him and M. Labori. The latter declared that Bertin himself, by remarks which he had made upon a certain occasion, convinced the lawyer of the innocence of Dreyfus. Counsel then recalled other words used by Bertin to the effect that M. Demange was counsel for the German embassy because he had defended others accused of espionage.

The witness admitted the correctness of M. Labori's quotation, whereupon M. Demange jumped up and protested against Lieutenant-Colonel Bertin's statement. Sharp words were exchanged, until Colonel Jouaust intervened and refused to allow any further discussion of a matter outside of the case.

Several minor witnesses followed.

Major Gendron was called to testify regarding an Austrian woman, Mme. Dely. He said he had taken tea at her house on a single occasion, and that he thereafter confined himself to exchanging a few polite words with her when they met, though the gallant officer asserted that the lady urged his revisiting her home. He thought that neither the age nor the beauty of the lady accounted for her stylish mode of dressing, nor for the mystery of her existence, nor for the presence of her child. All this, it appears, told the witness that he was dealing with an adventuress. He heard that she had fine acquaintances, including Dreyfus, and, in view of the fact that in such companionship Dreyfus was liable to commit some light, imprudent action, witness informed Lieutenant-Colonel Bertin of his fears.

Major Bosse, Captain Boulanger, Colonel Jeannel, and Major Maistre all testified. In the main their evidence was uninteresting.

Lieutenant-Colonel Jeannel repeated evidence which he had given before the Court of Cassation. He was very hard on Dreyfus, but while testifying he scarcely once looked the prisoner in the face.

Colonel Jeannel during his cross-examination threw some light upon the question of the Firing Manual, which, he said, he lent Dreyfus in 1894.

M. Demange wanted to know the exact date, and Colonel Jeannel said he believed it was in July, adding "in 1894." That would have been a point calculated to weaken the proof against Dreyfus, counsel pointing out that Colonel Jeannel was not examined in 1894, and asking the cause of this irregularity. The date of the bordereau was given as April of that year, namely, before Colonel Jeannel lent the Firing Manual.

The prisoner said that in 1894 he insisted at both the preliminary examination and at the court-martial that Colonel Jeannel should be examined.

"I obtained no satisfaction," Dreyfus added. "I was, however, sure of my facts. Colonel Jeannel's memory must be playing him false. Perhaps the confusion arises from the fact that I asked him to lend me the German Firing Manual."

Colonel Jouaust—Do you remember that, Colonel Jeannel?

Colonel Jeannel—No.

At this point M. Labori expressed surprise that it was not thought necessary in 1894 to examine a witness who now (August 22d), "out of pure caprice and for the convenience of the prosecution" had become an excellent witness. The court, counsel added, would deduce its own opinion.

The last witness of the day, Captain Maistre, read a letter from an officer, now at Nantes, affirming that while he was on the General Staff as a probationer, at the same time as Dreyfus, the latter told the officer of his visit to Alsace-Lorraine, and recounted how he had followed the German army manœuvres on foot and on horseback.

This was intended to show Dreyfus was not telling the truth when he denied having been present at any time at the manœuvres in Alsace-Lorraine.

Another part of Captain Maistre's evidence proved to be in favor of Dreyfus. In contradiction of other witnesses who declared Dreyfus frequently stayed at the office prying into other officers' duties, Captain Maistre declared that Dreyfus was disinclined to work, and often left the office before the regular time.

The prisoner, in the tone of calm moderation which again distinguished his utterances, replied to Captain Maistre's allegations, and added, with reference to M. Beaurepaire's accusations, that the latter's immorality would ere long be demonstrated before the court-martial. The court then rose for the day.

Maître Labori was immediately surrounded by friends, nearly every one in court wishing to shake hands with him. He was cheerful and smiling, and had a few well-chosen words for every one.   Madame Labori shared in the admiration expressed for her husband.   The brilliant lawyer returned home in a carriage as he had come, with an escort of two mounted gendarmes.   Policemen, gendarmes, and detectives were also distributed along the road, as a precaution against a fresh outrage.

Apart from the salutations of his personal friends, there was no demonstration while M. Labori was either going to or coming from the Lycée.

Chapter XXXVII.

GENERAL GONSE CORNERED BY M. LABORI

MAÎTRE LABORI, leading counsel for the defence, and Madame Labori were present in court when the trial of Dreyfus was resumed on August 23d. The session was comparatively uneventful. The depositions were not productive of any really thrilling incidents. Much of the time was occupied in reading the testimony of Esterhazy and Mlle. Pays before the Court of Cassation, during which many of the audience left the court.

M. Labori again distinguished himself in laying bare the weak points of the evidence. He was less fierce, however, than yesterday, though quite aggressive enough to arouse the latent hostility of the judges, which showed itself in various little ways.

During some of the depositions M. Labori appeared very nervous. He was unable to remain still an instant, twitching his fingers and shaking papers in his hands. He was almost too impatient to wait till the witnesses concluded their testimony.

The only dangerous opponent of Dreyfus was General Gonse, who mounted the stage with a quick step and apparently light heart. But he left it badly mauled by M. Labori.

General Gonse began by declaring he came to defend his honor against those "drivelling" against him. But when his cross-examination was finished he returned to his seat with his honor worse off than before, for M. Labori had driven him into a corner on the attempts of the General Staff to shield Esterhazy, and had shown that the General Staff, for which Gonse was responsible, had engineered Esterhazy's escape from the hands of justice.

Comptroller Ray, the first witness called, gave his impressions of Dreyfus, which harmonized with those of the generals who have already testified. But, the witness was unable to give a single specific fact to substantiate his impressions.

Major Drevieli testified to a long string of similar insinuations. He referred to Dreyfus's alleged boastfulness of his money and the prisoner's irregular attendance at his office.

After Dreyfus had rebutted one or two of this witness's statements, Major Du Chatelet was called. He described the alleged confidences of Dreyfus in regard to women and gambling.

Maître Demange expressed surprise at the fact that the witness had not mentioned this at the court-martial of 1894, to which Major Du Chatelet replied:

"What! Here was a man accused of one of the most heinous crimes, and you think I ought to have retailed his confidences in regard to women and gambling. Nonsense!"

Dreyfus briefly corrected some of Du Chatelet's statements, and then M. Dubreuil, who described himself as a private gentleman, took the stand. He testified as to how he was introduced to Dreyfus by a certain M. Bodson, at whose house the witness afterward dined in company with Dreyfus and a German attaché, whose name he did not remember.

Continuing, M. Dubreuil said he was greatly astonished at the "suspicious familiarity" between the attaché and Dreyfus, and that, perceiving they disapproved of his presence, M. Dubreuil ceased his visits to M. Bodson. When the latter asked the reason of this, saying, according to the witness, that Dreyfus was the friend and even the lover of his wife, and asking witness's advice as to how to get rid of her, witness asked M. Bodson if he had proofs, and Bodson is said to have replied:

"Proofs! Yes, I have even proofs enough to drive Dreyfus out of the French army."

Witness, however, was unable to learn what M. Bodson referred to.

When he was pressed to describe more clearly the alleged German attaché, M. Dubreuil replied that he did not know his name, but was told he was attached to the German Embassy.

M. Labori—Was he a military or civil attaché?

M. Dubreuil—I do not remember. I do not know. Let Maître Labori put himself in my place [laughter], and he will see the difficulty of remembering the name of a stranger he met thirteen years ago.

Dreyfus protested excitedly against the evidence of M. Dubreuil, who is a Parisian friend of M. de Beaurepaire; but Colonel Jouaust exhorted

him to be calm, promising the prisoner a chance to reply.   This arrived
shortly afterward, and Dreyfus thundered out:

"I won't speak here of M. or Madame Bodson, except to say that my
relations with Madame Bodson ceased in 1886 or 1887, since when I have
never seen her.   I wish simply to assert that the witness is lying.   I
never dined at M. Bodson's with any civil or military attaché.   The matter must be cleared up.   People must produce definite facts here, and not
mere tittle-tattle.   The name of the person with whom I am alleged to
have dined must be ascertained.   It must be known here who is lying
and who is speaking the truth."

Major Le Rond, a professor of the Military School, described his relations with Esterhazy and Picquart, telling how Esterhazy attended the
artillery manœuvres of 1894 and 1896, and touching upon Picquart's subsequent inquiry as to whether in 1894 Esterhazy could have obtained
secret documents relating to new inventions, to which the witness replied
in the negative.

The major added that during this interview Picquart said he spoke in
behalf of the Minister of War.   The witness added:

"Colonel Picquart's manner in speaking of Esterhazy left me so little
doubt that proofs of Esterhazy's guilt existed that I asked if he had been
arrested or was about to be taken into custody.   Colonel Picquart replied
that he had not yet obtained positive proof, but had the gravest presumptions."

Major Le Rond also said that when Colonel Picquart questioned him
in 1896 as to the possibility of Esterhazy's possessing knowledge of artillery matters, the witness replied that Esterhazy seemed anxious to learn
something about artillery, but his questions, while displaying intelligence
and alertness of mind, showed comparatively little acquaintance on the
subject.   Esterhazy, he added, could only have consulted the Firing Manual through the witness, and had he done so his action, though not irregular, would have remained in the major's memory.

Here Colonel Picquart jumped up and denied that he mentioned espionage to Major Le Rond, or that he spoke in behalf of the Minister of
War.   But the major adhered to his statements, and asserted that Picquart's memory was playing him false.

At this juncture Colonel Jouaust announced that it was Esterhazy's turn to speak, but that, as he was not present, the evidence which he gave before the Court of Cassation would be read.

The clerk of the court accordingly read Esterhazy's deposition.

The chief aim of Esterhazy, in his testimony before the Court of Cassation, delivered January 24, 1899, was to show that in 1897–98 he was protected by Du Paty de Clam, Henry, and their subordinates, acting under orders from Generals de Boisdeffre, Gonse, and de Pellieux. He refused to make any declaration in regard to the bordereau, in language which was interpreted against him by the Court of Cassation in its judgment regarding a revision of the Dreyfus case.

M. Labori asked that three letters addressed by Esterhazy to the President of the Republic should be read.

The following are passages from those letters. In the first letter he said:

"My house is illustrious enough in the annals of French history and in those of the great European causes, for the Government of my country to take care not to allow my name to be dragged in the mud. I address myself, therefore, to the supreme head of the army and to the President of the Republic, and I ask him to put an end to the scandal, as he can and ought to do.

"If I should have the sorrow not to be listened to by the supreme head of my country, my precautions are taken for my appeal to reach the ears of my heraldic chief, to the sovereign of the Esterhazy family, the Emperor of Germany. He is a soldier, and will know how to set the honor of a soldier, even an enemy, above the mean equivocal intrigues of politics. He will dare to speak out loud and strong to defend the honor of ten generations of soldiers. It is for you, as President of the Republic, to judge if you should force me to carry the question into that region. An Esterhazy fears not anything or anybody, if not God."

In his second letter Esterhazy said:

"I am at bay and compelled to use all means in my power. A generous woman, who warned me of the horrible plot woven against me by friends of Dreyfus, with the assistance of Colonel Picquart, has since been able to procure for me among other documents the photograph of a paper which she succeeded in getting out of that officer.

"This paper, stolen in a foreign legation by Colonel Picquart, is most compromising for certain diplomatic personages.   If I neither obtain support nor justice, and if my name come to be pronounced, this photograph, which is to-day quite safe abroad, will be immediately published."

In the third letter he said:

"This document is protection for me, since it proves the scoundrelism of Dreyfus, and is a danger for my country, because its publication, with the facsimile of writing, will force France to humiliate herself or to declare war.   You, who are above empty quarrels in which my honor is at stake, do not leave me under the obligation of choosing between two alternatives equally horrible.   Compel the Pontius Pilate of politics to make a clear, precise declaration instead of manœuvring to retain the voice of friends of Barabbas.

"All letters that I have written will shortly reach the hands of one of my relatives, who has had the honor this summer to receive two emperors.   What will the whole world think when it learns of the cowardly, cold cruelty with which I have been allowed to struggle in my agony without help, without advice?   My blood will be upon your heads."

General Gonse said he desired to reply to Esterhazy's statements. During the course of his observations, the general said Esterhazy's allegation that he was the right-hand man of the General Staff was absolutely false.

The general then proceeded to refer to his avoidance of Esterhazy during the Zola trial.

"I considered him to be a compromising person," said the witness, "and I was not wrong.   If Esterhazy was permitted to go free at the time of the judicial inquiry, it was by order of General Saussier, who would not accept the advice of the General Staff nor of the officers under him, however high their rank.   It was Major Du Paty de Clam alone who compromised the entire Headquarters Staff by his imprudence.   [Sensation.]

"If I now say so for the first time it is because the case against Du Paty de Clam had been dismissed.   I could not have spoken earlier without seeming to accuse a prisoner."

The general then attempted to explain the intervention of the Headquarters Staff in the choice of Esterhazy's witnesses at the time of his prosecution by Colonel Picquart, and said he, the witness, was convinced

Du Paty de Clam was only connected with the late Lieutenant-Colonel Henry and not with Esterhazy.

M. Labori said he desired to show if General Gonse did not consider himself in some measure responsible for the proceedings of Du Paty de Clam.

The general replied in the negative, and added that he was conscious that he had always done his duty. The witness admitted, however, that Du Paty de Clam was not altogether innocent of a share in the appearance of the "Dixi" article, which appeared in the *Libre Parole*, and gave the public the first information regarding the character of the secret dossier and the intrigues against Colonel Picquart.

When General Gonse was asked what he thought of Du Paty de Clam's interviews with Maître Tezenas, Esterhazy's counsel, he replied:

"Esterhazy was a sort of special prisoner. He retained his liberty, not because he was under the protection of the General Staff, but because General Saussier so ordered."

Thereupon M. Labori remarked that General Saussier acted in this matter because he had been deceived by the Headquarters Staff in regard to Esterhazy, adding:

"That is a point which it is very important to emphasize."

The general admitted that were two interviews between Du Paty de Clam and M. Tezenas, after which, witness said, he ordered them to stop.

General de Boisdeffre at this point took the occasion to re-defend himself.

"I ask leave," he said, "only to tell the court that I give the most absolute contradiction to Esterhazy's evidence."

Then turning to the counsel for defence, the general added:

"If I were not here as a witness I would ask permission to say, in regard to these falsehoods, that I despise them and repel them with the scorn they deserve."

General Lebelin de Dionne, governor of the Military College, then testified to Dreyfus's character at college. The prisoner, he said, displayed great intelligence, but had a deplorable temper. He recalled a remark of Dreyfus that the people of Alsace-Lorraine would be much happier under German rule than under the rule of France.

The prisoner, referring to the recriminations mentioned by General

Lebelin de Dionne, explained that during his first year at the Military College he attained very high marks, that the second year he almost held his place, when, he added, he heard that a member of the Examining Board had declared at a board meeting that, without knowing the pupils, he put mark 5 opposite the name of Dreyfus, simply because they did not want a Jew on the Headquarters Staff. The prisoner thought that his protests against this would, therefore, be readily understood.

Regarding the alleged remarks about Alsace-Lorraine, Dreyfus declared that the statement was the very opposite of his real sentiments.

M. Lanquety, a mining engineer of Boulogne, who told the Court of Cassation that he had seen Dreyfus at Brussels during the summer of 1894, followed. The witness said he could not now swear to when he saw Dreyfus there.

The prisoner, rising, declared that it was in 1886, at the time of the Amsterdam exhibition, adding that was the only time he visited Brussels.

"I met you, M. Lanquety," said Dreyfus, "at a restaurant in St. Hubert Arcade. We exchanged a few words."

M. Lanquety admitted that the prisoner's statement was true.

Chapter XXXVIII.

GENERALS GO DOWN UNDER COUNSEL'S FIRE

WHEN the trial of Captain Dreyfus was resumed at the Lycée on August 24th, Colonel Jouaust, president of the court, ordered that the evidence given by M. Penot, a friend of the late Colonel Sandherr, chief of the Intelligence Department, be read.

It was to the effect that Colonel Sandherr said the Dreyfus family offered him 150,000 francs on condition that he would clear Dreyfus.

Maître Demange, for the defence, disposed of this allegation by reading the actual note on the subject written by Sandherr, thereby proving that the Colonel's remarks had been distorted, Dreyfus's brothers only having said:

"We are convinced of the innocence of our brother, and will spend our entire fortune to discover the truth."

The testimony of the first witness of the day, M. Dinolle, a former official of the Government, was also in favor of Dreyfus, as it was in direct contradiction of what M. Dubreuil deposed yesterday regarding the alleged intimacy of Dreyfus with the German attaché at the house of M. Bodson, a mutual friend.

The president of the court then called the next witness, Colonel Maurel-Pries, who was president of the Dreyfus court-martial in 1894.

As M. Labori lashed him with pointed questions the colonel hesitated, and then answered in a short, choppy manner, and when M. Labori finally disposed of him, the witness left the platform with the pale face and scared look of a man who had been awakened from a nightmare.

The counsel had drawn from the colonel a confession that the secret dossier was communicated to the judges of the court-martial of 1894 by Colonel Du Paty de Clam. This avowal produced a sensation in court, and Maurel-Pries's declaration that he only read one of the documents did not affect the main fact, while his protestation that the reading of the document had no effect upon him, as his mind was already made up, was nullified by his subsequent declaration that this one document sufficed to convince him.

M. Labori pointed out the contradictions in the evidence of the officers of the Headquarters Staff regarding the importance and nature of the contents of the bordereau, and asked General Mercier where Dreyfus could have obtained particulars about the hydro-pneumatic brake?

The general hotly objected to being asked to repeat his evidence, and M. Labori, equally warmly, said:

"I am only asking for definite statements."

Mercier then said he thought Dreyfus might have had cognizance of the brake at Bourges, adding:

"In any case, he had a better chance to obtain such knowledge than Esterhazy could possibly have had."

M. Labori—General Mercier says, "Dreyfus might have had cognizance." I desire to emphasize that expression. We shall now prove Dreyfus could not have had cognizance of the brake.

Counsel proceeded to demonstrate how rigorously the secret of the construction of the brake was guarded, and asked why, in 1894, the charges regarding the Robin shells were not dwelt upon?

General Mercier—That arises from the simple fact that it was not known until 1896 or 1897 that information on the subject was being divulged. The existence of treachery in regard to the distribution of heavy artillery among the army corps was unknown until 1896.

The passages-at-arms between M. Labori and General Mercier were followed with the keenest interest. Both men were wary and mutual suspicious of each other, and there was considerable acerbity, Colonel Jouaust at times finding difficulty in preventing the discussion from wandering outside legal paths.

Continuing, M. Labori asked why General Mercier did not have a report prepared regarding the confessions Dreyfus is alleged to have made to Captain Lebrun-Renault.

General Mercier—The question of the confessions was of no importance, as a revision of the case seemed impossible.

M. Labori—What does General Mercier think of Esterhazy and the part he played?

General Mercier—I do not know Esterhazy, and I do not think about him at all.

M. Labori—Did he know you at his trial in 1898?

General Mercier—No.

Colonel Jouaust—General Mercier was not Minister of War then.

M. Labori—This is most interesting. General Mercier declares he knows nothing of the trial of 1898.

General Mercier—I know nothing of it. I leave that to the court-martial which tried Esterhazy. I have only to answer in court for my acts, and I refuse you the right to question me about my thoughts.

Colonel Jouaust, addressing M. Labori, said:

"You are reverting to the evidence of General Mercier?"

M. Labori—My object in interrogating the witness is to revert to his evidence.

General Mercier—I protest against the word "interrogating," for I am not a prisoner.

"Interrogatory," in French law, is generally applied to the examination of an accused person by a magistrate.

M. Labori—It is not a question of "interrogatory"; I used the word in the most respectful sense. Will General Mercier say what he means by the charge preferred against the partisans of Dreyfus of having spent 35,000,000 francs? What was this sum used for? The amount is simply ridiculous.

General Mercier—I might just as well ask you.

M. Labori—Do you mean to suggest that it was spent in advertisements and in buying consciences?

General Mercier—I say nothing whatever.

Counsel next wished to know why the bordereau was communicated to the court-martial of 1894, when it was considered impossible to show the other documents of the secret dossier.

General Mercier—Because the bordereau was not dated, not signed, and its place of origin could be concealed.

M. Labori pointed out that the place of origin had been mentioned in court, and then asked for explanations in regard to the perpetration of the 1894 forgery.

The cross-examination of General Mercier became more and more heated, and so rapid that it was difficult to follow, and many of the answers were confusing. As the questions of counsel touched upon the secret dossier and a certain document in blue pencil, General Gonse, General Roget, M. Gribelin, and Major Lauth also participated in the discussion, which almost degenerated into a wrangle.

Major Lauth said he believed a clue to the blue-pencil document existed before the trial of 1894, and M. Labori asked why, in that case, it was not produced at the trial, since it incriminated the prisoner?

General Mercier said he did not know of this clue, and Major Lauth disclaimed all responsibility in the matter, as he was not connected with the preliminary inquiry.

General Gonse said the document had been in the possession of Colonel Sandherr, [sensation] and it was by him placed in the secret dossier for comparison with other papers.

M. Labori asked for explanations in regard to the commentary on the secret dossier, and General Mercier admitted he destroyed it in 1897.

General Gonse, who was questioned on the same subject, declared that it was by order of General de Boisdeffre that he returned the commentary to General Mercier.

Answering further questions, Mercier said the Panizzardi telegram was not communicated to the court-martial in 1894. He was ordered by General de Boisdeffre not to include it in the secret dossier.

Counsel next discussed the three-page document, claiming that the false rendering of the Panizzardi telegram was. to correct it and point directly to Dreyfus as the traitor.

Mercier asked to be allowed to converse with General Chanoine before attempting to explain. General Chanoine thereupon advanced and explained about the document, which had been handed him by General Mercier. He said he noticed inaccuracies in it, and resolved not to use it. Witness, however, had been carried away in testifying, and read a page of the document, and it was after a friendly conversation with Maître Labori that he read the entire document in court, at General Mercier's request, and returned him the document.

General Mercier acknowledged the accuracy of General Chanoine's statement, adding that it was Colonel Du Paty de Clam who gave him the document.

Counsel had the document reread, and referred to the two versions of the two telegrams of November 2d, one designating Dreyfus as communicating documents to Germany.   M. Labori pointed out that M. Paleologue of the Foreign Office denied that the Ministry of Foreign Affairs had communicated this version, and asked why General Mercier had received it through Du Paty de Clam.

At this juncture General Roget mounted the platform and expressed surprise at this "idle controversy being resumed." [Cries of "Oh! Oh!"]

The general asked that Major Maton, who assisted in deciphering the telegram, be called, and counsel protested against the application of the word "idle" to any questions he thought proper to ask.

General Chanoine said that he communicated the document to General Roget, while enjoining absolute privacy on the subject.

When asked if he accepted responsibility for the document, General Chanoine replied in the affirmative, adding, however, the admission that he had made a mistake.

Colonel Jouaust intimated that the court ought to take no notice of the document in question.

Dreyfus here gave a detailed story of how he employed his time at Bourges from October, 1889, to February, 1890.   He said that as he was preparing for his examinations he had no time to go to cafés or to think of anything outside of his duties.   This was a reply to General Mercier's assertion that he could have learned the secret of the hydro-pneumatic brake there.   The prisoner said:

"I was promoted to be a captain on September 12, 1889, and remained at Bourges from October, 1889, to February, 1890, when the written examination at the Military College began.   I was then called to Paris, obtained two months' leave, was married in April, and I spent four months at Bourges.   As I was preparing for examination I had no time to go to cafés or to think of anything outside of my duties."

General Risbourg, who was commander of the Republican Guard in Paris in 1894, was the next witness.   He described the scene with Captain Lebrun-Renault, when the witness learned of Dreyfus's alleged confessions to Captain Lebrun-Renault the day after the prisoner's degradation.

In conclusion General Risbourg eulogized the services of Captain Lebrun-Renault, and said that before the incident of the confession there was nothing against him. He was an excellent officer, a good comrade, and incapable of injuring any one.

After being asked the usual question, Dreyfus protested against General Risbourg's evidence.

"I am surprised," the prisoner said, "that he, Captain Lebrun-Renault, could have made the statement attributed to him. On the way from the prison of La Sante Captain Lebrun-Renault shook hands with me, a fact which is in contradiction of his statement. Besides, when such a terrible charge has been hanging over a man who has resisted it for five years, witnesses should not come here merely to speak their beliefs, but ought to bring proofs, positive proofs. Otherwise I am completely nonplussed as to how I can reply." [Sensation.]

Continuing, Dreyfus said:

"Reference was also made to confessions. I will state the exact terms of the so-called confession of mine. The day Captain Lebrun-Renault and I were together in the room I said to him:

"'I am innocent. I will declare it in the face of the whole people. That is the cry of my conscience. You know that cry. I repeated it all thorugh the torture of my degradation.'

Afterward I added, referring to the visit of Du Paty de Clam: ' The Minister is well aware that I am innocent.'

"What I meant to intimate was that I had apprised the Minister, in response to the steps Du Paty de Clam had taken against me, that I was innocent. Du Paty de Clam visited me and asked for information. I replied to him:

"'I am innocent, absolutely innocent.'

"I replied verbally to Du Paty de Clam and in writing to the Minister that I was perfectly innocent. That is what I meant by the words: ' The Ministry is well aware that I am innocent.'

"Then I reverted to the visit of Du Paty de Clam, and said to Captain Lebrun-Renault:

"'Du Paty de Clam asked me if I had not given documents of no importance in order to obtain others in exchange.'

"I replied that not only was I absolutely innocent, but that I desired the whole matter should be cleared up. Then I added that I hoped that within two or three years my innocence would be established. I told Du Paty de Clam that I wanted full light on the matter; that an injury had been done, and that it was impossible for the Government to fail to use its influence to discover the whole truth.

"'The Government,' I said, 'has means, either through the military attachés or through diplomatic channels, to reach the truth. It is awful that a soldier should be convicted of such a frightful crime. Consequently, it seems to me, I who asked only for truth and light, that the Government should use all the means at its disposal to secure that light.'

"Du Paty de Clam replied:

"'There are interests at stake higher than yours. These channels cannot be employed.'

"He added, however, that the inquiries would be continued. It was on the strength of Du Paty de Clam's promise to try what means could be found to reach the truth and end this awful injury, that I said I hoped that in two or three years my innocence would be proved, for Du Paty de Clam told me that the investigation, which would be of the most delicate nature, could not be undertaken immediately.

"I think I have expressed my whole mind. If you still have any doubt, I ask you, Colonel, to present it to me."

The prisoner's remarks deeply impressed his hearers.

At the request of M. Demange, General Mercier was recalled and asked to explain why, having sent Du Paty de Clam to Dreyfus to discover the amount of the injury Dreyfus had done, he had not followed up his investigations.

General Mercier—I did not feel called upon to do so.

Colonel Jouaust—Tell us, General, why, when you were apprised of the confession, you did not send some one to Dreyfus to try to get a substantiation and discover what he had not told Du Paty de Clam.

General Mercier—Dreyfus had written me that he refused to discuss the confessions with Du Paty de Clam, and I took no further steps.

Colonel Jouaust—But, since the prisoner seemed to have begun making avowals of his guilt, why did you not follow the matter up?

General Mercier—I might, perhaps, have thought of it. But it did not occur to me.

The prisoner again protested that the inquiry ought to have served to destroy the fiction of a confession, to which such importance is now attached.   Continuing, Dreyfus said:

"Will you permit me, Colonel, to make a small remark with reference to the fiction of my confessions?   I remained in the prison of La Sante for two or three weeks and saw M. Demange during that period, and also then and while I was at the Île de Ré I wrote to the Minister of War and others.

"I believed the letters I wrote are contained in the secret dossier.   I believe I also wrote to the head of the state.   How is it I was never asked about the legend of my confession, that I was in a position to destroy immediately?   I never heard a word of it.   It was only four years later, in January, 1899, when interrogated by the commissioners sent by the Court of Cassation, that I heard of this fiction.   What I do not understand is that while I was still in France no one spoke to me of this fiction, which could have been disposed of before the egg was hatched by proving it a false legend and nothing more."

M. de Veruine, Special Commissary of the Minister of War, deposed that Colonel Picquart was ordered to have Esterhazy watched.   Witness informed General Gonse, and the latter was advised to continue the investigation discreetly.   On several occasions, witness continued, Esterhazy was seen entering the German Embassy, always quite openly, but dressed in civilian clothes.

M. de Veruine saw Esterhazy enter the German Embassy on October 23, 1897.   He stayed there an hour, and drove to the Crédit Foncier (a financial institution), whence he went to the office of *La Patrie*.

M. Labori—What does General Roget think of the part played by Esterhazy?

General Roget—I have said that the part played by Esterhazy escaped me completely.

M. Labori—General Roget, however, spoke of the syndicate as though it was a public institution.

General Roget—Exactly, it is a public institution.   Everybody talks of it.

M. Labori—But General Roget mentioned an offer of 600,000 francs to Esterhazy.   I insist upon asking General Roget what he thinks of Esterhazy's visit to Colonel Schwartzkoppen (the German military attaché) on

October 23, 1897, the same day as the interview in Mont Souris Park, a visit during the course of which it is known Esterhazy threatened to commit suicide if the German military attaché refused to declare that he (Esterhazy) was not the author of the bordereau?

General Roget—It is not for me to say what I think of it.

M. Labori, resuming his seat, said, "Very good." [Loud and prolonged laughter.]

Colonel Fleur, retired, testified to the numerous alleged inaccuracies in Colonel Sandherr's evidence before the Court of Cassation. Cordier told the witness that the dismissal of himself and Colonel Sandherr was a beginning of a Jewish revenge, and added that the Jews had influenced General de Boisdeffre. Cordier also said he had not doubted the guilt of Dreyfus.

The witness dramatically added:

"What was my stupefaction when, later, I heard Colonel Cordier express ideas diametrically opposite to those he expressed to me!"

Asked if he desired to reply to the witness, Dreyfus said:

"I have nothing to say. I only reply to facts. I will not reply to lies. If you attach the slightest importance to what has been said, I beseech you, with all my heart, to make a most complete inquiry for the most dazzling truth. That is what I ask of you, Colonel, and of the members of the court-martial."

Colonel Cordier, who was Deputy Chief of the Intelligence Office in 1894, was called. He protested against the conditions under which he was summoned, without being released from his oath of professional secrecy, and also protested at the manner in which the summons was worded.

The witness expatiated on the series of schemes of which he claimed he had been the victim, to the amusement of the court, until Colonel Jouaust invited him to curtail his recriminations and proceed with his testimony, to which Cordier genially replied:

"I am coming to that, Colonel. I'll reach it in less than five minutes. You will see how I shall cut it short!"

Colonel Cordier, who is said to be given to excessive drinking, caused shouts of laughter by interlarding his remarks with the expression: "Full stop. That's all."

Even the judges joined in shrieks of laughter at the colonel's testimony.

Colonel Cordier could only testify as to certain facts, since he was not released from professional secrecy.   Colonel Jouaust said he would ask the Minister of War to release Cordier from his oath, and that he would then be recalled.

M. George Charles Alfred Marie Millin de Grandmaison, deputy from the Saumur District of Maine-et-Loire, who is classed as a Royalist, though registered as a liberal Republican, next appeared as a witness and repeated the testimony he had given before the Court of Cassation.

He recalled a conversation he had with an English friend, Mr. Charles Baker, who said he was assured Dreyfus was innocent because he had seen a letter from Colonel Schwartzkoppen affirming the prisoner's innocence. Baker, it seems, also mentioned numerous documents showing that certain French officers, not including Dreyfus, were spies, and Baker asked the witness to publish the documents, but without proofs of their genuineness, as Emperor William did not wish to intervene.

The witness, after protesting against foreign interference in French affairs, repudiated the idea that a French officer could be sentenced because he was a Jew.

M. de Grandmaison concluded by saying:

"I adjure the Court to acquit the prisoner unhesitatingly if it believes him innocent, [laughter] and to convict him if it believes him guilty."

M. Demange bitterly complained that the witnesses of the prosecution were allowed to air their personal opinions and appeal to the gallery, at which M. de Grandmaison retorted:

"Anyway the defenders of Dreyfus are being assisted by foreigners. Their cause must be very bad to necessitate recourse to such help."

M. Labori invited the witness to define what he meant by foreign intervention, particularly pointing out the alleged contradictions in the statements of foreign personages.

The witness quoted the declarations of the German Minister of Foreign Affairs, Count von Buelow, according to one of which, he said, the German Government and Embassy were not acquainted with either Dreyfus or Esterhazy, while in another statement Von Buelow implicated the German Headquarters Staff and Embassy in connection with Esterhazy.   M.

Labori and the German Government might very well not know Dreyfus, but Esterhazy might be known to the German Espionage Bureau.

M. Mertian de Muller, a friend of M. de Beaurepaire, followed. He described a visit which he made to Emperor William's palace at Potsdam, and said that at one point the guide announced that they were about to enter the Emperor's room. At the bottom of the room witness noticed his Majesty's bed, and witness was admiring the canvases on the wall, when he remarked a small table, upon which was an army list and a newspaper, the *Libre Parole*, bearing a postage-stamp. Written on the newspaper, in blue pencil, the witness asserted were certain words in German regarding the meaning of which M. de Muller was certain. They were: "Dreyfus has been arrested."

M. Demange—You are quite sure you were in the Emperor's bed-room?

M. de Muller—I should think so. But his name was not written on the door.

Regarding the German word meaning "arrested," the witness, when cross-examined, could not positively say he had distinctly read or understood it.

M. de Muller, who is a paralytic, left the witness box assisted by an usher.

Colonel Fleur and M. de Grandmaison momentarily reappeared on the scene. But Colonel Jouaust, evidently wearying of the prolonged trial, quickly called the next witness.

Colonel Picquart's former orderly in Tunis, a man named Savignaud, testified to posting letters from Picquart to M. Scheurer-Kestner, the former Vice-President of the Senate, who has taken so much interest in the Dreyfus case, in May and June, 1897.

But M. Labori pointed out that M. Scheurer-Kestner absolutely denied the receipt of letters under those dates.

The court then adjourned.

Chapter XXXIX.

"EXPERT" BERTILLON ATTACKS DREYFUS

WHEN the session of August 25th was opened, the clerk of the court read a medical certificate, signed by two doctors whose names were unknown to the audience, declaring it was impossible for Du Paty de Clam to leave his bed and come to Rennes to testify.

Maître Labori asked President Jouaust to instruct two well-known medical men to examine Du Paty de Clam, but Colonel Jouaust refused.

Rowland Strong, an English newspaper man, was then called to the witness bar. He deposed to the fact that Major Count Esterhazy confessed to him that he wrote the famous bordereau.

Henri Weill, a former officer of the Headquarters Staff, was then called. But he was absent, and his deposition was read. M. Weill's statement, in substance, was that Esterhazy told him in 1894 that Dreyfus was innocent, but that this would not prevent his conviction, because he was a Jew.

The next witness was M. Gobert, an expert of the Bank of France, who could claim the honor of being the first man in France to have declared in favor of Dreyfus, having reported, on examining the documents in the case, that Esterhazy, and not Dreyfus, wrote the bordereau.

This witness opened his deposition with a brief personal statement protesting against being characterized as a "doubtful expert" by the military party.

"But," he added, in tones of profound pity, and turning toward Dreyfus, "I have no right to complain, and am silent when I see before me the unfortunate man who sits there."

A murmur of approval from the audience greeted these words of sympathy.

M. Gobert was most emphatic in attributing the bordereau to Esterhazy.   He declared the bordereau was written in a running natural hand, and said there was no tracing or other trickery.

M. Gobert protested against the insinuation that he was an interested witness.   He referred to his thirty years of service, during which he had reported on thousands of documents, and added, visibly affected:

"I protest against the term 'interested expert.'"

The court closely followed M. Gobert's exhaustive story of his examination of the bordereau and his interview with Generals Mercier, de Boisdeffre, and Gonse.

M. Gobert asserted that the handwriting of the bordereau was natural and fluent, but that it was almost illegible, whereas Dreyfus, even when writing rapidly, always wrote most legibly.

The witness had asked General Gonse if an envelope accompanied the bordereau, as he, M. Gobert, wished to see what the writer's careful caligraphy was like, explaining that the address of a letter is always in a firmer hand than its contents.

General Gonse had refused the request on the ground that the witness must not know the name of the addressee.

The General had also decided not to allow the bordereau to be photographed, alleging that if the War Office photographers were allowed to photograph it all Paris would be acquainted with the bordereau the next day.   [Laughter.]   Thereupon the witness had remarked:

"General Gonse, this is a very interesting confession."

M. Gobert had then suggested that the work be intrusted to the Prefecture of Police, where M. Bertillon is the photographer.

Until then, the witness also said, he had never heard of M. Bertillon as a handwriting expert, saying he became an expert for this special occasion, when he was called into the War Office.   [Laughter.]

General Gonse, it appears from the testimony, had been greatly enraged when he learned of the result of M. Gobert's examination of the bordereau, and visited the expert repeatedly.   The latter always insisted upon learning the name of the suspect.

"It was not proper," said M. Gobert, "for me to accuse any one without being perfectly cognizant of the facts, especially in circumstances of so grave a nature.   I would not accuse any one anonymously, for to do so would be contrary to the law."

Amid laughter in court, the witness described how, from an examination of an official report on Dreyfus, from which Dreyfus's name had been removed, M. Gobert had the malicious satisfaction of telling General Gonse the name of the officer they wanted to arrest.

It was after M. Gobert had refused to incriminate Dreyfus that M. Bertillon had been intrusted with the examination of the bordereau, and, after a few hours' study, M. Bertillon positively attributed the bordereau to Dreyfus. From that time forward M. Gobert had heard no more of the Dreyfus case. He was not asked to submit a report, but had described to the then Minister of Justice, M. Guérin, the circumstances in the case. M. Guérin, continued the witness, had intimated that "these were soldiers' affairs," which did not concern him as Chief of the Civil Judiciary.

General Gonse having alluded to certain undesirable acquaintances formed by M. Gobert, the latter replied, amid a sensation in court:

"I emphatically protest against the insinuations of General Gonse. There is not a single word of truth in what he says."

There was a further dispute between General Gonse and M. Gobert over circumstances in connection with the latter's examination of the bordereau. M. Gobert said that Colonel d'Abeville was present, but the colonel promptly advanced, and said he had never seen M. Gobert before to-day, adding:

"If M. Gobert's other recollections are as exact as this, the court will draw its own conclusions."

Dreyfus here declared in the most positive manner that he had never been at the Bank of France, where M. Gobert was employed, or had relations with any one there. The prisoner reasserted that his sole desire was to know the truth. He admitted he had been engaged in various financial operations, but said he had never asked either for written or verbal information from the Bank of France.

M. Bertillon, the noted specialist in the measurement of the human body, was called as the next witness. To the surprise of the audience, he entered the court-room without a single paper, carrying a high hat in his hand instead. But the astonishment was short-lived, the first words of M. Bertillon being a request to permit his diagrams and papers to be brought in.

The request was granted, and M. Bertillon retired for a moment. He returned at the head of a squad composed of an infantry sergeant and four privates, all staggering under the weight of immense leather satchels, bulging with documents, charts, etc., which they deposited on the stage as a roar of laughter echoed throughout the court.

Even the judges were unable to repress a smile as they gazed on M. Bertillon's stage properties strewed over half of the platform. A table was brought in, upon which the plans he was using could be placed.

The witness began by saying that only intelligent men could follow his explanations; and the court was half emptied as the audience, after smiling at his extraordinary words and expressions, soon became bored and went out.

M. Bertillon's deposition occupied the whole of this session.

The court-room presented a curious scene while M. Bertillon, whom the Dreyfusards, in their most indulgent moments, describe as a "dangerous maniac," spent the remaining hours of the session in explaining in unintelligible terms his "infallible system" of proving that Dreyfus was the author of the bordereau. The majority of the public, however, utterly unable to comprehend M. Bertillon's theories, had left the court-room. Even "La Dame Blanche" (the White Lady) abandoned her post.

In the mean while M. Bertillon, with gestures and in the shrill pitched voice of a quack at a country fair, continued his monologue, producing every few minutes some fresh paper covered with wonderful hieroglyphics. These papers he presented to the judges, who, with an expression of owl-like wisdom, carefully examined them, their heads clustered together, their eyes gazing on the long, wide strips of paper, while M. Bertillon leaned over their table trying to explain his mystifying diagrams. The copies were afterward passed to MM. Labori and Demange, who, however, apparently did not derive much benefit from their perusal.

Dreyfus gazed at the scene with a look of stupefaction.

The clearest utterance of M. Bertillon during the course of his demonstration was that the handwriting of the bordereau "obeys a geometrical rhythm, of which I discovered the equation in the prisoner's blotting pad."

The audience watched him as he bent over the desk busily drawing letters, the judges gazing at him, until at the end of ten minutes the people and the judges became restlessly impatient, and Colonel Jouaust remarked that it was not necessary to copy the whole bordereau, and that a few lines would suffice.

A few minutes later M. Bertillon arose, strode to the judges' table, and laid before them his copy. The judges, counsel, the Government Commissary, Major Carriere, and the clerk clustered around in one group, eager to see the result. Again the audience watched the strange spectacle until Colonel Jouaust shrugged his shoulders, and then the audience knew that M. Bertillon had failed to satisfy them.

M. Bertillon noticed this, and said, apologetically:

"I was too badly placed."

Maître Demange returned to the counsels' table and, in response to a look of inquiry from Dreyfus, whispered a few words to the prisoner with a shrug of his shoulders and a smile on his face. Dreyfus appeared perfectly satisfied.

M. Bertillon gave his testimony in the manner of a schoolboy reciting a lesson, to demonstrate technically how he reached the conviction of Dreyfus's guilt, reciting facts already published on April 22d. He said he proposed to prove to the court:

"First—That the bordereau was a doctored document.

"Second—That it could only be manufactured by the prisoner.

"Third—That it had been written in a free hand by means of a key-word placed beneath tracing paper in such a way as to be quite visible."

The witness, continuing, declared Dreyfus did not have recourse to imitating Esterhazy's free handwriting, because it required too long to study, and he used the tracing process because it was easier to learn and more likely to be successful.

Suddenly the wandering attention of those remaining in the hall was riveted by the cryptographic remark, enunciated by M. Bertillon in loud tones:

"We clearly have before us a fabricated document. The one word always rests upon the other, with a divergence of 1.25 millimetres and 2.25 millimetres. That is a phenomenon which is unnatural."

M. Labori watched the specialist for a few moments, and then returned to his seat, holding up both hands and exclaiming:

"It is most extraordinary."

M. Bertillon continued his explanations, and caused a whirl in the brains of his hearers. The audience, quite in the dark regarding the meaning of the technicalities, punctuated the queer expressions with peals of laughter. The members of the court-martial evidently tried hard to understand, while Dreyfus appeared fatigued, but endeavored to follow the arguments.

"My theory," continued the witness, "was, in 1894, considered by the Ministry of War to be favorable to the prisoner. If the defence accepted it, they said, the long magisterial investigation would have to be recommenced, and so," here the witness raised his voice and struck the table with his fist, "when the word 'grille' [perforated card used for cipher] was uttered at the court-martial of 1894, the prisoner's face contracted. When I spoke of the fabrication of the bordereau he exclaimed:

"'Oh, the wretch. He saw me write, then.'

"I did not hear the remark, but when it was repeated to me it was a revelation. For, if innocent, the word 'fabrication' would have delighted instead of frightened him."

Chapter XL.

MERCIER ACCUSES THE DEAD

WHEN the court resumed its sessions on August 26th, M. Alphonse Bertillon, chief of the Anthropometric Department of the Paris Prefecture of Police, resumed his testimony, which had been interrupted on August 25th by adjournment.

The comic aspect of M. Bertillon's performance again appealed to the risibilities of the audience, though the judges paid close attention to his demonstrations, which were concluded at 8:30 A.M., the witness saying, in a declamatory tone:

"I am convinced that the writer of the bordereau is the prisoner sitting there."

Drefyus heard him without flinching and with an expression of disdain, which he showed in a still more noticeable manner just before the specialist's testimony, when M. Demange handed him a paper which M. Bertillon had submitted to the judges as convincing proof of the guilt of the accused. The prisoner perused it for a few moments, and then handed it back with a shrug of his shoulders and without uttering a word.

Referring to his papers which were seized at the War Office, Dreyfus said it would not be strange to see notes, written by officers, altered. He added:

"I was shown yesterday (August 25th) a note relative to General de Miribel. There were in the document corrections, made by the chief of the department himself, which shows that immediately after having written a note he handed it to the chief of the department."

In regard to the so-called "blotting-pad letter," Dreyfus said:

"This letter is perfectly genuine. Madame Dreyfus can testify to that point. No one here will doubt the word of Madame Dreyfus, and you, gentlemen, less than any one," he added, looking steadily at the judges.

Captain Valerio of the artillery, called by the prosecution to explain

M. Bertillon's system and to give an opinion on the subject, said he thought M. Bertillon's evidence might be summarized in a sentence:

"The bordereau was doctored and the document fabricated by means of secret writing, or writing with a key, the key-word 'interest' being found on the 'blotting-pad letter' attributed to Mathieu Dreyfus.

"The system," continued the captain, "was evidently devised to offer the prisoner two means of escape. Either he would deny being the author of the bordereau by pointing to the difference of the handwriting, or he would contend it was a plot, by showing the documents were traced over his writings.

"However complicated the ingenuity of the human mind might appear," continued the witness, "I propose to show:

"First—That the document was fabricated.

"Second—That it was fabricated by means of the key-word 'interest.'

"Third—That documents written by the prisoner in the War Office contained words written by means of the same key.

"Fourth—That the forgery was intended to enable the prisoner to plead there was a plot against him.

"Fifth—That the prisoner alone could be the writer."

Captain Valerio then attempted to prove his hypothesis, traversing practically the same ground as already laboriously covered by M. Bertillon, during the course of which he pointed to what he alleged were conclusive proofs of the value of M. Bertillon's system.

The witness declared that as he wished to remain on scientific ground, he would not attempt to define the motive actuating the writer of the bordereau. But, he added, he was perfectly convinced it could only have been Dreyfus. Esterhazy had declared himself to be the writer, but that could not be true, because it had been proved the bordereau was forged.

In conclusion, Captain Valerio declared the court now had in its possession material proof of the prisoner's guilt. [Sensation.]

When Dreyfus was asked the usual question, the prisoner pointed out that the evidence of Captain Valerio was only a repetition of M. Bertillon's, and that, consequently, his reply to the latter applied equally to Valerio.

Reference having been made to doctored words in minutes written by him at the War Office, Dreyfus pointed out that these minutes were written in the presence of witnesses. He also dwelt upon the fact that he had already acknowledged the genuineness of the "blotting-pad letter," which he reaffirmed, adding that the hypothesis that he doctored the bordereau in order to have means of defence fell to the ground of itself, since he had never attempted to turn the system to use.

"All M. Bertillon's measures are false. All, without exception," exclaimed the prisoner vehamently, amid excitement.

There was a highly dramatic scene toward the end of the session. Maître Labori asked to have Captain Freystaetter, of the Marine Infantry, one of the members of the court-martial of 1894 which convicted Dreyfus, called in contradiction of the desposition of Colonel Maurel-Pries, the presiding judge upon that occasion, who had testified that he only read one of the documents out of the secret dossier communicated to the court-martial.

The captain, who is a finely built officer, and who has a handsome, honest face, ascended the platform with a firm step and a fearless air. When he was asked to recount what occurred, he said his conviction of the guilt of the prisoner was formed by the evidence of the experts in handwriting, the deposition of Colonel Du Paty de Clam, "and," he continued, "I must add, some slight influence was exercised over my mind by hearing the secret dossier read."

The witness was then questioned as to whether one or more of the documents were read, and he said they were all read. This was in direct contradiction of Colonel Maurel-Pries, and M. Labori once demanded the confrontation of Captain Freystaetter with Colonel Maurel-Pries. The latter mounted the stage, and presented a miserable spectacle, his shifty eyes blearing out beneath heavy eyebrows.

"How do you explain this?" asked M. Labori.

Then the colonel, at bay, replied savagely:

"I said I only read one document. I did not say only one document was read."

This statement called forth an outburst of hisses and indignant "Ohs!" from the audience, which looked upon it as an infamous confession.

The witness, trembling with shame, but evidently determined to fight to the last, threw a fierce look of hatred at M. Labori and the audience, as the gendarmes shouted:

"Silence! Silence!"

MADAME LABORI SUPPORTING HER WOUNDED HUSBAND.

RETURN OF DREYFUS: EN ROUTE TO RENNES.

SCENE BETWEEN GENERAL ROGET AND COLONEL PICQUART, AUGUST 18, 1899.

RETURN OF DREYFUS: FIRST LANDING ON FRENCH SOIL.

WITNESSES AGAINST DREYFUS.
General Zurlinden, Casimir-Périer, Billot, Mercier.

PANORAMIC VIEW OF DEVIL'S ISLAND.

THE SECOND COURT-MARTIAL: REMARKABLE SCENE DURING THE SESSION OF AUGUST 24TH.

Three witnesses, counsel for the prosecution, counsel for the defense, the prisoner, and the presiding officer in altercation.

THE CONFRONTATION OF CAPTAIN FREYSTAETTER AND COLONEL MAUREL-PRIES. JUDGES IN THE TRIAL OF 1894.

After this the audience listened spellbound as Captain Freystaetter, in a distinct, bold voice, told exactly what the documents of the dossier were, and how Colonel Maurel-Pries not only read these documents, but made comments on them. This was practically calling Maurel-Pries a liar, and the colonel glared at the captain ferociously.

Freystaetter, however, was not dismayed, and his words, spoken in a tone of candor and fearlessness, must have carried conviction to every hearer.

General Mercier then asked to be heard, and placed himself by the side of Maurel-Pries. The forbidding appearance of these two men, both dressed in civilian attire, was in striking contrast with the erect, unflinching attitude of Freystaetter, who wore the smart uniform of a captain of artillery, with medals on his breast. It was a remarkable scene.

General Mercier at once denied Captain Freystaetter's declaration that the Panizzardi dispatch was contained in the dossier. "It is a lie!" [Tremendous sensation.]

Captain Freystaetter, however, was undaunted, and replied, looking Colonel Jouaust straight in the face:

"I swear that what I have said is true. And," Freystaetter added, "I not merely remember the dispatch, but I have a vivid recollection of the fact that the first words were, ' Dreyfus is arrested. Emissary warned.'"

This emphatic declaration increased the sensation.

General Mercier then made the self-saving reply that he did not make up the dossier, which was made up by the late Colonel Sandherr, Chief of the Intelligence Department.

M. Labori was hotly indignant at General Mercier's equivocation, and asked Colonel Jouaust again and again to have special doctors make an official examination of Colonel Du Paty de Clam to see if he was really incapable of giving evidence. But the president of the court refused, whereupon M. Labori, beside himself, cried:

"Colonel Sandherr is dead; Colonel Henry is dead, and Colonel Du Paty de Clam won't come here."

Then counsel sat down, boiling with indignation. Colonel Jouaust told M. Labori not to make observations.

The scene this day showed both Colonel Maurel-Pries and General Mercier in an odious light. Maurel-Pries was shown, to put it mildly, not to have told the truth, while Mercier, when cornered, threw the awk-

15

ward responsibility for the illegalities of the court-martial of 1894 on dead men, as M. Labori pointed out.

The audience had their hearts in their mouths from the moment Captain Freystaetter opened his lips until the three confronted witnesses left the stage, and every moment a murmur of disgust and the general cry of "Oh!" burst from the hearers.

General Mercier accused Captain Freystaetter of lying in the matter of the Robin shell, concerning which there is a report accusing Dreyfus of communicating the details of the shell to Germany.

Freystaetter had said that it was included in the secret dossier.

"I have caught Captain Freystaetter in the very act of lying," said General Mercier, amid the greatest excitement in court, "for the Robin shell was not delivered until 1895."

Captain Freystaetter replied promptly, maintaining the truth of his previous statement, saying he referred to "a" shell and not to the Robin shell, and he spoke like an honest man.

Colonel Maurel-Pries, on the other hand, when driven to confess, told untruths, and tried to wriggle out of it. He presented a despicable appearance, his voice broken as though choking, while his limbs were shaking with suppressed, futile passion.

This incident, which terminated with the evidence of Captain Freystaetter, caused an immense impression on the audience. The Dreyfusards were jubilant.

Dreyfus said he had nothing to ask the witnesses. Colonel Maurel-Pries, General Mercier, and Captain Freystaetter then left the stage.

M. Paray-Javal, a draughtsman, was called for the defence. He was accompanied by a blackboard, upon which he proposed to refute a portion of M. Bertillon's problems. The witness said, amid laughter, that the demonstration would occupy no less than two hours. He then proceeded to chalk a number of caligraphic signs on the blackboard, and presented to the court photographs of the writing of the bordereau and the prisoner's handwriting, pointing out their dissimilarities and entering into elaborate explanations, which were not concluded when the court adjourned.

Chapter XLI.

THE EVIDENCE OF M. BERTILLON IS RIDICULED

THE fourth week of the trial of Captain Dreyfus opened in the Lycée Building on August 28th.

The first witness called was M. Paray-Javal, the draughtsman, whose evidence was interrupted on August 26th by the adjournment of the court.

With the aid of a blackboard M. Paray-Javal demonstrated the fallacy of M. Bertillon's calculations, and criticised the latter's unfairness in not submitting Esterhazy's handwriting to the same tests as the prisoner's writing. At the same time, the draughtsman declared, even if M. Bertillon had done so, the results would not have proved anything.

In conclusion M. Paray-Javal said, amid laughter, that he thought M. Bertillon was a very intelligent man, but that his system was false, and he, the witness, was convinced that only self-esteem prevented M. Bertillon from admitting his error.

M. Bernard, an inspector of mines, who took high honors at the Polytechnic School, who followed M. Paray-Javal at the witness bar, said he appeared to refute a portion of M. Bertillon's evidence which was based on false calculations. As a matter of fact, he added, it was on such a basis that the whole system rested.

In conclusion, M. Bernhard exhibited to the judges a plate representing a page of current handwriting, and said:

"If it was examined by M. Bertillon's system it will show certain peculiarities which would not be found upon the examination of fifty million other documents. M. Bertillon would therefore say the document was fabricated. But he would be wrong, for I borrowed the page from a report written by M. Bertillon himself."

M. Bertillon demanded permission to reply to the witness, and Colonel Jouaust replied:

"I cannot grant your request, and I will not grant such permission to any of the fourteen experts, except in the case of a personal explanation."

M. Bertillon—I wish to speak of the manner in which I reconstructed the bordereau.

Colonel Jouaust—Why, you are discussing the case. I cannot allow you to speak except in regard to a personal fact.

The president's statement aroused loud laughter, amid which M. Bertillon, disconcerted, resumed his seat.

M. Teysonnieres followed. He said he adhered in all respects to his report dated October 29, 1894, in which he expressed the opinion that the bordereau was the work of the writer of the documents seized at the prisoner's residence. For purposes of comparison, the witness lengthily criticised the bordereau letter by letter, pointing out resemblances to the prisoner's handwriting.

M. Teyssonieres, in finishing his testimony, said he thought it was impossible to find more tangible reasons than those which induced in him the belief, which he hoped the court would share.

Replying to the court, M. Teyssonieres said he had not noticed that the prisoner's handwriting was illegible, and he had never seen the document dictated to Dreyfus.

The copy of the bordereau made by Dreyfus was then handed to the witness, who declared it had never been given to him for purposes of comparison.

The witness added that he would require three days to give an opinion upon it. He could not conclude his examination on the spot. He must have time.

M. Charavay, the archivist and expert in ancient manuscripts, said:

"I, with two colleagues (MM. Teyssonieres and Pelletier), though acting under separate instruction, was commissioned to examine the bordereau and a number of documents for comparison unsigned and in different handwritings. I examined, first, the latter documents, and by the process of elimination fixed upon one resembling the bordereau. I was then furnished with specimens of the handwriting in question, but was not told the name of the writer. I asked if the document could be regarded as genuine, and was told the place whence it emanated, which could not be mentioned by me, and which could leave no doubt in regard to its value. I make this remark because I think it explains my opinion, for I could not consider a document of this nature which was not marked by a certain dissimilarity of handwriting. I therefore attributed to dissimilarity the differences I was careful to note in my report.

"Now I must inform the court, that, in view of the fact that handwriting which was not produced in 1894, and which is evidently akin to the handwriting of the bordereau and the handwriting of Dreyfus, has since been submitted to me, I cannot maintain with the same degree of certainty the conclusions of my former report, and I can only make one statement, namely, that these two handwritings resemble the bordereau. I should, however, point out one of the typical dissimilarities, upon which I laid stress, between the writing of the bordereau and the documents submitted for comparison, namely, that the double ' s ' is not found in the new handwriting. In other words, the double ' s ' of the bordereau is found in Esterhazy's handwriting."

After repeating the evidence he gave before the Court of Cassation, M. Charavay declared it was the new element, the handwriting of Esterhazy, which led him to declare he did not adhere to his conclusions of 1894.

In conclusion M. Charavay energetically protested against General Mercier's accusations, adding that what convinced him that he had made a mistake in 1894 was the publication of Esterhazy's letters, the discovery of the Henry forgery, the inquiry of the Court of Cassation, and Esterhazy's confession.

The conscience of the witness compelled him to say that in 1894 he was misled by similarity in handwriting.

"It is a great relief to my conscience," M. Charavay added, "to be able to say, before you and before him who is the victim of my mistake, that the bordereau is not the work of Dreyfus, but of Esterhazy."

An immense sensation was caused in court by this statement.

Replying to Colonel Jouaust, the witness said that the mere examination of the bordereau and the documents presented for comparison were sufficient to convince him that the bordereau was not written by Dreyfus.

The prisoner, on being asked the customary questions, requested M. Charavay to give further particulars as to the reasons which led him to modify his opinions in regard to the writer of the bordereau, whereupon the witness entered into a lengthy technical explanation. He told how he found unmistakable resemblances between the bordereau and Esterhazy's writing.

M. Pelletier, another expert, prefaced his evidence by saying he desired to make a definite statement on the point upon which he was in entire disagreement with General Mercier. The latter had testified that the witness refused to use certain documents submitted to him for comparison in common with the other experts, and said he had been led to regard M. Pelletier's work with some suspicion, because of certain incidents in which M. Pelletier, being summoned to appear simultaneously in two different courts, had written to both, excusing himself on the ground of attendance at the other.

General Mercier declared this made him suspicious of M. Pelletier's report in favor of Dreyfus, inferring that his failure to comply with the summons of the examining magistrates in November, 1894, was connected with his report, whereas the report, the witness pointed out, was handed in on October 26th.

"I have only to oppose facts to Mercier's inferences," said M. Pelletier. "On October 22d I was intrusted with the verification in question. I handed in my report October 26th, and it was only in November that I was summoned to undergo cross-examination on a complaint lodged by the military authorities. General Mercier, in short, had not the slightest reasons to suspect the conclusions which I had reached."

After replying to a question or two from the court, M. Pelletier continued:

"After settling this personal matter there remains nothing but to maintain in their entirety my conclusions to the effect that there is no likeness between the writing of the bordereau and that of the prisoner."

M. Couard, the official archivist and expert in the Esterhazy case in 1897, then testified that he was instructed by Major Ravary to examine expertly the bordereau and specimens of Esterhazy's handwriting. The witness insisted upon experimenting with the original bordereau and specimens of Esterhazy's caligraphy written by Esterhazy in the presence of experts. Beyond this the expert and Esterhazy had no relations. The latter therefore could not have influenced him, and the witness protested against M. Zola's accusations and adhered to his opinion of 1897, that the bordereau was not the work of Esterhazy.   He, the witness, would wager his head on this.

M. Couard said he was convinced the caligraphy of the bordereau was neither frank nor natural, and the writer, in his opinion, probably wished to imitate another person's handwriting.   The letter of August 28th, the witness continued, although declared genuine by Esterhazy himself, seemed doubtful to M. Couard, who added that he believed Esterhazy would say anything he was wanted to say.

Since 1897 the witness had not believed a word Esterhazy had said, and, he pointed out, there was nothing to prove Esterhazy would not a year hence say exactly the opposite of what he said now.

Replying to a question, M. Couard, while reasserting that the bordereau was not the work of Esterhazy, declined to commit himself in regard to Dreyfus, whose handwriting, added the witness, he had never been called upon to examine.

M. Varinard, with whom MM. Couard and Belhomme acted as experts in the Esterhazy case, was the next witness.   He adhered to his report that the bordereau was not the work of Esterhazy, and said he persisted in this opinion in spite of Esterhazy's statements to the contrary.

The court then adjourned.

Chapter XLII.

THE "LITTLE WHITE MOUSE" TESTIFIES

THE appearance of Colonel Cordier, formerly Deputy Chief of the Intelligence Department of the War Office, as the first witness at the Dreyfus court-martial, on August 29th, aroused great interest, as, since his previous appearance, the colonel has been released by the Minister of War from his oath of professional secrecy. Speaking in firm, audible tones, the colonel testified that on September 23, 1894, he left Paris on a fortnight's leave of absence, and that nothing was then known in the Statistical Department of the War Office of the discovery of treason.

Continuing, Colonel Cordier said that the day after he returned to Paris, Colonel Sandherr, who appeared greatly distressed, handed the witness a copy of the bordereau on foolscap paper. Sandherr and Cordier animatedly discussed the bordereau, Sandherr considering it ample evidence of treason.

The document was photographed and an investigation was opened, which resulted in arousing suspicions against Dreyfus. Prior to this there was no presumption of Dreyfus's guilt. It was on October 8th that the suspicions of the prisoner's guilt became definite.

The witness said he believed the bordereau arrived at the War Office after September 24th. He could not say who received it. Very few officers were then aware that treason had been committed. The witness thought it necessary to enter into these particulars in reply to the statements of his assistant, Major Lauth, before the Court of Cassation.

At this point, Major Lauth, rising in the centre of the court, exclaimed:

"I beg leave to speak, Colonel."

Proceeding with his testimony, Colonel Cordier said he believed the bordereau was handed to Colonel Sandherr by Colonel Henry.

Cordier then explained what was the "ordinary channel" by which information reached the War Office.   The "ordinary channel," the witness said, was a very clever spy, attached to the Intelligence Department, who had the habit of visiting great houses, but who preferred the company of servants to the company of their masters.

Cordier then described the method of piecing documents, and showed how the bordereau was pasted together by Henry, who was usually intrusted with this work.   The witness said piecing documents possessed fascination for the men who were engaged upon such work, "like the passion of fortune-telling by cards."

"Men who have once pieced paper," said the witness, amid laughter, "will always continue to do so."

Referring to the spy who has been dubbed as the "ordinary channel," Colonel Cordier said the former did not directly receive the documents from the Embassy from which they were abstracted.   A woman, he explained, served as an intermediary, and, the "ordinary channel" having been closed, it was found necessary to negotiate directly with the intermediary, otherwise the woman, with whom rendezvous were usually made in churches.   But, as the "ordinary channel's" services were still available elsewhere, his pay was continued.

Possibly, continued the witness, the spy endeavored to renew his relations with the Embassy.

Cordier, whose evidence greatly interested his hearers, described the various leakages.   He especially referred to a very serious case designated as "Leakage of St. Thomas Aquinas," in which a clerk of the church of St. Thomas Aquinas, Paris, was mixed up in espionage, and a serious leakage in the Minister of Marine.

The witness then referred to the spy Guénee's denunciations, to the effect that officers of the Headquarters Staff were guilty of treachery.   But, the colonel explained, it was very difficult to accept Guénee's statement as gospel.   The witness regretted Guénee's death, as, he said, the court would have been edified by his testimony in regard to the manner in which many things were fabricated.

Cordier described the events prior to the arrest of Dreyfus, and showed that only a single real leakage, namely, the plans of the fortresses, had occurred at the time of his arrest.   The document known as "Cette canaille de D——," he explained, was contemporaneous with this leakage.

"It has been said," continued the witness, "that I made a mistake on this point, and confounded the document with another containing the initial alone. I should like very much to see the document, in order to assure myself that it has not been tampered with. It is not, however, of any importance, except to show that General Roget's evidence concerning it is false from beginning to end." [Sensation.]

Reverting to the manner in which the suspicions against Dreyfus crystallized, the colonel described the efforts to pry into the prisoner's life, and said the information at first received was very bad and constituted strong proof against the prisoner. Later, however, it assumed quite a different aspect. It was admitted that before his marriage Dreyfus was not "unimpeachable morally, nor was he entitled to wear a wreath of orange blossoms." [Laughter.]

But, Cordier added, after his marriage Dreyfus was quite different.

The witness also said that while Dreyfus boasted of his conquests, he, Cordier, was of the opinion that those who boasted the most accomplished the least. [Laughter.]

Dreyfus, he continued, bragged a great deal, and probably now repented having done so, and Dreyfus's inquisitiveness, according to witness, was probably explained by his knowledge that he would not long remain on the Headquarters Staff, and he desired to obtain all the information which might be useful to him in after life.

"In 1894," declared Colonel Cordier, emphatically, "I had been reassured by the unanimity of the judges, and I was absolutely convinced of the guilt of Dreyfus. Now I am absolutely convinced of his innocence." [Great excitement.]

M. Labori questioned the witness in regard to the letter mentioned in M. De la Roche-Vernet's evidence referring to the spy "C. C. C.," which was dispatched to the War Office at the time of Colonel Picquart's arrival. Cordier explained that it was a letter from an Italian lady, with whom the department, at that time, was in correspondence through an intermediary at the Foreign Office.

"I greatly respect Italian ladies in general," said Colonel Cordier, "but not when it is a case of espionage, and I advised Colonel Picquart not to make too much use of the lady's offices, saying to him: 'There must be no petticoats.'"

Major Lauth commented upon Colonel Cordier's testimony, especially the statement that there were no Anti-Semites on the Headquarters Staff, remarking that there was one exception, and that this was Cordier himself, who was always expressing antipathy to the Jews, especially when there was a question of introducing Dreyfus to the department.

"Yes," exclaimed Cordier, "quite true. I was an Anti-Semite, but my opinions never went to the length of bringing false evidence against the Jews. [Sensation.] I am an honest man, and I have a conscience." [Renewed excitement.]

Colonel Fleur appeared in the witness box to refute Colonel Cordier's testimony. He declared that on August 23, 1898, Colonel Cordier said to him:

"Dreyfus is guilty. But there must be two others. There are three of them."

Colonel Cordier shrugged his shoulders, and admitted that on that date, just a week before the arrest of Henry, he said forgery had been committed at the Headquarters Staff. But, the colonel added, he told the same thing of others the day after the posting up of the speech of M. Cavaignac, then Minister of War, was voted by the Chamber of Deputies.

Archivist Gribelin also advanced and protested against Colonel Cordier's statement.

He was followed by General Mercier, who said it was necessary for Cordier to say what he knew about the arrangement of the secret dossier by Colonel Sandherr.

General Mercier caused a sensation by indorsing Colonel Cordier's statement with reference to the alleged attempt of Mathieu Dreyfus to bribe Colonel Sandherr. The general said:

"When Colonel Sandherr reported the interview and I asked his opinion of it, Sandherr replied:

"' He gave me the impression of being an honest man resolved to sacrifice everything for his brother.'"

The name of M. de Freycinet, known as "The Little White Mouse," was called, and amid suppressed excitement the former Minister of War, former Minister of Foreign Affairs, and former Premier took the witness stand.

Maître Demange proceeded to question the former Minister. Counsel recalled General Mercier's statement that M. de. Freycinet told General Jamont that 35,000,000 francs had been raised abroad for the defence of Dreyfus.

In reply, M. de Freycinet expressed the anguish which he felt at the sight of the trouble into which his country was plunged, and said his whole desire was to see peace and calm restored. In regard to the conversations referred to the witness said:

"General Jamont made me a visit of courtesy on the occasion of my quitting office at the beginning of May. I received many similar visits. I do not think that I exaggerate when I say I received a hundred such visits. I made no note of the remarks exchanged by my different visitors.

"In the case of General Jamont we, of course, talked about the case and the campaign of speeches and press utterances which had been proceeding in different parts of the world during the previous two years. In regard to the Dreyfus case I was led to say that our agents abroad reported that efforts had been made, on the initiative of private individuals, in behalf of this campaign. A very disinterested campaign in France, I am sure; but less so abroad.

"I reported the estimates I heard had been made by people who professed to be well acquainted with the question of advertising in regard to the probable money value of the whole campaign throughout the world since its inception.

"That, Monsieur le President, is a résumé, as complete and faithful as my recollection permits, of the conversation with General Jamont. What struck me most was the identity of our anxiety in regard to the army. We mutually expressed uneasiness, for it must not be concealed that the present attacks have had a profound echo which might eventually endanger the cohesion of the army.

"You know well, gentlemen, that there is a higher discipline than even the Military Code. As I said in the Chamber, it is that more rigorous discipline which comes from the confidence of the soldier in his chiefs. How can that confidence be maintained if those chiefs are depicted daily in the blackest colors? Was it not to be feared that at a given moment this confidence would disappear, and what would be the result if we were engaged in external difficulties? [Sensation.]

"I adjure those of my countrymen," continued M. de Freycinet earnestly, "who participate in these attacks under the impulse of generous passion and with the object of serving a noble, elevated idea—I have no doubt they are led away—to take heed of the dangers in which they may involve the country. As General Jamont said to me: 'It is high time to end it.'

"Let us cease throwing in one another's faces accusations which discredit us in the eyes of our rivals. Gentlemen, let us prepare—and I would that my feeble voice could be heard by all—let us prepare to accept your judgment with respect and silence. May the judgment of this French court, toward which the whole world has its eyes turned, open up the era of reconciliation which is so necessary. [Immense excitement.]

"Gentlemen, pardon me for telling you what I wish. It springs from a heart which has no longer much to desire here below, except to live and see the country great and honored.

"I have finished. I have given an exact account of the interview with the commander-in-chief of our armies in time of war. I have nothing to add."

M. de Freycinet had fully maintained his title to the nickname, "The Little White Mouse," which was bestowed upon him on account of his ability to speak lengthily without conveying much information.

Replying to a member of the court-martial, M. de Freycinet explained the part which he played in the Ministry to which he belonged. He said he confined himself to giving effect to the Government's decisions when the Supreme Court decided in favor of a revision.

M. Demange wanted M. de Freycinet to repeat in court his statements made in the Chamber of Deputies in regard to the small importance attaching to the alleged treason, but M. de Freycinet declined to repeat them, saying the court could, however, indicate the sense of his speech. In his opinion most of the leakages could only have been of infinitesimal importance, though the information relative to covering the troops might have been important. The publication of secrets relating to arming and explosives was also dangerous. But when the witness made his speech in the Chamber of Deputies he wished above all to avoid increasing public excitement.

M. Labori—Is M. de Freycinet aware of any fact which led him to

believe foreign money has played a part in the revision of the trial of
1894?

M. de Freycinet—No, no, Monsieur le President.

M. Labori—What does M. de Freycinet think of the accusations of a
certain section of the press against MM. Scheurer-Kestner, Tarieux, Brisson, and Ranc, and by another section against the Court of Cassation,
tending to attribute the opinion on the revision expressed by those persons
to the influences of corruption?

Colonel Jouaust—I refuse to put the question.

M. Labori insisted that he should at least be permitted to question M.
de Freycinet relative to M. Scheurer-Kestner, the former Vice-President
of the Senate, whose statements about the letters Colonel Picquart wrote
to him from Tunis have been contradicted by Savignaud, Picquart's former
orderly.

To this the president of the court replied that the good faith of M.
Scheurer-Kestner was not under discussion. Colonel Jouaust added that
M. Labori wished to import passion into the proceedings.

Counsel was defending himself against this aspersion, when M. de
Freycinet intervened and said he did not scruple to say that M. Scheurer-
Kestner was his friend, and that he had the highest opinion of his char-
acter.

M. Labori thanked the witness for this frank statement.

After leaving the witness-stand M. de Freycinet took a seat beside
General Billot, with whom he briefly conversed. The former Minister
then left the court-room, after having been excused from further attendance.

M. Gallichet, editor of the *Drapeau*, then testified. He expressed his
personal indignation at the charges of treason against Henry, and repeated
the gossip of a third party relative to an alleged remark Colonel Cordier
was overheard to make, namely:

"We have taken Dreyfus with his hand in the bag."

M. Belhomme, a former Inspector of Schools, seventy-eight years of
age, testified that he examined as an expert the bordereau in the Esterhazy case, and came to the conclusion that it was not the work of Esterhazy. The witness added that he adhered to his opinion even more positively now than before. Incidentally, M. Belhomme expressed surprise

at the fact that the Court of Cassation did not take the result of his examination into account. In conclusion M. Belhomme declared he never believed the bordereau was in Esterhazy's writing, and added that until he actually saw him make a fresh copy of the document, witness would have no remarks to make in regard to the handwriting of Dreyfus, which he had not sufficiently examined.

After M. Demange had asked a question or two, to which M. Belhomme did not reply, M. Demange pointed out the contradictions in M. Belhomme's original report and in his statements at this session.

The court then adjourned.

Chapter XLIII.

ESTERHAZY ACCUSED BY FOUR WITNESSES

M. Paul Meyer, member of the Institute and Director of the School of Ancient Manuscripts, was the first witness on August 30th. He deposed in favor of Dreyfus.

After MM. Molinier and Giry, and M. Picot, a member of the Institute, all of whom testified in favor of Dreyfus, General Deloye testified against the prisoner on the artillery references in the bordereau.

Then the court, on the application of the Government Commissary, Major Carriere, ordered that the opening part of the session of August 31st be behind closed doors for the purpose of discussing documents relating to the artillery.

The evidence of MM. Meyer, Molinier, and Giry, all of whom are handwriting experts of the first mark, was a strong point for Dreyfus. They were most emphatic in declaring the bordereau was written by Esterhazy, and created a better impression than M. Bertillon by not introducing the fantastic diagrams which the latter deemed necessary.

On the other hand, many persons thought General Mercier, fearing that the exposure of August 26th would discredit him altogether with the judges, had conceived the idea of giving way on certain points, and thus to some extent reinstating himself by an affectation of impartiality.

M. Meyer explained this in his evidence before the Assizes Court. He was unable to be so positive in regard to the writer because he had only seen a facsimile of the bordereau; but at the Court of Cassation he saw the original bordereau.

"I convinced myself," said M. Meyer, "by a magnifying glass that the bordereau was written in a free hand and without hesitation, whereas it is precisely hesitation in the formation of the strokes which reveals the use of a method of tracing. I can affirm that it is in the writing and in the very hand of Esterhazy. That is perfectly clear to me." [Commotion.]

At the conclusion of his testimony the witness gave a demonstration of the fallacy of the Bertillon system.

Professor Auguste Molinier, of the School of Ancient Manuscripts, gave similar evidence. He said that each fresh examination of the bordereau only served further to convince him that it was the work of Esterhazy.

Amid deep attention the witness demonstrated how the conclusions of the experts who attributed the bordereau to Dreyfus were mutually destructive, and dwelt on the defects of M. Bertillon's arguments, pointing out the striking resemblance of the alleged doctored handwriting with Esterhazy's writing, who, he added, in everybody's opinion, had relations with Colonel Schwartzkoppen, the former German military attaché at Paris, and the dissimilarities between the writing of the bordereau and that of the prisoner.

The members of the court-martial were apparently much interested, and asked Professor Molinier a number of questions, to which he replied, upholding his conclusion that Esterhazy was the writer of the bordereau.

General Mercier requested permission to speak, and called attention to the fact that in his testimony before the Court of Cassation Professor Molinier said a change was apparent in Esterhazy's handwriting after 1894, and asked that the professor's former evidence be read.

M. Labori then jumped up and inquired if General Mercier intervened with the object of verifying Professor Molinier's evidence. Counsel added that it seemed to him that General Mercier intervened less in the character of a witness than as a representative of the Government Commissary. He therefore would be grateful to the general if he would kindly explain the bearing of his remark.

Mercier replied that on this special point he desired to confirm the evidence of Professor Molinier, which, he said, corroborated M. Bertillon's statement that Esterhazy, the man-of-straw, changed his handwriting in order to replace Dreyfus.

In conclusion General Mercier said:

"Having emphasized the point in regard to the change in Esterhazy's handwriting in 1897, perhaps before, I am satisfied." [Commotion.]

Professor Giry, also of the School of Ancient Manuscripts, gave sim-

16

ilar evidence to that of Professor Molinier. He said the bordereau only
had a superficial likeness to Dreyfus's handwriting, and asserted that it
was certainly the work of Esterhazy.

The witness also said the bordereau was not written with the aid of
key-words.

M. Labori asked if the witness had noticed a change in Esterhazy's
caligraphy, and Professor Giry replied that he had studied the question,
but did not think there had been any marked change.

Counsel then asked whether General Mercier had meant to intimate
that Esterhazy's handwriting had become more or less like that of Dreyfus since 1894, to which the general replied that he had not wished to
express an opinion, but he reiterated that M. Bertillon had shown that
Esterhazy's handwriting had become more like that of the bordereau.

M. Picot, a member of the French Institute, said he had had an interview with a "certain military attaché" (Colonel Schneider, the Austrian
military attaché), and that the conversation turned upon the Dreyfus case.
The attaché expressed surprise at the "incorrect attitude of French officers
in doubting the word of foreign officers."

"My impression," added the witness, "was that he was anxious to assert firmly and unequivocally the absolute innocence of Dreyfus." [Sensa-
tion.]

"Regarding the bordereau," continued M. Picot, "the attaché said only
three documents, enumerated, were referred to, the real fact being that
the others were padding, meant to swell the dossier."

The witness noticed that the attaché employed the expression "hydraulic brake," and never "pneumatic brake."

In regard to Esterhazy, the attaché, M. Picot said, declared that he
considered him a swindler. The attaché also asserted that Esterhazy had
relations with Colonel Schwartzkoppen, who dismissed him because Esterhazy only brought information devoid of interest.

It was then, continued M. Picot, that Esterhazy tried to enter the
War Office, and almost succeeded, and it was then that he wrote to
Colonel Schwartzkoppen the letter since known as the bordereau. In reply to the writer of the bordereau, added M. Picot, Colonel Schwartzkoppen wrote the telegram card known as the *petit bleu*. But on reflection
he crumpled it up and threw it into the fireplace.

At this juncture General Roget asked leave to speak and, stationing himself beside the witness, said he must strongly protest against M. Picot's evidence regarding the military attaché's surprise that French officers did not believe their foreign colleagues.

"What does the witness think," continued General Roget, "of the foreign office, who, having caused the publication in the *Figaro* of an emphatic denial of a statement of General Mercier, was afterward obliged to acknowledge the authorship of a document?"

M. Picot retorted that he had only repeated statements made to him, and had abstained from comments on them. He had, therefore, nothing to say in reply to General Roget's questions.

M. Demange, intervening, asked General Roget if he did not think the Foreign Office's mistake was excusable, since the word "report" had been applied to a document not possessing the character of the report?

"It is not for me to accuse or excuse," replied the general. "I confine myself to pointing out to the court that the conversation repeated occurred in May, that is to say, at the time the result of the investigation of the Court of Cassation was already known. For my part, I only intervened because French officers have been arraigned, and when being accused, French officers have the right to reply." [Excitement.]

General Deloye, Director of Artillery at the War Office, was called to the witness bar. He repeated his explanations given before the Court of Cassation as to the various peculiarities of the artillery, particularly with reference to the brake of the "120 short" gun.

The witness said he considered that in 1894 it would have been impossible for any officer serving with his regiment to communicate anything in regard to the brake of this gun. He added that, although the gun was in use at Rennes, the officers forming the court-martial, among whom was an officer commanding a "120 short" gun, had only the vaguest ideas about this gun, while in 1894 the details of the "pneumatic brake" could only have been known to very few officers.

When Dreyfus was asked if he had anything to say, he replied:

"I do not intend to discuss the terms of the bordereau, nor advance theories about it. It must be known what is in the notes and what is their nature and their value before theories can be suggested.

"Mention has been made of the '120 short' gun. I state briefly for the second time all that I knew in 1889–90 at Bourges of this gun.   I knew the principle of the ' pneumatic brake.'

"General Mercier's deposition recalled the fact that he was Inspector-General at Bourges in 1890.   He must remember the lecture given in the presence of all the officers, both of the Gunnery School and the foundry, and all the departments of Bourges, and the officers of the garrison artillery.   He must recollect the final lecture given on the subject of the 'pneumatic brake,' of which he made the customary rough sketch.   This is to be found in the St. Cyr lectures.   All my knowledge of the 'pneumatic brake' was derived from the lectures.   As regards the brake itself, I have seen it twice, once in the courtyard of the Gunnery School at Bourges and once in the School of War.   I have not seen it in action.   I have not seen the '120 short' gun fired.   I have never been present at the firing trials.

"Mention has also been made of the shrapnel shell of 1891.   The knowledge of General Deloye on this point is much more extensive than mine, and everything he has said is quite correct.   In 1894 I studied the shell, and, in a necessarily incomplete study, reached the conclusion that the shell of the 1891 pattern was a shell in which the bullets were kept in place by a smoke-generating substance intended to produce dense clouds of smoke on bursting, in order to facilitate range finding.   These are the conclusions I reached in 1894, and I chronicled them in a report made at the time."

Chapter XLIV.

THE PRISONER BREAKS DOWN UNDER THE STRAIN

THE session of the court-martial of August 31st opened behind closed doors. Majors Hartmann and Ducros and General Deloye, all of the artillery, were present. The court discussed the secret documents relating to the artillery subjects of the bordereau. In addition to the usual cordons of troops in the streets leading to the Lycée, an extra guard was posted, so as completely to isolate the hall in which the judges met in secret session.

The public were admitted to the court at 9:30 A.M. The first witness called after the public session was opened was Captain Lebrun-Renault of the Republican Guard, who reiterated his testimony given before the court of Cassation, repeating the terms of the alleged confession of Dreyfus:

"I am innocent. In three years they will recognize my innocence. The Minister knows it. If I delivered documents to Germany, it was to have more important ones in return."

The witness's explanation that he did not refer to the confession of Dreyfus during his interview with President Casimir-Perier, because he overheard a conversation during the course of which he was called "traitor," "canaille," and "cur," came as a surprise, for he did not mention this in his evidence before the Court of Cassation, as Maître Labori, leading counsel for the defence, pointed out.

M. Labori also laid stress on the fact that Captain Lebrun-Renault should have kept his notebook, in which, he asserts, he made a note of his conversation with Dreyfus, for four years, and have destroyed it on the very day the matter was brought up in debate in the Chamber of Deputies. The captain's reply that he looked upon the copy made by M. Cavaignac, then Minister of War, as being sufficient, was considered rather lame.

Captain Lebrun-Renault is a well-built man of medium height, broad-shouldered, and wears a well-trimmed mustache.   But he has queer eyes. He spoke in a loud, clear voice.

Dreyfus, replying to the witness, began by calmly declaring that Captain Lebrun-Renault's statement that a certain Captain d'Attel was present during his conversation with Captain Lebrun-Renault was inaccurate.

The witness, however, maintained that Captain d'Attel was present, whereupon Dreyfus said that if he was present he, the prisoner, did not speak to him.

Dreyfus then raised his voice excitedly, and, accompanying his words with short, emphatic gestures of the right hand, which was quivering with his emotion, he declared that Captain Lebrun-Renault should not have repeated to his chiefs his utterances, which began with a protestation of innocence, without asking him to explain his words.

"Those are manœuvres," cried the prisoner, "which must fill all honest men with indignation."

This declaration of the prisoner made a deep impression on the audience.

Dreyfus spoke the last words through his teeth and was evidently laboring under the greatest excitement and indignation.   The audience broke into "Bravos!" which the gendarmes immediately suppressed.

Captain Anthoine followed and repeated what Captain d'Attel had said confirming the confession.   Dreyfus replied that he had not spoken to Captain d'Attel.

On being recalled, Captain Lebrun-Renault said this was true, but he added that Captain d'Attel was present and could have overheard the conversation.

M. Labori here pointed out that Captain d'Attel had not spoken to his chiefs on this subject, and General Mercier, who, like all the military witnesses, followed the proceedings with the keenest attention, rose and admitted that this was correct.

Colonel Jouaust told Dreyfus that he had not explained why he mentioned the term of three years, to which Dreyfus replied:

"I did not give three years as the term.   I only said I hoped that in the course of two or three years my innocence would be recognized.   And I wish to state, Colonel, that, as my letters to General Gonse show, my words did not have the sense evil minds have sought to give them."

M. Labori then had General Gonse called to the bar, and asked him if he had not used the alleged confession of Dreyfus in opposing Colonel Picquart's arguments in favor of a revision.

General Gonse replied that he had not, whereupon M. Labori asked that the letters exchanged between General Gonse and Colonel Picquart should be read.

The clerk of the court began to read a letter which began "My dear Picquart," when General Gonse interrupted him and asked that Colonel Picquart's previous letter be read first, but, as the letter was not available for the moment, the reading of all the letters was adjourned until September 1st.

Major Forzinetti, who was governor of the Cherche-Midi Prison during the time Dreyfus was imprisoned there, and who testified in behalf of Dreyfus, declaring he had never heard of the confession Dreyfus is said to have made, was the next witness called. He repeated his testimony before the Court of Cassation, adding that he frequently met Captain Lebrun-Renault and Captain d'Attel, and that neither of them ever alluded to the alleged confession.

The witness declared that he once taxed Captain Lebrun-Renault before General Gonse and other witnesses, with saying he had spoken to the witness (Major Forzinetti) of the confession, and Captain Lebrun-Renault did not reply. "Whereupon," Major Forzinetti said, "I seized his arm and cried: ' If the words repeated as yours are true, you are an infamous liar.' "

Major Forzinetti then declared that on visiting General de Boisdeffre to express fears about the health of the prisoner, the general asked him his opinion of Dreyfus, and the major replied:

"My General, had you not put that question to me I would have kept my counsel. But since you ask my opinion, I declare I believe he is innocent."

The witness then recounted Colonel Du Paty de Clam's theatrical devices to surprise Dreyfus, to which Forzinetti declined to be a party, and the major also said that on one occasion, when Dreyfus was in a crisis of despair, he, the witness, remained with the prisoner, consoling him, until three o'clock in the morning.

Colonel Jouaust asked Major Forzinetti if Dreyfus ever had ideas of suicide, and the witness replied that Dreyfus had asked for a weapon. and that also, after his condemnation was read to him, he was with difficulty prevented from dashing his head against the wall.

After the last visit of Du Paty de Clam to Dreyfus, continued Major Forzinetti, the prisoner wrote to the Minister of War a letter which concluded with the words:

"When I am gone, let them seek the culprit."

At the conclusion of Major Forzinetti's evidence, Dreyfus, on Colonel Jouaust's invitation, and after reference to the last interview with Du Paty de Clam, said, looking with gratitude at the major:

"There is a matter which Major Forzinetti has just recalled which has greatly moved me, and which I wish to recall, for I wish to say to whom I owe the fact that I have done my duty—to whom I owe having done it for five years after my condemnation.   I had determined to kill myself.   I had made up my mind not to undergo the frightful torture of a soldier from whom they wished to tear the insignia of honor.

"Well, then, let me say this: That if I went to that torture, I can say here that it was thanks to Madame Dreyfus, who showed me my duty, and who told me that if I was innocent I ought to go to it, for the sake of her and our children.   If I am here, it is to her I owe it, Colonel."

Here Major Forzinetti said:

"It is quite true.   In his last interview with his wife Dreyfus said: ' For her and for my children I will undergo this torture of to-morrow.' "

This declaration of Dreyfus that his life was due to his wife deeply stirred all his hearers.   He spoke in a broken voice, with emphatic gestures, swaying to and fro with emotion, and when he had finished he sat down abruptly, evidently to conceal his discomposed features from the gaze of the spectators in court, who when he was seated were only able to see his back.   Tears were glistening in his eyes, and he was clearly suppressing an outburst of sobbing.

General de Boisdeffre denied that Major Forzinetti had expressed to him his conviction that Dreyfus was innocent.   But the major maintained his assertion.

Lieutenant-Colonel Guérin, whom General Saussier ordered to attend the degradation of Captain Dreyfus and report upon it, said:

"At about 7:45 I saw the prison van arrive.   Dreyfus alighted and was taken to the office, where he was guarded by Captain Lebrun-Renault, whose name I did not know at that time. At 8:55 the adjutant of the garrison relieved Captain Lebrun-Renault, with four artillerymen and a corporal, composing the guard which was to conduct the prisoner to the place of degradation. At that moment I was at the door of the building.

"Captain Lebrun-Renault, when relieved from duty, saw me and immediately began to relate what Dreyfus had said. The three statements which struck him, because of their importance, remained so graven in my memory that I could never forget them,—namely, first, the prisoner's pride in the facings he had lost; second, his confession that he had delivered documents to a foreign power; third, that in three years justice would be done him. A group of officers were standing near, and as Captain Lebrun-Renault's conversation was not confidential, and the statement he had made me was of great importance and interest to us, I begged him to repeat to the officers what he had just told me.

"I must add that Captain d'Attel had been ordered to superintend matters, and his special duty required him to report everything which occurred in the office of the adjutant while Dreyfus was there, and until Dreyfus was conducted to the place of degradation.

"Throughout the ceremony the prisoner walked automatically. Afterward, when he was conducted to the prison van, I stood, in company with some officers, in the passage Dreyfus traversed, and Dreyfus, addressing the officers, repeated that in three years justice would be done him. He then entered the van and disappeared.

"After the ceremony I verbally reported to General Saussier the incident of the morning, particularly the statements made by Dreyfus to Captain Lebrun-Renault.

"During the day Captain d'Attel also told M. Wunenberger, archivist of the Paris Headquarters, that Dreyfus had confessed."

M. Demange—How do you reconcile his protests of innocence with the alleged confession?

Colonel Guérin—That is not my business.

M. Demange—You reported the confession to General Saussier?

Colonel Guérin—Certainly.

M. Demange—Was it suggested that steps be taken to verify the alleged confession?

Colonel Guérin—I do not recollect.

M. Demange—So there was no attempt to interrogate Dreyfus in regard to the alleged confession?

Colonel Guérin—The case had passed out of the hands of the military authorities, the prisoner having been handed over to the civil authorities.

Dreyfus, when the usual question was put to him, said he had nothing to add to the reply he had made to Captain Lebrun-Renault.

One of the judges asked the witness whether M. Weil, when attached to the Army Headquarters, had relations with Esterhazy, to which Colonel Guérin replied that he believed M. Weil had known Esterhazy for a long time.

The Judge—Do you think Esterhazy knew the prisoner?

Colonel Guérin—I do not know.

Dreyfus here remarked that he never knew Esterhazy.

Major de Mitry of the hussars testified to Captain Anthoine telling him of the alleged confession of Dreyfus.

Army Controller Peyrolles also testified that he heard of the confession from Colonel Guérin. The latter he added, introduced the witness to Captain Lebrun-Renault on their way to the Zola trial.

Continuing, Major de Mitry said:

"I said to Captain Lebrun-Renault, point blank: 'How is it the confession of Dreyfus was not reported to our President and Premier when you were summoned to the Elysée?'

"Captain Lebrun-Renault replied: 'I did not report it, through a kind of apprehension, because when in the anteroom I heard some one say "Who is this gendarme who is betraying professional secrets and feeding the press? He might smart for such indiscretions."'

"I replied: 'Renault, you have made a mistake. In your place I would have told the President.'"

When called upon to reply, Dreyfus declared he had never said his trial would be revised in three years.

"I do not understand these words," said the prisoner. "I should be very grateful to you, Colonel, if, in the interest of truth, you would make public the letter which I wrote to the Chief of the Headquarters Staff. It would then be seen in what terms I asked that an investigation should be made."

Colonel Jouaust—But why in three years?

Dreyfus—I have already told the court that I told Colonel Du Paty de Clam that the Government had the means of investigation, but that it required time to use them. I said, therefore, that before two or three years my innocence would be acknowledged. But I emphatically assert there was no sinister motive in my mind such as has been attached to these words. [Excitement.]

Dreyfus evidently referred to the General Staff's suggestion that when he used the expression "three years" he knew that Esterhazy would then appear as a man-of-straw and try to take Dreyfus's place.

Chapter XLV.

MORE TESTIMONY FOR DREYFUS

IMMEDIATELY after the opening of the session of the court-martial on September 1st, Colonel Jouaust aroused the interest of the audience by remarking:

"Maître Labori the other day asked that information be obtained regarding the character of a certain witness. I would not have acceded if the witness had not expressed a similar desire. Information which has now reached me will be read."

The clerk of the court accordingly read a report regarding M. Dubreuil, the Parisian friend of M. de Beaurepaire, who testified on August 23d that Dreyfus met a German attaché at the house of a mutual friend named Bodson, and whose cross-examination reflected severely on his reputation. The report was to the effect that M. Dubreuil never was a horse-dealer, as claimed by M. Labori, and that the character of the witness was most respectable, he being held in general esteem.

This was a very satisfactory session for Dreyfus. The Beaurepaire witness, Germain, who was to prove that Dreyfus attended the Alsatian manœuvres, found his statements denied by a reputable witness, while Germain himself, it was proved, had undergone two convictions for swindling.

In his deposition Germain declared he saddled a horse for Dreyfus to follow the manœuvres, and he said that his employer, Kuhlman, accompanied Dreyfus riding, and adding that the major told the witness the name of his companion.

Colonel Jouaust questioned Dreyfus on this point, and in reply to the usual question Dreyfus admitted that about 1886 or 1887 he spent a furlough at Mulhouse, adding:

"Every year, both while studying and attending the gunnery and artillery training schools, I passed one or two months at Mulhouse. But I can positively affirm that I never was present either in an official or semi-official capacity at the German manœuvres. I was never invited to attend the German manœuvres, and I never dined or lunched with any German officer. On each visit I called on the general commanding at Mulhouse with my regular passport, in accordance with my duty.

"I would like to point out, in regard to the manœuvring ground to which reference is made, that the Mulhouse ground is not ground over which manœuvres could be carried out. It is merely a small drill ground, nothing more than a clearing in the Hartz Forest on the road from Mulhouse to Basle. It is true that in the course of my excursions in 1886 I might have seen regiments drilling. But I emphatically declare that while out riding in 1886 or 1887 I never dined or lunched with German officers, was never even invited to do so by foreign officers, and never spoke to foreign officers."

Replying to Colonel Jouaust, Dreyfus said that while he was at Mulhouse he rode his brother's horse, and did not remember anything about the horse mentioned by Germain.

During the cross-examination M. Labori asked the groom, Germain, if he was acquainted with M. de Beaurepaire, and the witness replied that he was not acquainted with him, but he added that M. de Beaurepaire knew the facts to which he testified, through the witness's friends, and he also admitted having written to M. de Beaurepaire giving information which the latter had published in the *Echo de Paris*.

The next two witnesses, however, gave strong testimony in favor of Dreyfus, and sadly knocked Germain's testimony about.

Kuhlman, the livery-stable keeper, who employed Germain at this time, in his testimony said that he never rode with Dreyfus as stated by Germain; that he never went to the manœuvres in company with Dreyfus, and absolutely denied all Germain's statements. Germain, the liveryman added, was in his employ, and possibly the groom accompanied Dreyfus. But the witness had no knowledge of it.

In conclusion, Kuhlman emphatically reiterated that he never rode with Dreyfus. He said he was well acquainted with the whole Dreyfus family.

Major d'Infreville testified that he had known Germain since 1894. He added that Germain informed him that Dreyfus attended the German manœuvres. Witness had never said that an officer Germain saw in the Bois de Boulogne was Dreyfus, for the simple reason that he did not know Dreyfus.

Germain, on being recalled, asserted that he certainly thought Major d'Infreville told him the officer referred to was Dreyfus.

The next witness, Captain Le Monnier of the Headquarters Staff, who was a probationer at the same time as Dreyfus, deposed that while they were at the School of War in 1894, Dreyfus, in the course of a conversation referring to the.covering of troops in the Vosges region and the movements necessary for the invasion of Alsace, said that he was well acquainted with a certain position to which the Germans attached great importance as a means of checking a French advance. This position, witness continued, was westward of Mulhouse, and Dreyfus said he reached this opinion after following the German manœuvres on horseback.

The prisoner at this point quietly pointed out that the position mentioned by Captain Le Monnier was situated in an entirely different locality from where he, the prisoner, is supposed to have followed the manœuvres. Dreyfus added:

"Captain Le Monnier must have confused it with a position which I described from knowledge acquired when traversing the whole district on horseback while a youth."

The prisoner reiterated that he never attended the manœuvres in question.

The next witness, M. Villon, another of the friends of M. de Beaurepaire, declared that when in Berlin during the year 1894 he overheard a conversation of some German officers who were lunching in an adjoining room of a café in that city. One of the officers, the witness added, expressed indignation that a French officer was guilty of treason, and his companion replied:

"It is a good thing for us. You know we are getting the plans of mobilization from Dreyfus." [Murmurs of assent and dissent.]

At the request of M. Demange, M. Villon detailed the alleged conversation, and said he had not mentioned the conversation in 1894, because Dreyfus has been arrested, and, knowing him to be guilty, the witness foresaw he would be convicted.

The café, however, in which the above conversation is reported to

have occurred has since disappeared, and, as there are no means of verifying Villon's testimony, it certainly should not have had much effect on
the judges.

Two or three witnesses, in support of Dreyfus on artillery questions,
were next heard, and special Commissary Fischer of the Eastern Military
Railway System testified that he was charged to investigate the leakage of
documents at the gunnery school at Bourges, and found nothing to incriminate Dreyfus.

Fischer asserted that he was not long in finding out that a former
artilleryman named Thomas had communicated to a foreign power documents affecting the national defence. Thomas, he added, was sentenced
to death for attempted murder in 1886, but the sentence was commuted
to penal servitude for life. The witness went to Avignon and secured the
convict's confession that he communicated sketches of "shell 80 " of the
horse artillery and of the "120 siege-gun," for which he had received one
thousand francs.

Replying to Colonel Jouaust, the witness declared that, as Thomas was
arrested in 1886, he could not have been a spy at a later date.

Fischer was followed by Lieutenant Bernheim, who testified that, while
in garrison at Rouen, he furnished Esterhazy with information and documents regarding the artillery, in which Esterhazy was much interested.
The witness was never able to recover the documents. He supposed at
the time that Esterhazy was anxious to increase his military knowledge.

Replying to M. Demange, Lieutenant Bernheim said he had not testified at the Esterhazy trial, because his testimony was then considered to
be of no great value.

Lieutenant Brugere, of the Artillery Reserve, the next witness called,
said it was perfectly easy for any officer to inspect closely the "120-short "
gun. Moreover, he added, detailed explanations and information regarding the brake were given to the officers present when the gun was fired.
On two occasions, witness also said, when the gun was fired he noticed the
presence of a group of non-artillery officers. Therefore, the lieutenant
pointed out, it was plain that access to the gun was quite easy.

In May, 1894, Lieutenant Brugere continued, the new Firing Manual
was distributed. A copy was given to each battery, and, as the captain's
lectures were not fully understood, other copies of the Firing Manual were

printed, and all officers and non-commissioned officers so desiring could obtain as many as they liked.   In some regiments even the ordinary gunners secured copies, and among those favored regiments, Lieutenant Brugere pointed out, was the Sixth Artillery, stationed at Rennes.   [Excitement.]

The witness said he gave his copy of the Firing Manual to an infantry officer on May 17, 1894.   The *Société de Tir à Canon*, of Paris, also reprinted the manual and distributed it among its members.

Captain Le Rond here interposed, saying that no batteries of the "120-short" gun were at the Chalons camp in 1894, and Lieutenant Brugere retorted that he only referred to what he saw in the month of May. A lively discussion ensued, General Roget and General Deloye denying Lieutenant Brugere's statements.

General Roget asked Lieutenant Brugere if he was not the officer who had written M. Cavaignac, then Minister of War, a violent letter tendering his resignation and declaring it was a dishonor to serve in the French army.

This declaration caused a scene, for Lieutenant Brugere, turning to General Roget, cried:

"I protest against General Roget's words.   I affirm that I never said any such thing."

General Roget then backed down, saying:

"Well, that was the general sense of the letter."

A roar of disgust came from the audience at this apparent underhandedness upon the part of the general, and Lieutenant Brugere again emphatially declared General Roget was wrong.

General Deloye, to whom General Roget appealed, said he had been consulted by the Minister of War as to what ought to be done in connection with the letter, and witness read the report which he made on the subject to the President of the Republic, who, he added, immediately signed an order relegating Lieutenant Brugere to the Territorial Army.

After this Lieutenant Brugere again arose, and emphatically maintained that he made no statement in the sense indicated by General Roget, but had only alluded to some personalities, and had not mentioned the French army.   It would have been absurd to do so, he continued, since the French army consists of all citizens over twenty years of age.

Maître Labori and Colonel Jouaust agreed that the letter should be obtained from the Ministry of War and read in court. Lieutenant Brugere expressed satisfaction at this step, while General Roget returned to his seat with less buoyancy than he left it.

The next witness, Captain Carvalho, a handsome young artillery officer, proved an excellent reinforcement for Dreyfus. He gave his evidence clearly and boldly, and emphatically declared that there were no special precautions to keep the mechanism of the "120-short" gun secret. He said the gun was frequently operated in the presence of non-artillery officers, who were told everything that they desired to know, including a description of the hydro-pneumatic brake. Moreover, he added that in April, 1894, the artillery officers had a description of the hydro-pneumatic brake given them.

Regarding the 1895 Firing Manual, witness said copies were obtainable in 1894 in all the regiments of the army, and asserted that he had purchased a copy.

"Here," said Captain Carvalho, "is an actual copy of the manual, which I hand over to the court-martial."

M. Labori then had an animated discussion with Colonel Jouaust, who at first refused the counsel's request to read a letter which the latter had received on the evening of August 31st. After receiving a reluctant permission from the court, Labori read the letter, which proved to be from a spy named Corningue, stating that he had copied the Firing Manual in the room of Major Panizzardi, the Italian military attaché at Paris, in the presence of Colonel Schwartzkoppen, the German military attaché at Paris (referred to in the letter as A and B). Labori then said he was not certain whether this was the 1894 or 1895 manual, and begged the President to question Colonel Picquart on the subject.

Picquart said, in response, that he believed it was the 1895 manual, and that the copy was made in 1896 in Major Panizzardi's room in the presence of Major Panizzardi and another person. Colonel Picquart added that Major Lauth ought to know something about a certain mark on the manual. All the manuals at the Versailles garrison were ordered returned to headquarters in order to see which one was missing.

General Deloye admitted that he was not sure whether it was the 1894 or 1895 manual, and corroborated Colonel Picquart's statements.

Major Lauth expressed surprise at the fact that Colonel Picquart's rec-

17

ollections were so vague, and added that Picquart had relations with the spy, Corningue, who, he said, was a doubtful character.

Here M. Labori asked to what spy Major Lauth was able to give a good character, to which the major replied:

"Why, none." [Laughter.]

M. Labori then said that Major Lauth insinuated that Corningue was trying to levy blackmail. Was that his idea?

Colonel Jouaust refused to allow the question.

M. Labori then asked to be allowed to question Major Lauth further, but Colonel Jouaust refused. Counsel insisted, but Colonel Jouaust waved him down, whereupon M. Labori cried:

"You suppress all awkward questions." [Sensation.]

The Government Commissary, Major Carriere, said:

"I desire to point out that the defence is always asking to speak, while I am always refused permission to do so when I ask."

Colonel Jouaust, out of patience, retorted:

"I have heard enough. Be quiet. The incident is closed."

This cavalier treatment of the Government Commissary, who, however, made himself ridiculous whenever he opened his mouth, caused general laughter.

Addressing Colonel Picquart, M. Labori asked:

"When did you know that the Firing Manual was being copied?"

Colonel Picquart—During the summer of 1896.

M. Labori having remarked that this was all he desired to ask at present, General Hippolyte Sebert, retired, of the marine artillery, deposed. He preceded his testimony by saying he did not think he ought to withhold the evidence he was able to give, as he felt it would contribute to the reparation of a judicial error.

The general then criticised the bordereau from a professional standpoint, pointing out that the writer must have been a low-classed man, negotiating directly with a correspondent on whose doles he was dependent. He said he was probably an officer, but certainly not an artillery officer, adding that this was proved by the employment of expressions an artilleryman could not have used.

General Sebert entered into long explanations of his statements, pertinently pointing out that an artillery officer would have known the interesting parts of the Firing Manual, and would not have written in the bordereau, "Take what interests you." The witness gave a number of instances showing the dense ignorance displayed in gunnery technicalities by the writer of the bordereau, and amid profound silence General Sebert declared that his study of the case had led him to the conviction that the bordereau could not have been written by an artillery officer or by an officer belonging to a special arm of the service who had passed through the Polytechnic School. [Excitement.]

General Sebert referred to the satisfaction he felt at knowing that the experts of the highest standing in handwriting had confirmed his opinion, and he dismissed M. Bertillon's assertions, saying that on examination he, the witness, had easily found proof of the worthlessness of that demonstration.

"It is painful for me," added General Sebert, "to express so severe an opinion on the man whose name is connected with the application of the anthropometric method, which has been of great service to our country. But French science cannot give its authority to lucubrations so pretentious as those M. Bertillon brought here. I reassert most emphatically that the bordereau was not written by an artillery officer or by an officer who passed through the Polytechnic School. I have been sustained in giving my evidence by my firm belief in the entire innocence of Dreyfus, and I am glad I have had strength enough to bring here the stone which I have to lay on the edifice of reparation, and conscientiously, while holding aloof from outside passions. This edifice is a work of appeasement and peace, which will restore the country to an era of concord and union." [Prolonged excitement.]

General Sebert also expressed his opinion of Valerio's evidence in support of M. Bertillon's system, saying that, in spite of the latter's talent, he had not succeeded in converting a false theory into a true one.

As soon as General Sebert had finished his testimony, M. Bertillon bounced up, and asked to be allowed to speak; but Colonel Jouaust quickly turned to the usher and said, "Bring in the next witness," whereupon M. Bertillon, extremely annoyed, returned to his seat.

Major Ducros then deposed that he commanded a field battery; that he knew Dreyfus and offered him certain information. But, he pointed out, Dreyfus never asked him a question, although he knew he (the witness) possessed much interesting information, especially particulars about the hydro-pneumatic brake.

General Mercier here intervened, and said that, at the time Major Ducros was speaking of, the Ducros field-piece had been rejected in favor of the Deport cannon, and, he said, Dreyfus therefore could have no object in procuring particulars of the Ducros gun.

Major Hartmann of the artillery was the next witness for the defence. He asked permission to refer to certain of the documents which were produced during the secret session of the court on August 31st, upon which, he said, he had reached important conclusions. But General Deloye objected, as it was contrary to the instructions of the Minister of War.

The major then asked the court to sit briefly in camera, and Colonel Jouaust promised to render a decision later.

More support for Dreyfus was forthcoming, however, in this deposition of Major Hartmann, since he expressed the opinion that the author of the bordereau did not know what he was writing about, as he spoke of the "120-short" gun when he meant the "120-long" gun.

The major led the court through a maze of technical details about artillery, until Colonel Jouaust asked him to refrain from technicalities as far as possible, evidently fearing that Hartmann might reveal secrets of the service. His evidence was directed entirely to show that Dreyfus was not the author of the bordereau, and that the artillery information mentioned in it was accessible to many officers of all arms in the spring of 1894.

Proceeding, Major Hartmann testified on highly technical subjects, his evidence being the same as given before the Court of Cassation. He spoke in loud, energetic tones, and occupied the whole of the remainder of the session. The major's testimony was not concluded when the court adjourned.

So far as the depositions were concerned, Dreyfus certainly had every reason to be pleased with this day's proceedings.

Chapter XLVI.

MORE TESTIMONY IN FAVOR OF DREYFUS

THERE was a large attendance of generals at the Lycée at the opening of the session of September 2d.

The interest centred in the testimony of Major Hartmann, of the artillery, which was interrupted by the adjournment of the court on September 1st, and was resumed at this session. The major, who had done great service for the defence, resumed his important deposition regarding artillery matters, and the bringing out of points and phraseology in the bordereau indicating that the writer could not be Dreyfus.

The witness wished to enter into the question of the Robin shell. But, on General Deloye's objecting to a statement on the subject in open court, Major Hartmann asked to be allowed to give it behind closed doors, saying it would only take him a few minutes to call attention to the point he had in mind.

The president of the court decided to hear this part of the witness's testimony in camera at the end of the proceedings, or at the beginning of the session of September 4th.

In response to questions from Maître Labori, leading counsel for the defence, and M. Demange, Major Hartmann said any officer attending the Chalons camp would have obtained sufficient information to write notes on the covering of troops and Madagascar matters.

M. Labori then recalled General Mercier's attack on Captain Freystaetter, on the latter's declaration that the secret dossier communicated to the court of 1894 contained a document concerning a shell, for which General Mercier called the captain a liar. Major Hartmann affirmed that it was quite possible that particulars about a certain shell should have leaked out in 1894.

An interesting confrontation between General Deloye and Major Hartmann followed, the general declaring that he did not believe the major was keeping strictly to the truth.   Deloye then proceeded to point to what he said were inaccuracies in Major Hartmann's testimony.   He insisted that Dreyfus, in the course of conversations with artillery officers, could have secured information on the subjects mentioned in the bordereau, to which the major retorted that if any artillery officer had been questioned by Dreyfus he would already have come forward to say so as a matter of strict duty.

General Deloye, questioned by M. Labori and M. Demange, said the inventor of the Robin shell told him Dreyfus never asked him for particulars about his shell, except on a minor point.   The general added he came as a technical witness to show Dreyfus could be guilty, adding that it was not his business to say whether he believed him innocent or guilty.   He could only say that Dreyfus's contention that it was impossible for him to know certain matters referred to in the bordereau was untrue.

M. Labori asked General Deloye if he knew whether the documents which could have been betrayed by the traitor, especially by the writer of the bordereau, were important, whereupon the general turned to counsel and excitedly cried:

"Don't ask me.   Don't ask me!"

These exclamations created a sensation in court, which was doubled when General Deloye added that there was sufficient in the bordereau to establish that the traitor knew the importance of the documents he was giving up.   The witness added:

"When I read the bordereau I was dismayed."

Major Hartmann, in reply to General Deloye, reiterated that the author of the bordereau was ignorant of artillery matters.

"For," the major pointed out, "if he meant the '120' hydraulic brake, he gave particulars of what was long known, while if he meant the '120 short' he employed a wrong expression."

General Mercier reappeared in the witness box in an attempt to refute Major Hartmann's argument.   He accounted for the use of the expression "hydraulic brake" in the bordereau by the fact that the Germans used the expression to designate similar brakes.   Therefore, he added, it was natural that the correspondent of the Germans should employ the term.

General Deloye then said:

"I beg the court to allow me to say that in an army liable to find itself confronted by the enemy there is need of cohesion.   Consequently, all the officers of France must march hand in hand, as brethren.   I do not think it is good for it to be said that officers who have risen from the ranks should stop short at a certain point, and that individual merit should not count, and that there is a bar which cannot be passed.   No! no! that is not satisfactory any more than it is true.   Captain Valerio is an example.   He has made himself, and a large number of others similarly able have filled the positions to which they have risen.   Coming here as the representative of the Minister of War, I beg the court to allow me to say to one of our comrades who has risen from the ranks that these opinions are not ours.   I think it was necessary to say so."

After a brief discussion between General Mercier, General Deloye, and Major Hartmann on the German expression used to designate hydraulic brake, the trio returned to their seats.

This ended the deposition of Major Hartmann, who certainly was a very valuable witness for the defence, although the effect of his testimony was somewhat weakened by General Deloye's theatrical statement in reply to M. Labori.

The next witness, M. Louis Havet, a member of the Institute, took up the bordereau from a grammatical point of view, declaring it to be his conviction, after studying closely the styles of Dreyfus and Esterhazy, that the latter wrote it.   The witness entered into an interesting analysis of the phraseology of the bordereau, pointing out that certain phrases in it were met in Esterhazy's letters, but never in those of Dreyfus.   He then traced the influence exercised on Esterhazy by his linguistic acquirements, notably traces of German construction.

The Government Commissary, Major Carriere, who was always blundering, asked M. Havet if he had been present at sessions of the court before he had testified.

M. Havet said "Yes," to which the major, with great severity, said:

"You have been guilty of a grave breach of judiciary discipline."

To this M. Havet quietly remarked:

"But I had not been summoned as a witness at the time I attended the sessions."

Major Carriere sat down, checkmated.

The letters exchanged between Colonel Picquart and General Gonse, at the time the colonel wanted a thorough investigation into the case, were then read, and M. Labori pointed out to General Gonse that these letters never alluded to the alleged confession of Dreyfus.

General Gonse replied that it was because he always advised Colonel Picquart not to mix up the Esterhazy and Dreyfus cases. Dreyfus, he added, had been condemned, and his case could not be reopened, but they were bound to see if there was not another traitor.

The general then made a bitter complaint of the fact that his letters had been communicated to M. Scheurer-Kestner, former Vice-President of the Senate.

Referring to this published correspondence, General Gonse exclaimed: "When one procures the handwriting of a man one can get him hanged." [Laughter.] General Gonse referred to a well-known saying of a French judge, Laubardemont: "Give me four lines of a man's handwriting and I'll have him hanged."

Continuing, General Gonse said:

"When a man intends to publish another's letters he asks what the writer's meaning was. That is but fair. But, without doing so, Picquart handed my letters to M. Scheurer-Kestner without my knowledge or consent. These letters have been published in a book which can be found at every bookseller's, entitled "Gonse-Pilate.'"

M. Labori—Was not the bordereau, in conjunction with the *petit bleu*, the basis of Picquart's belief in Esterhazy's guilt?

General Gonse—I said to Picquart: "Don't let us trouble about hand-writings at present."

M. Labori—How could the Dreyfus and Esterhazy cases be separated, when both were based on a common document?

General Gonse—Because at that time Dreyfus had been convicted, and the bordereau was ascribed to him.

M. Labori—Was it not possible to reconsider an error?

General Gonse—There was nothing to prove to me that the bordereau was written by Esterhazy.

M. Labori—Will General Gonse repeat what Colonel Picquart told him concerning the conclusions of M. Bertillon?

General Gonse—I was not acquainted with M. Bertillon's conclusions, but Picquart seems to exaggerate them.

At M. Labori's request, Colonel Picquart was recalled, and said:

"In a brief letter which I wrote to General Gonse in regard to M. Bertillon's conclusions, I only referred to part of his observations, and the best proof that I did not wish to exaggerate them is the fact that I asked General Gonse to order a supplemental inquiry."

Colonel Jouaust—In what form did M. Bertillon communicate the result of his examination?

Colonel Picquart—Verbally, on two occasions. As regards General Gonse's letters I handed them to a lawyer when I understood that I was the object of abominable intrigues, and when I received from my former subordinate, Henry, while in Tunis, a threatening letter, which had been forwarded with the assent of General Gonse and de Boisdeffre. If this letter was published I cannot be held responsible for it. [Excitement.]

General Gonse maintained that the Henry letter was written without his assent and in reply to an insolent letter from Picquart. The latter, the general added, saw machinations everywhere. He alleged that he was sent to Tunis to be killed. The court could form its own conclusions.

Colonel Picquart remarked that he brought the secret dossier to General Gonse simultaneously with the bordereau, and that the general, consequently, was in a position to judge of the probabilities of the innocence of Dreyfus.

M. Labori asked if General Gonse knew of the plot hatched against Picquart, and if he knew that letters addressed to Picquart at Tunis were opened at the War Office? and the general admitted that a letter was opened in the Intelligence Department in November. He added that suspicious letters were always handed to him (General Gonse) by Lieutenant-Colonel Henry, so that he, the general, might report to the Minister of War on them.

M. Labori—Whom was the letter addressed to?

General Gonse—I do not know. No doubt to the chief of some department.

Colonel Picquart—It was addressed to me personally.

M. Labori—Does General Gonse know that the words in the letter in question were used for the purpose of fabricating a telegram intended to destroy the value of the *petit bleu?*

General Gonse admitted that the expressions seemed to him suspicious. If the letters were seized it was because they were addressed to Picquart as head of the department, and it was thought they might relate to official matters. He added that Picquart's letters were only opened when they looked suspicious.

Colonel Picquart retorted that it was curious his opened letters afterward reached him without a sign of having been tampered with.

Counsel then questioned General Gonse relative to the opening of the "Speranza" letter, and the general replied that this letter was not addressed to Picquart, but bore a curious address.

M. Labori—Why did General Pellieux ascribe the letter to Colonel Picquart, whom he had never seen?

General Gonse—I do not know.

M. Labori pointed out that the first letter, which was genuine, was forwarded to Colonel Picquart after having been opened, while the "Speranza" letter was retained. The latter could therefore be regarded as the work of a forger.

Colonel Jouaust—You are entering into a discussion.

M. Labori (sharply)—No, Monsieur le Président; by virtue of Article 319 of the Code, I merely say what I think in regard to the evidence.

General Gonse, replying further, dwelt upon the fact that it was necessary that the Intelligence Department should know the acts of Colonel Picquart, who had been removed on account of his conduct.

M. Labori—Does General Gonse think the Henry forgery was the result of a plot against Colonel Picquart?

General Gonse said he thought the forgery was "an unfortunate proceeding." [Laughter.] He would have prevented it if he had been consulted. But he did not believe there was a plot against Picquart. Henry desired to have fresh proof against Dreyfus, "though fresh proof was not really required, as the diplomatic dossier contained ample proof."

M. Labori protested against such a statement, and asked which document of the dossier implicated Dreyfus.

Colonel Jouaust refused to allow the question, and counsel thereupon remarked that he reserved the right to form what conclusions he thought proper on this point.

Colonel Jouaust—Form as many conclusions as you like.

M. Labori next referred to the attempt to bribe Commissary Tomps, and to erasures in the *petit bleu*.

General Gonse declared the *petit bleu* already had traces of erasure before it was first photographed.

This M. Labori vigorously denied, and asked that the evidence of the experts proving the contrary should be read.

Here General Roget reappeared on the scene, and, amid the keenest attention of all, described the forgery proceedings against Picquart as resulting from his (the witness's) discovery that erasures had been made in the *petit bleu*.

"It was General Zurlinden," Roget added, "who ordered Picquart to be prosecuted. I assume responsibility for all my own acts, but for my own acts alone. I am surprised that the defence should arraign me on this point."

M Labori declared that he merely wished to show that the erasures could not be ascribed to Picquart, and that therefore they ought not to have formed the basis of a prosecution against him. Then counsel again asked that the expert evidence on the subject be read, and Colonel Jouaust promised it should be read during a future session.

Upon three occasions M. Demange asked General Gonse to explain why Picquart, on seeing the *petit bleu*, proposed to lay a trap for Esterhazy, unless the *petit bleu* was addressed to Esterhazy. But counsel elicited no reply, until General Roget came to the rescue and said Picquart knew Esterhazy was coming to Paris in any case, and if he sent a decoy letter, Esterhazy would have appeared to come in response to it, whether he had done so in reality or not.

M. Labori declared this was untrue, and Picquart maintained that his conduct throughout was perfectly straightforward.

M. des Fonds-Lamothe, a former artillery officer, and now an engineer, was the next witness. He testified that he was a probationer simultaneously with Dreyfus. The witness said that in August, 1894, he borrowed the Firing Manual from Colonel Picquart and kept it as long as he liked.

"In 1894," M. des Fonds-Lamothe said, "Firing Manuals were given to whoever asked for them."

M. Demange—Can the witness, who was on the Headquarters Staff with Dreyfus, say whether, in 1894, he thought he would go to the manœuvres? [Excitement.]

M. Lamothe—I have only performed a conscientious act. I am convinced that not one probationer in 1894 could have believed he would go to the manœuvres.

M. des Fonds-Lamothe also stated that the probationers were informed by a circular dated May 15, 1894, that they would not attend the manœuvres. The object of antedating the bordereau, the witness added, was to make it a prior date to that of the circular. It had since been attempted to attain the same object by post-dating the circular.

As to the post-dating of the circular, witness said he did not doubt that different Ministers of War who had expressed opinions in the case were perfectly honest, but he thought they had made a mistake. [Excitement.]

The witness, who was a fellow-probationer of Dreyfus, proved one of the strongest witnesses for the defence, as he brought out in support of his contention that Dreyfus could not have written the bordereau the following argument:

"If, as at first asserted, the bordereau was dated May, Dreyfus could not have written, ' I am going to the manœuvres,' because a circular was issued in May informing the probationers that they would not go to the manœuvres; while if the bordereau was written in April, as now asserted, Dreyfus could not have spoken of the Firing Manual, which was only printed at the end of May."

Not one of the generals found a reply to the last argument, which looked like a clincher, General de Boisdeffre alone declaring that, although it was true the circular mentioned was sent to the probationers, the latter knew that they could nevertheless go to the manœuvres if they made special application. Generals Mercier and Roget then went on the stage and confronted M. des Fonds-Lamothe, and a heated discussion ensued. General Roget asked when the witness had altered his conviction in favor of Dreyfus, and M. des Fonds-Lamothe replied:

"From the time of the publication of the proceedings before the Court of Cassation. I was expecting proof of my comrade's guilt, and I was thunderstruck when I saw the date of the bordereau had been altered."

General Roget asked if Fonds-Lamothe had not on several occasions expressed his belief in Dreyfus's guilt?

M. des Fonds-Lamothe admitted that possibly he had done so, before the publication of the proceedings before the Court of Cassation, but not at the time of the prisoner's arrest, for that was kept secret.

Asked the usual question, the prisoner reminded the court that in 1894, when Colonel Du Paty de Clam had endeavored to make the date of the bordereau August, he had protested that he could not have written the sentence, "I am going to the manœuvres," since he would not be going on regimental duty until October, November, and December, and he dwelt upon the fact that at the time he handed M. Demange a note on the subject.

M. Demange corroborated the prisoner's testimony, and pointed out that the note mentioned by the prisoner had been added to the dossier by the Court of Cassation, while Dreyfus was still on Devil's Island, thus precluding all doubt as to its genuineness.

General Roget here interpellated that requests to go to the manœuvres were usually made verbally, so that it could not be proved whether Dreyfus had asked or had not asked to go to the manœuvres. The general, however, admitted that no inquiry had ever been made on this important point.

M. Demange created a stir by saying that it was most regrettable that no inquiry had been made by the War Office on a point of such importance.

General Roget was greatly excited during the foregoing scene, but M. des Fonds-Lamothe did not flinch. He retorted quickly to all the general's observations. The two men glared at one another, and once General Roget addressed M. des Fonds-Lamothe in such a bullying fashion that the audience hooted him.

M. des Fonds-Lamothe concluded with declaring that if the prosecution would follow up the pieces of evidence they would be absolutely convinced that Dreyfus did not write the bordereau.

The court briefly retired and afterward announced that it had been decided to hear the remainder of Major Hartmann's evidence in camera on September 4th.

The court then adjourned.

Chapter XLVII.

CONFLICTING TESTIMONY

THE fifth week of the second trial by court-martial of Captain Dreyfus began on September 4th, with the largest attendance yet seen in the Lycée.

The session opened very interestingly with the appearance of M. Cernuschi, an Austro-Hungarian refugee.

His letter to Colonel Jouaust, offering his testimony, stated that, having been mixed up in political troubles in Austria-Hungary, he had been obliged to seek refuge in France, where he had a friend who was a high official of the foreign office of a central European power. This friend, the witness said, told him that certain foreign agents in France might denounce him, the first name mentioned being that of Dreyfus. Another officer, a foreign general of staff, similarly warned him.

One day, the witness said, when he was visiting the latter, he saw him take from his pocket a voluminous packet containing military documents. The officer said that in France one could buy anything, adding:

"What is the good of Jews if you don't use them?"

Being questioned if he asked the name of the traitor in this case, the witness replied:

"No, because the officer had already said Dreyfus was his informant."

This answer and the tone in which it was delivered evoked a movement of incredulity among the audience. Major Carriere, representing the Government, asked that the court hold further examination of this witness behind closed doors, in view of the diplomatic side of his testimony.

M. Labori then arose and announced that since the prosecution had summoned the aid of foreigners he intended to make formal application to have complete steps taken through foreign channels to ascertain whether the documents mentioned in the bordereau were delivered to a foreign power, and if so, by whom.

The words of M. Labori created a deep impression, as they made it evident that counsel for the defence was on the war-path.

The second witness called was M. André, clerk to M. Bertulus, judge of the Court of Cassation, who received the confession of Lieutenant-Colonel Henry. M. André deposed that he overheard Lieutenant-Colonel Henry exclaim:

"Don't insist, I beg of you; the honor of the army must be saved before everything."

The next important witness was the well-known mathematician M. Painleye, who began by tearing M. Bertillon's system of argumentation to pieces.

M. Painleye exhaustively criticised Mr. Bertillon's cryptographic system, citing in support of his conclusions the opinion of M. Henri Poincaré, in his opinion the most illustrious mathematician of modern times, who, in a letter the witness read, examined seriatim the deductions of M. Bertillon and demonstrated their fallacy, also pointing out miscalculations made by M. Valerio. Professor Poincaré's letter fully supported M. Bernard's conclusions.

The reading of Professor Poincaré's letter having been concluded, M. Painleye repeated his evidence which had been given before the Court of Cassation. He vehemently protested against the false versions that had been published of his conversations with M. Hadamard, in which the latter was made to affirm the guilt of Dreyfus. On the contrary, the witness said, M. Hadamard never doubted the prisoner's innocence.

General Gonse intervened at this juncture. He was surprised, he said, at the importance attached to the evidence of MM. Hadamard and Painleye. There had been, General Gonse asserted, at least fluctuations in their views of Dreyfus's character, for which Dreyfus's own family were unwilling to give guarantees.

M. Painleye reasserted that both M. Hadamard and himself had always been satisfied that Dreyfus was innocent.

General Gonse replied, declaring that the whole matter was insignificant, and insinuated that the faith of M. Hadamard and M. Painleye in the innocence of Dreyfus must have been strengthened recently.

M. Painleye replied, warmly insisting that he never had any doubt of Dreyfus's innocence.

The two men then went at it hammer and tongs, M. Painleye facing General Gonse with his arms folded, and thrust home with his questions and retorts until General Gonse became red in the face. Then General Roget joined in the discussion.

As the altercation between General Gonse and M. Painleye was rapidly becoming heated, M. Labori intervened. A sharp passage of arms followed between M. Labori and Colonel Jouaust, leading to considerable excitement.

M. Labori asked General Gonse why he had incorrectly reported certain information he had collected.

Colonel Jouaust refused to put the question, and invited M. Labori to study moderation.

M. Labori retorted:

"The defence is using its rights with the utmost moderation."

Colonel Jouaust—No, you are not. I beg you not to drown my voice when I am speaking. Your very tone is wanting in moderation. Moreover, I consider the question unimportant.

There were prolonged murmurs of assent and dissent among the audience at this declaration by Colonel Jouaust.

M. Labori said he was surprised that General Gonse had included incorrect information in the secret dossier.

General Gonse—I composed one of the secret dossiers by means of annexed documents communicated to the ministry; but the minds of all the War Ministers were made up before they had any cognizance of these documents.

M. Labori—Does General Gonse assume responsibility for these secret dossiers to July, 1898?

General Gonse—Yes, I had charge of it.

M. Labori—How happens it, then, that a telegram from the French Ambassador at Rome, sent by the Foreign Office to the War Office, referring to payments to Esterhazy by an Italian agent, was not added to the secret dossier?

General Gonse—There were plenty of others. All were not included, but only the most important.

M. Labori—Was the information of the French Ambassador at Rome of less importance than the garbled conversation of M. Painleye?

Colonel Jouaust—I will not put the question.

M. Labori—Why was information against Dreyfus always included in the dossier, and never any incriminating Esterhazy?

Colonel Jouaust—I also refuse to put that question.

M. Labori—All right. I think the question itself fully answered the purpose.

M. Labori then asked General Gonse who compiled the secret dossier in question.

"I did," shouted Commandant Cuignet from the body of the hall.

Commandant Cuignet then came to the bar, and declared that he had omitted all documents from abroad, "because foreigners were interested in deceiving us." Several documents of this kind had been omitted, particularly one reciting a conversation between a foreign sovereign and a French attaché, in the course of which the sovereign was represented as saying that what was occurring in France was proof of the power of the Jews.

"That," added the major, "might be regarded as against Dreyfus; but nevertheless it was not included in the dossier."

As he made this statement, Commandant Cuignet turned to a brother officer sitting in the place set apart for witnesses, and smiled with the self-satisfied air of a man who had made a distinct score.

M. Demange rose immediately to express surprise that the document in question had not appeared in the War Office dossier.

Major Cuignet—It does not appear there because it was received at the Foreign Office.

M. Paleologue, intervening, said that the Foreign Office only acted as an intermediary in that matter.

M. Labori commented with astonishment upon the fact that alleged fresh proofs against Dreyfus were still spoken of, and demanded that all proofs be produced at the secret session of the court-martial at which M. Cernuschi was to be examined.

General Chanoine was asked by Colonel Jouaust if he had any explanations to offer, and replied that his duty was merely to produce the secret dossier, and that he could not say anything regarding documents outside the dossier.

The question of the report drawn up by Commandant Cuignet and Offi-

18

cer Wattines, dealing exhaustively with the secret dossier, was then introduced.

General Billot, formerly Minister of War, mounted the platform and said he was glad that reference had been made to the secret dossier, as it enable him to protest against the insinuation that he had handed Major Cuignet a docment from the secret dossier.

"I gave this report," he said, "to M. Cavaignac, the former Minister of War."

"Then," said M. Labori, "let us have M. Cavaignac's explanation of what became of the report."

Colonel Jouaust called for M. Cavaignac, but the former Minister of War was not in the court-room, and an officer was sent to seek him.

Meanwhile the testimony of two minor witnesses was heard.

The proceedings to this point were very exciting, as at one time, when General Chanoine and M. Paleologue were brought upon the stage to explain Commandant Cuignet's statements, there were five witnesses at the bar, all speaking at once and interrupting one another. The testimony throughout was interspersed with heated scenes between M. Labori and Colonel Jouaust.

M. Demange during the day read a letter from Rabbi Dreyfus denying that he had ever heard a number of scandalous statements which, it had been alleged, were made to him.

Since M. Cavaignac could not be found in the precincts of the Lycée, it was decided to hear him on September 5th.

M. Mayer, who is on the staff of the *Temps*, testified that the spy Guénee informed him that the War Office had indisputable proof of the guilt of Dreyfus, and mentioned a snapshot photograph representing Dreyfus conversing with a millitary attaché at Brussels.

After a brief recess of the court-martial Dr. Peyrot deposed that he met M. Bertulus, judge of the Court of Cassation, at Dieppe after the arrest of Lieutenant-Colonel Henry, and that M. Bertulus narrated to him the dramatic scene in his office with Henry. M. Bertulus was very jubilant over Henry's arrest, and said he was convinced that, if Henry were detained, everything would be known in due time.

A commissary of the secret police, named Tomps, was then called by the defence, and it was admitted at the end of the proceedings that he proved indirectly a strong witness for Dreyfus and a correspondingly damaging witness for the General Staff. His evidence brought out a glaring instance of duplicity on the part of the staff office in suppressing documents which must weaken its own case.

Commissary Tomps was called to the General Staff office to investigate a case of espionage, and naturally had consultations and close relations with officers of the bureau.

The commissary began his testimony by paying a high tribute to Lieutenant-Colonel Picquart's correct attitude and uprightness in the Dreyfus inquiry, while other officers sought to undermine him by insinuations. Lieutenant-Colonel Henry, the witness asserted, tried to induce him to attribute to Picquart the communication of the bordereau to the *Matin*, in which journal the bordereau was first published.

M. Tomps, who was also a special commissary of the railway police, deposed that he photographed the bordereau by order of Colonel Sandherr. He had not manipulated the plate with a view to concealing marks upon the document. When the facsimile of the bordereau was published Lieutenant-Colonel Picquart ordered the witness to discover who had supplied the photographic copy. While engaged in the investigation of this matter, Lieutenant-Colonel Henry upon one occasion approached the witness and clearly evinced great uneasiness at the successive revelations in the Dreyfus matter. Henry told the witness that the revelations could only have emanated from an individual who had the documents in his hands. Henry, the witness testified, added:

"They can only emanate from our office, where only Picquart, Lauth, Gribelin, or myself could have revealed them. I am sure that neither Lauth, Gribelin, nor myself have been so indiscreet. You would do well to discover who is responsible."

M. Tomps detailed successive steps in his investigations, showing how Lieutenant-Colonel Henry and Major Lauth had brought pressure to bear to make him implicate Lieutenant-Colonel Picquart, and their angry threats when the witness's report did not suit them. They accused the witness of being influenced by some one.

Replying to M. Demange, M. Tomps said that he had only once mixed up Esterhazy in connection with the report. Esterhazy had been seen at a foreign agent's residence, which had two exits, and he had other suspicious relations. Witness had found corroboration of this.

Answering a question of M. Labori, M. Tomps further detailed Lieutenant-Colonel Henry's pressure upon him with a view to having the communication of the bordereau to the *Matin* ascribed to Lieutenant-Colonel Picquart. Witness did not know if the leakages at the War Office continued after Dreyfus left.

Then Commissary Tomps came to the most important portion of his testimony, which led to a restricting of his revelations. The witness was asked if he had ever investigated the Paulmier affair, which was as follows:

Paulmier was the valet of Colonal Schwartzkoppen, the German military attaché at Paris, and it was alleged that he saw on Schwartzkoppen's desk documents signed by Dreyfus. The General Staff had declared that an effort would be made to get at the truth of this story, but Paulmier disappeared, and therefore, although the General Staff could not prove the story, it could not be disproved.

To a question regarding this case, Commissary Tomps replied that he had not investigated the affair, whereupon M. Labori suggested that M. Hennion, sub-chief of the Political Police, who was now in Rennes superintending the precautions for the safety of witnesses, may have been intrusted with the inquiry into this case.

Colonel Jouaust called to Hennion, who was present in the court-room: "Come here and testify."

M. Hennion ascended the platform and took the oath. He declared that he did investigate the case, and actually found Paulmier, who told him there was not a word of truth in the whole story. He never saw any paper bearing the name of Dreyfus. Thereupon M. Hennion had furnished a typewritten report on the subject, stating that Paulmier never saw, or said he had seen, such documents.

M. Labori immediately called attention to the fact that the General Staff had suppressed M. Hennion's report in favor of Dreyfus, and only declared that the report had been received representing Paulmier as untraceable. M. Labori also pointed out that the Headquarters Staff had alleged that the detective only reported that Paulmier had disappeared, and that his address was unknown. Probably, M. Labori suggested, the gentlemen at Headquarters merely misunderstood the report of the detective.

Commandant Cuignet and Captain Junck then arose and insisted that only a report that Paulmier could not be traced had been received at the office of the General Staff.

M. Hennion replied, reiterating that he had forwarded a report to the General Staff, giving Paulmier's emphatic denial of the whole story.

M. Labori asked Commandant Cuignet and Captain Junck where the report was that they said had been received by the General Staff stating that M. Paulmier could not be found. The officers interrogated were obliged to admit that they were unable to find the report.

M. Labori much regretted that this report could not be found, and added, amidst much excitement:

"But this is always the case. It is always impossible to get at the bottom of interesting incidents owing to documents being missing."

Major Lauth reappeared with the view of refuting the evidence of M. Tomps. Lauth declared that no one in the Statistical Section dreamed of suspecting Picquart when the inquiry was ordered as to how the *Matin* secured the bordereau. Suspicion attached rather to a civilian clerk who was on friendly terms with Tomps.

After Commissary Tomps had replied, the court retired to deliberate on the subject of holding another secret session.

When the members of the court returned Colonel Jouaust announced that there would be a sitting in camera on September 5th.

The name of Mr. Serge Basset was then called. Mr. Basset is the London correspondent of the *Matin*, who furnished the Esterhazy interviews, and MM. Labori and Demange pointed out that Esterhazy's confessions were too important to be discussed at the fag-end of this session.

Upon suggestion of counsel for the defence, the court therefore adjourned.

Chapter XLVIII.

APPEAL TO EMPEROR WILLIAM AND KING HUMBERT

MAITRE LABORI telegraphed personal appeals to Emperor William and King Humbert to grant permission to Colonel Schwartzkoppen and Major Panizzardi, German and Italian military attachés in Paris in 1894, to come to Rennes to testify at the trial of Captain Dreyfus. The appeals were couched in eloquent terms, invoking the assistance of their majesties in the name of justice and humanity.

The demand of Maître Labori that the court-martial should issue process, subject to the approval of the two sovereigns, came like a thunderbolt on September 5th. The step was fraught with momentous consequences, as it afforded Emperor William an opportunity again to assume his favorite rôle of arbiter of the destinies of the world.

Colonel Jouaust told Maître Demange at the close of the session that if he received official notification that Colonel Schwartzkoppen and Major Panizzardi were coming to depose he would be prepared to adjourn the trial pending their arrival.

A remarkable circumstance, and one that was significant of the relations between the two eminent advocates who are conducting the defence, was the fact that Maître Labori telegraphed the German Emperor and the King of Italy on his own initiative, without consulting or advising Maître Demange.

The Minister of War, General the Marquis de Gallifet, on September 5th sent orders to the generals and other military witnesses to leave Rennes and return to their respective posts within two hours after the conclusion of the depositions, and not to be present during the pleadings.

M. Cernuschi, the political refugee, who appeared before the court-martial on September 4th, as a witness for the prosecution, was not examined by the court during the time it sat behind closed doors on September 5th. The examination of the secret espionage dossier, mentioned by Captain Cuignet at the sitting of September 4th, occupied the great part of the secret session of the court.

When the open session of the court-martial began Maître Labori submitted a preamble and motion in the following terms:

"As I had the honor to announce on September 4th, I beg to submit to the court-martial the following conclusions:

"May it please the court, in view of the fact that at its sitting on Monday, September 4th, the president of the court-martial, by virtue of his discretion and power, called as a witness Eugene de Cernuschi, a former lieutenant of cavalry in the Austrian army, residing at 37 Rue Chambon, Paris, who represented, notably, that Dreyfus had been signalized to him not only by the chief of a department in the foreign office of a central European power, but also by an officer of the Headquarters Staff of another central European power, as an informer in the service of foreign nations; and, considering that the intervention in such circumstances of a former officer of a foreign army against the French officer renders necessary that the defence abandon the reserve they have hitherto imposed upon themselves, and move for the communication to the court of the documents enumerated in the papers called the bordereau, all of which communication to the court will be of such nature as to prove in a striking manner the innocence of the accused with regard to allegations which cannot entirely or immediately be refuted except by official documents, I therefore move that the Government Commissioner request the Government to ask the power or powers concerned through diplomatic channels for communication of the documents enumerated in the paper called the bordereau."

After reading the preamble M. Labori proceeded to inform the court that he did not intend to develop conclusions which in themselves were sufficient.

"I am well aware," said counsel, "that we are face to face with a peculiarly delicate situation; but as I have no control over decisions of the court with regard to the conclusions I have the honor to submit, I beg to state that I have notified the Government Commissioner to name Colonels Schwartzkoppen and Panizzardi as witnesses whom I consider it necessary to call before the court-martial at Rennes if they are willing to testify before it. I beg to point out that it is only now and for exceptional reasons that we are obliged to have recourse to the testimony of foreign officers. I add that in view of present circumstances there is nothing in this course that can cause anxiety. It is in conformity with precedent. The moment is very near when truth and light are about to break forth, showing the innocence of the accused."

Major Carriere, in objecting to M. Labori's request, said:

"We cannot prejudge the issue of a trial in the conclusions submitted by M. Labori. One point seems to be extremely delicate. These conclusions amount to a request that the court instruct the Government Commissioner to ask the French Government to submit to a foreign government, though diplomatic channels, a request for the production of documents which are peculiarly non-diplomatic and possess little official character. Therefore this mission imposed upon the French Government is of a very delicate kind. I do not know if the Government Commissioner is qualified to perform such a function. Certainly the diplomatic point of view seems to me morally and materially impossible. I cannot conceive of one government addressing to another such a request. I think the end now in view cannot be attained. The defence, which has powerful means behind it, might obtain these documents in a semi-official manner, but I think there are reasons to believe the Government cannot undertake such a mission. I make all reservations, then, in this respect.

"As regards notification to me of the names of Colonels Schwartzkoppen and Panizzardi, I see no reason why the gentlemen should not be examined by the court if they care to attend. The court will determine what course will be taken with regard to the request presented by the defence concerning documents to be obtained abroad. This seems to me beyond our jurisdiction. The court will judge. I beg the president to retire with the judges to a private room and decide the question."

M. Paleologue, the representative of the Foreign Office, supported Major Carriere's views. He said:

"I understand perfectly the importance the defence attaches to the production of the documents enumerated in the bordereau, seeing that the whole case turns upon them. But even if the request of the accused appears to be based upon logic and justice, it seems inadmissible from a diplomatic point of view. Considerations of the highest order are opposed to the Government's taking the initiative it is requested to take with regard to a foreign power."

Colonel Jouaust then said that the court would announce its decision in this matter later.

Serge Basset, the first witness called, testified that the *Matin* sent him to London on five occasions to interview Major Esterhazy, who furnished a mass of interesting information concerning the Headquarters Staff. Esterhazy declared that he was not the author of the bordereau, though the witness did not believe him. Esterhazy complained bitterly of the generals, who, he said, had thrown him overboard, adding that there was nothing left for him but to blow out his brains. The witness advised against suicide, and urged Esterhazy to the utmost endeavor to reveal the truth and the part he had played. Finally, while walking in Piccadilly, Major Esterhazy said to the witness point blank:

"Well, Ribon [the witness's pseudonym], I am going to tell you what nobody knows. It is I who am the author of the bordereau. I wrote it in 1894 at the request of my friend Sandherr. There was a traitor at Headquarters, Dreyfus, whom Sandherr told me they wanted to catch. I did not hesitate to do what I was asked."

Mr. Basset added that, with Esterhazy's consent, he had each of Esterhazy's statements verified, Esterhazy saying he had decided to make the avowals because he was disgusted with his abandonment by the generals. In conclusion, the witness referred to offers of money to Esterhazy.

Lieutenant-Colonel Brongniart, a member of the court-martial, asked:

"Did Esterhazy tell you Dreyfus was guilty?"

M. Basset—Yes.

Colonel Jouaust—The two statements of Esterhazy are incompatible.

M. Basset—It is not for me to reconcile them.

Major Carriere here made an extraordinary protest against Major Esterhazy's insinuations against Colonel Sandherr.

"I protest," he cried, "in the name and memory of Colonel Sandherr against the insinuations introduced against him. I have made it a rule not to enter into discussion with witnesses, but, as M. Basset states that Major Esterhazy asserted that Colonel Sandherr told him to write the bordereau, I, on behalf of Colonel Sandherr's memory, protest against such insinuations. He was incapable of such an order."

M. Labori—I hope this protest is not addressed to the defence.

Major Carriere—It is not addressed to counsel for the defence; it is addressed to the man who was capable of launching such a statement.

M. Labori—Does M. Basset know that Major Esterhazy addressed letters to General Roget?

M. Basset—I do not.

M. Labori—General Roget, perhaps, will tell us.

Counsel then called upon General Roget to testify regarding letters he had received from Major Esterhazy since the opening of the trial.

General Roget looked the ghost of his former assertive self. His face was careworn, and showed little of that fighting spirit which first characterized his appearance upon the stage.

General Roget said: "I did receive a letter from Major Esterhazy in August, and informed the president of the court-martial of the fact, asking him to make what use he liked of it. I refused to open further letters as soon as I recognized Esterhazy's handwriting."

On M. Labori asking to see the letter, Colonel Jouaust said he would not put the letter in evidence, because it contained only abuse and recriminations.

As M. Labori protested, General Roget said he had handed all the letters to the president of the court-martial, because he did not wish to be compromised by Esterhazy, which was evidently the latter's intention.

Colonel Jouaust said he had not included Esterhazy's letters in the evidence, because he did not wish the proceedings to be unduly protracted, but, as the defence insisted, the letters would be produced.

General Roget read the one Esterhazy letter which he admitted having opened. In this letter Major Esterhazy said he could not prove the existence of the alleged syndicate organized in the interest of Dreyfus, and complained that the General Staff had refused to give him a fair hearing.

M. Labori put a series of questions intended to bring out the fact that the General Staff had made use of Major Esterhazy, even after he was known to be unreliable. General Roget said he had not considered Major Esterhazy's avowal to be of any value.

Counsel sought to question General Roget more closely on his statement that none of the generals of the General Staff had any relations with Major Esterhazy, but Colonel Jouaust declined to allow further discussion.

This led to another scene between the president of the court and counsel for the defence, M. Labori declaring that General Roget, who came more as a public prosecutor than as a witness, refused to reply to probing questions.

M. Labori—Does General Roget consider the confessions of Esterhazy valid?

General Roget—No; all versions given by Esterhazy are quite incorrect. He is an impostor concerning whom I prefer to express no opinion.

M. Labori—Does General Roget consider Esterhazy a man-of-straw?

General Roget—I have no proof of the fact, but I am inclined to believe he is.

M. Labori—Was he a straw-man in 1894?

General Roget—No, I do not think so.

M. Labori—When, do you think, did he first contemplate playing the part?

General Roget—I have made no investigation on that point. Contrary to Esterhazy's assertions, the generals of the Headquarters Staff had no relations with him.

M. Labori—Why was Major Esterhazy's rôle of straw-man not mentioned in the trial of 1898?

General Roget—I was not present, and do not know.

Considerable discussion ensued between Colonel Jouaust and M. Labori, the former attempting to protect General Roget from too close questioning. M. Labori insisted, however, and gained his point. The examination proceeded:

M. Labori—Since General Roget expresses an opinion on this case, upon what does he base it?

General Roget—On the part generally played by Esterhazy.

M. Labori—How do you explain the fact that Esterhazy made no confession during the Zola trial?

General Roget—I do not know.

M. Labori then expressed surprise that there was no mention of a man-of-straw until so late a day, while all the acts of which Esterhazy is accused were long known.

At the request of M. Labori the report of the Court of Inquiry, which decided whether or not Esterhazy should be cashiered, was read. According to this report, the court was not permitted to go outside of specific questions submitted to it by the Minister of War.   One of the questions, referring to Major Esterhazy's letter to President Faure, caused Du Paty de Clam to admit that he inspired those letters.   This made a great impression upon the Court of Inquiry, which finally concluded that there was ground for clemency.

When the reading of the report was concluded M. Labori vainly tried to question General Billot concerning the "document liberateur" which secured Esterhazy's acquittal, Colonel Jouaust declaring he would not permit General Billot to be re-examined.

General Zurlinden, at that stage of the proceedings, ascended the platform, dressed in the uniform of his rank, and with his inseparable eyeglass.   He spoke a few words respecting the General Staff's belief in Major Esterhazy.   M. Demange said he could not understand why it was alleged that the defence desired to compromise the Headquarters Staff, and asked whence arose the suggestion that Major Esterhazy was a mere dummy.

General Roget replied that one reason which induced the belief that Esterhazy was a man-of-straw was that his confession that he had written the bordereau was absolutely inadmissible.   General Roget was perfectly convinced that Esterhazy was entirely innocent of treason.   [Murmurs of asset and dissent.]

General Roget next attempted, but without success, to refute the evidence given on September 2d, by M. des Fonds-Lamothe relative to the sentence, "I am going to the manœuvres," saying the circular issued may have been indefinite.

Dreyfus arose and in a clear voice emphatically insisted that the circular of May 17, 1894, announcing that the probationers would not go to the manœuvres, was written in the clearest language, which the court would see if it were read; that the court possessed the circular and consequently could judge whether it contained definite instructions.   The prisoner recalled the fact that in August the probationers were asked which regiments they desired to join.   The situation was very clear.   All the probationers at the Staff Headquarters had participated in the June journey made by the General Staff.   He did not know whether or not certain officers retained doubts, but he was absolutely certain he had never asked for leave to attend the manœuvres. The sentence in the bordereau, "I am going to the manœuvres," expressed a positive idea. He not only never went to the manœuvres, but never could have attended them. He reiterated that he had never asked to go to the manœuvres, for he was absolutely convinced that such a request would not be granted.

M. Deffres, a reporter for the *Temps*, of Paris, then testified that he saw Esterhazy in London, and that the latter confessed that he was the author of the bordereau. The witness added that he raised the question of the letters to Mme. Boulancy, and brought away the impression that Esterhazy wrote the "Uhlan" letter.

Senator Trarieux, formerly Minister of Justice, was the next witness. He made a long deposition in favor of Dreyfus, reviewing the history of the case and his own part in connection therewith. M. Traireux showed himself to be an excellent speaker, with a good presence. He had iron-gray hair and mustache, and spoke with a clear, resonant voice, which was heard outside the court-room.

M. Trarieux looked straight at the judges while testifying. He preceded his evidence by saying he wished to throw light upon his conduct in this case. When Dreyfus was convicted, the witness said, he was convinced, like everybody else, of the prisoner's guilt; but violent diatribes on the fact that Dreyfus was a Jew awakened his suspicions. He therefore consulted M. Hanotaux, former Minister of Foreign Affairs, and the latter informed the witness of the existence of the "Cette canaille de D——" document, though M. Hanotaux failed to inform him that it had been imparted to the judges of the first court-martial, unknown to the prisoner. This fact the witness learned later.

Continuing, M. Trarieux, whose statement was practically an impassioned speech for the defence, denounced the secret communication of the documents to the court-martial as a monstrous illegality and a violation of the most sacred rights of the defence. The witness described as impossible the hypothesis advanced by M. Teyssonieres, the handwriting expert, to convince the witness that Dreyfus was guilty. The witness said his doubts were confirmed when he heard that M. Scheurer-Kestner had secured proofs of the innocence of Dreyfus and the guilt of another.

M. Trarieux dwelt upon the noble ideal of M. Scheurer-Kestner, who had passed sleepless nights, tormented with the thought that an innocent

man was shedding tears of blood.   When M. Scheurer-Kestner revealed
what he knew, the witness was greatly surprised, especially when he
learned that Colonel Picquart had not succeeded in obtaining the support
of the chiefs of the army.   The witness said he was amazed that the latter
had not eagerly grasped the opportunity to work together for the rehabilitation of an innocent man.

During the course of his deposition M. Trarieux said he could not
agree to a single conclusion reached by General Gonse in his correspondence with Picquart, and said the latter's removal from the Secret Intelligence Department was the result of underhand plotting by some one opposed to revision.   The witness enumerated in support of this statement
various forged documents which, he asserted, had emanated from the Secret Intelligence Department, namely, the "Cette canaille de D——"
document, in which the name of Dreyfus had been substituted for the hypothetical "de D——," the Weyler forgery, and the publication of a facsimile of the bordereau.

"Lastly," said M. Trarieux, "there appeared the cynical Henry forgery.
All these facts created a great impression regarding the Headquarter Staff.
I accuse no one, but assume that the chiefs were deceived."

The witness pointed out that if any proof of the guilt of Dreyfus existed in 1896, General Gonse would have given Picquart an order to stop
the investigation.

After an interview with M. Scheurer-Kestner, M. Trarieux added, he
became convinced of the guilt of Esterhazy, and saw his duty as a conscientious citizen and senator, and perhaps as an ex-Minister, and that to
fulfil his duty he must devote himself to a work of justice.

In describing the steps taken in support of revision, M. Trarieux mentioned an interview he had with a foreign ambassador, who, in tones of
the most profound and affecting sincerity, declared that Dreyfus never had
relations with him or with any military attaché or officer of the army of
his country.   M. Trarieux asserted the importance of this statement to
the ambassador, who energetically reaffirmed the absolute innocence of
Dreyfus.   The ambassador added that he had investigated and found nothing to implicate Dreyfus.   Further, the ambassador said he had seen in
the hands of Colonel Panizzardi a letter from Colonel Schwartzkoppen
proving the guilt of Esterhazy, who, his excellency added, generally com-

municated information of minor value. Moreover, at the time of M. Scheurer-Kestner's revelations Major Esterhazy called upon Colonel Schwartzkoppen, and it was then that a dramatic scene of violent recriminations and threats occurred. The ambassador also showed the witness that the "Cette canaille de D——" phrase did not apply to Dreyfus.

As he proceeded M. Trarieux became more and more impassioned, and walked back and forth upon the platform. He explained that, notwithstanding the confidential nature of his revelations, the ambassador had accorded him permission to communicate it to the judicial authorities. In a subsequent interview which the witness had with the same ambassador the latter had informed him that the Henry forgery, which had just been discovered, had been long known to his Government, and that the French Government had been aware of it for a year.

M. Trarieux continued:

"Exception may be taken to certain passages of what I have asserted, but among men of honor who listen there is not one who doubts the sincerity of my language or the truth of what I have said. It may be said that I should not adduce here the evidence of a foreigner. That is M. Cavaignac's opinion, and I do not oppose it, but it has no foundation either in fact or in law. The testimony of foreigners is not disallowed by law, which does not restrict the field of investigation of a judge, to whom it merely says: 'See, investigate, enlighten yourself.' Moreover, Major Panizzardi was cited to appear in a case of swindling at Versailles. This country should be bold and proud enough to seek the truth everywhere.

"Besides, was there not yesterday somewhat unexpected evidence of a foreigner who related remarks of a foreign sovereign? Why should the testimony of foreign representatives be opposed here? Even the supreme head of the army, the gallant soldier, General the Marquis de Gallifet, has not shrunk from adducing before the Court of Cassation the testimony of General Talbot."

M. Trarieux said he suspected neither the sincerity nor the probity of the judges of the court-martial of 1894, but only the nature of the documents submitted to that tribunal.

Criticising General Mercier's rôle as a witness, M. Trarieux said he was surprised that the ex-Minister of War had not included in the dossier the official version of the Panizzardi cipher telegram.

With regard to General Roget and Captain Cuignet, the witness declared that their allegations that Major Panizzardi had informed his ambassador that Colonel Schwartzkoppen had relations with Dreyfus were absolutely unfounded.   On the contrary, the witness asserted, Panizzardi expressly stated that Dreyfus had no relations with any foreign attaché. General Roget and Captain Cuignet had therefore mis-read—he would not say misinterpreted—the report upon which it was alleged they had based their statements.

General Roget attempted to intervene, but M. Trarieux continued, reasserting the truth of all he had stated.   The ambassador already referred to, M. Trarieux declared, said, " Esterhazy is the traitor."

Continuing, M. Trarieux said: "The Supreme Court has given its decision, and our eyes confirm its judgment."   He then proceeded to show that Esterhazy's confession must be genuine.   "If," said he, "an ideal of the type of traitor is sought, he is the man.   He is overwhelmed with debts, and is a man of loose habits.   He wrote the 'Uhlan' letter to Mme. Boulancy.   He had not even the soul of a Frenchman.   And yet he is placed on a level with a young captain of irreproachable conduct, against whom nothing but secret documents has been brought.   Doubt is no longer possible."

After demonstrating, in this way, why question of the innocence of Dreyfus was impossible, M. Trarieux concluded:

"This is no longer the time for pleading falsehoods; it is the hour for pacification.   It is also the hour for justice, which has declared that small as well as great, without distinction of sex or person, shall have their rights."

The deposition of M. Trarieux closed the public session.   At its conclusion the court-martial went behind closed doors and examined the secret espionage dossier.   The court also deliberated upon the application of M. Labori for a order upon the Government Commissary to request the French Government to invite foreign governments to supply the documents enumerated in the bordereau.   After a brief interval it was unanimously decided to reject the application of M. Labori, on the ground that the court did not consider itself competent to pronounce a judgment which might entail diplomatic action by the Government.   It was also decided unanimously to examine M. de Cernuschi on September 6th, behind closed doors.

The court then adjourned.

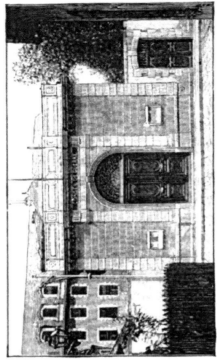

MILITARY PRISON AT RENNES: ENTRANCE TO COURT-ROOM.

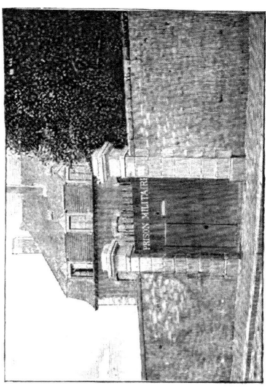

MILITARY PRISON AT RENNES: THE ENTRANCE GATE.

MILITARY PRISON AT RENNES: SCENE IN THE
COURT-YARD.

ARRIVAL OF MADAME DREYFUS AT RENNES.

FRENZY OF PARIS: READING THE NEWS IN THE STREETS.

AGITATION OF PARIS: RUSH ON THE BOULEVARDS FOR EVENING PAPERS ANNOUNCING THE VERDICT.

THE MOB RAMPANT IN PARIS.

CAPTAIN DREYFUS LEAVING THE COURT-MARTIAL FOR THE MILITARY PRISON.

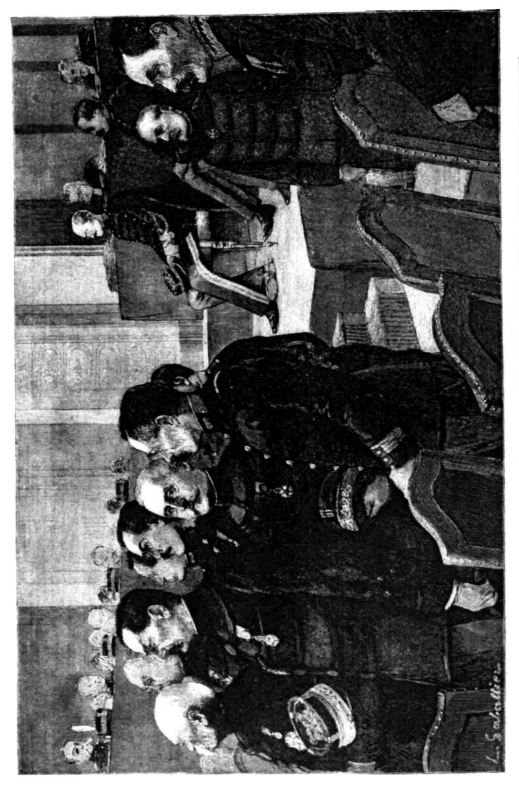

THE TRIAL AT RENNES: MILITARY WITNESSES LEAVING THE COURT AFTER GIVING THEIR TESTIMONY.

RETURN OF DREYFUS: DRIVING FROM THE QUAI TO QUIBERON.

Chapter XLIX.

M. LABORI THREATENS TO WITHDRAW FROM THE CASE

IT was said on September 6th, that the salvation of Dreyfus was then hanging on a word from Emperor William. If the Kaiser consented to allow Colonel Schwartzkoppen, the German military attaché, to testify before the court-martial, or to send a deposition, or, what was considered still more probable, to allow his deposition to be accompanied by the actual documents mentioned in the bordereau, then Dreyfus was saved.

If the Emperor, however, should decide that it was not in the interests of Germany for Colonel Schwartzkoppen to intervene, then Dreyfus's case was pronounced hopeless and his condemnation certain.

Maître Labori insisted that the appearance of Cernuschi on the witness stand was quite without precedent, but the anti-Dreyfusards pointed out, and with a certain amount of reason, that the counsel for the defence were really the first to introduce foreign testimony, as they summoned the English journalist, Rowland Strong, on the question of Esterhazy's confession that he wrote the bordereau.

The public proceedings of September 6th were marked by three important episodes.

The first was General Zurlinden's admission that the erasure and restitution of Esterhazy's name in the *petit bleu* could not have been perpetrated by Colonel Picquart, and consequently must be attributed to some one inside the General Staff.

The second was the declaration by M. Paleologue that the secret dossier contained a document which showed that Colonel Schwartzkoppen admitted his relations with Esterhazy, and that Schwartzkoppen, in the opinion of Paleologue, sent to Esterhazy the identical *petit bleu* for which Colonel Picquart was detained ten months on a charge of forgery.

The third was General Billot's insinuation that Esterhazy and Dreyfus were accomplices, which led to an impassioned protestation on the part

19

of the accused, and to a thrilling scene between M. Labori and Colonel Jouaust, resulting in the lawyer's excited denunciation, tantamount to an accusation of open partiality.

From a spectacular point of view, however, the great event of the sitting was the battle royal between Maître Labori and Colonel Jouaust over certain questions which counsel wished to put to General Billot. M. Labori here lost control of himself under the influence of his deep feeling of indignation, and his belief that Colonel Jouaust was deliberately gagging him in the interest of the military clique. His voice, which at first resounded through the court-room, became choked with emotion. The spectators held their breath as he retorted defiantly to Colonel Jouaust's refusal to put the questions, his words drowning Jouaust's voice in an irresistible torrent, whose force was heightened by his passionate gestures.

When he finally fell back in his seat with a look of hopeless indignation, his face was blanched and his fingers twitched spasmodically—a speaking testimony to the high tension to which his nerves had been wrought by fruitless combat with the iron ruling of the bench.

Dreyfus too, in his vehement protest against General Billot's insinuations of his complicity with Esterhazy, recalled his anguished outbreak early in the trial.

It was a strange contrast to hear him a little later, when he had apparently mastered his feelings, deliver an argumentative reply to Major Gallopin, of the artillery, in a calm, moderate tone. Indeed, one was almost tempted to imagine that his emotional outcry in reply to General Billot was a piece of theatricality.

Gallopin's evidence left a decidedly unfavorable impression, despite the plausibility of the explanation given by Dreyfus.

Two hours of the opening of the sitting of September 6th were spent behind closed doors. The length of time occupied in the examination of Eugene de Cernuschi, the Austrian refugee and witness for the prosecution, was the subject of much remark, as being indicative of the fact that the court found this witness to be worthy of more consideration than it had been supposed he deserved.

Senator Trarieux, former Minister of Justice, resumed his deposition, which was interrupted by the adjournment of the court on September 5th. He took up the testimony of Savignaud, the former orderly in Tunis of

Colonel Picquart, and witness for the prosecution, who had claimed to have seen letters addressed to M. Scheurer-Kestner, formerly Vice-President of the Senate, by Picquart, while in Tunis. M. Trarieux declared that Savignaud was a perjurer, and that two officers visited Savignaud before the court-martial opened. M. Trarieux hinted that the officers drilled Savignaud on the testimony he was to give.

Savignaud replied, reiterating the truth of his previous testimony.

Colonel Picquart then repeated his denial of Savignaud's story.

M. Trarieux reviewed the question of the *petit bleu*, which, he said, he was convinced was authentic. He proceeded to comment upon the questionable rôle played by Major Lauth in the affair.

Major Lauth interrupted the witness, asking that he be allowed a hearing, and on the conclusion of M. Trarieux's deposition Major Lauth confronted him. The major declared that he had acted honestly throughout, and that he had not the least doubt of Picquart's falsification of the *petit bleu*, in order to incriminate Esterhazy.

A striking incident occurred when Lauth, a moment later, asserted that Picquart had always shown the greatest contempt for the officers of his bureau, asserting that on one occasion Picquart had brought to the General Staff, in the presence of Mesdames Henry and Lauth, a woman, Mme. D———, who was the wife of a magistrate, and, Lauth intimated, Picquart's mistress.

Picquart arose and cried: "I protest absolutely."

At the same time there arose from the spectators a chorus of indignant cries of "Oh!" "Canaille!" "Cochon!" ("Pig!"), and "Misérable!"

The gendarmes were ordered to repress the outbursts of indignation which had been evoked by the conduct of Major Lauth in publicly naming a woman in a scandalous connection.

General Zurlinden, formerly Minister of War, followed Major Lauth at the witness bar. Zurlinden spoke in justification of his action while he was Military Governor of Paris and Minister of War in the matter of the prosecution of Picquart, taking the ground that the measure was absolutely necessary in order that the court should clear up the charge of forgery brought against Picquart. Moreover, General Zurlinden said, the Minister of Justice had persuaded him to send Picquart before a military court.

General Zurlinden, during the day's testimony, amid intense excitement, admitted that the Tavernier inquiry showed that the *petit bleu* had not been scratched when it reached the statistical section of the Intelligence Department, and that consequently the erasure was not the work of Picquart.

M. Trarieux replied to General Zurlinden, reproaching him with Colonel Picquart's ten months in prison.

M. Labori then asked a question of General Zurlinden regarding the *petit bleu*. Colonel Jouaust refused to put the question, on the ground that the court was engaged in the trial of Dreyfus, and not of the Picquart affair.

Counsel, however, insisted, taking the ground that the *petit bleu* demonstrated the guilt of Esterhazy, and that consequently it was very important for Dreyfus.

The lawyer proceeded with his attack on General Zurlinden, who admitted that the magisterial inquiry showed that the *petit bleu* was not tampered with when it first arrived at the Intelligence Department, and that consequently Picquart could not have been guilty, as alleged, of distorting the document.

M. Labori asked that M. Paleologue, the representative of the Foreign Office, be consulted with reference to the reading before the court of diplomatic documents which established irrefutably the authenticity of the *petit bleu*.

M. Paleologue, who sits behind the judges, came to the front of the stage and said that he did not know to what documents M. Labori alluded.

"The document," replied M. Labori, "in which is recounted a conversation between M. Delcasse, the Minister of Foreign Affairs, the former Count von Munster-Ledenburg, German ambassador to Paris, in the course of which the ambassador said Colonel Schwartzkoppen had admitted that he sent Esterhazy a number of telegraphic cards or *petits bleus*."

M. Paleologue replied that what M. Labori said was quite true, and that the document belonged to the diplomatic dossier. As to the *petit bleu* in question, added M. Paleologue, Colonel Schwartzkoppen could affirm whether he wrote it himself or whether he had not seen it; but in any case, M. Paleologue said, he believed it was sent by Colonel Schwartzkoppen.

This declaration by the representative of the Foreign Office created a marked sensation in court.

M. Trarieux then read a letter, which he wrote to General Billot, June 1, 1898, protesting against these falsehoods. To this letter General Billot had replied that he had not instituted the inquiry. The judges intrusted with the investigation of the Esterhazy case, notwithstanding their conscientiousness, were, M. Trarieux asserted, absolutely deceived by stories then current. The judges accepted as gospel all the lies of Esterhazy, who, though acquitted, was not tried.

Replying to M. Labori, M. Trarieux dwelt at length upon the charges, which he described as fairy tales, against Picquart, who had been alleged to be an agent in the pay of the Dreyfus family, and whose object, as asserted, was to put Esterhazy, an innocent man, in the place of Dreyfus the culprit.

M. Trarieux again entered upon a long statement, in the course of which he said Esterhazy was acquitted, not judged.

Colonel Jouaust stopped the witness, saying he must not speak in that way of judges. M. Trarieux replied that he had not referred to judges, but to "la chose jugée."

Colonel Jouaust then pointed out that M. Trarieux was taking M. Labori's place and making a regular speech for the defence.

General Billot then confronted M. Trarieux, and, in reply to the latter's criticism of him, the general was much affected, and spoke in a husky voice. He began by declaring that M. Trarieux had delivered an eloquent oration, but that it was special pleading for Dreyfus and Picquart, and an arraignment of former ministers.

The General praised Picquart for his services in the army, and declared that he had the greatest confidence in him—a confidence which, however, he has since been compelled to withdraw. Then, discussing Picquart's investigation of the suspicions against Esterhazy, the general said:

"Even if Esterhazy should be proved a traitor, that would not prove Dreyfus innocent; for in cases of espionage it very often occurs that there are several accomplices."

M. Labori wished to question General Billot, and an altercation with Colonel Jouaust ensued. Finally M. Labori cried:

"Allow me to remark, Monsieur le President, that it has never been said that Dreyfus had an accomplice in Esterhazy."

Dreyfus, who heard General Billot's statement with evident excitement, also sprang to his feet, and shouted:

"I protest against this odious accusation."

M. Labori again insisted that he be allowed to question General Billot. Colonel Jouaust still refused, and a heated wrangle once more ensued.

M. Labori made a passionate protest against the attitude of Colonel Jouaust, who then said:

"I decline to allow you to speak."

Counsel retorted excitedly:

"I bow to your ruling, but I take note that every time I put a question which is irresistible you refuse to allow it."

This declaration M. Labori delivered in a ringing voice, punctuating his utterances with striking gestures. The audience burst into loud applause. The greatest excitement prevailed, and Colonel Jouaust said:

"If this demonstration is renewed I will have the court-room cleared. Have you anything more to say, Maître Labori?"

M. Labori—No, because—and I speak with the utmost respect—I am prevented from putting any questions touching the core of the affair. I reserve the right to take such action as regard for my responsibility compels me to take up."

This sentence was the climax of the strained relations which have prevailed between the president of the court-martial and M. Labori.

Major Gallopin, an officer of the artillery, was then examined. He proved a rather unfavorable witness for Dreyfus, whom he declared he once met on the Boulevard St. Germain, carrying a voluminous package, which he said contained secret papers treating of mobilization, and which he was carrying to the Geographical Bureau.

Dreyfus was questioned regarding this statement, and admitted that he sometimes took documents home to facilitate work; but he said that he did not recall the particular incident to which Major Gallopin referred. This admission by Dreyfus made a bad impression, especially when the next witness, Major Hirschauer, deposed that he heard Dreyfus express a desire to go to the manœuvres. The major, however, could not remember the exact date.

Dreyfus replied:

"It is very possible that I expressed regrets that I should be unable to go to the manœuvres, and, what is certain, we all knew that none of the probationers could go."

Colonel Picquart was called to the witness stand, and said that Dreyfus never applied to him for leave to go to the manœuvres, adding that he was surprised no inquiry had been made upon his point to the chief of Dreyfus's bureau.

Colonel Jouaust read a letter from the colonel of the one hundred and thirty-eighth regiment of infantry, dated September 2d, recalling the date of the report on Madagascar, which had enabled him to fix the date of the bordereau as August, 1894. This report, he added, was drawn up in the Third Bureau of the General Staff, and consequently an indiscretion might have been committed by an officer employed in the bureau.

The deposition of Colonel Du Paty de Clam, which was taken by Major Tavernier, was then read. It was more remarkable as being a repetition of Du Paty de Clam's former evidence, than as containing any new revelations. This was what the defence feared, and the reason they declared they had little faith in the result of an *ex-parte* examination.

In his deposition Du Paty de Clam replied to the attacks made upon him as a soldier and citizen. He complained that slanderous statements unsupported by proof had been made regarding him. The witness laid stress upon the fact that the charges had been dismissed, and expressed the opinion that the sole object of the slanderers was to impugn the judges who condemned Dreyfus in 1894. He denied that he ever had relations with Lieutenant-Colonel Henry, or that he was concerned with the publication of the article in the *Éclair*, or with furnishing Esterhazy with the "document liberateur."

Du Paty de Clam admitted that he had had relations with Esterhazy, and repeated the explanations with reference thereto which he gave before the Court of Cassation.

With regard to the Dreyfus case, Du Paty de Clam declared that he was not connected with the discovery of the bordereau. It was only on pressure, the deposition continued, that the witness accepted the task of investigating the charges in this case. After detailing the course of this investigation, Du Paty de Clam said that the order for the arrest of Captain Dreyfus had been distinctly issued quite independent of the dictation test.

Du Paty de Clam then described the famous dictation scene, in the course of which, he said, Dreyfus displayed an emotion regarding the cause of which there might be differences of opinion, but the fact, witness asserted, was undeniable that M. Cochefert, the chief of the detective department, who was present, regarded the prisoner's agitation as an indication of his guilt. Dreyfus manifested his excitement by nervous movements of the jaw, and complained that his fingers were cold.

Du Paty de Clam defended himself against the charge of being a torturer of Dreyfus and his family. The deposition contained copies of letters from Madame Dreyfus establishing the fact that Du Paty de Clam's relations with her were always courteous.

With regard to the date of the bordereau, Du Paty de Clam expressed the opinion that it must have been written between the 15th and the 30th of August, 1894.

The witness denied all statements attributed to him with regard to the incorrect versions of the Panizzardi telegram.

Later in his deposition, Du Paty de Clam referred to the preparation, by himself and Colonel Sandherr, of a secret commentary intended to show who was the traitor among the officers at the headquarters of the General Staff, "who must be a a Captain D——." None of the documents accompanying the commentary mentioned the Panizzardi telegram nor the manufacture of a shell.

Regarding the interview with Captain Dreyfus, Du Paty de Clam declared that he never said to Dreyfus:

"The minister knows you are innocent."

The Minister of War never spoke of delivering documents in order to obtain others. What Dreyfus said was:

"No, no, Major, I do not wish to plead extenuating circumstances. My counsel has promised me that in three, five, or six years, my innocence will be admitted."

Later Dreyfus said:

"Major, I know your belief. I have not opposed it. I know you are an honest man, but I assure you you have made a mistake. Seek what you call my accomplices, and what I call the culprits, and you will find them." The prisoner's last word to him was: "Seek."

The deposition of Du Paty de Clam made no reference to cases connected with that of Dreyfus. The witness swore that everything contained in his statement was true.

The court-martial then adjourned.

As a result of the scene between Colonel Jouaust and M. Labori the latter wished to retire from the case. He was convinced that the judges were utterly hostile to him, and it is said that he had conceived the idea of a dramatic withdrawal at the opening of the session of September 7th. A meeting of the friends of M. Labori was held at his house during the afternoon to decide whether such a step would be advisable.

Chapter L.

JOUAUST REFUSES TO TAKE EVIDENCE OF ATTACHÉS

A VERY pessimistic feeling was produced among the friends of Dreyfus on September 7th, by the decision of Colonel Jouaust not to allow the evidence of Colonel Schwartzkoppen and Major Panizzardi in the case.

It was predicted that it meant the certain condemnation of Dreyfus. This was the unanimous opinion of the anti-Dreyfusards, and it was the impression of a majority of the Dreyfusards, whose last hope was that Colonel Jouaust only dared to refuse to take the evidence of Colonel Schwartzkoppen and Major Panizzardi, because the court had already made up its mind to acquit the prisoner.

At the opening of the day's session of the court-martial Maître Labori announced that Colonel Schwartzkoppen and Major Panizzardi would be unable to appear personally before the court, and so he proposed that a rogatory commission should be telegraphed to receive their depositions.

In making his motion for the appointment of a rogatory commission, M. Labori said:

"I have received notice that, for reasons of public policy, Major Panizzardi and Colonel Schwartzkoppen could not come to Rennes to testify before the court-martial. But I am also informed from the same quarter that they would answer the questions of a commission sent by the court-martial. I therefore beg the court to direct, as in the case of Colonel Du Paty de Clam, that Colonel Schwartzkoppen and Major Panizzardi be examined by commission.

"The court will certainly understand that the defence must submit to the necessities of public policy, which are, I have no doubt, similarly understood by the Government of the republic. I shall, therefore, be glad if you will ask M. Paleologue if, in this case, the telegraph may be employed. I think such a method would be exceedingly rapid, and I am convinced that the president of the court-martial and the court-martial itself will not refuse to allow the defence to ascertain the truth."

Counsel added that he would make a formal application to this effect.

Colonel Jouaust, president of the court, then invited the opinion of M. Paleologue, who replied:

"It is clear that considerations of public policy stand in the way of foreign military attachés appearing in a French court to testify in regard to facts of which they had cognizance in their diplomatic capacity. Colonel Schwartzkoppen and Major Panizzardi will not attend the court-martial.

"As regards the dispatch of a commission, I believe the Foreign Office will not oppose it. But I must make all reservations regarding the use of the telegraph. I do not know if that would be a regular proceeding."

M. Labori—But couriers can be employed.

M. Paleologue—I do not think the telegraph can be used.

Major Carriere—I do not oppose the appointment of a commission. It is a matter for the president to decide. There are no legal objections, provided we respect the provisions of the Military Code, which do not permit an interruption of the trial. Such procedure must not be allowed to hinder the progress of the trial, and must, therefore, be rapid.

M. Labori—I think it possible to make the procedure I propose very rapid. The Military Code provides for a suspension of forty-eight hours. On the other hand, the court might shorten its sittings, reducing them four hours each. In any case, I shall have the honor of formulating an application which I will submit to the court.

He then drew up a formal application that Colonel Schwartzkoppen and Major Panizzardi be cited as witnesses, and that eight questions should be telegraphed them, to which they should reply under oath.

While M. Labori was drafting his motion, a member of the court-martial remarked that certain documents mentioned in Du Paty de Clam's depositions could not be found either among the records or in the statistical department of the War Office.

To which M. Demange replied that perhaps they were under seal.

M. Labori then read the terms of his formal application, which stated that as considerations of public policy prevented the appearance of Colonel Schwartzkoppen, and Major Panizzardi before the court-martial, commissions should be sent to examine them, in order to permit these officers to state under oath all that they knew in regard to the case.

Counsel furthermore requested the court to have the following questions put to each of the two officers:

"First—On what date did you receive the documents mentioned in the bordereau?

"Second—Are these documents in the same handwriting as the bordereau, which you know from a facsimile?

"Third—What did these documents contain?

"Fourth—Did you receive the Firing Manual, either in the original or a copy?

"Fifth—Did you receive the graduation bar?

"Sixth—Since what date did you receive those documents?

"Seventh—Was it to the same correspondent to whom you address the *petit bleu* that was referred to in the conversation between Count von Munster and M. Delcasse?

"Eighth—Have you had direct relations with the accused?"

M. Labori urged the importance of the evidence of these two witnesses, whom, he declared, he would not have cited if Cernuschi had not been called. Counsel pointed out it was possible to suspend the proceedings long enough to obtain replies to the questions, which he considered indispensable.

The court made no answer at once, but retired to deliberate on M. Labori's application. Every one in court stood up when the judges returned fifteen minutes later.

Colonel Jouaust gave the order "Present arms" to the guard of soldiers at the bottom of the hall, while he, standing, and with the other judges standing on either side of him, read the decision that the president, Colonel Jouaust, was competent to order a rogatory commission, but that the judges as a body, according to the Military Code, were not competent to do so.

M. Labori thereupon asked Colonel Jouaust if he still maintained his refusal to appoint the commission, the colonel, when M. Labori submitted his conclusions, having said he was opposed to the application.

Colonel Jouaust replied, "Yes"; and by this decision the evidence of Colonel Schwartzkoppen and Major Panizzardi, who were prepared, it was said, to swear they never had relations with Dreyfus, was thus excluded.

The refusal of Colonel Jouaust seemed inexplicable, because it appeared to be his duty to receive all evidence directly bearing on the case, and more especially the evidence of the two attachés, the refusal of whose testimony was thought to be equivalent to a slight on their respective countries.

The chief of detectives, M. Cochefert, the first witness of the morning, deposed favorably regarding the attitude of Dreyfus when Du Paty de Clam dictated the bordereau to him. The witness said Dreyfus appeared not to be troubled until afterward, when Du Paty de Clam questioned him.

M. Cochefert referred to a revolver found on a table near the desk at which Dreyfus was then seated, and he recounted how the prisoner, on perceiving it, cried:

"I will not kill myself. I will live to establish my innocence."

The clerk of the court then read a letter from Captain Humbert to the effect that Dreyfus had expressed a keen desire in 1894 to enter the Statistical Section of the War Office, and saying that he met Dreyfus once carrying some voluminous packets of maps and documents, and remarked that he was acting very imprudently.

In reply to the usual questions, Dreyfus said that Captain Humbert's recollections were not exact, adding:

"In regard to the papers mentioned, perhaps it would be advisable to have the Commissariat Tables of Plan 13 produced, when you will see that they are of no great importance. It is certain I was acquainted with five or six tables, the printing of which I was instructed to superintend."

Colonel Jouaust—Did you apply to Colonel Sandherr with the view of entering the Statistical Section?

Dreyfus—No, no.

Colonel Jouaust—Did you not express such a desire to your comrades?

Dreyfus—No.

Savignaud, the former orderly of Colonel Picquart, and one of the witnesses, asked the court to certify that Senator Trarieux, the former Minister of Justice, had called him an impostor and a perjurer.

M. Trarieux rose and insisted that Savignaud's evidence was a contradiction of the evidence of Colonel Picquart, M. Scheurer-Kestner, and M.

Roque, proving, he claimed, perjury somewhere, but not by the last trio of witnesses.

M Trarieux added that his statements were in accordance with the dictates of his soul and conscience, and, if he was amenable to the law for them, there was also a law against perjurers.

General Mercier here reappeared on the scene. After saying that the evidence of Captain Freystaetter must have greatly influenced the judges, he referred to the attacks on himself made by the revisionist newspapers, saying that in consequence of Freystaetter's assertions he had been described as a forger, and it was great satisfaction to him now to be able to reply to Captain Freystaetter by adducing, in addition to the testimony of Colonel Maurel, an addition to his own testimony, which was confirmed by Colonel Du Paty de Clam's deposition.

Continuing, the general said that information which he had happily been enabled to obtain would completely enlighten the judges. He maintained that in 1894 he gave orders that the various translations of the Panizzardi telegram received from the Foreign Office should not be taken into account, and he declared that the testimony of General de Boisdeffre and M. Gribelin on this point agreed with his.

The sealed envelope handed to the court-martial of 1894, the general also said, was made up in his presence, and did not contain the Panizzardi telegram. It was sealed by Colonel Sandherr, and Colonel Du Paty de Clam was entrusted with conveying it to the court-martial.

He, the witness, had questioned the officers who acted as judges of the court-martial of 1894, in regard to the presentation to the court of a secret envelope. All, with a single exception, had assured him that they did not remember reading the Panizzardi telegram, although they could not declare under oath that it was not among the documents.

Three officers apologized for the vagueness of their recollections after the lapse of five years. Mercier asseverated that these statements themselves constituted proof, but he thought it necessary to point out contradictions in the evidence of Captain Freystaetter. He read an old letter from Freystaetter to a friend, in which the captain expressed his belief in the guilt of Dreyfus.

The general quoted a number of statements to the same effect, alleged to have been made by Freystaetter.

General Mercier, continuing, said he reproached Captain Freystaetter for engaging in newspaper discussion, which, perhaps, resulted in mixing his ideas so that others were being substituted for his personal recollections, which indicated a certain mental derangement. In support of the theory of lunacy, Mercier mentioned that Freystaetter, while in Madagascar, was once guilty of disobeying his commander, and on another occasion the captain executed thirty natives without trial.

The allegations of General Mercier caused so much excitement in court that Colonel Jouaust requested the general not to enlarge on the subject.

In conclusion Mercier invited the judges to pay no attention to Captain Freystaetter's statement, but to accord to the evidence which he himself had had the honor to give, all the confidence and moral authority they would have reposed in it if the Freystaetter incident had never happened.

M. Demange said he agreed with General Mercier that the Freystaetter incident could be dropped without injuring the case of Dreyfus.

"Thank God," said the lawyer, "I am here in a court of justice, where the question of justice is being discussed before honorable men and loyal soldiers. Then let this incident be forgotten."

The reports of experts were next read, showing that the tracing paper on which the bordereau was written was similar to paper used by Esterhazy, and official records were produced, showing that Dreyfus was wrong in regard to the number of probationers in 1894.

The prisoner admitted that his recollections were perhaps not precise.

M. Labori said he regretted that Cernuschi was not present, as counsel desired to question him, and, in any case, he wanted to add to the dossier certain letters showing that Cernuschi had suffered from insanity, and was destitute of moral sense. The defence had discovered that applications had been made for Cernuschi's extradition, and that he was pronounced to be altogether worthless and unreliable. Counsel also said that, although representing himself to be a political refugee, if Cernuschi had not left Austria he would have been placed in an asylum for the insane.

M. Labori then asked that a letter received from the witness Grenier should be read. The Government Commissary admitted receiving it, but said that the letter was of no importance. Counsel thought otherwise, and read a copy of the letter which Grenier had sent him simultaneously with one to Major Carriere. The letter referred to a letter from Esterhazy showing the latter's great interest in questions outside of his duties, that Esterhazy had in his possession official documents, that he concerned himself with the mobilization of the troops, and that he had expressed supreme contempt for the French army.

Colonel Jouaust remarked that if the letter had reached him he would not have made use of it, as it had nothing to do with the Dreyfus case.

This called forth murmurs of assent and dissent, and M. Labori retorted that he was of quite an opposite opinion. He said that General Chanoine had handed the court a latter from Colonel Schwartzkoppen to his government, announcing that he was about to send them information regarding the real effectiveness of the Russian army, and this was also referred to in Esterhazy's letter. Colonel Schwartzkoppen had also mentioned the Paris and Toul manœuvres, which would explain the phrase, "I am going to the manœuvres." This letter was written a fortnight after the arrest of Dreyfus, and M. Labori declared that he would be glad to hear the generals on that point.

General Roget accordingly marched to the platform. In regard to the mobilization of the Russian army, he said that a well-informed article on the subject had appeared in the *Revue Bleue*, owing to the indiscretions of a certain person he would not name, as he, the general, did not wish to compromise him.

Captain Cuignet confirmed General Roget's statement, adding that it must not be concluded that the information furnished to the German general staff did not emanate from Dreyfus. The fact that it took a fortnight to reach its destination proved nothing.

General Mercier also intervened to show that any information furnished by Esterhazy could have had no value.

Colonel Picquart offered explanations of the leakage in 1893, and General Mercier again jumped up and protested against indiscretions committed in favor of a former minister being called leakages.

At the request of M. Labori, the testimony given by the witness named Ecalle before the Court of Cassation was read. It described how Esterhazy employed Ecalle to execute a sketch of a rifle, which afterward, Esterhazy said, he had sent abroad with an imaginary plan of mobilization.

After further testimony on this point, a letter from Esterhazy to General Roget was read, in which the writer complained that no use was made of his information, and violently attacking M. Bertillon, who, according to Esterhazy, ought to be in an asylum for the insane.

Esterhazy complained of his miserable condition, described General de Boisdeffre as a scoundrel, and the *Echo de Paris* as a "dirty Jew sheet," adding that it was a mistake to abandon him and then prosecute him.

After repeating his threats, Esterhazy wrote that if he were the moral author of the bordereau he could not have supplied the information contained in it, and expressed surprise that nothing had been said in regard to the rôle played by Colonel Picquart. He then attacked, turn about, all the officers of the General Staff.

At this juncture M. Labori said that he thought that the court had heard quite enough of this edifying letter, and asked that the rest of it be not read. But Major Carriere objected, remarking that the letter was most interesting.

M. Labori—They are all interesting, and I would like to have them all read.

Major Carriere—They are all of the same degree of interest. They are all rot.

The reading then proceeded. In a letter containing a long string of bitter recriminations and violent insults, particularly in regard to certain members of the court-martial, whose impartiality was impugned, Esterhazy declared in conclusion:

"I will say or do nothing to increase the dangers of the situation. But I, an old and faithful servant, have been denounced and have fallen beneath the blows, after having been basely abandoned by the Boisdeffres, Billots, and other generals."

After Major Hartmann had briefly refuted General Mercier's statement that the Germans always termed the hydro-pneumatic brake the "hydraulic brake," which Hartmann declared to be absolutely untrue, Colonel Jouaust, though requested by M. Labori to allow M. des Fonds-Lamothe to be re-examined, refused to hear any further testimony.

Thereupon on September 7th, at 10:30 A.M., the Government Commissary, Major Carriere, began his speech closing the case for the prosecution. He concluded at 11:50 A.M. His speech, lasting only an hour and a quarter, was generally characterized as one of the weakest and most

20

ridiculous orations ever heard in a court of law. His absurd arguments, colored by his grotesque mannerism, evoked continual outbursts of derisive laughter.

Major Carriere, after reading the judgment of the Court of Cassation, and the questions referred to the present court-martial, said:

"Colonel and Councillors: By a judgment, June 3d, last, of the Court of Cassation, the Dreyfus case was sent before a court-martial at Rennes. I read the judgment at the beginning of the trial. It quashes and annuls the judgment of December 22, 1894, convicting Captain Alfred Dreyfus, and sends him before a court-martial at Rennes to be tried on the following question:

" Is Captain Alfred Dreyfus guilty of having in 1894 practised machinations for the benefit of a foreign power, by delivering the documents mentioned in the bordereau?

" The task of the court-martial at Rennes is the same as that of 1894. The trial has been public, and has been conducted with all the fulness possible to answer the requirements of justice and public opinion. It is my duty to discharge the task of justice with moderation. I have no personal opinion to defend. I have carefully examined the documents, seeking scrupulously to ascertain the truth, without malice, without passion, and without fear."

Major Carriere then entered upon a review of the case. He defended the secret sessions as being necessary, while they did not injure the diffusion of light; traced the espionage plot, recalled the discovery of the bordereau and the investigation which was said to show that the traitor was Dreyfus, and reviewed his prosecution and trial and the judgment of 1894.

"The proceedings," said Major Carriere, "were conducted according to the prevailing conditions. I will say nothing more in regard to the moral character of the prisoner, the question of his gambling or consorting with loose women. It has been said that we military men are not clever, and are not tactful. Maybe that is so. But we are a simple and upright people, who proceed direct toward our duty, and our acts are always characterized by good faith."

The major then proceeded to examine the bordereau, saying that apart from the question of the handwriting, upon which even the experts fell out, he thought that the reference to covering of troops and the artillery formation were very significant. Esterhazy, he pointed out, would have had no difficulty in securing the Firing Manual, therefore he could hardly have written that it was difficult to get; while Dreyfus could not easily have obtained it.

Discussing the sentence about going to the manœuvres, which has caused so much controversy, Major Carriere declared that it would have been impossible for Esterhazy to write it. He referred to the complexity of the prisoner's character, and proceeded to dilate upon the impartiality with which he had examined the whole case, upon which, he asserted, he had entered with his opinion wholly unformed.

"I said to myself, let us take the bull by the horns. It was Picquart who brought about the revision. Let us study Picquart. I found his case perfectly constructed, and for a moment hoped we might acquit and reha-bilitate an innocent man. It would have been all to our advantage and no trouble to repair a judicial error of the judges of 1894, whose honor has never been impugned. That would necessarily have pacified the public mind. But closer investigations of Picquart's case showed fissures. My momentary conviction of the innocence of Dreyfus was transformed into a stronger belief in his guilt, which has been confirmed by the testimony of the witnesses; and I come here to tell you, on my soul and conscience, that Dreyfus is guilty, and I demand the application of Article 76 of the Penal Code."

The last statement of the Government Commissary caused a great deal of excitement in court, which was afterward adjourned for the day.

When Major Carriere had concluded, and Colonel Jouaust had ordered the adjournment of the court, Dreyfus rose quickly and apparently not de-jected.

As the prisoner was passing counsel's table, M. Labori stopped him and whispered, "Courage." Dreyfus smiled and nodded, and, as he proceeded, M. Jaures, the Socialist leader, and a number of others seated on the benches before which Dreyfus passed, repeated M. Labori's word of en-couragement.

The most elaborate police measures were to be taken during the last day of the trial. Eight gendarmes were to be distributed in the court-room. Twenty gendarmes and a detachment of infantry were detailed for duty in the courtyard; the cordons of troops and gendarmes in the vicinity of the Lycée were ordered tripled and placed farther back; detachments of gendarmes were to be posted on the squares and bridges of the town, and mounted gendarmes had been instructed to patrol the principal streets of Rennes.   Also the garrisons of neighboring towns were held in readiness to be despatched to Rennes at a moment's notice.

Chapter LI.

PLEADING FOR THE PRISONER

THE development of the Dreyfus case on September 8th was marked by three distinct matters, namely, the opening of the speech of Maître Demange for the defence; the decision of Maître Labori not to make a speech for the defence, as he feared to irritate the judges; and an official statement from Berlin that German agents never had any relations with Dreyfus. The latter was issued in the following terms:

Berlin, September 8th.—The *Reichsanzeiger* this evening, in the official portion of the paper, publishes the following statement:

"We are authorized to repeat herewith the declarations which the imperial Government, while loyally observing the reserve demanded in regard to internal matters of another country, has made concerning the French Captain Dreyfus.

"For the preservation of his own dignity and the fulfilment of a duty to humanity, Prince von Munster, after obtaining the orders of the Emperor, repeatedly made in December, 1894, and in January, 1895, to M. Hanotaux, M. Dupuy, and M. Casimir-Perier, declarations to the effect that the Imperial Embassy in France never maintained either directly or indirectly any relations with Dreyfus.

"Secretary of State von Buelow, in the Reichstag January 24, 1898, made the following statement:

"'I declare in the most positive manner that no relations or connections of any kind ever existed between the French ex-Captain Dreyfus, now on Devil's Island, and any German agents.'"

At Rennes this announcement was not received until late in the evening of September 8th.

The hall of the Lycée was crowded at the opening of the session of the court-martial September 8th. At an early hour a long line of people awaiting admission was formed outside the door. Standing-room at the back of the court commanded fifteen and twenty francs for places, and the demand was increasing as the trial approached its end.   Among the privileged persons in attendance was Baron Russell of Killowen, Lord Chief Justice of England, who was conducted to a seat by General Chanoine and M. Paleologue, of the French Foreign Office.   The chief justice came to Rennes especially from Paris, where he had attended the sessions of the Anglo-Venezuelan boundary arbitration commission, in order to see something of the trial.

Maître Demange at once began his speech for the defence.   He pointed out the strength of the testimony against Esterhazy, and during the course of his remarks he cried: "Do you think if Dreyfus and Esterhazy had been before the court-martial in 1894, that the court would have condemned Captain Dreyfus?"

As he asked this question, counsel pointed to the prisoner sitting before him and added: "No."

The voice of M. Demange was beautifully modulated, sometimes soft and persuasive and at other times sharply argumentative.   Then again he frequently filled the hall with his stentorian tones, as he thundered with indignation at the charges against Dreyfus, the shameful weakness of the prosecution, and in denunciation of Esterhazy.

Captain Dreyfus listened to the oration of M. Demange with a mask of impassibility resembling his attitude during the first days of the trial. Whatever the prisoner's feelings were as he heard M. Demange pleading for his liberty, he carefully concealed them.

It was generally noticed that when Maître Labori entered the court that morning he spoke to M. Demange in a deprecating tone, and a sharp discussion ensued, almost bordering on a dispute.   The same thing took place during the usual brief suspension of the sitting.   The two lawyers apparently were at loggerheads about the best method of conducting the case, which, it was said, boded no good for Dreyfus, and nobody was astonished when it was announced that M. Labori would not address the court in behalf of the prisoner.

The following, in substance, was the plea of M. Demange:

"However solemn the occasion may be, I must at the outset protest with all my soul against the allegation which one of the witnesses did not shrink from uttering.   The witness said that whoever advocated the revision of this case, that is to say, whoever believed in the innocence of Dreyfus, was working against the army and against the country. I here declare that he does not know me, and that he does not know Maître Labori. Neither M. Labori nor myself would be here if those statements were true. Let me tell you simply this: The day on which, amid the shock of furious political passions, I saw let loose over our country this tempest of madness, when I saw everything I had learned to revere and love since childhood imperilled, I, a Frenchman, the son of a soldier, endured every torture. When I turn my eyes toward Devil's Island, where was buried alive one who, from the bottom of my heart, I believe to be a martyr, I began to wonder if Divine justice had not abandoned him. Since then I have recovered. I have hearkened to the voice of my conscience, and have pursued an undeviating course, free from anger or passion, not heeding hatred or prejudice. I have done my duty. You will do yours, which is to mete out justice."

Continuing, M. Demange said he wished to define clearly the prisoner's position. On this subject he said:

"When the case of the revision began, Dreyfus was a convict, and serious presumptions of his innocence were necessary before the case could be taken up by the Court of Cassation. To-day it is for the Public Prosecutor to prove his guilt. Let no one blame us, therefore, if we have not proved the innocence of our client. The task was not incumbent upon us. It is for the Government Commissioner to show that he is guilty of the abominable crime imputed to him."

Counsel then protested against the suggestion that an attempt had been made to put Esterhazy on trial, explaining that all the defence desired was that the innocence of Dreyfus should appear. M. Demange added that he was satisfied that the judges of 1894 were honest, like the present judges. But if the former had seen Esterhazy's handwriting, he asserted, they would have pronounced a different verdict.

Counsel then entered into details, dealing with the information collected regarding the prisoner in 1894, during the course of which he remarked:

"The only real information is that found in the cries from his soul. Even before his conviction, what was his first cry? 'I will not take my life because I am innocent.'"

Proceeding, M. Demange dilated upon the prisoner's increasing protestations of innocence, and his touching letters to his family, exclaiming:

"In them you see his soul, which speaks. Alone in his tomb he communes with himself. He cherishes the hope of seeing his innocence acknowledged."

Among the letters of Dreyfus read by M. Demange was one in which, after asserting his innocence, and declaring that he always served the tricolor flag with devotion and honor, the prisoner complained that he was treated on Devil's Island like an ordinary convict. It concluded: "I wish to live."

"That is a soldier's soul," exclaimed M. Demange, "and it is that man you call a traitor. That is the man who, in your presence, restrains his sobs and his emotions. Ah, gentlemen, I would rather defend guilty men who are clever dissemblers, than an innocent man who is too sincere."

After this, other letters of the prisoner were read, all breathing the same desire to live to see his honor restored, though the writer was broken down in health and spirit. One letter, written in 1897, appealed to General de Boisdeffre to lend his generous aid in securing for the writer restoration of his liberty, of which he had been robbed. Writing to his brother, the prisoner said:

"While one or more scoundrels are walking free, it would be a happy release for me to die. But it would be a disgrace to Lucille and my children."

The letter concluded urging his brother to find the culprits, while carefully protecting the interests of the country.

"Is not that the cry of an innocent man?" asked M. Demange, added: "Yet, though General de Boisdeffre received the letter, he did not forward it to Mathieu Dreyfus. Five Ministers of War pronounced Dreyfus guilty, while admitting that it was impossible to produce proofs. General de Boisdeffre, General Gonse, and General Roget also affirmed their belief in his guilt. But, happily, they stated reasons, and, instead of proofs, only accumulated presumptions."

Counsel, after pointing out that the generals only studied the case at the very moment when public aberration had reduced the whole question to a conflict between Dreyfus and the army, thus making it impossible that the generals should not be prejudiced, and probabilities and presumptions seemed to them to be proofs, said:

"I must acknowledge, however, the honesty and honorable conduct of the generals, who could not have acted otherwise than they have done."

M. Demange then paid an eloquent tribute to the "honesty of purpose" manifested by the generals. Dealing next with the alleged confessions, counsel read the report of Captain Lebrun-Renault, of the Republican Guard, who had the prisoner in custody previous to his degradation, and maintained that the exact words of Dreyfus, which were now known only to reflect the ideas which Colonel Du Paty de Clam had previously expressed to the prisoner, point out that, although Du Paty de Clam maintained the contrary, it was certain that imagination had played a much greater part than reason in his acts. It was also significant, counsel said, that the report drawn up by Du Paty de Clam on the day following his interview with Dreyfus had disappeared. Du Paty de Clam, counsel intimated, had evidently forgotten his remarks to Dreyfus, as he had forgotten other facts.

M. Demange then said that he was surprised at the attitude of General Gonse toward the alleged confessions, and marvelled at the fact that Captain Lebrun-Renault, who was sent to the Elysée palace expressly to repeat the confessions, did not mention them. It was likewise inexplicable that General Saussier and General Mercier took no steps to verify the so-called confessions, which were lost sight of until M. Cavaignac, as Minister of War, sprung them upon the Chamber of Deputies as proof of the guilt of Dreyfus. The Court of Cassation, the lawyer also said, had justly decided that they were not confessions.

Discussing the secret dossier, M. Demange examined the documents one after the other. He said that all interpretations of the document commencing "doubt proof" were hypothetical, but they applied much more easily to Esterhazy than to Dreyfus. It was so with the other documents. There was nothing to indicate that Dreyfus was concerned any more than any one else. The leakage ascribed to Dreyfus could only refer to the plans of fortresses, and this leakage continued until 1897.

The document containing the words "Cette canaille de D——," according to M. Demange, only indicated a "poor devil," and could not be ascribed to a man whom another letter described as a friend in the Second

Bureau. No credence could be attached to some of the documents, while others were wholly inapplicable to the prisoner.

Counsel said the sixth document was a letter written from Germany by Count von Munster-Ledenburg, the German Ambassador to France, to Colonel Schwartzkoppen, the military attaché of Germany at Paris, containing the words, "As regards Dreyfus, we are easy." M. Demange pointed out that the Dreyfus case was the universal topic of discussion in Germany at the time, and at first the German officials might have been uneasy, but had evidently reassured themselves.

M. Demange was indignant at the fact that, because Count von Munster-Ledenburg had not expressly declared Dreyfus was innocent, the prosecution should have deduced from his words an avowal of his guilt.

Referring to the letters of November 2d and November 11th, sent by Major Panizzardi to his chief, it had been alleged that they proved that Dreyfus had relations with Colonel Schwartzkoppen, whereas in reality Major Panizzardi merely denied that Dreyfus had any relations with Italy. It was impossible to doubt the authenticity of these facts. It was incredible that Colonel Schwartzkoppen and Major Panizzardi deceived their governments. The omission of Esterhazy's name from these letters was intentional.

In concluding his examination of the secret dossier, M. Demange remarked that he felt compelled to refer to these documents emanating from foreigners, as General Mercier relied upon them to support the guilt of Dreyfus. The statements of the military attachés, that they had no relations with Dreyfus, had been confirmed by the statement of the Minister of State in the Reichstag, who could not have been deceived by his attaché at Paris.

"I have finished," then said M. Demange, "my examination of the secret dossier. All France knows the worthlessness of its contents. Yet, it is owing to it that the country has been distracted for months, and it has been thought that there were documents and proofs in it which might bring France to blows with a neighboring power. You are now acquainted with it. The secret dossier has been exploded. You will pardon me the loss of time I have imposed upon you. I will now take up the circumstantial evidence."

M. Demange then discussed the circumstantial evidence adduced in

1894. He said the perturbation of Dreyfus at the dictation scene had nothing to do with producing the idea of guilt in the minds of those present. Colonel Du Paty de Clam, M. Cochefert, chief of detectives, and Major Gribelin were all convinced beforehand of his guilt as a result of evidence which they considered unimpeachable; so much so that they wished Dreyfus to blow his brains out, but Dreyfus declined because he was innocent.

Continuing, counsel for the defence successively showed the hollowness of the stories of Mathieu Dreyfus's attempt to corrupt Colonel Sandherr, the late Lieutenant-Colonel Henry's theatrical denunciation of Dreyfus as a traitor at the court-martial of 1894, and the reports of the detectives. He pointed out how the prosecution had advanced as proof the alleged statements of individuals, who were not in the pay of the War Office, but whom they carefully abstained from producing for examination; especially dwelling upon Henry's statement in 1894—which has since been admitted to be false—that a certain War Office employee informed him that Dreyfus was the culprit.

M. Demange then showed the emptiness of the gambling and libertine charges against the prisoner, and said that the simplest actions of Dreyfus were misconstrued, even his legitimate desire to obtain knowledge being imputed as a crime.

After demonstrating the falsity of the testimony of M. de Beaurepaire's witnesses, Mueller, Dubreuil, Villon, and Cernuschi, counsel said that the only proof left was the bordereau. Who could have sent it? Who wrote it? Complete light could only be shed on it by the production of the notes enumerated in the bordereau. This had been said by General Zurlinden himself. But counsel asked the court to remember, with reference to those notes, that all General Deloye could say was that it was not impossible that Dreyfus might have possessed them. This was all he could say when it was a question of high treason. M. Demange added:

"You will find this phrase in the mouth of a witness entitled to your entire respect, and it is upon the strength of such a statement that Dreyfus is to be proved guilty. I will not attempt to obtain such light on the documents, but since theories have been promulgated I will suggest one. I will seek to show that you must put aside even the technical value of the bordereau and the last effort of the prosecution.   I will seek to combat the circumstantial evidence it has invoked."

At this point M. Demange paused to announce that he would need another two hours and a half to finish his plea, and as it was then already eleven o'clock the court adjourned until 7:30 A.M., September 9th, thus fixing the opening of the court of that day an hour later than usual.

The general impression formed was that the speech of M. Demange must have had a certain effect on the judges, as it was a strong effort argumentatively.

Great interest was aroused during the day by the arrival at Rennes of Max Regis, the ex-mayor of Algiers, the notorious Jew-baiter.   He was attended by a couple of Algerians in native costume, and a crowd of people followed him about.   He stopped to take some refreshment at the principal café, and the place was immediately invaded by a gaping crowd. M. Regis was present in the court-yard of the Lycée during the morning, and discussed the situation with the leading anti-Dreyfusards.   His presence was not considered a good omen for the peace of the town.

The local papers published an open letter from M. Regis to the Premier, M. Waldeck-Rousseau, declaring that he, M. Regis, intended to preserve the greatest calm, but adding that if an attempt was made to arrest him he would resist.

Chapter LII.

AGAIN FOUND GUILTY

WHEN Rennes awoke on September 9th, the appearance of the streets left no doubt that the final crisis of the great trial had been reached. The whole town bristled with soldiers; all the streets near the court were guarded at intervals by double lines of infantry; two companies of infantry sat on the church steps adjoining the Lycée, with their arms stacked in front of them, while in the courtyard of the prison and at various other points cavalry could be seen in readiness. Every one entering the court was subjected to the closest scrutiny. Even the few women who attended the session were deprived of their small sunshades before being permitted to pass.

A larger crowd than usual witnessed the passage of Dreyfus from the prison to the Lycée. But the crowds were nowhere large, and, aside from the presence of the military, the town was as tranquil as usual.

The prisoner looked flushed and in ill health, apparently suffering from the great strain.

M. Demange resumed his speech for the defence, which was interrupted on September 8th by the adjournment of the court. The audience listened to his remarks with the most serious attention, and he was also closely followed by the judges. In his appeal to them he strongly accentuated the words: "Why, you must not say a thing is possible. A judge must have proof. No doubt must rest on the conscience of a judge."

In the second row of the privileged public, facing the judges, sat Mathieu Dreyfus, brother of the prisoner, whose sunken eyes and careworn face reflected his anxiety and anguish. It was evident that he had not slept during the night.

The prisoner sat behind a captain of gendarmes, and as M. Demange refuted the arguments made in the speech of the Government Commissary, Major Carriere, the prisoner continually turned his face toward Mathieu,

to watch the effect it had upon him.   Dreyfus, however, did not display
the intense emotion with which his heart, on this critical morning, must
have been bursting.

Gendarmes were plentifully sown among the audience, and were posted
in the gangways around the court-room.   There was a pleasant contrast
in their pretty blue uniforms with white cord trimmings, to the sober
attire of the majority of the spectators.   They kept their eyes roaming over
the court, and their hands rested on the black leather cases in which nes-
tled big army revolvers.

The silence was only broken by the occasional rustling of a reporter's
notebook, or the neigh of an artillery horse picketed in a street beside the
Lycée.   Now and then there was the sound of the rattling of a rifle or the
clanking of the sword of some officer hastily crossing the court-yard where
the troops were stationed.

The peroration of M. Demange was a splendid piece of oratory.   His
voice thundered through the court, echoed outside, and the officers and
troopers stationed in the court-yard crowded around the entrance hall,
standing on tiptoe to catch a glimpse of the speaker, while inside the hall
many of the audience were moved to tears.

The speech was very skilfully arranged, and was devoted to demolish-
ing stone by stone the arguments of the prosecution.   Counsel began by
saying :

"When yesterday's (September 8th) sitting was ended I was about to
deal with what is called the direct evidence, namely, the technical value
of the bordereau.   The prosecution, by taking separately each of the notes
containing information supplied by the writer of the bordereau, deduced
the opinion that he alone could have communicated information of the
documents.   If he had in his possession proof of this, he should have given
it.   It devolved upon the Public Prosecutor to prove that Dreyfus possessed this information, and nobody but he.   That is how the question
must be put.   We are before a court of justice, in which suppositions have
no place.   In order to produce proof, I must ask, and we must know, what
was the information supplied.   Consequently, we must have the notes delivered.   Otherwise we have to deal with a hypothesis.   That is my first
objection, to which I challenge the Public Prosecutor to reply."

M. Demange, remarking that the hypothesis accepted in 1894 could not now be maintained, proceeded minutely to examine the theories of the Headquarters Staff, especially General Roget's, whose arguments he refuted seriatim. He similarly analyzed the evidence of General Mercier, reiterating the arguments as to the utter improbability of an artilleryman employing the incorrect terms used in the bordereau in connection with artillery matters.

He then reviewed the well-known facts in the case, showing that Colonel Schwartzkoppen, the German military attaché at Paris, supplied information to his government, years before, regarding the "120-short" field-gun. He said that only the internal construction of the brake of this gun remained secret, but Dreyfus knew nothing about it, and never asked for information on the subject from the few officers knowing it. Therefore, counsel contended, Dreyfus could not have betrayed this secret.

Regarding the practical tests of the gun, M. Demange continued, Dreyfus was similarly ignorant. General Mercier's statement that Dreyfus attended the trials could be dismissed, as it had been proved that the only leakage resulting from those trials had been furnished by the spy Grenier. It was thus apparent into what error all the witnesses supporting the prosecution had fallen. Their opinions had been imperfectly formed, and the judges must be on their guard against it, honest and sincere as it doubtless was.

After refuting the imputations against Dreyfus based on the Firing Manual, which he said were purely hpyothetical, M. Demange continued, emphatically:

"The prosecution has no right to rest content with hypothesis. We are in a court of justice. The defence alone has the right to say it is possible or not possible. As General Deloye declared, it is the duty of the Public Prosecutor to produce evidence. But he had adduced none against Dreyfus."

After showing that the prisoner had never seen the "120-short" field-gun fired, counsel read letters from Esterhazy proving that the latter attended the Chalons camp, and probably attended the trials.

"But the prosecution," M. Demange added, "has not to choose between Dreyfus and Esterhazy. It has only to prove Dreyfus guilty, and could not do so. On the contrary, we have shown that Dreyfus did not possess the documents communicated nor the information contained in them."

Dealing with the note referring to the covering of troops, M. Demange pointed out General Mercier's change of front on this subject. In 1894 the general contended that it was in reference to the commands of these troops that the leakage occurred, while he now asserted that it was regarding the mobilization and transport of the troops. The prosecution had thus advanced two versions, which must cause the judges terrible searchings of conscience, especially as no proofs had been furnished. What right had the prosecution to advance statements without corroboration? Counsel put it to the conscience of the judges, and he had asked this of General Mercier himself.

Continuing to plead with great warmth and eloquence, and with clear, closely reasoned arguments, which were followed with breathless interest by the entire audience, M. Demange declared that he did not believe in the complicity of Henry and Esterhazy, for Henry was honorable and loyal. If he had been the accomplice of Esterhazy, Henry would have destroyed the bordereau. Possibly Henry had inadvertently divulged information to Esterhazy, under the impression that he was conversing with an honorable, straightforward man like himself, and, discovering in 1898 that he had placed his hand in a traitor's, he committed a crime upon which counsel declined to enlarge, since the perpetrator had already paid for it with his life. What other explanation could be given of the suicide of this man, with whom the whole army sympathized? Even after the discovery of the crime Henry had spoken of scoundrels. Was one of these not Esterhazy and the other Weil, the latter having unconsciously betrayed information? General Saussier had every confidence in Henry's loyalty, and Esterhazy might have received information from Henry or Weil, who were unconscious informers.

A loyal soldier, General Billot, had moreover said that the traitor was not alone. In his mind he connected the names of Esterhazy and Dreyfus. Counsel did not profess to clear up the matter, but he wished it to be cleared up. It must be proved that Dreyfus knew Esterhazy and Weil. M. Demange did not fear whatever light could be thrown on the case. Three men were in the Intelligence Department—Henry, Esterhazy, and Weil. Esterhazy had even placed the others under pecuniary obligations, and all these were closely bound together.

Replying to the hypothesis deduced in the note relating to the modifi-

THE ALTAR OF ST. JOSEPH (WRECKED BY THE MOB, AUGUST 20, 1889).

CAPTAIN DREYFUS: "THAT I AM ALIVE TO-DAY I OWE TO MY WIFE."

THE TRIAL AT RENNES: COLONEL JOUAUST READING THE ARRAIGNMENT AT THE BAR.

THE FUNERAL CORTÈGE OF COLONEL HENRY.

M. BERTILLON DEMONSTRATES HIS "SYSTEM."

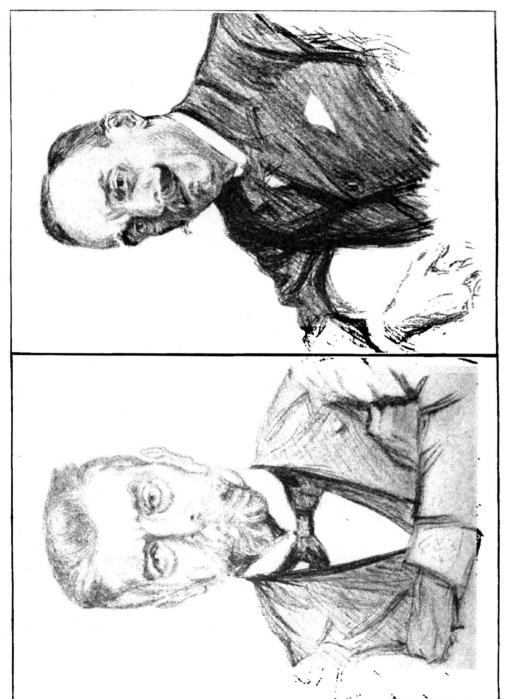

MAJOR FORZINETTI.

M. BERTULUS, MAGISTRATE OF INSTRUCTION AT THE POLYTECHNIC INSTITUTION.

MAÎTRE DEMANGE ADDRESSING THE COURT IN BEHALF OF DREYFUS.

cation of the artillery, M. Demange pointed out that the information could have been obtained by Esterhazy at the Chalons camp, while, regarding the Madagascar note, Dreyfus had never had possession of it, though one of his most bitter prosecutors, Colonel Du Paty de Clam, had it in his office.

Returning to the Firing Manual, counsel showed how Esterhazy secured a copy of it, and pointed to the fact that his government had asked Colonel Schwartzkoppen for supplementary information, which showed that the original intelligence was incomplete, and supplied by an incompetent person, not an artilleryman. The memorandum to Colonel Schwartzkoppen asked for the Firing Manual, which must, therefore, have been offered, and to the graduation bar, which Esterhazy had obtained from a friend and kept.

Had all these proofs existed against Dreyfus, how strong would have been the case for the prosecution! But their hypotheses were not even probable, while the theories of the defence were all supported by documents culled from the secret dossier.

Dealing with the last line of the bordereau, " I am going to the manœuvres," counsel produced a note, written by Dreyfus, proving that he knew in May, 1894, that he would not attend the manœuvres with his regiment.

Counsel dwelt upon the importance of the fact that the probationers absolutely knew they would not attend the manœuvres, though certain individuals cherished the hope that exceptions might be made in their favor. Only one actually applied to General de Boisdeffre for permission, but the latter did not promise anything. M. Demange protested against the Government Commissioner's assertion that it had been agreed that the probationers should attend the manœuvres as officers of the Headquarters Staff, and said he wished to know if Major Carriere adhered to his statement on the subject.

Major Carriere recalled that General de Boisdeffre had declared that he had promised to do his best to satisfy the probationers.

M. Demange—And you call that an agreement?

Major Carriere—Certainly.

M. Demange—Then we do not agree as to the meaning of the word in the French language.

21

Continuing, M. Demange exclaimed:

"Hear what the author of the bordereau writes: ' I am going to the manœuvres.'   Is that only a belief?   Isn't it rather a certainty?   Well, gentlemen, I have shown you that Dreyfus could not have written that. On the contrary, Esterhazy's regiment was at the manœuvres, regarding which information was supplied.   Was Esterhazy there?   I do not know. But what is certain is that Dreyfus, if he was the author of the bordereau, could not have written at the end of August: ' I am going to the manœuvres,' since he knew the probationers were not going.   I think I have shown that when all the points of the accusation are examined they vanish.   So much for the technical value of the bordereau.   I have argued foot by foot with my honorable friends on the other side, and I have shown the fallacy of the mental process whereby they reached the point that they were able to affirm on their soul and conscience that Dreyfus was guilty.   I might therefore say with pride that I have demolished the case of the prosecution.   But I am not entitled to do so.   I merely say to the court, be careful.   You must be certain, and before you can say Dreyfus is guilty you must, on your souls and consciences, be able to declare that there is no doubt that no one but he had the documents enumerated in the bordereau.   But you do not know what the documents are. That is my last word on this portion of the case.   I have now to deal with the material evidence."

Counsel next dissected the handwriting evidence, and reminded the court of the groans with which M. Scheurer-Kestner was greeted when he displayed the handwriting of Esterhazy in the tribune of the Senate.

"'Is that all you have?' disdainfully asked the Senators.   To-day the prosecution has no more."

Referring to M. Bertillon, M. Demange said he did not understand his conclusions.   "He produced in court a monumental work," said the lawyer.   "But I am convinced, and hope to prove, that M. Bertillon's system is false.   But, I must do him the justice of saying that when the Prefect of Police applied to M. Bertillon he appealed to a man of genius who, by the creation of the Anthropometric Department, conferred upon society an inestimable benefit.   Still, I can only say, ' You have fallen into error which may be fatal to an innocent man.' "

Proceeding, M. Demange demolished M. Bertillon's theories, dealing at great length with the different contentions, admitting that some of them might content certain scientific minds. But, he added, it must not be forgotten that genius had a dangerous neighbor. It did not do to have too much genius, and M. Bertillon's work was liable to land the judges in serious error. The statements of scientists, the evidence of common sense, and the declarations of M. Bertillon himself showed that the experts had not proved the guilt of Dreyfus. If the handwriting of the bordereau was disguised, how could Dreyfus's exclamation, "This handwriting has a frightful resemblance to mine," be explained?

Counsel said he was convinced that the bordereau was written, in his natural hand, by Esterhazy. The paper on which it was written also condemned Esterhazy.

M. Demange next examined at length the theory that Esterhazy was a straw-man, and showed this was rendered quite untenable by every action of Colonel Picquart, who was accused of trying to effect the substitution. How, if Esterhazy was a straw-man, could he have lost his head at the moment of his arrest to such an extent that he contemplated suicide? The lawyer contrasted the lives of Dreyfus and Esterhazy, saying there was nothing but idle tales against the former, while the latter was always in search of a five-franc piece. When the time arrived for the judges to say whether the bordereau was in the handwriting of Dreyfus, they would have to remember that all the experts admitted that it was not, while all of them admitted that it showed traces of Esterhazy's handwriting. They would also have to compare the demeanor of Dreyfus during the past five years with the demeanor of Esterhazy to-day: One, on Devil's Island, constantly turning his eyes toward France and appealing to General de Boisdeffre against his conviction, demanding only justice; the other full of recriminations and bitter abuse, writing insulting letters to the generals.

M. Demange, after reverting briefly to the charges in connection with the Robin shell, protested against General Mercier's refusal to discuss motives, as being merely a psychological question, while it was in reality a question of common sense. There was an entire lack of motive in the case of Dreyfus, while there was every motive upon the part of Esterhazy. Dreyfus was rich and happy, he had two children who were his pride and joy, and a wife of whose devoted courage all were aware—everything a man could desire. Why should he have risked all that?

"Believe me," added M. Demange, "my conviction comes from an honest heart. I am convinced that the judges, with the doubt which will remain in their minds, will find it impossible to declare the prisoner guilty, for they will rather turn their eyes to the men hiding on the other side of the Channel. I ask you once more whether the noble, dignified bearing of the prisoner since 1894 is not that of an honest, loyal soldier?"

After this, M. Demange, with his voice broken with emotion, tears streaming down his face, and hands trembling, concluded his brilliant flight of oratory.

"Ah, gentlemen," said he, "I must now close in order to restore you to your well-earned repose, for I have now been addressing you for two days. But, there is one thing which detains me. When I have finished, the last word of the defence will have been said, and you will go to your private room to consider your verdict. Once there, what are you going to ask yourselves? If Dreyfus is innocent? That is not the point. But is he guilty? You will ask yourselves, 'Are we going to say he sent these documents when we do not even know what they contain?' and when you say to yourselves, after having heard that the defence is powerless, it is true, to throw complete light on the matter—but, believe me, speaking from sincere, honest conviction, we do not know what he sent. Another may have given these documents; but he, no, no! These were things he could not have given—"when you say to yourselves further that this writing is not his, when you say to yourselves that there is over there on the other side of the Channel a man of whom we have to say, 'It is he,'—will there be, gentlemen, no doubt in your minds? That doubt will be sufficient for me. That doubt will mean his acquittal. It will not permit honest, logical consciences to say this man is guilty. Very well, gentlemen, I ask only one thing, and that is that at this moment you cast one more backward glance. Remember what the prisoner was on Devil's Island. Remember how, for five years, this man, in spite of the most horrible sufferings, notwithstanding the most cruel torture, was never for a single moment alone, a guard with him night and day, and never allowed to exchange a syllable with a fellow-creature. I am not speaking of the torture of his being placed in irons; I am speaking of the terrible mental torture to which he was subjected. Well, gentlemen, the spirit which these sufferings, these tortures could not curb, that spirit which remained proud and high, I ask you, is it the spirit of a traitor? I ask you if it is not that of a loyal, tried soldier? I ask if the man who only lived for his children, that they may bear an honored name, this man here who has the cult of honor in his family, I ask if you can believe him to be a villain and a traitor to his motherland? No, I have no need to proclaim his innocence. I say your verdict will not be a verdict of guilty, for you have been enlightened. The judges of 1894 had not been so enlightened. They have not before them Esterhazy's writing. But you had it. That is the conducting wire, as God has permitted you, gentlemen, to have it.

"My task is now accomplished. It is for you to do yours. I pray God," exclaimed counsel, lifting his arms toward Heaven—"I pray God that you will restore to our France the concord of which she had so much need!" Then, turning to the audience, in which every eye was fixed upon him, M. Demange added, in conclusion:

"As to you, whoever you may be, Frenchmen, be you with me or against me, finding inspiration in the sublime idea of M. Mornaud before the Court of Cassation, I say to all, we are Frenchmen. Let us then be united in the common sentiment of love of country, love of justice, and love of the army."

As he reached this climax, the counsel's voice swelled like the tones of an organ, and the close of his impassioned peroration was followed by an outburst of applause, which was immediately suppressed by the president.

M. Labori then said he did not desire to speak.

Major Carriere, however, claimed the right to reply.

When the court resumed its session after a brief adjournment, the Government Commissary began his reply. He promised to be brief, and said he desired to submit to the court-martial a simple observation:

"Weigh the importance of the two categories of witnesses, those for and those against the prisoner. Weigh their importance, and judge, in all the independence of your character and all the strength of soldiers. Proof is everywhere. The hour of supreme decision has sounded. France anxiously awaits your judgment. I also await it, confidently and fully maintaining the conclusions already announced. I demand the application of Article 76 of the Penal Code and Article 267 of the Military Code."

The demand of the Government Commissary caused a sensation in court.

M. Demange rose to reply, with his voice hoarse from fatigue. He said:

"The Government Commissioner, in reminding you of the text of the law, has also reminded us of what we already knew—namely, that you are only answerable to your consciences and God for your verdict. This is my last word in this case. I feel that as men of honor and loyalty and as military judges you will never admit as proofs the hypotheses and presumptions advanced here; consequently my last word is the same I spoke this morning. I have confidence in you because you are soldiers."

Colonel Jouaust, president of the court, asked Dreyfus if he had anything to add in his behalf. The prisoner rose, and in a voice choked with emotion declared he had only one thing to say, but of that he was perfectly assured. He said:

"I affirm before my country and before the army that I am innocent. My sole aim has been to save the honor of my name, the name borne by my children. I have suffered five years of the most awful torture. But, to-day, at last, I feel assured that I am about to attain my desire, through your loyalty and justice."

Colonel Jouaust—Have you finished, Dreyfus?

Dreyfus—Yes, Mr. President.

The court then retired to deliberate, and the prisoner left the hall, never to return, as, in accordance with the law, the verdict was rendered in his absence.

After about two hours' deliberation, the court, by a vote of five to two, found the prisoner "guilty, with extenuating circumstances," and sentenced him to ten years' detention.

The text of the judgment was as follows:

"To-day, the 9th of September, 1899, the court-martial of the Tenth Legion Army Corps, deliberating behind closed doors, the president put the following question:

"'Is Alfred Dreyfus, brevet captain Fourteenth Regiment of Artillery, probationer on the General Staff, guilty of having in 1894 entered into machinations or held relations with a foreign power, or one of its agents, to induce it to commit hostility or undertake war against France, or procure it the means therefor, by delivering the notes and documents mentioned in the document called the bordereau, according to the decision of the Court of Cassation of June 3, 1899?

"The votes were taken separately, beginning by the inferior grade and youngest in the last grade, the president giving his opinion last.

"The court declares on the question, by a majority of five votes to two, 'Yes,' the accused is guilty.

"The majority agreed that there are extenuating circumstances, in consequence of which and on the request of the commissary of the Government, the president put the question and received again the votes in the above-mentioned form.

"As a result, the court condemns, by a majority of five votes to two, Alfred Dreyfus to the punishment of ten years' detention."

The judgment then quotes the Code and the Constitution under which the sentence was delivered, with the article of the law enjoining the Government Commissary to have the judgment immediately read in the presence of the prisoner, before the assembled guard, under arms, and to notify him that the law allowed a delay of twenty-four hours in which to lodge an appeal.

The silence was immediately broken by a rush of the reporters to drop their previously prepared telegrams into the letter-box in the street, where a gendarme received them and gave them to the respective messengers for transmission by wire.

The noise called forth a stern cry of "Silence!" and again all sound was hushed until Colonel Jouaust finished speaking. He concluded by saying the court would remain sitting until the room was cleared. He asked the audience to go out quietly and not to raise a shout of any sort.

The gendarmes then closed around the audience and pressed them outside. Not a cry or a word was raised by any one. Everything passed off with complete calm.

As the people emerged the gendarmes kept them moving away from the court. The small crowd outside cheered.

The pent-up feelings of the audience were expressed in a long, deep-drawn "Oh!" when Colonel Jouaust reached the word "guilty." The

word was pronounced under his breath.   Owing to the threat of vigorous
punishment for uttering any cry there was no outburst, but the faces of the
majority of the spectators reflected an expression of anguished surprise.

Maître Labori heard the verdict with a pallid visage, while Maître
Demange fell back in a chair as though horror-stricken.   Colonel Jouaust
read the judgment without a tremor of his voice and apparently unmoved.

After the verdict M. Demange said:

"Terrible! Unbelievable! It was the most awful shock I ever received
in my life.   I am trying to put myself in those men's places and view
the problem as they did.   Try as I may, I cannot grasp how they reasoned
it out."

"It is as I expected," said M. Labori.   "I was convinced from the first
that we were dealing with an unconscionable set, and I handled them accordingly.   My views were not fully supported, and I consented to yield.
Now it is not for me to speak.   The fight was not carried on as it would
have been if I had been in full charge.

"Now we must bend all our energy to secure a reversal and obtain a
new revision.   I am leaving with M. Demange at twelve to-night to present an appeal in Paris.   Monira alone stays here to get the signature of
Dreyfus on certain papers."

Zola telegraphed to M. Labori, saying:

"You were right, we were wrong.   Your plan of making this crime
impossible by disqualifying thoroughly all the military witnesses showed
you had penetrated them more than we.   Henceforth count me as a most
determined partisan for a vigorous fight, and no mercy to the foe when we
have him down.   From this day I re-enter the arena, never again to
leave it."

M. Clemenceau also telegraphed to M. Labori.   He said:

"Congratulations, nevertheless.   You know what I think and how I
feel now.   We must never rest till the five men now branded before an
offended world are securely lodged in a penitentiary for wilful abuse of
sacred laws trusted to their hands."

Max Nordau said:

"No words would fitly express my indignation."

M. Jaures, the Socialist leader, said:

"Military tribunals must be abolished, and will be.   They are a survival of mediæval prejudices. All citizens must be equal before the law. The danger of allowing one caste to consider itself separate from the rest of the nation and above common law was vividly exemplified in to-day's monstrous decision."

Octave Mirabeau said:

"This marks the beginning of a protracted political convulsion. Either we shall sink to the insignificance of Spain or rid our country of the clerical obscurantism which does not pervade the army alone, but a large portion of our people."

M. Marcel Prevost, the able correspondent at Rennes of the New York *Herald*, cabled to his paper:

"Dreyfus is condemned. You will read the new conditions of the sentence he has to undergo. They extenuate a little the rigor of his former judgment. But he is condemned. He is going to be degraded once more.

"This sentence was received with death-like stupor. Alas! for several days I have foreseen it only too clearly, but my conscience refused to believe it possible.

"Don't ask me for any comment on such an event as this. My heart as a man and a Frenchman is too full of grief. It seems to me as if my country had just heard a condemnation pronounced upon it."

Counsel for Dreyfus immediately prepared an appeal, which the prisoner signed at noon, September 10th.

After the verdict the health of the prisoner failed steadily, and it was said he was only able to take the very lightest nourishment, eggs and milk. But, sustained by the loving and wise counsels of his wife, who was allowed to see him in prison daily, Dreyfus bore up, and his friends continued their efforts in his behalf.

On September 19th, it was announced from Paris that the Council of Ministers had decided to pardon Dreyfus "in principle," and that the pardon would take effect a few days later. It was also announced that Dreyfus had relinquished his appeal for a reversal of the judgment of the court-martial. This was in accordance with the advice of his friends, who were anxious to secure his release, almost at any cost, in view of his failing health. But, it was added, this did not by any means indicate that the efforts to establish clearly the innocence of Dreyfus, and find the

really guilty man, would be abandoned.   On the contrary, it was said that
the search for the real culprit would be continued until Dreyfus was
cleared of all suspicion of treason.

Dreyfus was released from his prison at Rennes at three o'clock on
the morning of September 20th, and proceeded to Vern, with his faithful
brother, Mathieu Dreyfus, where he took a train bound for Nantes.   At
Nantes the two brothers took a train for Bordeaux and Carpentras, in the
department of Vaucluse, sixteen miles northeast of Avignon, where he
took up his residence at the home of his brother-in-law, M. Valabregue, a
well-known cloth-merchant, who has been established there for over a
quarter of a century.   There was no demonstration at Carpentras when
Dreyfus arrived there.

Carpentras is situated on the River Auzon, in a fertile district at the
foot of Mont Ventoux.   The town is surrounded by walls, flanked by
towers, and has four gates.   Outside the walls is a broad esplanade planted
with trees.   In 1313 Pope Clement V. fixed his residence there, and made
it the seat of the Pontifical See.   The present walls were built by Pope
Innocent VI., fifty years after that event.   The principal public buildings
of Carpentras are the cathedral, a Gothic edifice; a museum, the Porte
d'Orange; the Palace of Justice; a Roman triumphal arch; the hospital,
erected in 1751; the theatre, prisons, and a library containing 25,000 vol-
umes, 6,000 medals, and various antiquities.   The aqueduct, a massive
structure which crosses the valley of the Auzon by forty-eight arches,
was finished in 1734.   Carpentras has a population of about 10,000
souls.

When Dreyfus first met his children, on September 23d, the Saturday
after his arrival at Carpentras, the liberated man stood outside the garden
at the end of the carriage drive leading to the Valabregue villa.   On seeing him his little boy and girl, Pierre and Jeanne, jumped out of the carriage which was bringing them, with their grandparents, M. and Mme.
Hadamard, from the railway station whence they had arrived from Paris,
and ran toward their father.   Pressing them both in his arms, Dreyfus
kissed them passionately, and pressed them again and again to his heart,
tears of joy coursing down his face as he did so.   He was overwhelmed
with emotion and unable to speak a single word.   This first interview
with his children, after five years' separation, affected him so deeply that

he remained completely prostrated with nervous exhaustion during the rest of the day.

Of course the verdict of the court-martial alone practically established the fact that the charges against Dreyfus had not been proved, therefore the light sentence and the rider of "extenuating circumstances." This was confirmed by the action of the Cabinet Council in deciding to pardon the prisoner. Dreyfus, although condemned, was, to all intents and purposes, shown not to have been guilty as charged.

The future efforts in behalf of this seeming martyr and apparent victim of French military incompetency will be watched with the greatest interest throughout the world.

It is sad to add that, on the very day it was announced from Paris that the prisoner was to be pardoned, there came at exactly the same hour another despatch from the French capital saying that M. Scheurer-Kestner, the former Vice-President of the Senate and great champion of the cause of Dreyfus, was dead. He had been suffering from typhoid fever for some days previously, and expired without the consolation of knowing that his great work had triumphed.

Dreyfus was deeply grieved when informed of the death of his champion, M. Scheurer-Kestner. He was especially grieved that M. Scheurer-Kestner did not live long enough to receive his thanks. One of Dreyfus's first acts after he was freed was to order a wreath for M. Scheurer-Kestner's coffin.

Dreyfus wrote the following letter to M. Marcelin Pellet, son-in-law of M. Scheurer-Kestner, on September 21st:

SIR:—My first thought immediately after my liberation was for M. Scheurer-Kestner. What, therefore, was my profound grief on learning yesterday *en route* the great sorrow which has befallen you. I was impatiently awaiting the moment when I should be able to pay to M. Scheurer-Kestner the respectful homage of my admiration for his character, his loyalty, the generous ardor with which he took in hand the cause of an Alsatian innocent of the abominable crime for which he had been condemned. I beg you to be so kind to express this homage to all the members of his family, and to assure them how deeply I share with them their affliction. I shall never forget all I owe to M. Scheurer-Kestner. I shall teach my children that if honor has been rendered to their father it is thanks to his admirable devotion, and I shall teach them to love and venerate his memory.

Also the same day and about the same hour came a trumpet note from Cardinal Vaughan, the great English prelate, who, in a public letter on the Dreyfus case, published in London, said the Roman Catholic Church condemned the persecution of the Jews and of every other race. He added:

If Jews or Christians practise usury and extortion, or do any other hurtful thing, let laws be passed, not against Jews, but against the malpractices complained of, and let the law strike Jew or Gentile with equal severity.

It is unjust to identify the Catholic Church with the act of injustice, whereby Dreyfus was condemned at Rennes without clear evidence of his guilt. The case has been, from beginning to end, a state affair of military interest and of state treason, in which the Church has had no place.

I do not wish one word I write to be taken as an approval of the Rennes verdict. On the contrary, I share the indignation expressed against it, because it was unjustified by the evidence, and it is within the right of any man in any country to say that upon the evidence before him the verdict is infamous; but, having denounced the judgment pronounced by the officers, it is simply monstrous that foreigners should at once rush in and, before the judgment has been considered by the supreme authorities of the state, denounce the whole nation as savages.

The *Figaro* said: "Dreyfus will devote the rest of his life to the recovery of his honor. He is afraid, however, that he will die before this can be accomplished."

Mme. Dreyfus received hundreds of telegrams of congratulations on her husband's pardon. Most of these messages came from Great Britain and the United States.

The anti-Dreyfus newspapers were frantic over the prisoner's pardon.

The *Éclair* said it had hopes that the country would be spared this disgrace.

The *Gaulois* said: "Nothing can justify the pardon. Public opinion may not understand it, but the army will, for it had its revenge at Rennes."

The *Journal* said: "Dreyfus is a traitor, and his pardon will not alter that fact."

The *Intransigéant* said it proved that "if Dreyfus was a traitor Presiden Loubet was another."

The *Petit Journal* remarked that it is merely a sop to the "Triple Alliance Syndicate."

The *Aurore* said the Government has shown its "horror at the denial of justice by the Rennes court-martial."

The *Éclair* stated that a monster petition from Jewish people, headed with the names of the Rothschilds, had been presented to President Loubet asking for Dreyfus's rehabilitation.

Chapter LIII.

INDIGNATION THROUGHOUT THE WORLD

THE announcement of the second verdict in the Dreyfus case caused a wave of indignation to sweep around the world.

Paris heard the news calmly. But the general opinion was that it was only the end of another chapter in the history of this famous case, and that the bitter fight would be continued.

M. Drumont, in the *Libre Parole*, said the members of the court-martial presented a beautiful spectacle. They are warriors, without fear and without reproach. Nothing could disturb them, neither outrages nor flatteries which were still more insulting. Nor did the Government's blackmail succeed in extracting by force the acquittal of the most flagrant of traitors.

The *Petit Journal* said: "The guilty officer struck down tries to continue the agitation despite his promises to respect the court-martial's verdict."

The *Croix* declared that the verdict confirmed France's military justice. It was dealt without fear or favor, and without passion except such as was inspired by justice.

The *Courier du Soir* demanded that everybody accept the verdict. It prayed the Government to accord mercy to the prisoner on account of the expiation he has already made. It added that only extremists would persist in agitation, which, in any case, would henceforth be without nourishment.

The *Éclair* reminded the country of President Loubet's declaration that he would bow before the judgment of the court-martial. It said that no organized society can live without respect for the decisions of justice.

The *Temps* contrasted the calm manner in which the verdict was received in Paris with the excitement it caused in foreign countries, which, it says, are giving the matter far greater importance than it deserves.

The *Soleil* declared that nobody will contest the impartiality of the judges' verdict, which must be accepted.

M. Jaures said in the *Petite République Française* that the verdict is a monstrous defiance of conscience and reason.

The *Gaulois* congratulated the court-martial on its victory against the enemies of the army and France.

The officers of the *Libre Parole, Intransigéant, Le Soir, Petit Journal,* and other anti-Dreyfus organs were decorated with flags and brilliantly illuminated.

The verdict caused a sensation throughout France, especially in Lyons, Bordeaux, Nice, Nancy, Marseilles, and Lille, where the public crowded around the bulletin boards.

In Berlin the Dreyfus verdict caused a feeling almost of stupefaction. It had been hoped that the statement of the *Reichs-Anzeiger*, as emanating directly from Emperor William, would have rendered impossible the repetition of what is described as "one of the greatest judicial and political crimes of any age."

It was universally agreed that the second verdict is a grave political blunder, a violation of the laws of civilization, and an act of moral cowardice which the world will find it difficult to pardon.

The German press unanimously described the verdict as cowardly and impolitic, not to say criminal.

The Cologne *Gazette* said:

"It is a cowardly verdict, in the barbarous spirit of the Middle Ages. By this crime the judges have imposed a line of demarkation between France and the rest of the world, which, although it will not prevent diplomatic intercourse or stay the common exchange of products, will, according to all the notions of right, justice, honor, tolerance, and ethics which the civilized world bears with it in the twentieth century, form a barrier only to be removed by time and laborious effort."

The other leading journals commented upon the verdict in similar strains.

Indignation was evoked throughout Great Britain. Special prayers were offered throughout Saturday, September 9th, in all the London synagogues on behalf of Dreyfus, and as soon as the verdict was known Jews and Jewesses were seen at every street corner, expressing execration, and many sobbing bitterly.

At the music halls, especially the Palace Theatre, where cinematograph pictures of the incidents and leading actors of the Dreyfus affair were exhibited, the news was greeted with groans and hisses.

In almost all the London places of public worship pulpit references were made on September 10th to the verdict. Canon Scott-Holland, at St. Paul's Cathedral, said:

"A nation is on its trial. France stands at the judgment bar. All civilization is waiting to know whether to-morrow's news may add anything to qualify the naked cruelty of a bare telegram, anything to relieve staggered conscience."

The Rev. Hugh Price Hughes, the well-known Wesleyan divine, preaching at St. James's Hall, said:

"Five unhappy judges have already taken their places, in the judgment of the human race, beside Judas, Pilate, Judge Jeffries, and other foul creatures. They have sentenced their victim to a decade of imprisonment, but they have decreed themselves forever to the scorn, derision, and execration of the human race. Unless France shakes off this infamy, she will be left without an ally or a friend."

The Rev. Arthur Robins, chaplain in ordinary to the Queen, preaching at Holy Trinity, Windsor, said:

"The civilized world is aghast at this great crime of five abject judges."

The Daily Mail said:

"Rennes is France's moral Sedan."

The Daily Graphic said:

"The Rennes verdict will live forever as the supreme effort of human wrong-headedness."

The Daily Chronicle said that Mercier issues from the case one of the blackest scoundrels in history.

The Daily News remarked:

"It is no longer Dreyfus, but France herself that is on trial."

The Morning Post declared that "the mitigation of the sentence will be interpreted all the world over as evidence that the judges who condemned Dreyfus really believe him innocent."

The Daily Telegraph said:

"This infamous judgment disgraces France, dishonors her army, insults the Kaiser, and offends the best principles of humanity. There seems nothing left for France but a revolution and a war that will reduce her to the level of Spain."

The Standard said:

"We are watching by the sick-bed of a great nation, none knowing what new and deadly form the malady may assume."

The Times observed:

"We do not hesitate to pronounce it the grossest and most appalling prostitution of justice the world has witnessed in modern times. All the outrageous scandals which marked the course of the trial pale into insignificance beside the crowning scandal of the verdict."

Even the Russian press joined in the chorus, although perhaps the Jews are nowhere more hated than in Russia. The judges were everywhere described as criminals, and gloomy speculations were indulged as to what future is in store for France.

Papers of all nationalities began to fall in with the idea of boycotting the Exhibition.

At Budapest, Hungary, the following semi-official statement was issued:

"A movement is on foot against sending exhibits to the Paris Exposition of 1900. Many intending exhibitors have withdrawn their notices of participation on the ground that the present state of things in France renders it unsafe to send exhibits."

The Cathedral Chapter of Grau, capital of the county of the same name, on the Danube, and the residence of the Catholic Primate of Hungary, has cancelled its decision to send exhibits, giving as a reason its unwillingness to endanger works of art worth millions of florins.

In the United States the feeling was intense.

Plymouth Church, Brooklyn, following its time-honored custom of taking definite action with regard to all great public questions, considered the Dreyfus case on September 10th, and adopted resolutions condemning his sentence and expressing sympathy for the unfortunate captain and his family, and sorrow for France. The famous old church was crowded to the doors, and every sympathetic reference to Captain Dreyfus made by

22

the speakers, among whom was Dwight L. Moody, the evangelist, was received with warm applause. There was a particularly enthusiastic demonstration when a communication from the representatives of the Congregational churches of Great Britain, who have just arrived here to attend the International Council in Boston, was read.

Mr. Moody, after the close of the opening service, said:

"Our friends who are going to the council in Boston, having learned of Captain Dreyfus's fate on their arrival here, want to express an opinion on the great Dreyfus trial in France and to offer their sympathy for that unfortunate man. Fortunate, rather, for he is suffering for his race. I am glad that they have the opportunity to express that opinion."

The Reverend Horace Porter, assistant pastor of Plymouth, then introduce G. W. Cowper Smith, one of the delegates, who read the following communication from himself and his associates:

"That we, the undersigned, representatives of the Congregational churches of Great Britain, deputed to attend the International Council in Boston, having learned on our arrival in the United States of the fresh condemnation of Dreyfus, hereby record our amazement and sorrow at the verdict, unsustained as it is by public evidence, and express our fervent hope that a sense of justice may yet be aroused among the people of France that will lead them to repudiate the decision of a military court, and thus vindicate the rule of national righteousness."

Mr. Smith then said:

"I thank you for this opportunity of being able to introduce in historic Plymouth Church, which has so many happy associations with the English people, the expression of opinion which I have just read."

Mr. Porter, in behalf of Plymouth Church, read the following resolution, which was unanimously adopted:

"We who are here for Christian worship would remember with sympathy the undeserved suffering of Alfred Dreyfus and his family, and declare our sorrowful surprise at the manner of his recent trial and renewed condemnation, which we trust and pray may yet be overruled by higher authority, acting for the honor of France, for the love of justice, and in the fear of God."

Mr. Moody prefaced his sermon, as he had done at the morning service, by a sympathetic reference to Dreyfus and his family.

A mere glimpse of the handsome red and blue uniform of a French army officer on the stage of the Criterion Theatre during the evening of September 9th, the day of the verdict, drove one of the most fashionable audiences of the season to fury, and caused one of the greatest pro-Dreyfus demonstrations that has occurred in New York. Reserved and good-mannered men and women suddenly assumed the deportment which might be expected of an audience at a Bowery melodrama. Men in evening dress sprang to their feet, deriding the French army, and women hissed in scorn. Cries of "À bas l'armée!" "Shame on France!" and "Long live Dreyfus!" were heard all over the house. People in the orchestra and boxes were as demonstrative as those in the gallery. The confusion lasted fully three or four minutes, during which the play was interrupted.

At Louisville, Ky., about twenty-five citizens met at the office of Dr. P. G. Trunnell, on September 10th, to perfect the organization of what is to be known as the "Dreyfus Sympathizers." Dr. Trunnell, one of the organizers, said that the object of the organization was to interest the United States Government in the case of Captain Dreyfus, who, they believe, had been wrongfully punished.

A resolution was offered to the effect that the organization appeal to the Congress of the United States asking that body not to make any further appropriation for the Paris Exposition, and an amendment was offered appealing to the citizens of the United States who champion Captain Dreyfus's cause, to avoid France in every way possible, and thus administer a rebuke to that nation for the injustice to one of its subjects. The ministers of all denominations in Louisville were asked to assist in promoting the interests of the body.

The Marion Club, of Indianapolis, consisting of one thousand Republicans of that city, put itself on record on September 10th, as in favor of boycotting the Paris Exposition. The following telegram was sent by the officers to Senators Beveridge and Fairbanks and Representative Overstreet, all of whom belong to the club:

"The Marion Club, as a club which is a lover of justice and fair play, urges you, as a just rebuke to military despotism, which has convicted Captain Dreyfus, an innocent man, to use your influence with President McKinley to get him to withdraw the American Commissioner to the Paris Exposition."

In Philadelphia the verdict was condemned on every side.

Former Postmaster-General John Wanamaker said:

"While the Dreyfus episode is the business of France, the widespread interest in the case makes it impossible not to hold an opinion upon it. The larger jury of the people throughout the world will not agree with the verdict rendered, unless it is intended that the pardoning power will promptly remit the unexpired portion of the ten years' sentence."

Former District Attorney George S. Graham said: "I am not surprised at the finding of the court-martial, but, in my opinion, it is the most unjustifiable verdict ever rendered in any civilized community."

Dr. Solomon Solis-Cohen: "To my mind the Dreyfus question is not a Jewish one. Dreyfus was never identified with his people, either racially or religiously, prior to his persecution. The fact of his Hebrew birth has been used by his enemies and those of justice and the republic to intensify the prejudice against him, and effect his condemnation. The Dreyfus affair is in no sense a Jewish matter, but involves the liberty and conscience of all mankind."

Morris Newburger, president of the Jewish Publication Society of America: "The condemnation of Dreyfus was a foregone conclusion. Every one realized that the trial from its beginning until its ending was a travesty upon justice."

Ralph Blum: "I have always felt that poor Dreyfus was made the victim of a conspiracy, because he was born a Hebrew."

Chicago was equally indignant.

L. B. Wright, of Wright's Iron Printing Company, said:

"I have discharged all the Frenchmen in my employ, for one of them said Dreyfus should be hanged. The judges violated every principle of law and justice."

Clarence Buckingham, a prominent member of the Stock Exchange: "The verdict is an outrageous one, and every one in the United States thinks so. Those who prosecuted Dreyfus are smirched."

Frank O. Lowden, a lawyer and representative of the George M. Pullman estate: "A republic can do more injustice than a kingdom or an empire."

George Gibault: "It is a perversion of justice."

Theodore Prouix: "The French papers have printed everything unfa-

vorable, and the American papers all that was favorable, to Dreyfus.
Three-fourths of the French people believe him guilty. There will be a
revolution in France, but the army will suppress it."

French Consul Henri Merou: "The verdict will have no effect upon
the Exposition."

E. G. Keith, President of the Continental National Bank: "The verdict is unfair."

Rabbi E. G. Hirsch, of the Sinai Congregation: "I expected this verdict. It was necessary to prevent the overthrow of the republic, but the
army now will save it. France has passed through a dangerous crisis,
but the republic will stand. This verdict is an infamous one, but it decides the question of a republic, a kingdom, or a royalty. For a time at
least the republic is safe."

Eli B. Elsenthal: "There was no evidence of guilt whatever. The so-
called honor of the army of France was placed above truth and justice."

Levy A. Eiel: "There was no evidence against Dreyfus."

B. J. Rosenthal: "French judges do not consider evidence."

A. M. Rothschilds: "It was simply an outrage of justice."

A. J. Nathan: "This verdict is infamous."

Boston was not behind in expressing its indignation.

General William A. Bancroft said the whole trial had been remarkable for the kind of testimony accepted as evidence. The judge were military. Civil judges might have decided otherwise.

Colonel Melvin O. Adams said:

"If such judgments as this in the Dreyfus case can stand in a country, safety of the individual is a mere name. I have no opinion whether
Dreyfus be in fact innocent or guilty, but his condemnation by such means
is monstrous."

In the Hebrew quarter of Boston the opinion is summed up as follows:

"Of course, Dreyfus is not guilty. If he were they would shoot him,
and the fact that they have given him a ten years' sentence shows that he
is innocent."

Jay Hunt, recently in Paris, says:

"The verdict was to uphold the government and army. The president
of the court was prejudiced from the start."

Upon learning the verdict of the Dreyfus court-martial Assistant District Attorney Maurice B. Blumenthal, of New York, took steps for the organization of a committee of citizens, irrespective of religious belief, and including clergymen of different denominations, to hold a mass meeting to protest against the conviction of Captain Dreyfus.   A representative committee was appointed to wait upon President McKinley and petition him to appeal to the President of France to pardon the unfortunate victim.

This extraordinary outcry of all Christendom against the heinous outrage done to justice and humanity at Rennes was classed as "The Fifth Act" in a powerful contribution to the *Aurore*, signed by Émile Zola, on September 10th.   The article read as follows:

THE FIFTH ACT.

I am in mortal fear.   It is not anger, avenging indignation, the need to proclaim the crime and demand its punishment in the name of truth and justice that I feel now; it is terror, the sacred terror of the man who sees the impossible being realized, the rivers flowing back to their sources, the earth turning without the sun; and what I fear is the distress of our generous and noble France.   My dread is of the abyss into which she is falling.

We had fondly imagined that the Rennes court-martial was the fifth act of the terrible tragedy which we have been living for close upon two years past.   All the dangerous stages seemed to us to have been passed. We thought we were approaching a "dénoûment" of pacification and concord.   After the dreadful battle the victory of right became inevitable; the play must end happily, with the classic triumph of the innocent.

And we have been deceived!   A new stage opens before us, and that the most unexpected and the most terrifying of all, still further darkening the drama, prolonging it and urging it toward an unknown termination, before which our very reason trembles and grows weak.

The Rennes trial was only the fourth act, and, great God! what will the fifth act be?   What new tortures and sufferings will it bring?   To what supreme expiation will it force our people?   For is it not certain that the innocent cannot be twice condemned, and that such an ending would blot out the sun and arouse the nations?

Ah! that fourth act! that trial at Rennes!   In what mortal agony did I not live through it, in that solitude where I had taken refuge in order to disappear from the scene like a good citizen desirous of giving no cause for passion and disorder!   With what a tightening of the heart did I not await telegrams, letters, papers; and what revolt and what pain did their perusal not cause me! The days of that splendid month of August were blackened, and never have I felt the gloom and chill of mourning under skies so glorious.

Assuredly, for two years past, I have had my share of suffering. I have heard the mob shouting death at my heels. I have seen at my feet an ignoble mire of insult and menace. For eighteen months I tasted the despair of exile. Then there were my two trials—lamentable spectacles of villainy and iniquity.

But what are my trials in comparison with the trial at Rennes? Idyls, refreshing scenes where hope flowers.

We had been witness of monstrous things—the prosecution of Colonel Picquart, the inquiry into the Criminal Chamber of the Court of Cassation, the "loi de dessaisissement" which resulted from it. But all that seems childish now. The inevitable progression has followed its course. The Rennes trial stands out above all like the abominable flower growing atop of all these heaped-up dunghills.

We have seen the most extraordinary collection of attempts against truth and justice—a band of witnesses directing the course of the trial, making their plans every night for the cowardly ambush of the morrow, pressing the charge, in place of the Public Prosecutor, with lies; terrorizing and insulting those who contradicted them, imposing with the insolence of their stripes and their plumes upon a tribunal knuckling down to this invasion of their chiefs, visibly annoyed at seeing them in criminal posture, acting in obedience to a peculiar mental process; a grotesque Public Prosecutor, who enlarges the bounds of imbecility and leaves to future historians a charge whose stupid and murderous emptiness will be an eternal cause of wonder; a man of such senile and obstinate cruelty that it seems to be irresponsible, born of a human animal not yet classed; a defence which it was at first endeavored to assassinate, which was afterward made to sit down every time it became troublesome, and which finally was refused permission to produce the decisive proof which it demanded, the only witnesses who know.

And this abomination lasted for a whole month, in face of the innocent —that piteous Dreyfus, the poor shreds of whose humanity would make the very stones weep. And his former comrades came and kicked him, and his former chiefs came and crushed him with their rank so as to save themselves from the galleys. And there was never a cry of pity, never a throb of generosity in those shameful souls!

And it is our sweet France that has given this spectacle to the world!

When the complete report of the Rennes trial is published there will exist no more execrable monument of human infamy. This is beyond all.

Never will a document of such wickedness have been furnished to history. Ignorance, folly, cruelty, falsehood, crime are displayed there with an impudence that will make future generations shudder. There are in that collection avowals of our baseness at which human nature will blush.

And it is this that makes me tremble, for in order that such a trial should have been possible in a nation, that a nation should lay itself open to the world for such a consultation upon its social and intellectual condition, it must be undergoing a terrible crisis.

Is it death that is approaching? And what bath of truth, of purity, of equity will save us from the poisonous mud in which we are agonizing?

As I wrote in my letter to the President of the Republic after the scandalous acquittal of Esterhazy, it is impossible for a court-martial to undo what a court-martial has done. That would be contrary to discipline, and the judgment of the Rennes court-martial—that judgment which in its Jesuitical embarrassment has not the courage to say yes or no—is the plain proof that military justice is powerless to be just, since it is not free, since it defies evidence almost to the point of again condemning an innocent man rather than cast doubt upon its own infallibility. Military justice is seen to be nothing more than a weapon of execution in the hands of the commander. Henceforward it can but be an expeditious form of justice in time of war—it must disappear in time of peace. The moment it showed itself incapable of equity, of simple logic, and of mere common sense it condemned itself.

Has thought been given to the atrocious situation in which we are made to stand among the civilized nations?

A first court-martial, deceived in its ignorance of the law and its want of skill in sifting evidence, condemns an innocent man. A second court-martial, which likewise was deceived by a most impudent conspiracy of lies and frauds, acquits a guilty man. A third court-martial, when light has been thrown on the matter, when the highest magistracy of the country consents to leave to it the glory of making reparation for an error, dares to deny the full daylight, and a second time finds the innocent guilty.

This is irreparable. The last crime has been committed. Jesus was condemned but once.

But let final ruin come, let France fall a prey to faction, let the country be aflame and perish in the embers, let the army itself lose honor rather than confess that some members of it made a mistake, and that certain generals were liars and forgers. The ideal shall be crucified; the sabre must remain king!

And so we find ourselves in this glorious condition before Europe, before the world! The whole world is convinced of the innocence of Dreyfus. If a doubt had remained in the minds of some far-away race the blinding glare of the Rennes trial would have carried the full light there. All the courts of the Powers that are our neighbors are well informed, know the documents, have proof of the worthlessness of three or four of our generals and of the shameful paralysis of our military justice.

A moral Sedan has been lost—a Sedan a hundredfold more disastrous than that other one where only blood was spilt.

And I repeat, what fills me with dread is that this defeat of our honor seems irreparable, for how are we to quash the judgments of three courts-martial? Where shall we find the heroism to confess our fault, to march onward with head uplifted proudly? Where is the government with courage to be a government of public safety? Where are the chambers that will understand and act before the inevitable final crash?

The worst of it all is that we have come to a reckoning day of glory. France desires to celebrate its century of labor, of science, of struggle for liberty, for truth and for justice. No century that has passed has been marked by more superb effort; this will be seen later on. And France has called together in her capital all the peoples of the earth to glorify her victory, liberty won, truth and justice promised to earth.

Thus, a few months hence the peoples will come; and what they will find will be the innocent twice condemned, truth trampled upon, justice assassinated. We have fallen beneath their contempt; and they will come and laugh at us in our very faces. They will drink our wines, they will kiss our maid-servants, as people do in the low-class inn which is not above that sort of thing.

Is all this possible? Are we going to allow our Exhibition to be the foul, despised place where the whole world is willing to seek its pleasures only?

No! a thousand times no! We must have, and that at once, the fifth act of the monstrous tragedy, even if we have to lose our flesh and blood in the effort. We must have our honor restored before we salute the visiting peoples in a France healed and regenerated.

This fifth act haunts me, and I am ever recurring to it. I am working on it; I build it up in my imagination.

Has it been noticed that this Dreyfus affair, this gigantic drama which moves the universe, seems to be staged by some sublime dramatist desirous of making it an incomparable masterpiece? I will not recall the extraordinary incidents that have stirred our souls. At every fresh act passion has swollen, horror has grown more intense. In this living piece it is Fate that has genius. Destiny is there, actuating the players, determining the incidents under the tempest it unchains; and assuredly it wants the masterpiece to be complete, and is preparing for us a fifth act—a superhuman act which will make France glorious once again and replace her in the forefront of the nations.

For you may be sure of this—it was Fate that decreed the supreme crime—the second condemnation of the innocent. The crime had to be committed for the sake of the tragic grandeur, the sovereign beauty, the expiation, perhaps, which will allow of the apotheosis, the final transformation scene.

And now that we have sounded the uttermost depths of horror, I await the fifth act, which will end the drama by delivering us, by restoring us to health and fresh youth.

I will now speak plainly of my fear. It has always been, as I have allowed it to be understood on several occasions, that the truth, the decisive, overwhelming proof should come to us from Germany. We must look the possibility of Germany bringing out the fifth act of the drama in a thunderclap squarely and courageously in the face.

Here is my confession.

Previous to my trial, in January, 1898, I learned with certainty that Esterhazy was the traitor; that he had supplied M. de Schwartzkoppen with a large number of documents; that many of these documents were in his handwriting, and that a complete collection of them was to be found in the War Office at Berlin.

From that time on I have, as a good Frenchman, been in constant dread. I thought with terror that Germany, our enemy of to-morrow, would perhaps slap us in the face with the proofs in its possession. Accordingly, with Labori, I decided to cite as witnesses the foreign military attachés. We were well aware we were not likely to bring them to the bar, but we desired to let the Government know we knew the truth, in the hope that it would take action.

No heed was taken. Mock was made of us. The weapon Germany has in her hands was left there, and matters remained unchanged up to the time of the Rennes trial.

On my return to France I hurried to see Labori. I insisted, with the energy of despair, on steps being taken to bring the matter before the Cabinet, to demonstrate the dreadful character of the situation, and to ask if the Government would not intervene, so as to obtain the documents for us. That was certainly a most delicate matter. Then there was that unfortunate Dreyfus to be saved, so that we were prepared to make every concession for fear of irritating public opinion, already at a high pitch of excitement. If the court-martial acquitted Dreyfus, it thereby deprived the documents of their nocuous virus; it shattered in the hands of Germany the weapon she might have used. The acquittal of Dreyfus meant the recognition of an error and its reparation.

My patriotic torment grew more intolerable when I felt that a court-martial was about to aggravate the danger by again condemning the innocent—the man whose innocence would one day be cried aloud by the publication of the documents in Berlin.

That is why I have never ceased to act, begging Labori to demand the documents, to cite M. de Schwartzkoppen, who alone can throw full light on the matter; and the day that Labori took advantage of the opportunity given him by the accusers bringing to the bar an unworthy foreigner, the day he arose and demanded that the court-martial hear the man from whom a single word would close the affair, he did his duty. His was the heroic voice that nothing can reduce to silence. His demand has survived the trial, and must inevitably reopen it and end it once for all by the only possible solution—the acquittal of the innocent.

The demand for the documents has been made. Their ultimate production is a certainty.

You see the awful, intolerable danger in which the president of the Rennes court-martial has put us by refusing to use his discretionary power to prevent the publication of the documents. Never was anything more brutal! Never was the door so wilfully shut upon the truth! And a third court-martial was added to the two others, in which the error was so blinding that the denial from Berlin would now condemn three iniquitous sentences.

The Ministry forgot that government is foresight. If it does not wish to leave to the good pleasure of Germany the fifth act, the "dénoûment," before which every good Frenchman should tremble, it is the Government's duty to play this fifth act without delay in order to prevent its coming to us from Germany. The Government can procure the documents. Diplomacy has settled greater difficulties than this. Whenever it ventures to ask for the documents enumerated in the bordereau they will be given, and that will be the "fait nouveau" which will necessitate a second revision before the Court of Cassation, which will be this time, I hope, fully informed, and would quash the verdict "sans renvoi" in the plenitude of its sovereign majesty.

But if the Government still hesitates, the defenders of truth and justice will do what is necessary. Not one of us will desert his post. Invincible proof we shall finally end by obtaining.

On November 23d, we shall be at Versailles. My trial will recommence, inasmuch as it is to recommence in all its fulness. If, meanwhile, justice is not done we will again have to do it. My beloved, my valiant Labori, whose honor has but increased, will pronounce at Versailles the address which he was unable to pronounce at Rennes. And thus, as you see, nothing will be lost. He will merely have to tell the truth, without fear of injuring me, for I am ready to pay for it with my liberty and my blood. Before the Seine Assize Court I swore to the innocence of Dreyfus. I swear to it before the entire world, which now proclaims it with me; and I repeat, truth is on the march. Nothing will stop it. At Rennes it has just made a giant's stride.

I no longer have any fear except that I may see it arrive in a thunderclap of the avenging Nemesis.   ÉMILE ZOLA.

Chapter LIV.

VINDICATION

MATHIEU DREYFUS, in an interview, in Paris, September 11th, was quoted as saying:

"Yesterday, before leaving Rennes for Paris, I talked for two hours with my brother, Captain Dreyfus. He is a marvellous man. After all these years of suffering he is as strong to-day in declaring his innocence as he was on the Champ de Mars, when first condemned.

"Those who spread rumors that he intends to commit suicide know not that an indomitable spirit animates his attenuated frame. When I heard the horrible report in Paris this morning that he had committed suicide, I could not help thinking one of his bitter enemies had circulated it in the hope that it might reach his ears, and that he would act upon the suggestion, as weakened men sometimes do. But his enemies will never have that grewsome pleasure. He is full of hope and looks fearlessly to the future.

"He does not need to-day the soothing voice of Mme. Dreyfus to induce him to continue to live. Mme. Dreyfus is similarly hopeful.

"Maîtres Demange and Labori, both of whom have gone to the country for some much needed repose, have given the whole family much encouragement. I, who have been charged by my brother with the rehabilitation of our name, have firm faith in the near future.

"The recent trial practically rehabilitates him. Outside a very limited circle his name is as fair as though the Rennes court-martial had declared him innocent. Suppose the son of Captain Dreyfus were to travel in the United States when he grows up to manhood, do you think there is one throughout the length and breadth of the land who would point to him as the son of a traitor? On the contrary, they would say, 'This is the youth who for years was unjustly robbed of his father,' and they would honor him as the son of a martyr.

"My brother's innocence is believed by everybody outside of France and by most people in France."

Maître Labori has been resting at Sammois, a short distance from Paris. He said, in an interview:

"We have won a great deal, considering that the most important evidence was excluded. Imagine where we are to-day, as compared with two years ago. If you ask me what do I think the most important gain of all in this fight for justice, I should answer, 'It is the world's awakening to the justice of our cause.'

"The great newspapers of all lands have taken such a keen interest in the question, and caught such a thorough grasp of it, that they are sure to continue speaking in the name of humanity and civilization. For it is not the cause of Dreyfus alone which is at stake; it is the cause of humanity and civilization. The great newspapers have already given ample evidence that they understand this, and if they follow up their broad and generous grasp of the question by reminding the Emperor of Germany that he owes a duty to humanity and to civilization, he is not the kind of a man to shirk it. That duty is to deliver to the French Government the documents mentioned in the bordereau. As soon as this responsibility, not to an individual, but to humanity and civilization, is made clear to him, the German Emperor is man of spirit and heart enough to act up to it.

"The verdict as it stands is neither yes nor no. Obviously the court had little knowledge of law, and less of evidence.

"We have gained much in other ways. His first condemnation was for twenty years, his second for ten; his first, to Devil's Island, permitted cruel and inhuman treatment; his second permits communication with the outer world; his first condemnation was unanimous: his second is given in such a way that even the five who declared him guilty showed they were not sure.

"Dreyfus's name is no longer stained before the civilized world, and in a short time there will be fewer still who believe him guilty."

Chapter LV.

FIRST FREE UTTERANCES OF DREYFUS.

THE *Figaro*, of Paris, secured the first interview with Dreyfus after his release from arrest. It was printed in the New York *Herald*, on September 22d, and read as follows:

"I do not know where to begin the story of emotion which I have just lived through, so much has the flood overflowed my mind and my heart. It has been given me to share for twenty-four hours—all that is best in me—in the most terrible suffering that it is possible to imagine in the destiny of a human being with whose fate the *élite* of the civilized world has united itself for two years, and against whom all the ignorance and malice of men have been leagued. This being, whom one would say was accursed, is my brother, whom my saddened thoughts went out to join and compassionate across the seas; he is there in the presence of my real deep sympathy.

Every precaution had been taken for Dreyfus to leave Rennes without inconvenience. Advised in the evening, he had passed his time—being unable to sleep—in packing his trunk. At half-past two in the morning M. Viguie, directeur de la sureté générale, accompanied by one of his controleurs, came to fetch him in a carriage at the gate of the Manutention, and they went to the station of Vern, situated ten kilometres from Rennes.

"Nothing suspicious had been seen in the neighborhood of the prison, but after a few hundred yards had been traversed M. Viguie, leaning out of the window of the landau, noticed a red lantern following, evidently that of a journalist. How was he to throw the intruder off the scent? The driver whipped up his horses, which broke into a gallop. They thus came to within four hundred metres of the station of Vern, and it was perceived they had a big start of the man who was following.

"The carriage stopped at the corner of the road. The passengers got out quickly and hid themselves behind a house by the roadside, and the carriage, which now contained only the chef de cabinet of the prefect of Île et Vilaine, rolled on into darkness.

"This stratagem escaped the notice of the man following. His carriage soon passed by the invisible group, and followed the other landau at full speed. Then they walked quietly to Vern Station, and got into the 4:36 A.M. train from Rennes to Chateaubriand. The latter place was reached at 6:14 A.M.

"The travellers changed carriages and arrived at Nantes at seventeen minutes past eight o'clock. I was on the platform at the arrival of the train. It would take too long to relate how I was able to foresee this itinerary. Nevertheless I was not without uneasiness as to the success of my plan. The platform was deserted. Had I made a mistake? I soon saw two men dressed in black approaching, and I immediately recognized them. They were Mathieu Dreyfus and his nephew, Paul Valabregue.

"My tips were good. My mind was relieved. Should I go up to Mathieu Dreyfus, whom I knew well, or should I hide to follow him at leisure? I hesitated between these two alternatives, and watched the two men. They looked to right and left, as though they were afraid of being recognized.

"I made up my mind at once and approached. What was the stupefaction, I may almost say the distress, of Mathieu Dreyfus, when I approached him! I quickly understood his fears and quieted them. I assured him that the train that was about to carry his brother away would have only one more passenger, and that no indiscretion on my part would interfere with the success of their journey.

"He begged me to keep my vow, and I have kept it.

"At this moment Captain Dreyfus is hidden in the midst of his own people. I may now relate this touching Odyssey, all the details of which will remain forever fixed in my memory.

"Here is the train from Chateau Briant coming. It stops, the door opens, some men get down.

"Mathieu Dreyfus stands aside. Then when they are twenty metres off he follows them. I go with him.

"'Did you see?' he asked.

"I saw nothing but a group of four or five persons carrying bags and rugs, and it would have been impossible for me to recognize Captain Dreyfus among them.

"' Look!' said his brother, ' there he is with that rug.'

"I saw a bowed back, dressed in black, making its way to the buffet of the station.

"In a moment we entered. Already the passengers are at the tables. In a small room at the further end Captain Dreyfus is seated eating. His brother draws near. He rises. His mouth opens in an affectionate smile, and the brothers meet with a long embrace, without speaking a word. No one but myself witnessed this scene, so touching in its melancholy sympathy.

Mathieu introduced me to his brother. Captain Dreyfus holds out his hand. I press it and speak of the profound joy which his freedom will give to so many beings to whom it will be like a personal deliverance. He wears a navy blue suit and over it a black overcoat, the collar of which gapes behind, and on his head a soft, black felt hat.

"' It is in order not to be recognized,' he says, smiling, ' but it annoys me. I am not used to it, and I see nothing in it.'

"' Make haste,' says his brother, ' for we are going to start.' He seats himself again obediently, and empties his cup of milk, for his stomach cannot bear anything else.

"During this time M. Viguie has reserved seats in two compartments, for at present the service of surveillance is composed of three inspectors, chosen from among the best men of Hennion's brigade, who accompanied him to Rennes, and on whom falls the heavy responsibility of the long journey we are about to make.

"Captain Dreyfus enters the sleeping-car compartment with M. Mathieu Dreyfus, M. Paul Valabregue, his nephew, and myself.

"M. Viguie has just made his last suggestions, for he goes no further. Captain and Mathieu Dreyfus congratulate him on the skill and prudence he has displayed since their departure from Rennes, and the common wish is expressed that the rest of the journey may pass off equally well.

"The train moves at two minutes of nine. I am seated facing Captain Dreyfus. I never remove my eyes from him for an instant. I am surprised at the effect he produces on me. I expected, whatever my sentiments might be as to his case, to find myself confronted by a being who

23

awakened no sympathy.   He has been described as a haughty and disagreeable person, with a harsh voice and wandering eyes.   I had imagined him as hard, mistrustful, gloomy, if not bearing hate at least bitter; and I own that I was ready to forgive him all those things.   I find before me a man with fine, regular features, with a calm and mild expression.   He is pink of face, which would give him an expression of extreme youth if the top of his head were not absolutely bald, and if the hair on each side were not quite gray.   This being is enfeebled by anæmia, and what blood there is left in him flows toward the head, the last refuge of his prodigious vitality.   His neck is thin, his hands are long and bony, and the knees are pointed like nails through the blue cloth of his trousers.

"His chest is hollowed, his entire body is that of a vanquished being but for the energy of the mouth, the square jaw, and the will expressed in the look of his eyes.   They are blue, charming and mild, limpid and clear.   Far from shunning one's look, he fixes his eyes on you with assurance behind his eye-glasses, and his look is not that of a man of whom a monster of hypocrisy has been made, of whom one scoundrel has said that ' he sweated treason.'

"The train rolls on toward Bordeaux.   M. Mathieu Dreyfus looks at his brother with tender eyes.

"' Well,' he asks, ' are you comfortable?   You are not cold?'

"'Oh, no!   I am well covered up with my flannel vest, two wool shirts, my coat and overcoat.   I am very well—and then you forget the freedom.   It is good to feel free, free, free!   Not to feel people everlasting round you spying each movement, each gesture.   That, mind you, is the odious, insupportable thing.   To be shut up one can bear, though it is painful after a long time; but the eye of that man whose hostile examination of the smallest movements of your body you have felt every minute for five years—oh! it is horrible!'

"' Do not tire yourself too much,' observed Mathieu, paternally. 'You must be very tired.'

"'Let me alone,' replied the captain, ' I feel the want of speaking. Just think that I have not spoken for five years.   Then I feel so well—no fatigue, no pain—excitement probably—and to-morrow I shall suffer for it, but to-day I mean to do what I please.'

"He smiles, with a fine and thin smile which is far from being one of gayety, but which has rather the air of an unbending of the nerves of the mouth, which have so long been contracted.

"Laugh? How could Captain Dreyfus ever laugh? His life, suddenly overwhelmed under the deluge of adversity and catastrophe, under the terrible chaos of misfortune, will always retain the crushing weight of sadness. His impoverished blood will never again course joyously through his cold veins, and between happiness and him will always intervene the black muslin of melancholy.

"Already it sufficed to make sadness suddenly appear in his eyes that a name should be pronounced—that of General Mercier, mentioned by chance in the conversation.

"'Mercier,' I asked Dreyfus; 'what impression did his depositions make upon you?'

"Said he sharply: 'He is a malicious man and a dishonest man, but I do not think he is conscious of the extent of the evil he has done. He is too intelligent for me to be able to say that he is unconscious, but if he is mentally conscious, he is morally unconscious. He is a man without moral sense.'

"The train rushes on through the fertile land of this admirable country of the Vendean Bocage. Captain Dreyfus looks at the country.

"'How pretty this country is!' he says. 'Look at that little village, those cocks, those hens, those fine trees, outlined by the mist! Think that during a year I have seen only the sky and sea, and during four years the sky only, a square of brilliant blue, metallic, hard, and always alike, without a cloud! And, when I came back to France, you know how it was—by night in the midst of a terrible storm, taken from a ship into a boat, from the boat into a carriage, thence into a wagon, to arrive at last at a prison at dawn. So these are the first trees I have seen.'

"The landscape unfolds itself. Here is a sparkling stream, bordered with poplars, a large wood, fresh and green, more pine spaces out on the slopes. An old woman is washing linen on the banks of a pond. White steeples and red steeples, golden ricks, ruins, a peaceful little village, which seems half in mourning with its white house-points and slate roofs, sad meres full of reeds and faded water-lilies, and, suddenly, wide barren spaces with a few meagre pines and brambles growing between the rocks.

"Captain Dreyfus looks at all these as if they were indeed something new to him. He devours them with his eyes.

"'I should be as pleased as a child,' he says, 'to run about in those meadows and amuse myself with nothing. I am like a convalescent coming back to life.'

"Since the start he had never left off smoking.

"'You smoke too much,' said his brother.

"'Let me smoke; let me talk. It is so long since.'

"We talk of the death of Scheurer-Kestner. He told us the infinite sorrow he had felt at the thought that he would never be able to thank him, that he would never see the man who had done so much for him, and to whom he owed his liberty. He seemed to dream for a moment. Then he said:

"'What fine characters have displayed themselves in this affair!'

"'Have you written many letters since you returned?' I asked.

"'None; I have not had time, but now I am going to write those that I ought to write. Think! I have received more than five thousand since my return to France, without counting those that my wife has received on her side—very humble testimonials, besides very high ones. Oh, it has done me good! Officers, even on active service, have written to me and signed their names. One of my comrades in promotion wrote me the simple words, "Glad at your return; glad at your approaching rehabilitation." That consoles me for many desertions and for the unexpected hostility of many of my comrades.

"'Ah! What I suffered from those depositions in which they came spontaneously to say things which had no connection with the trial, but which they thought might injure me! And, mind you, I do not think it was out of malice against me—no, it was merely to please the chiefs. Ah! there are natures which conserve a very strange idea of duty. Instead of understanding by discipline obedience on the field of battle or in barracks, they extend it to the degradation of reason and moral liberty.

"'For me, I never could bend myself to such discipline, and I never could have believed that it was possible for officers to do so.'"

Chapter LVI.

EXPLAINS ANIMOSITY AGAINST HIM

"'How do you explain this animosity against you since 1894 in the offices of the General Staff?'" continued the correspondent.

"' I think that the cause of it is rather complex. First, and above all, I was believed to be guilty. It could never have been suspected that they could have plunged so lightheartedly into error. Then there was anti-Semitism in a latent state. Lastly, my manner may perhaps have had something to do with it. Yes, it was rather curt, but only with my chiefs, for, of course, I strove to show as much consideration as possible to my inferiors. I scarcely associated with any one, and when I entered the General Staff I had paid no visit to any one. I contented myself with sending cards by my orderly to the chief and sub-chief of the General Staff and the chief and sub-chief of my office, and that was all.

"' In my dealings with my chiefs I always retained my outspokenness and independence. If a plan or any piece of work seemed to me to be badly conceived, I did not hesitate to say so aloud, instead of considering myself obliged to approve everything in advance, as I saw done all around me, when it was a chief who spoke or acted.

"' I know that people don't like that. Colonel Bertin Mourot said something with deep meaning at Rennes, speaking of that admirable man, that hero, Colonel Picquart. It was felt that this officer did not walk behind the chiefs. That is their psychology and all their morality.'

"' Walk behind the chiefs as if it were in war or at the manœuvres?'

"' Yes, certainly, but when it is a question of honor and duty is there any need to walk behind any one? Has one not one's own conscience?'

"The hour for luncheon was approaching. We reach La Roche-sur-Yonne. They brought us some well-stocked baskets, containing hard-boiled eggs, cold meat, two biscuits, some chocolate, white wine, mineral water, and two little flasks of cinchona and rum. All these were carefully packed in tiny boxes or wrapped up.

"Mathieu wanted to prevent Alfred eating the meats. ' You know quite well that Delbet forbade you.'

"' What does it matter for once? To-morrow I will be good, but to-day is a holiday. Be easy; I feel so well. It is like a new life '—and Mathieu Dreyfus agrees to everything like a good-natured parent to a loved child whom he wishes to restore to health.

"The conversation now rolled on everything at haphazard.

"And Esterhazy—what do you think of him?'

"In quiet, measured accents, slightly doubtful, even like a savant propounding an hypothesis, he replied:

"' I think he is a swindler, a *chevalier d'industrie*, who has swindled his country—it is not even his country—just as he swindled his cousin and his tradesmen, but without in the least realizing that he did so. He wanted money. That was the motive, for,' he continued with animation, 'for every crime there must be a motive.'

"' What could it have been in my case? No one ever saw me touch a card, so I was not a gambler. It was said that I had led a fast life. How can you explain, then, that I took the ninth place on leaving the college? Don't people know what arduous work these examinations mean? How can work be allied with debauch?

"' General Mercier said that the search for a motive for a crime belonged to the domain of psychology, and that we were on the judicial domain. What does that mean? I was never in the law, but it seems to me that the first thing to be done when one suspects a criminal is to discover the motive for his crime. That is what I call sound sense.'

"He shrugged his shoulders, and his grave voice rose high in the silence of the stopped train. Then, lowering his voice, he repeated several times, accentuating each word, ' Sound sense. Simple, sober sense.'

"The train started, and the captain went on:

"' As to the theory of the court-martial upon the extenuating circumstances, it is just like this: Treason against his country is the greatest crime a human being can commit. A murderer, a thief may find some excuse for themselves; their crime is one against an individual. Treason is a crime against a collectivity. There are no extenuating circumstances. It is a monstrosity.'

"' What effect did the verdict have upon you?'

"The voice was at once lowered, and sadly he said: ' It was first of all intense anguish, then stupefaction, then very comforting when I learned that two officers had had the courage to declare me entirely innocent. I swear that those two brave officers were right.'

"In speaking Dreyfus uses two gestures. When he reasons his thumb and first finger touch, forming a circle. When he is impassioned or carried away his hand opens out with the fingers apart, as in the case of all sincere and frank persons.

"His brother now questions him.

"'What is exactly the climate over there?'

"Forty to fifty degrees [Centigrade = 104° to 122° Fahrenheit] by day, and never below twenty-five [77° F.] at night. That is the most terrible and most exhausting thing about it, for at a stretch one can bear heat provided one breathes a little fresh air from time to time; there—never.'

"' And you never knew anything of what was being done in France for you?' I asked.

"' Never a word; not a single word. From time to time the rigors were redoubled. I know now that that coincided with the declarations of the Ministers of War. Every time one of them ascended the rostrum and declared that I had been justly and legally condemned, I felt the effects through the medium of my jailers. They cut off my food, or my reading, or my work, or my walk, or the sight of the sea, and, finally, moving about with the aid of the double ' boucle.'

"' M. Mathieu Dreyfus regarded his brother with emotion.

"' Is it not awful?' he said. ' Happily, we knew nothing about it here, for our efforts would have been hampered thereby. If we had known that every step toward the truth brought him suffering, perhaps our ardor would have been diminished. But what pretext did your jailers give you?'

"' None, and I did not ask for any. I did not wish to be beholden to those people in any way. Besides, I did not wish to discuss my sentence or its execution in any way, for to discuss it would have implied to recognize it.'

"These words were said with extraordinary firmness, almost with harshness.

"' Yet one day,' he went on, ' the day when they put irons on my feet, I asked the reason of the barbarous treatment. They replied, "Precautionary measure." It was the day following that when a denial had been given of the bogus attempt to escape.

"' Ah, I well remember that night. It was not nine o'clock. I was in bed, when I heard musketry fire and a great commotion all around me; I sat up in bed and cried, "What is it? Who is there?" No one replied; my guard was silent. I did not stir, thanks to I know not what instinct. It was a good thing I did not, for I should have been instantly shot.'

"' And so you imagined that General de Boisdeffre was looking after your interests?'

"' Yes. I see now that I was mistaken.'

"' Would you re-enter the army if legally you had the right?'

"' No; I will resign the very evening of my rehabilitation.'

"' In short, do you think it has been an error or a conspiracy?'

"' I think that at the beginning, up to the time of the court-martial of 1894—that is to say, toward the end of this investigation—they believed—at least, the majority of the persons connected with it—that I was guilty, but at the court-martial it was different. I am certain that from that moment, as they felt they had made a mistake, they were afraid of being accused of carelessness, and they accumulated against me all kinds of machinations. The proof of this has been given by Captain Freystaetter.

"' They have provided behind my back documents that they knew were false, in order to secure my condemnation. When Captain Freystaetter said this at Rennes, and uttered the words "Panizzardi despatch" in his calm tones, I shuddered in all my being. How could they do such a thing as that?'

"In telling me this Captain Dreyfus's eyes opened wide with a frightened kind of stare, and he moved toward me as if the better to impress on me the horror that he felt.

"I questioned him again:

"' You speak in certain letters of your fear of madness. How, indeed, inactive as you were, ill in body and mind, without books and not knowing what your fate would be—how did you succeed in warding off insanity?'

"' In 1896 and 1897, as I had resolved to live, I removed from my table the photographs of my wife and children, the sight of whom made me suffer and weakened me. I no longer wished to see them, and I ended by only regarding them as symbols without the human figure, the thought of which unnerved me too much. I did not want to weaken. When one has a duty it must be accomplished to the end, and I wanted to live for my wife and children. It was the same during the trial at Rennes. When I was in so much need of strength—well, I would not re-read my diary of Devil's Island, so as not to unnerve myself and to preserve my energy, for (and he repeated this several times) when one has resolved to do one's duty one must go on to the end.'

"His fist strikes the seat, giving emphasis to his words.

"' Do you know,' he continued, ' what is most fatiguing in struggles like mine? It is a passive resistance. To have struggled like my brother for five years is indeed exhausting, but at least the effort leads to result. You move, go here and there, cry, but you act; while a passive resistance which mine had to be is more exhausting, and still more depressing because it exacts the effort of every minute in your life without resting a single minute. It is that, together with the lack of fresh air, which has exhausted me most.'

"'But you must have had terrible nightmares?'

"'Oh, yes. I wrote them down in my diary afterward, but I could not recall them at present. When the guard heard me talking aloud in the night he would come to the foot of my bed to listen to my words, in order to report them next day in his report to the governor.'

"We were nearing Bordeaux. The captain once more looked out on the country.

"' Oh, the beautiful vineyards!' he exclaimed, and continuing he said: ' It is so sweet, so quieting. When evening falls just see what charm there is about those light mists encircling the trees.'

"'What are you going to do now, captain?' I asked.

"'To live alone with my wife and children henceforth. My children are my greatest joy on earth. The elder, it seems, remembers me. The girl was only a few months old in 1894, so I do not know her. I did not wish to see them at Rennes in order not to leave the sad impression of the prison on their young minds. One should not darken a child's imagination; but I am going to see them with great joy in two days' time. I want to bring them up myself, and in common with their mother to supervise their instruction and education, because I am opposed to boarding schools.

"' When my children were small it was a holiday for me to talk with them, to form them from their earliest age. Unfortunately, events did not permit it, but I hope to catch up.'

"Bordeaux—Is the journey going to last thus to the end? Not quite. Alas! the *Gironde* had received from Rennes a despatch announcing that Captain Dreyfus had left for Nantes, and local men inferred therefrom that he was going to alight at Bordeaux.

"Here they are indeed trying to recognize the captain, but we pass quickly through the crowd, and Mathieu Dreyfus alone is recognized. We at once enter the Hotel Terminus, which adjoins the station, and go upstairs for a wash. We are spotted. All the hotel knows about it straightway, as we can tell by the faces of the servants scrutinizing us. Still, we must dine and continue our route. We have the meal served in a salon, and dine with some gayety under the curious eye of the head-waiter, who is flustered. The captain is in good spirits. He asks me point-blank:

"' Do you wish to know my opinion on the "affaire"?' and as we all laugh over this outburst, he says to me, half serious, half gay:

"' Well, the fact is, I do not yet understand how they could accuse me of such a crime.'

"The agents of the detective department send us word that they are in waiting. Our tickets are taken for Cette.

"The station master is informed that we are going there to embark for Spain, and we hope he will spread the news, in order to lead the curious off the track. But all is in vain. A hundred people are stationed on the quay in front of the Hotel Terminus.

"The detectives decide to have us go into the street and go on to the platform by a public entrance, which is now deserted. This is what we do, and the surprised crowd has barely time to see us shut ourselves in our compartments without being able to distinguish the object of its curiosity. Five minutes more we stay there. The crowd does not utter a single cry. What a sign of calmer days!

"Then at thirty-eight minutes after seven o'clock the train starts without the shade of a murmur. Fifty yards away a railway employee cries, ' Bravo!' while on the other side of the platform a voice cries, ' Down with Dreyfus!'

"Captain Dreyfus, who hears both cries, makes a reflection worthy of a mathematician that equals things up.

"From now on it was known that the train had Captain Dreyfus on board, and calmly stretched out by the side of his brother Mathieu, in a sleeper, the blinds of which were drawn, the captain was trying to sleep for the first time as a free man.

"The night passed off well, and when in the morning at five o'clock we saw the captain again, he seemed rested, content and happy, as on the night before, even happier at the approach of the final goal. I have not yet said that this goal was Carpentras, where the Valabregue family owns a beautiful place, well situated and surrounded by other friendly families, and where Mathieu Dreyfus and Mme. Lucie Dreyfus had decided to shelter the captain directly he was liberated.

"The day breaks. The sun rises amid purple clouds on the horizon. I go forward to say farewell to the captain, who is watching the marvellous spectacle through the carriage window. I had a few words from him as to the present state of his mind. He says to me:

"'I have been the victim of ideas. I feel no bitterness. I nourish no hatred for those who have wronged me so deeply. I feel only pity for them. What we must know is that never again can such misfortune befall any man.'

"I ask him: 'Are you aware of the intensity of feeling that your misfortune has aroused? You know that people hate you, but you know that there are many others whose hearts have bled for your sufferings.'

"'I cannot take it myself. I represent in the eyes of sensitive people part of the human suffering, but part only, and I understand perfectly that it is the kindness of my fellow-beings which moved them at this symbol that I personify.'

"'Do you intend to live at Carpentras?'

"'Yes, until my health is restored and I have completely rested. I would not go abroad as I was asked to do. The reception I might have had would have had the air of reprisals against the country, and I could not make up my mind.'

"We had not spoken of the pardon. It was time to do so.

"'I did not ask for the pardon,' he said, 'but I accept it as an acknowledgment of my suffering and that of my wife, for we both need a little respite, but this pardon in no way affects my resolution to seek my rehabilitation.   I will not know either insult or menace, but I will know no weakness—I mean mental weakness.   Must not the soul dominate over the body?'

"Avignon.   The train stops.   We all get off.   In twenty paces we go out of the station.   Two landaus are in waiting.   A servant takes the luggage.   The captain, M. Mathieu Dreyfus, and M. Paul Valabregue get into one carriage, the detective and inspector into the other.

"We exchange a last shake of the hand through the window, and the historic procession quickly disappears around the great trees.

"Carpentras is twenty kilometres from Avignon.   This morning the prefect of Vaucluse telephoned to the mayor of Carpentras to inform him that Captain Dreyfus was within his walls, and to beg him to order police measures to be taken for his security and for keeping order.

"The mayor replied that he was sure of the sentiments of the majority of the population in regard to the Valabregue family, and that he would be answerable for quiet and order."

Chapter LVII.

"THE INCIDENT IS CLOSED"

THE *Aurore*, the *Petite République*, and the *Siècle*, of Paris, published on September 21st the following declaration from Captain Dreyfus:

The Government of the Republic restores me my liberty. It is nothing to me without honor. From this day forth I shall continue to seek the reparation of the judicial error of which I am still the victim. I wish that France as a whole should know by a final judgment that I am innocent. My heart will not be at rest until there is no longer a Frenchman who imputes to me the abominable crime which another has committed.

ALFRED DREYFUS.

The report of the Minister of War, General the Marquis de Gallifet, to the President of the Republic proposing the pardon of Dreyfus was as follows:

MONSIEUR LE PRESIDENT:—On September 9th the court-martial of Rennes condemned Dreyfus, by five votes against two, to ten years' detention, and by a majority it granted extenuating circumstances. After appealing to the Council of Revision Dreyfus withdrew his application. The verdict has become definitive, and henceforth it partakes of the authority of the law, before which every one ought to bow. The highest function of the Government is to enforce respect for the decisions of justice without distinction and without reservation. Resolved to fulfil this duty, it ought also to take into account what clemency and the public interest counsel. The verdict of the court-martial itself, which admitted extenuating circumstances, and the desire immediately expressed that the sentence might be mitigated are so many indications that ought to solicit attention. As the result of the judgment pronounced in 1894 Dreyfus has undergone five years' transportation. This judgment was annulled on June 3, 1899, and a penalty less severe both in its nature and its duration has been applied. If one deducts from the ten years' detention the five years served on the

Île du Diable—and it cannot be otherwise—Dreyfus will have undergone five years' of transportation, and ought to undergo five years' of detention. It has been suggested whether it was not possible to assimilate transportation to solitary confinement in a prison, and in that case he would have almost completely purged his sentence. Legislation does not seem to permit this. It follows, therefore, that Dreyfus ought to undergo a higher penalty than that to which he has been actually condemned.

It results from information obtained that the health of the condemned man has been seriously compromised, and that he could not, without the greatest peril, bear a prolonged detention. Apart from considerations of a nature to arouse anxiety, others of a more general order tend to the same conclusions. A higher political interest—the necessity of calling up all their powers always exacted from governments after difficult crises and in regard to certain orders of facts—suggests measures of clemency or of oblivion. The Government would ill respond to the desire of a country desirous of pacification if, by the acts which it behooves it to accomplish, whether on its own initiative or by a proposal to Parliament, it did not take steps to efface all traces of a painful conflict. It is for you, Monsieur le President, by an act of supreme humanity, to give the first pledge of the work of pacification which public opinion demands, and which the welfare of the Republic dictates.

For these reasons I have the honor to propose for your signature the following decree.

GENERAL DE GALLIFET, Minister of War.

The decree in question was thus worded:

"ARTICLE 1.—There is accorded to Alfred Dreyfus remission of the rest of the penalty of ten years' of detention pronounced against him by decree of the court-martial of Rennes dated September 9, 1899, and also of military degradation.

"ARTICLE 2.—The Minister of War is charged with the execution of the present decree."

General de Gallifet also sent to the military governors of Paris and Lyons, as well as to army corps commanders, the following general order:

TO THE ARMY:—The incident is closed. The military judges, the object of universal respect, have delivered their verdict in complete independence. We have, without any sort of reservation, bowed down before their decree. We shall likewise bow down before the act which a sentiment of profound pity has dictated to the President of the Republic. It is impossible that any question of reprisals of any sort whatever should henceforth arise. So I repeat, the incident is closed. I ask you, and if need be I should order you, to forget the past in order to think only of the future. With you, who are all my comrades, I cry heartily "Vive l'armée!" the army which belongs to no party but only to France.

GALLIFET.

Germany, on the whole, was pleased at the news of the compromise arrived at in the Dreyfus case. It was recognized with deep regret at Berlin that the unfortunate officer, by withdrawing his notice of appeal, abandoned, for the time being, his hope of securing a legal and formal vindication of his innocence, but the opinion was held that the trial at Rennes convinced all who were open to conviction, and that the main things to be considered after the trial were the tranquillity of France and the health of the prisoner.

The clerical *Kolnische Volks-Zeitung*, which had regarded the Dreyfus case with almost complete indifference, considered that it was an act of patriotism on the part of Dreyfus to accept the pardon. There were not wanting voices, however, which denounced the compromise as cowardly and even unwise.

The *Cologne Gazette* regarded the pardon as "an official recognition of the cowardly and disgraceful judgment at Rennes as the scornful answer of a common court-martial to the plain order of the court of highest instance in the country," and as "a victory of the military party over the civil institutions."

The *Vossische Zeitung* thought that the only excuse for the action of the French Government was that it was anxious to place the person of Dreyfus in safety as soon as possible, for fear of the consequences if an anti-Dreyfus ministry should come into power.

Chapter LVIII.

IS THE "INCIDENT" CLOSED?

WHEN the French Minister of War, General the Marquis de Gallifet, announced that the Dreyfus "incident" was closed, he probably believed he was stating the truth.   But he differs in this respect from the famous Paris correspondent of the London *Times*, M. de Blowitz, who, under date of September 24th, telegraphed to his paper as follows:

"For the honor of humanity and of France we must not fancy that, as General de Gallifet has said in a phrase which would seem to have been written on a drumhead, ' L'incident est clos.'   No; the heat of the battle, perhaps, is over, but the incident is not ended, for the simple reason that it is not an incident but a colossal chapter the episodes in which are stages in the history of civilization, and which is bound to continue if humanity does not intend to abdicate its right to progress.   For the foreigner as well as for France the sacred interests of justice, which are our common patrimony, are at stake.   Whoever deals an arbitrary blow at justice is nothing more nor less than a malefactor.   He is like a man who fells an immense tree across a railway line to stop the progress of the train at the risk of killing all the passengers.   No; neither for the foreigner nor for France is the incident ended.   The foreigner, it is true, has not himself to aim at reprisals, but in his shoulder-to-shoulder advance with the rest of humanity he has certain rights and certain laws to defend.   It would be to our common shame if after these five years of anxiety and doubt, if after these two years of anguish and of battle, we were to say calmly to one another, seated in the shadow of the beech-trees, ' Now that the prisoner is at liberty let us wash our hands of the whole matter and take breath.'   No, let us not lie down in idleness, content with the work already done.

"In the first place, Alfred Dreyfus, although no longer in prison, still remains condemned in the eyes of the law, mortally wounded in his honor, and, whatever the disdain manifested by public opinion throughout the world for the verdict of these Rennes judges, who had not the slightest idea that their mission was to rehabilitate before civilization and history the honor of military justice, Dreyfus has, nevertheless, come forth from Rennes gravely touched in his honor, ' sans lequel,' as he said, ' la liberté ne m'est rien.' The foreign Press, to be sure, has not to intervene in the efforts of Dreyfus to obtain the annulling of this verdict. Such a result, although not admitted by his peers, would efface the judicial stain which still remains upon his honor, and, as for his military judges, it is perfectly clear that their mental attitude is so utterly different from that of other reflecting beings that it is futile to appeal to them in the hope of obtaining a verdict in conformity with the ordinary principles of human justice. It is, nevertheless, necessary for the greater good of civilization that human society as a whole should draw from this event, which General de Galli-fet calls an incident, such conclusions as will hasten our common progress and remove from the path all the obstacles in the way. It is, further-more, imperative that history should treasure up the names of those who have with such effrontery conspired against truth, and have succeeded in transforming Justice into a strumpet obedient to their every heat, instead of allowing her to remain the virgin, haughty and serene, ' who renders verdicts and not services.'

"I venture to hope that my readers will not blame me for not taking my ease in the tranquillity of a work well done, and that they will allow me to point out to them that in France, as elsewhere, the men ready to defend insulted justice and outraged truth are still numerous and alert. This morning's *Figaro* contained a letter from M. Jonnart to M. Cornély, and I extract from it certain passages which may serve as the eloquent conclusion of what I have been saying, for M. Jonnart, a liberal-minded man, enamoured of justice, belongs to the group of a chosen few, to the band of young public men who are the hope of the Republic, those in whom the encroachments of ambition have not yet had time to stifle the voice of the heart, which makes itself heard simultaneously with that of reason. Although still young, M. Jonnart has already climbed well to the top in political life. It is he who, as one of the members of the com-mittee of the Progressist section of the Centre, wrote to M. Méline a few days ago a very plain-spoken letter in reply to the ex-prime minister's

24

effort to add one more embarrassment to those in which France is now involved.   M. Méline desired the immediate convocation of the Chamber, hoping to pile up a few ruins, on the summit of which he would take his place as master of the situation with his portfolio under his arm.

"Let me give now certain extracts from M. Jonnart's letter:

"'The incomprehensible verdict of the Rennes court-martial, against which good sense, logic, and the law itself protest, becomes the most striking justification of your articles, and condemns those whom it pretends to save.   For three years I have been unable through ill-health to ascend the tribune of the Chamber, and I am quite unable to express how much I have suffered at not being able to tell in public all my anxieties, my profound pain and distress, and at not being able to put my political friends on their guard against the indifference or the want of foresight of their chiefs.   There have been moments when I have ardently desired that Dreyfus should be found guilty.   I have read everything, studied everything, examined everything, with the hope of finding the proof of his guilt.   I refused to believe in the odious machinations in this abominable crime.   This proof I have not found; it does not exist.   I was then seized with a poignant doubt, and then, when my conviction had been formed on the documents themselves so that it could not be shaken, I felt that something had given way within me, and an evil wind seemed to be carrying away the ideals of my youth.   For I am a Republican and always have been so.   I believe in the Republic—that is to say, in justice and in liberty.   I have fought for these ideas in a modest place in the Republican ranks, but with a passionate sincerity, with a joyous spirit and enthusiasm no longer known to the young men of to-day, buoyed up by the indomitable hope of a better humanity.

"' Alas! does not what has taken place during the last three years in our unfortunate country make one doubt the progress of the human spirit? For me it is the shattering of certain illusions which had remained persistent amid the agitations of my political life.   The barbarians who conducted the savage campaign which has led up to the verdict of Rennes may make merry, their joy will not be long.   I have written this to a few friends many a time; you have said the same for yours in marvellous articles in which you blended all your heart with all your talent.   The Dreyfus affair is only an incident, but the audacious enterprise for which it has served as a pretext will have political consequences as to which the moderates of the Conservative and the Republican parties have made the great mistake in not concerning themselves. They will not say in excuse that they could not anticipate them. Ah no; these shortsighted politicians have been sufficiently warned. . . .

" ' . . . The insensate persons who have revived in this country the racial and religious wars cherish the illusion of keeping the conflagration within bounds. The sectarian fools who tremble with joy at the cry "Mort aux juifs!" and let loose civil war with the secret hope of stopping it at the exact point where their appetites and rancors were satisfied, have sown the wind to reap the whirlwind. And I note with painful surprise that Denys Cochin and many another Catholic like him whom I like and for whom I have a profound respect, did not utter in the thick of the battle, I will not say a cry of indignation—that we did not ask of them—but even a cry of pity. The religious bodies dispersed in 1880 have been reestablished almost everywhere, that of the Jesuits in particular. Only a short time ago a bill intended to enforce the famous decrees, and this time to apply them seriously, would have disturbed nobody and would have piteously failed. Now, you may imagine, it will have some chance of success. And, indeed, what force is given by recent events and by the propaganda of the *Libre Parole* and of the monkish leaguers of the *Croix* to the arguments of those who consider that the Republic, like the monarchy, cannot permit to thrive in its midst certain unauthorized religious bodies, certain rich and powerful associations, unrecognized by the State, completely outside its control, and constantly conspiring against its security and public order—incorrigible conspirators, beaten on May 16th, beaten with Boulanger, beaten always, yet always returning to the assault of Republican institutions with the same sophisms, the same pretensions, the same ambitions, and the same weapons—defamation and falsehood.' "

Chapter LIX.

THE HOPE OF FRANCE

A HISTORY of the Dreyfus case would be incomplete without a sketch of General the Marquis de Gallifet, the Minister of War at the time of the Rennes court-martial, and "the Hope of France." This combination of Royalist and Republican, gallant soldier and aristocrat, stern disciplinarian and statesman, was born in Paris, on January 25, 1830. He entered the French army in April, 1848, and reached the rank of sub-lieutenant December 30, 1857. He was promoted captain in 1860, major of cavalry in 1863, lieutenant-colonel in 1867, and general of division in 1875. De Gallifet (whose name, in some books of reference, is spelled Galliffet) served with great distinction in the Crimea, before Sebastopol, where he was commended for his bravery. The general was badly wounded by the explosion of a shell at Puebla, in 1863, during the Mexican war, and distinguished himself in the Algerian campaigns of 1860, 1864, 1865, and 1868.

In the Franco-Prussian war General de Gallifet served with the Army of the Rhine, and won the admiration of the invaders of France while at the head of the Fifth Regiment of African Hussars. He was captured by the Prussians at the battle of Sedan and was imprisoned in Germany. After the Franco-Prussian War, De Gallifet was made a general of brigade, and took a most active part in the second siege of Paris, then held by the troops of the Commune, and in the suppression of the Communards. Upon that occasion he acted with the greatest severity, but the circumstances seem to have justified him in so doing. When his victorious troops entered Paris, he caused thousands of Communards, caught red-handed, to be shot on the spot, and restored order by the unlimited use of rifle, bayonet, and rapid-fire gun. Any man of the Communards caught wearing a uniform, part of a uniform, or even military shoes, was promptly executed, and the hands of all the prisoners captured were examined for powder marks. If such traces of resistance to the troops of the Versailles Government were found, the curt order, "Shoot him," was issued, and a few minutes later the man so condemned was dead.

In 1871 General de Gallifet was sent to Africa, and took a prominent part in the pacification of the insurgent tribes. He commanded the El-Goliah expedition, and, overcoming the most serious obstacles in the way of the transportation of troops, he executed a rapid march through the desert and vanquished the Arabs.

Later, De Gallifet, who had become a great friend of M. Gambetta, was appointed to command the Eighth Army Corps; in 1875 he was made general of division, and in 1879 he was given the command of the Ninth Army Corps. He was promoted to the command of the Twelfth Army Corps in 1882, and in 1885 was made a member of the Supreme Council of War.

During the autumn of 1891, General de Gallifet conducted his part of the army manœuvres so brilliantly that the Military Medal, a high distinction in France, was conferred upon him. After conducting the fall manœuvres of 1894, the general retired from active service.

General de Gallifet was decorated with the cross of the Legion of Honor in 1855, was made officer of the Legion of Honor in 1863, commander of the Legion of Honor in 1873, grand officer of the Legion of Honor in 1880, and grand cross of the Legion of Honor in 1887. He has also been inspector-general of many army corps.

De Gallifet succeeded M. do Freycinet as Minister of War on June 22, 1899, becoming part of the non-partisan Cabinet formed to handle the crisis in France caused by the agitation for and against Dreyfus. His advent upon the scene apparently calmed the passions of all parties. Although originally a Royalist, De Gallifet is above all a loyal soldier, and all parties, remembering his extreme severity, to put it mildly, in suppressing the Commune, recognized that for once France had the right man in the right place, a man who might be counted upon fearlessly and relentlessly to uphold law and order, even if he had to make the gutters of the French capital, for the second time, run with human blood.

As to his Royalist leanings, it is an open question as to whether the kid-gloved but iron-handed soldier would not handle the followers of the Duke of Orleans, if they attempted a revolutionary movement, as roughly as he handled the Communards in the past.   In any case an officer and a gentleman in every sense of the words, De Gallifet is counted upon by his admirers to uphold the regularly constituted authorities in France at all costs.

With supreme confidence in his own nerve, De Gallifet looked with quiet scorn upon the turbulent parties of France, and openly defied the anti-Dreyfusites after the verdict, by promptly promoting Captain Frey-staetter and Major Hartman, the two officers who gave the most fearless, outspoken testimony in favor of Dreyfus, and in announcing that after investigation he had found no ground for suspicion of Colonel Picquart's conduct of the Intelligence Department.   This was practically saying that Freystaetter and Hartman had, in the general's firm opinion, testified to the truth, and that Picquart was an honest man.

It is said, in addition, that the general's private relations with ambassadors and others enabled him to convince himself that Dreyfus was innocent.

This firm stand of the general won him the respect, at least, of his worst enemies, and people throughout the world began to look toward him as likely to be the Moses capable of leading France out of the wilderness of corruption, incompetency, and general rottenness into which she had drifted, step by step, with open eyes, during past years.   France, her best friends know, needs a strong man at the helm of State—a brilliant man, a man who can excite the admiration of the world, a man who can command respect at home and abroad.   Such a man is General the Marquis de Gallifet.   As Minister of War he has proved very successful.   Will France recognize this by bestowing further honors upon him?   Let us wait and see what the future has in store for the gallant soldier-statesman.

Chapter LX.

WHAT EUROPE THOUGHT OF THE "PARDON"

THE "pardon" extended to Dreyfus was considered by a large section of the Austrian public to be a not unworthy counterpart to the verdict of treason with extenuating circumstances given by the Rennes court-martial. It was classed in Vienna as a compromise of a not particularly elevated or manly character, which went to show that the ministerial champions of justice in Paris had at least one point in common with the instruments of military violence at Rennes. Both were lacking in the courage of their opinions. The general feeling on the subject in Austria found unreserved expression in the *Fremdenblatt*, which remarked that the compromises effected involved a grave depreciation of moral dignity for all the principal factors concerned, adding:

"The Government in adopting this expedient proved that it had not the courage to take the straight road and proceed to the revision or cassation of the sentence. It remains to be seen whether the advantages of that expedient will outweigh the danger of such a confession of weakness,"

In the opinion of the Vienna semi-official organ, the main object of the French Cabinet was to detach the army from the enemies of the Republic, also saying that it was concerned for the fate of the Exhibition, which it did not wish to see prejudiced or endangered by subversive movements.

In Rome, the liberation of Dreyfus was hailed with general satisfaction, and was interpreted as an official disavowal of the iniquitous sentence of Rennes.

The London *Times*, otherwise the "Thunderer," commenting upon the release of Dreyfus, said:

"The release of Alfred Dreyfus from his long and barbarous captivity was accomplished yesterday, not as a public act of reparation, but as if it were something of which the Government that 'pardoned' him might possibly be ashamed. In the early hours of the morning M. Dreyfus was removed from his prison at Rennes, and, in company with his brother, who has stood by him so faithfully all through this cruel ordeal, left for a destination that is at present unknown. The persecution of an innocent man—practically declared to be so by the inept judgment of the Rennes court-martial and by the action of the chief of the State—has thus been exhibited, at last, to the world in its scandalous unrighteousness. It began in illegal methods of procedure, adopted, as the inquiry at Rennes has shown, to secure the conviction of the accused, and carried out by illegal methods of physical and moral torture from which even mediæval brutality might have recoiled. It is to be hoped, for the sake of France herself, that the victim of a plot as base and odious as any recorded in history will now have at least a chance of recovering a certain measure of health and strength in retirement and seclusion. Whether or not M. Dreyfus will proceed to an appeal before the Court of Cassation for the annulling of the Rennes verdict we cannot say. The moral effect of that pitiable decision has already been destroyed, not only by the force of public opinion, but by the resolution of the French Government not to act upon it. At the same time it is felt that justice is outraged when an innocent man has to slink away under cover of a 'pardon,' while the vile conspirators who did their best to send him back to Devil's Island are even now swaggering about in their uniforms and their cassocks as if they had the fortunes of France in their polluted hands.

"France will bitterly regret the apathy with which she has treated the most abominable of crimes, the systematic perversion of justice to secure the ruin of an individual. She has displayed the backwardness of her jurisprudence and the weakness of her moral fibre. In an interesting letter Sir Herbert Stephen points out that France is still in the stage out of which this country passed hundreds of years ago, when a trial was based, not on evidence, but on 'compurgation.' Unfortunately, the moral basis of compurgation, the truthful backing of a man by his honest neighbors, does not exist in a corrupt modern society.

"The effect of what has been said and done at Rennes on the minds of independent foreigners is strikingly shown in a letter from M. Zakrevsky, a well-known Russian jurist and a member of the Imperial Senate, which is the High Court of the Empire. M. Zakrevsky has studied the proceedings at Rennes, and is appalled to see what they mean. The conclusion he draws from ' this unheard-of spectacle ' is that ' modern French society has definitely fallen from the rank it occupied among civilized peoples. Where the sentiment of justice is atrophied by the intensity of political and religious passions grafted on to a monstrous national vanity passing itself off for patriotism, there is, I contend, no room left for the moral elements indispensable to a well-ordered form of society.' Nor will M. Zakrevsky admit that only the five unjust judges of Rennes and their chiefs should be held responsible ' for the iniquitous acts which have revolted the whole world.' He dwells, not without force, on the lamentable want of moral courage displayed by the nation. ' Take one instance amongst many. See how men who call themselves statesmen, who belong to the cream of society, like the Casimir-Periers, the Freycinets, when called upon to give evidence, to tell the whole truth, instead of throwing light upon important facts, are content to fence, or make oracular speeches. They think above all of themselves; their chief anxiety is not to depreciate their own value in the eyes of their great audience,—*i.e.*, of the country which listens to them.' Just as little does the Russian jurist mince his words concerning the motives which have led France to seek the alliance of his own country: ' Unable in her vanity and thirst for prestige to recognize in her defeats of 1870-71 all that was irremediable and even just, protesting that she would never accept the Treaty of Frankfort as final, prating of her re-vindications, of her hopes, without venturing to strike a blow, France has gradually cut herself adrift in the helplessness of political disorder from the other Western nations, to which, with their great liberal traditions, the ties of centuries united her, and she has sunk amorously into the arms of Russia, of a country which represents and practices more than ever principles entirely opposed to those which France boasts of holding. From the Russian alliance she has inevitably and logically drifted into anti-Semitism, into anti-Protestantism, into oppression of the weak, into a recrudescence of brutal militarism, and, finally, into the Dreyfus affair, crowned by the proceedings at Rennes.'

" No critics in this country or elsewhere have written anything so cruel and crushing as these and other even more uncomplimentary messages, for which we prefer to refer our readers to the French text. Yet it is plain that these views, so decidedly in unison with those of the great majority of Germans, Austrians, and Italians, as well as of Englishmen and Americans, are shared by Russians of every school. M. Zakrevsky is a Liberal; but a very eminent representative of old Russian ideas, M. Pobiedonostzeff, the Procurator of the Holy Synod, has come to the same conclusion about the Dreyfus case. He has said that ' for all impartial observers the proceedings at Rennes proved the innocence of Captain Dreyfus,' and has expressed his agreement with the contention of *The Times*, borne out by many independent testimonies, that the root of the mischief lies in the false education of the young in France.   Even the most rabid anti-Dreyfusards will hardly contend, we suppose, that the Russians have also joined the great ' cosmopolitan syndicate of treason.' "

Chapter LXI.

ECHOES OF THE TRIAL

THERE were many remarkable exhibitions of feeling throughout the world after the second conviction of Dreyfus, and a number of strong statements were made on the subject.

Archbishop Ireland, at St. Paul, Minn., said in an interview September 13th:

"It is my belief that public meetings in America such as it is proposed to hold for the purpose of protesting against the sentence of the Rennes court-martial are untimely, unfair to France, and likely to breed regrettable ill-feeling between that country and our own.

"I shall not deny that I have always had in my heart deep sympathy for the unfortunate officer who has been under trial in Rennes, and that I had wished and hoped that the sentence of the court would have been one of acquittal.

"But it is another question to face the verdict of the court the moment that verdict has been declared with the assertion that it is plainly against truth, and that the court from which it issues is guilty of base injustice and sacrilegious perjury. And it is, still more so, another question to lay upon France the crime of the verdict, if crime there be in it, and throw at a whole people and at their Government insulting epithets. Let us wait.

"This whole matter belongs to the internal life and to the internal administration of France, and international courtesy as well as justice bids us talk about it very carefully and very slowly. France is a proud, sensitive nation. She will deeply resent, as it is her right, undue criticism and hasty judgment of her acts by a foreign people, and especially will she resent, as it is surely her right, any uncalled-for interference with her internal administration and any imprudent challenging of her national honor.

"France has been our friend for ages. She was our friend when no other nation befriended us. She is our friend to-day. She is a sister republic. We should pause long and seriously before blaming, suspecting, or offending France.

"I can well understand the present happenings in America. The American people are most easily roused to sentiments of justice and humanity. Prudence, however, is the queen of all virtues, and we should strive to make it ours.

"In what I say I speak as an American, for what I believe the good of America. I make no plea for France, although, because I know France, I love her despite her faults, and I hope for her, despite her perils."

Governor Theodore Roosevelt, of the State of New York, in a speech at Walton, N. Y., September 13th, remarked:

"Something recently happened which I want to speak about. I think it a rare thing for the whole nation to watch the trial of a single citizen of another nation. We have watched with indignation and regret the trial of Captain Dreyfus. It was less Dreyfus on trial than those who tried him. We should draw lessons from the trial. It was due in part to bitter religious prejudices of the French people. Those who have ever wavered from the doctrine of the separation of Church and State should ponder upon what has happened. Try to encourage every form of religious effort. Beware and do not ever oppose any man for any reason except worth or want of it. You cannot benefit one class by pulling another class down."

In Washington, September 12th, a mass meeting was held at the Masonic Temple to protest against the verdict of the Rennes court-martial in the Dreyfus case. The speakers included men of all creeds—Jews, Protestants, and Catholics. The meeting adopted a set of resolutions affirming belief in the innocence of Dreyfus, condemning the proceedings of the court-martial, and pledging those present to use every lawful and proper means to prevent the co-operation of this country in the Paris Exposition. The resolutions, after expressing sympathy with Dreyfus and his family, continued:

"Remembering all the ties and traditions that bind us to France, and not forgetful of the glorious days of Lafayette and Rochambeau and of the gallant efforts of Picquart, Zola, Labori, and Demange, we do not despair of final victory for justice. We invoke all American citizens to co-operate to the end that justice may finally be done and the sentiments of the American people brought home to the Government and the citizens of France. In the mean time we will take measures as citizens to emphasize by word and act our deliberate intention not to co-operate in the Paris Exposition of next year, and do whatever is legal and proper to prevent our Government from official recognizing said Exposition."

The resolutions concluded by calling on the President of the United States to convey to the French Government, in whatever form he might deem proper, the views of the American people on the Dreyfus verdict, as voiced by that country and other meetings throughout the country.

Reference was made in one of the resolutions to the testimony of ex-Minister Lebon before the court-martial, in which he said that the rigorous treatment of Dreyfus was due in part to the understanding that there was a plan on foot to rescue the prisoner by a party of Americans. The resolution called upon Secretary of State Hay to obtain an official copy of this testimony "in order to refute this slander."

President McKinley did not take any action in the matter, as it was impossible for him to do so, as pointed out at the time by the New York *Times*, which said, editorially:

" If France were to suffer some national calamity, as she did in the death of her president, it would be quite proper for Mr. McKinley to express the sorrow and sympathy that we should all feel or to forward through our Ambassador the resolutions of any public bodies. But when it comes to criticism and protest our people must content themselves with individual utterance or with the utterance of and through the press. It is an accepted rule in all the relations of governments with each other that each is entirely independent in the conduct of its internal affairs, and none is at liberty to comment officially thereon unless prepared to take the consequences of an unfriendly act. There must always be a distinct reason in the peculiar interests of the criticising power to make criticism even plausible, and the power criticised need make no excuse for resentment.

" Our Government has no opinion as to the Dreyfus case, and has no right to any, any more than France would have a right to an opinion in regard to something that might arise in this country to offend the moral sense of its people—the lynching of colored men, for instance, or the whitewashing of the late Secretary of War. It does not by any means follow that the American people are not entitled to have a perfectly clear opinion on the subject and to express it in any form they choose, except through the Executive. As a matter of fact the American people have formed and expressed an opinion to which France will in its own way and in its own time listen. At the moment it is not pleasant to hear, but it is inspired by a sense of justice and it is not really unfriendly. There is no reason why we should conceal it. There is every reason why, soberly and temperately, we should express, explain, and enforce it. In the long run it will have its effect, and the effect will be salutary."

In New York City there was much indignation against the verdict of the Rennes court-martial, and the Municipal Assembly, September 12th, adopted the following resolution unanimously:

"*Whereas*, Since the last session of the Municipal Assembly the intelligent people of the world have been startled by the report of the conviction of Captain Alfred Dreyfus; and

"*Whereas*, We feel that his conviction was unjust, and not sustained by the reported facts and testimony—

"*Resolved*, That the Municipal Assembly of the city of New York extends to Captain Dreyfus its profound sympathy, and that in the interest of justice and humanity and of republican institutions this Assembly expresses its hope that this great injustice be corrected by the French Republic to the end that truth and justice may yet prevail."

Liberty Hall, East Houston Street, New York City, was crowded on September 12th with Jewish residents of the East Side, gathered under the auspices of the Englander Family Society, a benevolent and charitable organization, to protest against the verdict rendered in the Dreyfus trial.

The president of the society is J. Spero, and the secretary Irving Kline. Osias Maller presided at the meeting. A letter was read from Alexander S. Rosenthal, ex-United States Consul to Italy, in which he wrote:

"France has committed a crime by her unjust verdict rendered against Captain Dreyfus. The entire civilized world is convinced that the verdict is based on bigotry, intolerance, and prejudice."

The following resolutions were adopted by a unanimous vote:

"*Resolved*, That through the United States Ambassador in France we appeal to the President of the French Republic, that he right the wrong

done to an innocent man, not by pardoning Captain Dreyfus, but by intervening to secure for him a new trial; and should this request be refused,

"*Resolved*, That we appeal to President McKinley that he should take
measures to prevent the forwarding of any national exhibits by the United
States at the French Exposition in Paris in 1900."

The Central Republican Club, of New York City, at a meeting September 12th, unaniomusly passed the following resolution:

"*Whereas*, In common with the whole civilized world, we have observed with amazement the extraordinary trial concluded at Rennes and
its final judgment, and since it is the sacred interest of all men to defend
and maintain courts for the administration of justice in any country which
is frequently visited by foreigners, that lives and property may be secure
under the full intercourse of our times, we declare our unqualified censure
of the hateful methods of injustice which were employed to obtain the
second unrighteous condemnation of Alfred Dreyfus by a French court-
martial, and we declare that such methods and such tribunals are a perversion of justice and are more fitted for barbarous lands than for a country boasting to possess the civilization of the French Republic."

A copy of the resolutions was mailed to Mme. Dreyfus.

The State G.A.R. reunion of Nebraska, September 13th, adopted the
following resolution:

"*Resolved*, As a convention of soldiers who have fought in wars undertaken in the interests of a common humanity, having for their object the
redress of wrongs perpetrated on the weak and defenceless, we desire to
express our abhorrence of a verdict, as in the case of Captain Dreyfus,
that consigns an innocent man to ignominy, shame, and pain, and that be-
speaks the spirit of a bigoted past rather than that of an enlightened present."

The following message was sent to President McKinley by the Episcopal clergy of San Francisco, September 12th:

"The clericus of the Protestant Episcopal Church of San Francisco,
profoundly moved by the verdict in the Dreyfus case, most earnestly request your excellency to take such action toward a reversal of the sentence as is possible and compatible with the diplomatic relations existing
between the two nations."

The following message of sympathy was telegraphed to Mme. Alfred Dreyfus at Rennes by the summer residents of Northeast Harbor, Maine:

"MADAME: The heart of the whole world is toward you. The trial has made evident the innocence and the noble character of your husband, and the great public, which has followed this struggle with anguish, now renders to him and to his children the honor for which he has struggled till now, for which he is still struggling in France."

The message was signed by William Croswell Doane, Bishop of Albany; S. K. Doane, Eliza G. D. Gardiner, Winthrop Sargent, Aimé Sargent, Ellen W. Boyd, Margaret Condit, Marguerite Junod, Theodora W. Woosley, B. W. Frazier, Arthur Hugh Frazier, the Rev. Dr. W. R. Huntington, Rector of Grace Church, New York; K. F. Gray, James T. Gardiner, Andrew L. Wheelwright, Sarah C. Wheelwright; A. de Viti de Marco, Professor of Finance in the University of Rome; E. de Viti de Marco, Katherine Dunham, Ellen Vaughan, George W. Folsom, Etheldred Folsom, L. L. M. Limoges, Helen Ellis, and Dr. Theodore Dunham.

As a result of the feeling of sympathy with Dreyfus at Wichita, Kansas, Miss Sadie Joseph, a beautiful Jewish girl, was nominated, September 13th, for Queen of the Flower Parade at the Fall Carnival. In a few hours votes enough were cast for Miss Joseph to put her in the lead of the other candidates. Voting for other candidates was almost stopped, and enthusiasm for Miss Joseph ran over the city like wildfire.

In London, England, the Dreyfus Movement Auxiliary Society was organized soon after the Rennes verdict became known, about one hundred prominent Jews becoming members. Dr. A. Zuhn was elected president, and committees on subscriptions and speakers for mass meetings were appointed.

The London correspondent of the Manchester (England) *Guardian*, telegraphed to his paper, September 11th:

"I have known the East End ghetto many years, yet I never saw it exhibit such evident signs of woe and bereavement. The very mourning worn by both men and women seemed to indicate that they were suffering great personal sorrow. The news arrived about an hour before the termination of the Jewish Sabbath. In that hour there was a great outpouring of people, all of whom expressed sympathy with the prisoner. A venerable rabbi assured me that he had never seen the community, rich and poor alike, so moved. ' This,' said the rabbi to me, ' is the bitterest day of modern Judaism.' "

Esterhazy, in an interview in a London afternoon paper, September 11th, was quoted as saying:

"Dreyfus was justly condemned, as the inevitable result of the evidence collected by General Mercier. This bore conviction to the minds of the judges, and the court-martial, following the previous finding, declared Dreyfus guilty and I innocent. I believe the sentence was in accordance with an understanding with the Government. Dreyfus is in a position to claim a reduction of his sentence by one-half. The whole business was a farce, arranged in advance, and doubtless he will soon be liberated."

The Jewish Day of Atonement was celebrated on September 14th, in London, with Dreyfus demonstrations, especially in the East End. A procession with a banner inscribed "Dreyfus, the Martyr. All the Civilized World Demands His Instant Release," marched through Spitalfields.

The Great Synagogue in London, September 14th, presented a striking spectacle. It was crowded from morning until night, and thousands were unable to enter.

Dr. Adler, the chief rabbi, delivered a sermon referring to the Dreyfus case. He said what was morally wrong could not be politically right. Right, justice, honor, and mercy belonged to the immutable law. Falsehood and injustice might prosper for a time, but certain retribution would follow those who forsook the path of right and justice. It had been so with the colossal empires of antiquity, and with Spain in our day.

Dr. Adler declared that Saturday was not, as had been said, the bitterest day in the history of modern Judaism on account of the Dreyfus verdict. It was a memorable penitential Sabbath, ever to be remembered with the keenest disappointment, in which all felt the deepest pity for the prolonged agony of Dreyfus and his wife, but it was not a day of unalloyed bitterness for Jews. To France it was a day more disastrous than Waterloo, more humiliating than Sedan. France, which first allowed to the Jews the rights of citizenship, had defiled the golden vessels of God's temple, and branded an innocent man as an odious traitor to the country he loved so well. Even in France every one had not been hypnotized by the unholy blend of clericalism and militarism.

25

"Let the majesty of the law be vindicated," he concluded, "and let them not seek a pardon, which should be rejected with scorn; for where no crime was committed, how can a pardon be granted?"

Throughout New York City, the news of the pardon of Dreyfus was hailed with satisfaction. This was particularly so on the east side and in the French quarter.

The feeling in favor of Dreyfus has always been strong among the French residents in New York, and the rejoicing over the prisoner's pardon was general.

At Temple Emanu-El, after the services of the Feast of Tabernacles, Rabbi Gottheil, in his sermon, commenting on the fact that this was one of the three Jewish festivals on which it was a divine duty to "be happy and rejoice," deplored the misfortune of Captain Dreyfus, whose situation prevented him from fulfilling the divine behest. He fervently hoped, however, that justice would soon prevail.

At this point his associate, Dr. Silberman, handed Rabbi Gottheil a cablegram which contained the news of Dreyfus's pardon. Rabbi Gottheil read the message to the congregation, who demonstrated their satisfaction by loud applause.

Dr. Gottheil uttered a prayer of thanks and praise to God. Continuing his address he said:

"Among all those who have been roused in all parts of the world to righteous indignation by the injustice, none have shown such unprejudiced sympathy for and implicit belief in the innocence of Dreyfus as have the press of this country. They were among the first to proclaim their certainty of his innocence, and they were fearless and indefatigable in their advocacy of him."

Chapter LXII.

PROPOSAL TO BOYCOTT THE PARIS EXPOSITION

ONE of the outcomes of the Dreyfus verdict was a pretty general proposal to boycott the Paris Exposition of 1900. A sort of "holy alliance" against France was even suggested, but wise counsels prevailed and the matter was dropped. The New York *Herald*, referring to the boycott suggestion, said in an editorial September 15th:

"The newspapers are filled with threats of a sort of 'holy alliance' against France and of boycotting the great Exposition of 1900. This would be more than a mistake; it would be a gross injustice. Foreigners are perfectly free to criticise the affairs of France, just as Frenchmen have a right to express their opinion on anything that takes place in no matter what country.

"To criticise and condemn is one thing, but it is another and very different matter to interfere in the internal affairs of a country, as the would-be boycotters threaten to do. Any one can think what he pleases about the Dreyfus case. Everybody is privileged to discuss the Rennes decision and to approve it or stigmatize it. But to go far beyond that by threatening to punish Frenchmen and injure France because of an unsatisfactory verdict by a court-martial for whose action neither France nor the French people are to blame is pushing matters to an extreme beyond all right, justice and reason.

"'You cannot indict a people,' said Edmund Burke. No more can you with any show of reason or justice boycott or indiscriminately condemn a nation or a people. Those who are so zealous in fomenting this absurd agitation must remember that they are striking as well at all those who have been battling in behalf of Dreyfus. To boycott the Exposition would be to boycott France, whose highest court annulled the condemnation of 1894 and may yet annul that of 1899, whose Government is known to have desired an acquittal, whose press in large measure has protested against the conviction, and many of whose people condemn the Rennes verdict.

"It is these agencies in France—the government, the judiciary, the press and the people—that brought about revision, and it is these that are still desirous of attaining what they believe to be truth and justice.

"The threatened boycott is, moreover, as foolish as it is unjust, since it would be as detrimental to the interests of the boycotters as to those of the boycotted.

"The movement to boycott the Exposition is already losing ground in Germany. The proposed resolution by the Municipal Council that the city of Berlin should not send any special exhibit to Paris has been abandoned. The *Tageblatt* in an article on the subject reminded German exhibitors that by staying away from the great Exposition they would only be giving an advantage to their competitors.

"The effort to get up a mass meeting in this city to boycott the exposition has been also abandoned by its advocates, as the prominent citizens they approached refused to participate on the ground that it was ill-advised.

"Fortunately there is reason to expect that all ill-advised newspaper manifestations will pass away like a fit of bad humor, and that the Exposition of 1900 will have the great success it merits in view of the prodigious efforts it has called forth and the world-wide benefit it must prove. Both the United States and the German governments have refused to lend any official countenance to the foolishly threatened boycott, and we trust their commendable example will be followed by every nation represented in the grand enterprise."

The English press devoted columns of space daily to the telegrams from all parts of the world relating to the proposed boycott of the Paris Exposition. Germany, Austria, and Italy also came to the front. But the German government organs were quick to issue a warning against the proposal.

"Germany has no occasion to take the lead in this matter," says the *Cologne Gazette.* "She ought to leave this to other States, which, perhaps, would not consider it undesirable that Germany, of all powers, should adopt a hostile attitude toward France in this matter."

According to the *The Daily Mail*, of London, which was a strong advocate of a general boycott of the Paris Exposition as a protest against the Rennes verdict, Baron Suffield, president of the Article Club, an organization including in its membership the Colonial Agents General and representing commercial firms with an aggregate capital of £2,000,000,000, favored a boycott.

The English papers were full of letters from individuals and several firms announcing their withdrawal from the Paris Exposition, and urging the Government to do likewise, but the British Government never contemplated taking such a step.

M. Max O'Rell (Paul Blouet) wrote a letter to *The Daily Chronicle* of London, saying that a public expression of sympathy would go against Dreyfus, adding:

"For God's sake, use your influence to stop it.   But for the universal sympathy shown for Dreyfus, whom I personally believe to be innocent, in England and Germany, he would have been acquitted.   It is a terrible thing to say, but I say it and am not afraid of contradiction."

Sir Charles Dilke, M.P., a well-known authority on foreign affairs, in an interview in London, September 13th, deprecated the expression of resentment by foreigners in regard to the Dreyfus verdict.   Such action, Sir Charles said, was likely to make the situation worse for Colonel Picquart and other Dreyfus witnesses.

The secretary of the British Commission to the Paris Exposition said the same day that intimations of withdrawal had been received from only twelve intending exhibitors, while nearly 2,000 applications for space had been received from individuals and firms in Great Britain, India, and the British Colonies.

In many parts of the United States steps toward a boycott of the Paris Exposition were taken.   Many Western firms and individuals who had contemplated making exhibits at the Paris Exposition changed their plans for a time.   Among the concerns which were said to have cancelled their orders for space were the California Canneries of San Francisco, the biggest fruit-canning concern on the Pacific coast, which is controlled by an English syndicate, and the North El Paso and Northeastern Railway of New Mexico, which planned a fine mineral exhibit.   It was also reported that the feeling on the Dreyfus case was so strong in Los Angeles that a demand would be made for the repeal of the act passed by the last legislature appropriating $130,000 for the California exhibit.

The Boston School Board at its session September 13th passed an order which practically meant the boycotting of the Paris Exposition, for which a large school exhibit was planned.   But this was subsequently revoked.

Many manufacturers of Troy, N. Y., who had made application for space for exhibits at the Paris Exposition decided for a time to take no part whatever in it.   William Conners, proprietor of the Troy Paint and Color Works, had made preparations for an elaborate display, while collar, cuff, and shirt manufacturers had in process of manufacture many specimens that were to comprise a special department at the French metropolis. The result of the Dreyfus court-martial caused a cessation of preparations, but they were subsequently resumed.

The United States Commissioner-General to the Paris Exposition, Mr. Ferdinand W. Peck, said in an interview at Chicago, September 13th, that notwithstanding the newspaper statements that merchants in several parts of the country had refused to send exhibits to the Paris Exposition on account of the Dreyfus verdict, none had indicated to him any desire to do so.   When asked if he would refuse information if any of the exhibitors should withdraw, Commissioner Peck said he was not ready to answer that question, but he said he did not think it was right for him to disclose anything about the American exhibitors until their exhibits were installed. Some two hundred persons have applied to him for lists of the American exhibitors, but he has refused to furnish them.   As he has refused to disclose the names of those who have taken space, he thought he ought also to refuse to tell if they relinquish it.

Rabbi Joseph Leucht, of Newark, N. J., was quoted as saying on September 13th:

"The punishment for this outrage will surely come.   France is on the verge of revolution to-day; a bloody day of rebellion is not far off.   As far as the Jews in this country are concerned, I do not think any concerted action will take place to resent the dastardly deed.   France will have to meet the outburst of indignation of the whole civilized world.

"People are now questioning whether they should visit the exhibition of a land where human rights are trampled upon, and possibly governments will reconsider their participation in the affair.   I hope, at least, that free America will take some official act to register its disapproval of this crying shame.

"The Jews of this country will stay away from the Paris Exposition, and if some of them disregard this warning they will speedily rue it when arriving there.   The cry "À bas les Juifs!" will greet their ears wherever they go.   As for poor Dreyfus himself, this trial has brought him a greater vindication than he could ever hope for."

Chapter LXIII.

DREYFUS TRIAL REPORTING

THE correspondent of the New York *Sun*, Mr. H. R. Chamberlain, who described the Dreyfus trial for his paper, writing from Rennes under date of September 11th, described the strange experiences of the army of newspaper correspondents there. He said:

"It is for the pleasure of writing something from Rennes which shall include nothing about Dreyfus and his cause that I am sending this letter. For five long weeks the three hundred newspaper men assembled here from all parts of the world where a public press exists have seen, heard, thought, dreamed, discussed, written—nothing but Dreyfus. Two or three times, while driving or cycling within a few miles of the Breton capital, I have come across intelligent, contented peasants who had never heard the name Dreyfus, and I envied and congratulated them. In an hour or two I shall leave Rennes, never, I hope, to return, but before I go I want to tell what a nice town it is and describe for them two or three odd incidents which have added a touch of comedy to the serious business of our mission here.

"As for Rennes, most guide-books tell us that it is the cleanest if not the healthiest city in Europe. One's eyesight tends to confirm the claim. They even skim the surface of the almost stagnant river in the centre of the town every morning. One's nostrils suggest doubts on the subject, and one's experience of existence in so-called first-class hotels yields only cynical incredulity. I will not dwell upon the matter beyond remarking that scarcely any of those whose duties compelled them to remain in Rennes during the whole five weeks escaped one or more sharp attacks of illness.

"As for the people of Rennes (always excepting two or three of the principal hotel-keepers) their visitors have words only of grateful acknowledgment of kindness, courtesy, and most patient forbearance. American readers will not appreciate the significance of the latter phrase.   Here is a provincial capital, outside the line of tourist travel, inhabited by a sturdy, honest, intensely religious but narrow-minded people.   They saw their town almost taken possession of five weeks ago by a small army of foreigners and Jews.   They hate each of these classes with the ignorant but accumulated hatred of generations.   Moreover, they believed these invaders had come for the purpose of overthrowing a just judgment.   Any other verdict than that given yesterday would have been an outrage upon justice in their ignorant eyes.   And yet for five weeks the people of Rennes tolerated the presence of these unwelcome visitors, saw their streets, and cafés and public institutions almost monopolized by them, and said no word of insult, discourtesy, or resentment—except in their newspapers.   I prefer to believe that the newspapers of Rennes, which in several instances heaped vile abuse and obscene invective, especially upon the correspondents of the foreign press, represent only the low, venal minds of their writers, who, alas, typify only too faithfully the degeneration of journalism in France.

"It is not often that the professional side of a newspaper correspondent's work becomes a matter of public interest, but perhaps this unique experience here at Rennes is entitled to rank as an exception.   No previous event in the world's history has called together a corps of chroniclers so representative in its scope.   None, it should be remembered, came by invitation, as at the coronation of the Czar or the crowning of the little Queen of Holland.   Even the Queen's Jubilee in London failed to draw such an international gathering of journalistic clans.   Papers in Japan and even in Turkey sent correspondents to tell this story at Rennes.   A paper which I had never heard of in Norway spent $100 a day to give its readers an account of the trial, and a single journal in Vienna expended more than $20,000 in telegraph tolls at 'urgent' rates during the five weeks.

"Every disposition to facilitate the work of the correspondents was shown by the authorities.   We learned after a few days that each one of us had been quietly photographed, and full descriptions, with all that could be learned of our antecedents, had been sent to Paris in a special dossier by the omnipresent 'agents of the State'; but nobody could object to this harmless and flattering attention.   Neither could we find any fault with the assignment of places in the trial hall, which relegated the foreign correspondents to the seats most distant from the stage, where the testimony of many witnesses was inaudible. After all, the case to be heard was primarily a domestic French affair, and I doubt if in any other country on earth the same consideration would have been shown to foreign newspaper men, whose presence the great majority of Frenchmen regarded as an intrusion.

"I explained in one of my earlier despatches that each foreign correspondent received half a ticket to the Lycée. This was an immense concession from Colonel Jouaust's first dictum, which was : 'Assign one ticket to each group of ten. That will enable each man to attend one session in ten, and it will be quite enough for him.' Fortunately, the French military idea of journalistic needs did not prevail, and the committee of the 'Presse Judiciare' was able to induce the doughty president to take a more liberal view of the situation. Even the half-ticket regulation was modified to some extent, and each morning admission was granted to as many of the banished moiety of foreign correspondents as there remained empty seats after the ticket holders had entered. Finally the difficulty in hearing the evidence was partially overcome by securing reports of the testimony sheet by sheet from French reporters near the witness-stand, and thus the actual proceedings in the court-room were prepared for readers abroad.

"The authorities of Rennes provided also a great hall with a special telegraph office, for the use of visiting correspondents. The Bourse du Commerce was transformed into a vast editorial room. One hundred and fifty writing tables, nailed to the floor to prevent noise and confusion, comfortable chairs, pens, ink, and paper, and courteous attendants were all at the disposal of French and foreign writers during the five weeks.

"The problem of quick communication with the outside world was an ever-present difficulty from the first day of the trial until the last. There were available six telegraph and four telephone wires from Rennes to Paris, two wires to Brest, the landing-place of the French Cable Company's lines to America, and one wire to Havre, where the Commercial Company's cables touch. The best apparatus and most skilful operators in France were assembled at Rennes for the tremendous task of conveying the news of the trial to the four quarters of the world. Considering the facilities available, the result was probably the best accomplishment in telegraphy in this or any other country. On the first day more than 650,000 words were transmitted by telegraph alone. This quantity was exceeded on the day Labori was shot, and on other days it varied between the maximum and a minimum of 350,000 words.

"It would be unfair, perhaps, to criticise the quality of the work in view of its overwhelming quantity. And operator who sends at highest speed long messages in any of half a dozen languages which he does not understand can hardly be blamed if the despatches fail to arrive letter perfect at their destination. I confess I groaned in anguish of spirit when copies of *The Sun* reached Rennes containing my despatches sent during the early days of the trial. There was great improvement later—the French operator would probably be unkind enough to say this was due solely to my painstaking attempts to write a legible hand. When it is considered, however, that nearly one-half the matter sent over the wires from Rennes was written in English, German, Italian, Russian, Spanish, or Swedish, it must be admitted that the accomplishment of the Rennes telegraph corps was something stupendous.

"There were some amusing incidents in connection with the sending of the news of the trial, and one or two will bear repeating. The correspondent of a London evening paper rushed to the telegraph office on the afternoon of the day Labori was shot, and handed in a despatch of about nine hundred words. All correspondents had deposited in advance ample funds to cover the cost of telegrams in order to avoid the delay of frequent payments. The receiver, therefore, accepted the despatch with the customary ' Merci, monsieur.' The sender happened to wait for a moment, and presently saw the telegraph clerk pick up his message, cross the room, climb on a chair, and carefully place the despatch on top of a cabinet. The man returned to his seat, received a few more telegrams from the persons waiting at the window, checked them, gave them to a messenger to take to the operating room, got up again and carried a heavy ledger over to the cabinet and deposited it on top of the London man's despatch. The correspondent was mystified, but did not interfere until the clerk had received a few more telegrams and had carried a few more miscellaneous articles across the room and piled them upon the cabinet. Then the Londoner remonstrated gently:

"' Aren't you going to send my despatch?'

"' Your despatch has been sent, Monsieur,' was the calm reply.

"' No, it hasn't. It's over there on top of that cabinet,' insisted the correspondent.

The clerk looked at him as if he thought he had been bereft of his senses.

"' Nothing of the kind. I sent your despatch to the operating-room as soon as you handed it to me,' was the polite but firm reply.

"The Englishman began to get angry, and in rather peremptory tones asked the clerk to verify his words by examining the top of the cabinet. The clerk was sure by this time that his interlocutor was crazy. He muttered something about these English, and sharply asked the insistent disturber to stand aside and not block the line at the window. The enraged journalist hurried off, and found a French *confrere* of influence, to whom he explained the situation. Together they returned to the telegraph office and sent for the chief. The case was laid before him. He went to the cabinet, lifted down a heap of things on top, and there at the bottom of all lay the despatch. Then, naturally, the Londoner began to say things, but the chief interrupted him:

"' Now, be reasonable, you mustn't be angry with this poor fellow. Have a little consideration of the circumstances. He has been in tears all day ever since he heard Labori had been shot. He doesn't know what he is doing. Really it isn't fair for you to be cross with him.'

"And what could the correspondent do after that explanation?

"How to communicate the news of the court-martial's verdict most expeditiously to the waiting world has, of course, been the problem uppermost in every correspondent's mind for days past. Many schemes were devised for securing a few seconds' precedence, and some of them were sufficiently ingenious to deserve success, but in the end pure chance proved to be the controlling factor. This applies to the despatches announcing the judgment filed by the correspondent here after the decision had been announced in court by Colonel Jouaust. These telegrams poured into the Rennes telegraph office in a perfect avalanche, and, as usually happens in times of such excitement, the order of dispatching did not follow the exact order of receipt. In fact, the last was sometimes first. Those of us who have had experience of similar confusion at presidential elections at Ver-

sailles and other occasions had prepared for this emergency. We wrote
our despatches in duplicate, filed one at the earliest possible moment, and
waited to slip the other into the distracted clerk's hand at the moment
when he handed over the swelling pile of telegrams for transmission. The
chances were that the top or last message would be sent first.

"It is probable, despite all the rush at Rennes, that the first news of
the verdict reached New York via London. Some of us learned yesterday
morning that the decision would be telephoned to the home office in Paris
a few minutes before it was publicly announced in the court-room at
Rennes. As a matter of fact, at the moment when the decisive words
were being read to the assembled audience in the Lycée, the news had
been received at London, and had been transferred to the cable, which delivered it in New York three minutes late.

"The fate of two plans of rival American correspondents for beating
their fellows deserves to be recorded. They were not satisfied with conveying the news from the court-room to the telegraph office—a distance of
less than a quarter of a mile—by foot or bicycle; so they arranged sys-
tems of signals. In one case, a series of boys stationed at intervals along
the route was to pass along the signal of 'guilty' by holding the right
hand high in the air, while both arms in that position would signify 'innocent.' The boys were carefully drilled, and the system worked perfectly
until the fateful moment came. Then the first boy gave the signal properly, but the second lost his head. Instead of raising his hand he
clapped both arms to his sides and started pell-mell for the telegraph
office. His employer saw him coming and ran to meet him, unable to
imagine what had happened. The boy simply flung himself into the
newspaper man's arms. Too much excited himself to think of any French,
the correspondent shook the little wretch and shouted in English:

"'What is it?'

"Then the boy bethought himself. Up went his right hand high in
the air. 'Coupable,' he yelped, and trotted with his arm still up behind
his employer the rest of the way to the telegraph office.

"The other incident was no less tragic. Another series of boys were to
wave red discs if the verdict was guilty, blue ones for the four-to-three
verdict of dishonorable acquittal, and white for innocent. The correspondent who relied on this scheme made the fatal mistake of stationing a very

small boy at the Lycée end of the line. A crowd of more than a hundred men and boys was waiting at the slot beneath a window through which the word was to come. All broke and ran at the same moment when the news was received, and the small boy with a red disc was simply knocked down and trampled on by the crowd before he could give the signal."

DICTIONARY

OF NAMES, DOCUMENTS, ETC., IN THE DREYFUS CASE

THE following Dictionary of the Dreyfus case contains ready references to the leading actors and documents in the famous drama:

ABEVILLE, COLONEL D'—Former Deputy Chief of the Fourth Bureau.

BEAUREPAIRE, M. QUESNAY DE.—Former President of the Civil Section of the Court of Cassation, who resigned and bitterly attacked Dreyfus.

BERTILLON, M.—Chief of the Identification Department of the Paris Prefecture of Police. He testified at both of the court-martials as an expert in handwriting, against Dreyfus.

BERTIN, LIEUTENANT-COLONEL—Chief of Dreyfus's bureau at Military Headquarters, 1894.

BERTULUS, M.—The magistrate who made the preliminary examination of the Esterhazy case. He received the late Lieutenant-Colonel Henry's confession of forgery.

BILLOT, GENERAL—Minister of War (April, 1896–June, 1898) during the time of the Henry forgeries. To him Scheurer-Kestner opened up his doubts on the validity of the conviction of Dreyfus. Billot played him false, and took his stand on the "authority of the *chose jugée*."

BERTRAND, M.—Representative of the government at Zola's second trial. He violated the law for the purpose of saving Du Paty de Clam, the forger.

"BLANCHE" AND "SPERANZA" TELEGRAMS—Two telegrams forged by Du Paty de Clam and Esterhazy, and sent to Picquart with the object of "bluffing" him into the belief that a lady, who was in the "plot," had given away the "secret" that he forged the Esterhazy "petit bleu." The "Speranza" despatch was sent to Picquart especially with the object of inspiring official circles with the belief that he was an agent of the Dreyfus syndicate.

BOISDEFFRE, GENERAL DE—Chief of the General Staff at the time of the Dreyfus prosecution. He resigned because Henry deceived him. He was in touch with all the Esterhazy trickeries.

BORDEREAU—The document found in bits among the waste paper at the German Embassy, pieced together, and attributed to Dreyfus, though undoubtedly Esterhazy wrote it. It offers secret information, and is, of course, unsigned and undated.

BOULANCY, MME. DE—A relation of Esterhazy and an acquaintance of Colonel Picquart. Esterhazy tried to drag her into the conspiracy hatched against Picquart by suggesting that she wrote certain letters. It was absolutely false.

BRISSET, MAJOR—Government Commissary, or prosecutor, at the court-martial of 1894.

BRUGERE, LIEUTENANT—An officer of the Artillery Reserve; witness in 1899.

CARRIERE, MAJOR—Government Commissary (prosecutor) at the Dreyfus court-martial of 1899.

CARVALHO, CAPTAIN—Officer of the Artillery; witness at Rennes.

CASIMIR-PERIER, M.—President of the Republic at the time of the Dreyfus trial. He had the courage to speak out to the Court of Cassation and announce that the prisoner was convicted on secret evidence.

CASTELIN, M.—Member of Assembly, from the district of Aisne. He gave notice of an interpellation of the Government in 1896, which stirred the authorities to renewed activity and helped to bring about the revision of the case.

CAVAIGNAC, M.—Minister of War (October, 1895–April, 1896; June, 1898–September, 1898). He announced the discovery of Henry's forgery, but reaffirmed his belief in the guilt of Dreyfus. He is a cousin of Du Paty de Clam.

CERNUSCHI, EUGENE DE—An Austro-Hungarian refugee who testified at Rennes.

"CETTE CANAILLE DE D——"—A phrase in one of the documents of the secret dossier. It does not refer to Dreyfus, but to a subordinate, whose name is said to be known to the French War Office (said to be Dubois).

CHANOINE, GENERAL—Minister of War (September 18, 1898–October 25, 1898). He was chiefly memorable for his stagy resignation in the Chamber.

CHARAVAY, M.—Archivist and expert in ancient manuscripts. He testified at both courts-martial.

CHAUTEMPS, M.—Minister of Colonies in 1894. He tried to mitigate Dreyfus's sufferings in his exile, but without success.

COCHEFORT, M.—Chief of the French Detective Department.

COMMINGES, MLLE. BLANCHE DE—"La Dame Blanche" (The White Lady"), a wealthy lady who has attended all the court scenes in the Dreyfus drama.

CORDIER, COLONEL—Deputy Chief of the Intelligence Department in 1894.

COURT DE CASSATION—The French Court of Appeals. The body which decreed the re-trial of Dreyfus.

CUERS, RICHARD—A spy in the Government service.

CUIGNET, CAPTAIN—He discovered Colonel Henry's forgery, and was satisfied with the rest of the documents of the secret dossier, which he collected and filed.

DARIUS, M.—Procureur-General of Cayenne, where Dreyfus was in exile. He first announced to Dreyfus the order for revision of his case.

DARRAS, GENERAL—He commanded the troops and officiated at the degradation of Dreyfus.

DELAGORGUE, M.—President at the Zola trial. He made history by his stock saying in favor of the War Office party : "The question shall not be put."

DEMANGE, MAÎTRE—Dreyfus's counsel at the court-martial and during the Rennes trial.

"DIXI ARTICLE"—Written by Esterhazy in the *Éclair*, bitterly attacking Piquart on private information illegally lent him by the War Office.

"DOCUMENT LIBERATEUR" — The letter beginning "Cette canaille de D——." This was the famous one which Esterhazy threatened President Faure he would disclose, unless protected against Picquart. He alleged it had been stolen by Picquart for a foreign embassy. Esterhazy eventually returned it to the War Office, after it had served its purpose.

DOSSIER, THE SECRET—A collection of more or less private documents bearing on the case, only one of which, unless the War Office has manufactured any more forgeries, mentions Dreyfus by name, and this is absolutely commonplace and innocent.

DREYFUS, M. MATHIEU—The brother of the captain, was one of the pioneers of the campaign for revision. It was he who first denounced Esterhazy as the writer of the bordereau.

DRUMONT, M.—Editor of the *Libre Parole*, who first published details of the discovery of the bordereau.

DU PATY DE CLAM, LIEUTENANT-COLONEL—The melodramatic villain of the piece. He set a trap to surprise Dreyfus by dictating to him the text of the bordereau. He was a warm supporter of Esterhazy, and acted the part of the "Veiled Lady." He assisted in forging telegrams to entrap Picquart, and did the dirty work of the War Office.

26

ECHEMANN, LIEUTENANT-COLONEL—Member of the court-martial of 1894.

ESTERHAZY, COUNT WALSIN—One of the chief opponents of Dreyfus. M. Mathieu Dreyfus having denounced him as the writer of the bordereau, he was tried and acquitted, amid an anti-Jewish manifestation. He was subsequently arrested on a charge of forging the "Speranza" and "Blanche" telegrams, but liberated on a technical point. He was, however, expelled from the army, and has since gravitated between Holland, London, and Paris, at one time fully admitting he wrote the bordereau by desire of his superiors, and then denying he ever said so. There is little doubt but what he did write it. With Du Paty de Clam, he stooped to any anti-Dreyfus trick, no matter how mean, but he played all parties equally false.

FABRE, GENERAL—Former Chief of the Fourth Bureau of the General Staff.

FAURE, M. FELIX—Ex-President of the French Republic, and an unqualified supporter of the General Staff against Dreyfus.

FLORENTINE, MAJOR—Member of the court-martial of 1894.

FONDS-LAMOTHES, M. DES—A former artillery officer—now an engineer.

FORZINETTI, COMMANDANT—Director of the Cherche-Midi prison, where Dreyfus was first confined. He denied the prisoner made any confession, and eventually, for affirming a belief in his innocence, fell into disgrace.

FREYCINET, M. DE—Former Premier and former Minister of War, known as "The Little White Mouse."

FREYSTAETTER, CAPTAIN—A member of the court-martial of 1894, and a fearless defender of Dreyfus at Rennes.

GALLET, MAJOR—A member of the court-martial of 1894.

GALLIFET, GENERAL THE MARQUIS DE—Minister of War at the time of the Rennes court-martial. Called "The Hope of France," on account of his fearless adherence to truth and enforcement of strict discipline.

GALLOPIN, MAJOR—Officer of the Artillery, who testified at Rennes.

GERMAIN, M.—A groom in the employ of Kuhlman, a stable-keeper in Alsace.

GONSE, GENERAL—Assistant Chief of the General Staff. He was the immediate superior of Picquart, against whom he was, after a moment's hesitation, a consistently warm supporter of Esterhazy. He had doubts about Dreyfus's guilt till the influence of Headquarters made him solid with the other generals, since when he bitterly opposed revision.

GRANDMAISON, M. GEORGES CHARLES ALFRED MARIE MULLIN DE—Deputy from the Saumur District of Maine-et-Loire, a friend of M. de Beaurepaire. He made a sensational speech at Rennes.

GRIBELIN, M.—Principal Archivist of the Headquarters' Staff, and an abettor of Du Paty de Clam.

GUENEE—A private detective.

GUERIN, M.—Former Minister of Justice.

GUERIN, LIEUTENANT-COLONEL—He was ordered to attend and report on the degradation of Dreyfus.

HADAMARD, M.—The father-in-law of Dreyfus, a rich Paris diamond merchant.

HANOTAUX, M.—Former Minister of Foreign Affairs.

HARTMANN, MAJOR—Officer of the Artillery, witness at Rennes.

HAVET, M. LOUIS—A member of the Institute and a Professor of the College of France, who testified at Rennes.

HENNION, M.—A detective; Chief of Secret Police at Rennes.

HENRY, LIEUTENANT-COLONEL—Picquart's successor in the Intelligence Department. To supply non-existent evidence he forged a telegram which was inserted in the secret dossier. On discovery and arrest he cut his throat in Mont Valerien prison.

HENRY, MME—Widow of the late Lieutenant-Colonel Henry.

JOUAUST, COLONEL—President of the Dreyfus court-martial of 1899.

KUHLMAN, M.—An Alsatian livery stable-keeper, who testified at Rennes.

LABORI, MAÎTRE FERNAND—Counsel of Dreyfus, Zola, and Picquart.

LEBON, M.—Former Minister of the Colonies, during Dreyfus's exile.

LEBRUN-RENAULT, CAPTAIN—An officer to whom, so it was at one time alleged, Dreyfus made a confession. As a matter of fact he did nothing of the kind; only the War Office, by purposely distorting the captain's report on the circumstances, made it appear that he did.

LE MONNIER, CAPTAIN—One of the Headquarters' Staff.

LE ROND, MAJOR—A professor at the Military School.

MAUREL-PRIES, COLONEL—President of the Dreyfus court-martial of 1894.

MERCIER, GENERAL—Minister of War (November, 1893–January, 1895) when Dreyfus was arrested. He was his bitterest foe, and utterly implacable. It was he who laid secret evidence before the court-martial judges.

MULLER, M. MERTIAN DE.—A friend of M. de Beaurepaire.

MITRY, MAJOR DE—Officer of the Hussars, who testified at Rennes.

D'ORMESCHEVILLE, MAJOR BESSON—He drew up the "act of accusation" for the court-martial of 1894. He assumed allegations of guilt to be guilt.

PALEOLOGUE, M. — Foreign Office expert, and correct translator of the Panizzardi telegram, which Henry falsified.

PANIZZARDI, MAJOR—The Italian military attaché, supposed, erroneously, to have had relations with Dreyfus. He sent the telegram to his government on which Henry based his forgery.

PARAY-JAVAL, M.—Handwriting expert, who testified at Rennes.

PAYS, MME. DE—The mistress of Esterhazy.

PATRON, MAJOR—Member of the court-martial of 1894.

PELLIEUX, GENERAL—One of the French General Staff. He supported Esterhazy and used the Henry forgery in the Zola trial as an "absolute proof" of the guilt of Dreyfus.

PELLETIER, M.—Handwriting expert.

"PETIT BLEU"—A telegram found at the Germany Embassy, written by Colonel von Schwartzkoppen, the German military attaché, to Esterhazy, inviting him to call. It was torn up and thrown into a waste basket, the writer having changed his mind about sending it. It was found there by secret agents. Esterhazy contended that it was a forgery.

PICARD, M. LEMERCIER—War Office agent and forger of the humbler type. He laid a trap for the Dreyfus party, which failed. He was imprisoned and was said to have hanged himself. Other reports say he was murdered.

PICQUART, LIEUTENANT-COLONEL—Ex-head of the Intelligence Department. He took up the cause of Dreyfus on the ground that the evidence was insufficient, and he also produced the famous "petit bleu" (telegram) alleged to have been written to Esterhazy by the German attaché, Colonel von Schwartzkoppen, making an appointment but which was not sent. He was removed from the army and imprisoned on a charge of forging the "petit bleu" himself, but was since liberated.

POLYTECHNIC SCHOOL—The school where French officers are educated, corresponding to West Point in the United States.

RAVARY, MAJOR—He drew up the blundering report at the time of the Esterhazy court-martial.

RISBOURG, GENERAL—Commander of the Republican Guard in Paris in 1894.

ROCHE, CAPTAIN—Member of the court-martial of 1894.

ROCHEFORT, M. HENRI—Editor of the *Intransigeant* newspaper.

ROGET, GENERAL—The alleged manufacturer of nearly all the War Office reports about Dreyfus, the revision of whose trial he bitterly opposed. He was the savior of the General Staff in its most illicit machinations, and that was why M. Déroulède tried to induce him to march on the Elysée.

SANDHERR, COLONEL—Former Chief of the Intelligence Department of the French Army. He died from brain disease soon after the first trial, at which he played a prominent part.

SAUSSIER, GENERAL—Military Governor of Paris.

SAVIGNAUD, M.—A former orderly of Colonel Picquart.

SCHEURER-KESTNER, SENATOR—The former Vice-President of the Senate, since dead. He was the first public man who prominently took up the cause of revision (in July, 1897). He was an able champion of Dreyfus, and was not afraid of consequences.

SCHNEIDER, COLONEL—Former Austrian military attaché at Paris.

SCHWARTZKOPPEN, COLONEL—The German military attaché in Paris, to whom the bordereau was sent, and who was alleged to have written the "petit bleu" to Esterhazy.

SYNDICATE, THE—A figment of the imagination of the Anti-Semites, who came to the conclusion that a number of wealthy persons were financing and "working" the Dreyfus campaign.

TEYSONNIERE, M.—Handwriting expert, who testified at the 1894 court-martial.

TRARIEUX, SENATOR—Former Minister of Justice, witness at Rennes trial.

TOMPS, M.—A special Commissary of the Railway Police, who first photographed the bordereau.

VALABREGUE, M.—Captain Dreyfus's brother-in-law, residing at Carpentras, with whom he is living with his family after his release.

"VEILED LADY," THE—This was Du Paty de Clam, disguised, who handed the "document liberateur" to Esterhazy near the Arc de Triomphe. It was suggested that Esterhazy thought the lady was inspired by revenge on Picquart.

VEUGMON, DR.—Physician in charge of Dreyfus at Devil's Island.

VIGUIE, M.— Director of General Safety, French Government Police.

WEILL, HENRI—A former officer of the Headquarters' Staff.

WEYLER LETTER—A forged letter, incriminating Dreyfus, sent to the War Office. The author, probably, was Du Paty de Clam.

ZOLA, ÉMILE—The novelist. He published the now famous letter of accusation ("J'accuse") against the entire French General Staff, accusing them, in point of fact, of a gigantic conspiracy to convict Dreyfus. He was put on trial, convicted, fined, and sentenced to imprisonment. He appealed, and his sentence was quashed. He was again prosecuted on a sentence in his article which barred any reference to the Dreyfus case. Hence he permitted judgment to go by default, and, being condemned, left the country, appealed, and lived in England, returning only recently to France. His celebrated denunciation is now proved to have been founded on absolute truth.

ZURLINDEN, GENERAL—War Minister (January, 1895–October, 1895). Ex-Military Governor of Paris. He is chiefly memorable for his expression in the Chamber of Deputies of absolute conviction of the guilt of Dreyfus.

Lightning Source UK Ltd.
Milton Keynes UK
11 April 2011

170705UK00001B/6/P